THE BORDER COOKBOOK

Other Cookbooks by Cheryl Alters Jamison and Bill Jamison

The Rancho de Chimayó Cookbook

Texas Home Cooking

Smoke & Spice

THE BORDER COOKBOOK

Authentic Home Cooking
of the American Southwest
and Northern Mexico

CHERYL ALTERS JAMISON
AND BILL JAMISON

THE HARVARD COMMON PRESS
Boston, Massachusetts

THE HARVARD COMMON PRESS
535 Albany Street
Boston, Massachusetts 02118

Printed in the United States of America

Library of Congress Cataloging-in-Publication Data
Jamison, Cheryl Alters.
    The border cookbook : authentic home cooking of the American
Southwest and Northern Mexico / by Cheryl Alters Jamison and
Bill Jamison.
        p. cm.
    Includes index.
    ISBN 1-55832-102-0 (cl.) — ISBN 1-55832-103-9 (pbk.)
    1. Cookery, American—Southwestern style. 2. Cookery, Mexican.
I. Jamison, Bill. II. Title.
TX715.2.S69J35 1995
641.5979—dc20
                                                        95-10799

Special bulk-order discounts are available on this and other Harvard
Common Press books. Companies and organizations may purchase
books for premiums or for resale, or may arrange a custom edition, by
contacting the Marketing Director at the address above.

Cover and text illustrations by Sara Love
Cover and text design by Joyce C. Weston

10 9 8 7 6 5 4 3 2 1

For Lenore Tapia and family

CONTENTS

FOREWORD BY MARK MILLER

The history of the U.S.–Mexican border area makes it one of the world's great culinary regions, similar to the great feeding grounds of the oceans, where currents of different temperatures meet. Just as this mixture produces waters teeming with all kinds of creatures, so the migrations of different peoples to the border area have created a region of rich cultural exchange, between Indians and Spanish, *vaqueros* and cowboys, and Hispanics and Anglos.

The Border Cookbook is the finest collection of recipes from this great culinary area of the Americas. In reading this book, I have relived my own taste experiences over and over again: the lobster and fish tacos in the fishing villages of Baja, the nopales, the *albóndigas*, the soups of corn and shrimp with their fiery broths, the enchiladas with shredded dried beef, the *huitlacoche*, the blue crab soups, and the stuffed squash blossoms—all of the dishes I have come to know and love.

The homey, gutsy foods of the border are full of big flavors, flavors that feed the soul and the spirit. These are the dishes that have sustained the peoples of the Southwest—from the early natives to the tourists who come from the city on weekends to see the "real America." Here, where sunsets are a hundred miles wide, where you can ride for days and never see anyone, where the coyotes howl and the stars are overwhelmingly beautiful, the foods have to be big in spirit. This amphitheater of nature is no place for timidity; the people are strong and honest, and the food here reflects the spirit of both the land and its people. These dishes need no fancy names or pretty presentations. They do not have to be served on fancy china or at "in" restaurants to be appealing. Wherever they're found, these foods refuse to be overlooked. "Here I am,"they say. "This is what I stand for. Take me or leave me."

I remember my first experience eating Mexican food as a child. One Sunday morning I returned from church to smell a new aroma in the house, wafting from the kitchen. It wasn't something familiar, like my grandmother's French Canadian breakfasts of baked beans with molasses, eggs, and homemade breads with country honey and butter. It wasn't my godmother's spicy pasta sauce with Italian sausage. The aroma was much stronger, hanging in the room like a string of Christmas lights. In the kitchen I found my mother cooking juicy red sausage. Slowly sizzling in the skillet, it was loose and rich. This was the source of the intriguing smell. Impulsively, I took a bit on a fork and blew on it to cool it down. When I put it in my mouth, there was an explosion of flavors, and then a quiet blast of heat. This was my first encounter with chorizo. That morning I had my first of many breakfasts of scrambled eggs, chorizo, corn tortillas, and hot chocolate. I was hooked. My experience of food had become enlarged, and this experience enlarged my world.

Like many Americans who grew up on the East Coast, I was unaware of the rich history and cuisine of the West, a land that was settled by Europeans well before the Mayflower landed. I was unaware of Thanksgiving celebrations by the early explorers of the Southwest, five generations before the Pilgrims' first feast. I knew only the America east of the Mississippi.

Over the past thirty-five years I have traveled widely, studying, cooking, and eating the foods of "the Border." They represent some of my fondest eating memories, some of the tastiest down-home good times. Their excellence is no longer a secret, of course. Three hundred and fifty years after whites began settling the East, the foods of the West have come to symbolize America. Salsa has overtaken ketchup as the top-selling condiment, and tacos can be found from Paris to Sydney. The foods that originated in the border area have become icons of American cuisine.

These foods can be found in so many places today, in fact, that often they have lost some of their original character and flavor, or they have become misunderstood. Cheryl and Bill Jamison's book puts all of these foods back into their setting—into the context of their history, their geography, and their people. Reading *The Border Cookbook*, I was impressed at how Cheryl and Bill have captured the feel and flavor of this land and its people. Each page taught me something new about the history of border food—where cheese was first made in Mexico by the Mennonites, what plants the Spanish nurtured in the mission gardens in Arizona and Sonora, and the surprising tale of why there are Chinese influences in Baja cuisine. The Jamisons trace the development of each recipe, sometimes all the way from its pre-Columbian origins to its modern adaptations.

This book is not just historical, though. It is about a living culture and cuisine—a culture that is constantly in transition, a cuisine that is always modifying its flavors. Border food reflects not only how people have lived, but how they live now. In lovingly presented sketches, Cheryl and Bill describe today's heroes of the cuisine. People like Jo Ann Casados, who makes New Mexican food the same way it has been prepared in her family for generations. People like Norman Fierros, a Phoenix chef who creates new incarnations of old dishes while keeping the spirit of the original intact. These people—home cooks, famous chefs, teachers, sheepherders, artists, and tortilla makers—define their cuisine as it defines them. The food and the people are one and the same.

Most books on Southwestern and Mexican cooking make the political border separating the United States and Mexico the boundary of their subject matter. In treating the region and its culinary heritage as a whole, the Jamisons show that the way people eat, more than their political allegiance, defines who they are. This book shows how the dishes of the border unite the people of Mexico and the southwestern United States in one kitchen.

Just as people of the border area have learned and borrowed from one another to enjoy life more, the Jamisons, with true Southwestern hospitality, share their knowledge of how to add these culinary pleasures to your life and how to share them with your family and friends. Cheryl and Bill exhibit an encyclopedic knowledge not only of the region's history, people, and culinary traditions, but also of culinary methods and the botany of food plants. As a professional chef, and as one who has spent a long time learning about these great traditions, I am glad to see the wealth of information on cooking techniques, equipment, and ingredients, especially Southwestern foods such as chiles. (If this book had been written twenty years ago, my life would have been a lot simpler!) The recipes, carefully collected from the best sources, are for quiet home-cooked meals as well as for celebrations and special events. The list of sources in the back of the book alone makes it worth having.

The Border Cookbook is a book that anyone who is interested in the cuisines of the Americas, or anyone who wants to cook great dishes from this area, should have. If you are an armchair (or a dining-room-chair) traveler, you will get hungry just reading about all the cafés, truck stops, taco stands, tortilla stores, and restaurants described in this book. I want to try each dish at every place the Jamisons tell about. I want to eat a picadillo plate at the H & H Car Wash & Coffee Shop in El Paso, and have *cabrito al pastor en cerveza* at El

Azteca in Austin. I want to try the real tampiqueña steak and the crab salpicón.

Like the Tarahumara Indians of Mexico, I mistrust anyone who doesn't eat chiles. With this book, I know the border foods I treasure will have a long life and will continue to nourish us for a long time. Thank you, Cheryl and Bill, for sharing your knowledge of the cooking of the border. Your book is not just another cookbook, but a work of love.

Mark Miller is chef and owner of the Coyote Cafe restaurants in Santa Fe, Las Vegas, and Austin, and of Red Sage in Washington, D.C. He has written five cookbooks, including Coyote Cafe, Coyote's Pantry, *and* Mark Miller's Indian Market Cookbook.

THE BORDER COOKBOOK

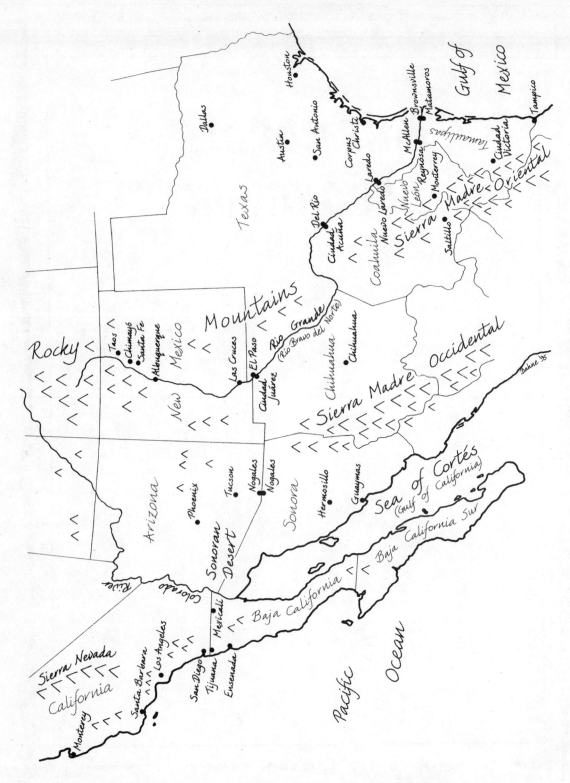

THE BORDER REGION

Gulf of Mexico

Dallas

Houston

Austin

San Antonio

Corpus Christi

Brownsville

Matamoros

McAllen

Reynosa

Nuevo León

Monterrey

Ciudad Victoria

Tampico

Tamaulipas

Sierra Madre Oriental

Laredo

Nuevo Laredo

Del Rio

Ciudad Acuña

Coahuila

Saltillo

Texas

Mountains

Rio Grande

(Rio Bravo del Norte)

El Paso

Ciudad Juárez

Las Cruces

Rocky

Taos

Chimayó

Santa Fe

Albuquerque

New Mexico

Chihuahua

Chihuahua

Sierra Madre Occidental

Dahne '95

Arizona

Phoenix

Tucson

Nogales

Nogales

Sonora

Hermosillo

Guaymas

Sonoran Desert

Sea of Cortés

(Gulf of California)

Baja California Sur

Colorado River

Mexicali

Sierra Nevada

California

Los Angeles

Santa Barbara

San Diego

Tijuana

Ensenada

Baja California

Pacific Ocean

Monterey

THE MOVEABLE FEAST

When Ernest Hemingway called his life in Paris "a moveable feast," he immortalized a phrase that also captures the essence of food traditions along the border of the United States and Mexico. In its most intrinsic, hearty form, the home cooking of the American Southwest and northern Mexico is a feast of vibrant and varied flavors developed over centuries of cross-cultural migrations.

A culinary border never existed in this vast region of deserts and mountains. If there was a boundary at all, it encircled rather than divided the area, producing shared traditions that date back at least twenty-five hundred years to the early period of permanent Native American settlement. The peoples who populated the borderlands in pre-Hispanic days had more in common with each other than with other Native groups to the north or south, and that remained true of their Spanish conquerors later, when the whole region was a rugged subsistence frontier for the Crown's New World empire.

Nothing much changed after Mexico established its independence from Spain in 1821. The present U.S. states of Texas, New Mexico, Arizona, and California became part of the fledgling nation, and the Mexican government treated them like all the rest of northern Mexico, as a coarse outback. An invading U.S. Army pushed the official border south in the 1840s, but the old cultural bonds didn't budge as easily as the lines on the map.

The parts of the American Southwest that the Spanish colonized centuries ago retain important ties to northern Mexico, particularly in cuisine, where the two areas are still as closely linked with each other as they are with other sections of their respective countries. In each case, in fact, the cooking wins national acclaim as a distinctive regional style, which in the United States is usually known as "Mexican" or "Southwestern" and which Mexicans call "norteño."

Cooks on both sides of the border borrow from each other, and they also reach away increasingly in different directions for culinary influences from their own country. Norteños adopt notions from Mexico's urban south, and Anglo-Americans bring diverse customs to the Southwest from all corners of the United States. The national cultures meet at the border, making it a place of contemporary confluence as well as shared historic traditions. The region is a fertile breeding ground for food ideas, a ferment of old and new, Native and Hispanic, Mexican and American.

To fully appreciate the connections and crosscurrents, you have to look at the whole. Other cookbooks, in English and Spanish too, deal with parts of the picture, with personal, state, or multi-state surveys of the cooking. This book covers the entire region, on both sides of the border, from the Gulf of Mexico to the Pacific Ocean, from the Sonoran Desert to the Rocky Mountains and the Sierra Madres. We look for the commonalities that bind together the area—and therefore the two countries—as well as the significant local differences that produce permutations such as Tex-Mex, New Mexican, and Sonoran cooking.

The historical overview that follows introduces these subjects, and then we address them more fully in the recipe chapters in hundreds of stories about specific dishes, ingredients, and cooks. The junctions and divergences are enlightening on their own, but our ultimate purpose is to discover the top culinary contributions of the region overall, to break down artificial barriers in search of the best food and most enduring flavors of the borderlands. We discuss what is typical and conventional, but we focus on dishes that thrive and delight both inside and outside their embryonic environment.

The style of cooking comes originally from home kitchens and can be re-created in home kitchens anywhere in the United States or Mexico. You find the robust fare in a multitude of borderland cafés today, but it's nothing like the commercial fast-food imitations that have swept the United States or the ersatz restaurant concoctions that bury poor ingredients under mounds of sour cream, cheese, or chiles.

Our recipes are authentic, evolved outgrowths of long-standing home traditions, though most of them are our renditions of a dish, enhanced for contemporary tastes in many cases. Sometimes the recipes reflect influences from professional chefs who have developed impressive, innovative interpretations of

Southwest and norteño food, but the book is not about elegant, fussy preparations and presentations.

We stick with the home heritage because it's the original source of inspiration for everyone, and still a moveable feast of flavorful and festive cooking.

THE NATIVE AMERICAN AND SPANISH ROOTS

The Spanish came to the New World in search of gold and glory, and found Mexican food instead. They made other accidental discoveries as well, including tons of silver, but one of the first and most amazing revelations was the Native American cooking.

Many of the basics of Mexican cuisine as we know it today were already in place in 1519, when Hernán Cortés landed at the Veracruz harbor and began his conquest of the Aztec homeland in the lush central Valley of Mexico. The chroniclers of the Spanish expedition described the Aztec food in detail, reporting on corn tortillas in all shapes, tamales with a multitude of fillings, a dozen kinds of beans, fish and lobster dishes, turkey feasts, chocolate drinks, and much more. Corn was the core staple of the diet, and a sacred icon, but life certainly didn't lack spice. The variety and uses of chiles alone staggered the Spanish. Friar Bernardino de Sahagún wrote that market vendors sold chiles in every color and condition, from mild reds to hot greens, from local products to specialties of remote regions, from smoked versions to bunches strung in *ristras*.

In addition to corn and chiles, the Aztecs cultivated and harvested beans, squash, cacti, tomatoes, avocados, and other fruits. They domesticated turkeys, ducks, dogs, and bees for food, fished the great lake that surrounded their capital of Tenochtitlán, transported seafood from the coast, and hunted deer, rabbits, wild birds, and other game. Their larders brimmed, particularly in the court of Moctezuma, and many of the dishes they ate were similar to those of today.

The Spanish added to the bounty, introducing pork, lamb, beef, milk, cheese, butter, lard, wheat, rice, and other European essentials. The conquerors also brought Old World cooking concepts and techniques, especially after the establishment of convents and the arrival of nuns. Over time the collaboration between Native cooks and Spanish sisters produced the sophisticated cuisine of central and southern Mexico, featuring cream sauces, *moles*, and other rich, complex preparations.

When the Spanish moved north from the land of the Aztecs and Mayas, they found a different food situation, with fewer resources and simpler diets. The indigenous peoples of the present-day borderlands raised the Native American staples of corn, beans, and squash, but the arid climate imposed limitations on agriculture and restricted the diversity of edible wild plants and game. European imports ultimately had a greater overall impact on the style of cooking, particularly beef, cheese, and wheat.

By the time the Spanish pushed north, however, and settled in any substantial numbers, they were no longer exactly European themselves. In eating habits at least, the Aztecs had won the day, converting their conquerors to Mexicans. The colonists brought chiles with them, in much greater variety than existed in the area before, and they came with an enduring enthusiasm for such basic Native American dishes as tortillas and tamales.

LIFE ON THE NORTHERN FRONTIER

The borderlands of today were once the "Wild West" of the Spanish empire in the New World. The conquerors began exploring the vast region within a couple of decades of their victory over the Aztecs, but settlement lagged and remained sparse for centuries. As in the American West in a later period, it took months to reach the frontier on wagon trains, the conditions demanded rugged self-sufficiency, and nomadic warriors such as the Chichimecas, Apaches, and Comanches posed a constant threat.

The economic lures that ultimately prevailed—land and treasure—were similar as well in the two areas. The Spanish discovered silver in Chihuahua in the mid-sixteenth century, and then found more in Sonora. The northern mines paid well for labor, attracting workers from the south who became known for their independent and extravagant ways.

Hacendados (the landed gentry) followed the miners north, originally to provide food for the isolated boomtowns that developed around the mines in Chihuahua and Sonora. Through colonization incentives and aggressive expansion, the *hacendados* soon moved into Coahuila and Nuevo León as well, establishing immense ranches across much of the frontier. The climate was the best in New Spain for raising wheat, and the grassy plains of the region offered ample free feed for cattle. The lives of the *vaqueros* (cowboys) and *charros* (gentlemen-horsemen) on the open range gave rise to the shared ranching traditions of Mexico and the United States, which spread later to Texas and the rest of the American Southwest.

The other major motive for heading north, besides land and silver, was saving souls for Christ. That constituted part of the mission in New Mexico, the first permanent Spanish enclave in the Southwest. After an early exploratory expedition discovered a concentration of Pueblo villages along the upper Rio Grande, the Spanish came to colonize the area in 1598. They sought gold initially, but ultimately stayed to convert the Pueblos to Christianity. In the end, their biggest success may have been converting the people to chiles, which became and remain a mainstay of the New Mexico diet.

A century later, Father Eusebio Francisco Kino and other Jesuits set out to bring salvation to isolated Native groups in Sonora, Baja California, and Arizona. Kino alone traveled seventy-five thousand miles across the frontier in twenty-four years and helped to found more than one hundred local churches and missions. Along with the religious message, the Jesuits brought cattle, sheep, goats, and chickens to the region, and a scattering of Spanish settlers planted wheat, grapes, and Old World vegetables wherever they would grow.

Within a few decades, in the middle of the eighteenth century, Franciscans and small bands of soldiers carried the same goods and goals farther north into California, known then as Alta (Upper) California. Inspired by Father Junípero Serra, the priests built a chain of twenty-one missions that stretched six hundred fifty miles up the Pacific coast from San Diego to Sonoma. Following a set pattern, Native laborers erected a chapel in a fortified village quadrangle, and on the outskirts Spanish colonists established ranchos to feed the missionaries and their converts.

Far to the east in Texas, a similar plan yielded fewer results. Largely in response to French encroachments from Louisiana, the government of New Spain envisioned a series of presidio-missions reaching across the territory from the Rio Grande all the way to the Sabine River, which formed the Louisiana boundary. Many of the settlements failed, though the tiny mission at San Antonio grew gradually into an important town, where the earliest Anglo-American pioneers in the Hispanic borderlands learned to love Mexican food.

When the Anglos arrived in the nineteenth century to tame their wild West, they prided themselves on their independence and ability to master harsh conditions. They were not fully aware of it, but their Spanish and Mexican predecessors possessed the same qualities and had to maintain them over a much longer period in even greater isolation. As much as a half-year's journey from Mexico City, and sometimes impossibly remote from each other, each outpost on the northern frontier of New Spain had to survive on its own resources. The settlers everywhere shared a life of hardy self-reliance and subsistence simplicity. That created a common bond in experience and character that no future border could completely erase.

THE POROUS BORDER

From the early years of nationhood, leaders of the United States talked about the country's "manifest destiny" to expand to the Pacific Ocean. A fervent and somber James K. Polk campaigned for the presidency on that goal in 1844 and started a war with Mexico two years later to accomplish it. He got his way in the Treaty of Guadalupe Hidalgo, which extended the United States south as well as west by acquiring half the territory that the young nation of Mexico had recently inherited from Spain.

The war left lasting prejudices on both sides of the new border, reinforcing the worst stereotypes that each country held about the other. Jingoistic propaganda in the United States created the persistent but perverse image of Mexicans as lazy and devious, and in Mexico the dismemberment of the homeland resulted in a virulent Yankeephobia. The tensions affected relationships along the border, but less so than in the two capitals because of the cultural and culinary ties between the old frontier states.

People in nearby areas continued to move freely across the boundary line, which became a problem in Mexico long before immigration developed into an issue in the United States. By the late nineteenth century, railroad transportation expedited commerce over the border, and lax legal safeguards during the long tenure of Mexican president Porfirio Díaz allowed U.S. companies to exploit the natural resources of Sonora, Chihuahua, and Coahuila to their own advantage. The states boomed economically, but most of the profits went north along with a range of products, from cotton to copper.

The inequitable situation produced serious discontent on the Mexican side of the border, and that helped fuel a political revolution in the country in 1910. Many of the leaders of the upheaval—including Francisco Madero, Francisco Villa, and Álvaro Obregón—grew up in the north and saw the disparities firsthand. Typical of their region, they tended to blame the distant government in Mexico City more than the American capitalists.

The revolution resulted in stringent restrictions on foreign investment in Mexico—now eased in the North American Free Trade Agreement—but it didn't stem other movements and exchanges across the national boundary. During the United States' ill-fated experiment with Prohibition in the 1920s, Americans from the Southwestern states flooded over the line to drink and do more, fashioning a border-town reputation that major cities such as Tijuana, Ciudad Juárez, and Nuevo Laredo are still trying to overcome.

The tide that arouses the United States today, the extra-legal immigration from the south, has its roots in centuries of cultural continuity and geographical closeness. In most cases the immigrants come from northern Mexico and their destination is the American Southwest. They are moving between adjacent areas of the Hispanic borderlands, and the flow of people now is probably not much greater proportionate to population than at any other point in the past twenty-five hundred years. If we need to lay blame, perhaps it goes to President Polk and the arbitrary line his soldiers drew.

The cross-fertilization in the region has always benefited the two countries in culinary traditions at least, and that continues to be so. It nourishes the common historic roots of the cooking, which have branched out in many different directions over time, and encourages fresh awareness of the feast of local variations and specializations that characterize the food of the borderlands today.

SEPARATE PATHS TO THE PRESENT

The ranchers and cowboys who first settled large areas of northern Mexico continue to dominate the style of life in Chihuahua, Coahuila, and Sonora. Even workers in a modern automobile factory in Hermosillo are likely to wear cowboy hats, boots, and blue jeans, and their fare of choice remains close to what their ancestors ate on the range. Ask residents of Mexico City to describe the people of the north and they will portray them as frontiersmen still— earthy, gritty, and guileless—like Texans, one person told us. The depiction from an urban bias isn't always meant as flattering, but inevitably the next breath heaps praise on the food, particularly the beef and cheese.

Angus, Herefords, and Holsteins have replaced the lean, mobile Spanish cattle of yesteryear—just as the longhorns gave way to better breeds in

Texas—but the norteños continue to eat their beef in the old ways. They enjoy flame cooking and the flavor of wood smoke, reminiscent of campfire days. They prefer the robust taste of cuts such as brisket and *arracheras* (skirt steak) to delicate, naturally tender steaks. And they still relish dried beef in the form of *carne seca* and *machaca*, even though the development of refrigeration now eliminates the need for dehydration as a preservation process.

Dairy products are also common in the cooking. Sour cream or even rich clabbered cream tames the heat in some dishes, and cheeses fill quesadillas and bubble in the bowl in *queso flameado*. Mennonite farmers from the region created the most famous cheese in Mexico, known simply by the name of their home state, Chihuahua.

Norteños love tortillas as much as anyone in the country, but they are far more likely to make them with the locally grown wheat rather than corn. Often, even the shape is unfamiliar to other Mexicans. Sonorans in particular make huge, paper-thin flour tortillas, much larger than the versions usually sold in the United States. When one of any size is wrapped around beef, beans, or other ingredients, you have a burrito or burro, a dish found far more frequently north of the border than south of Sonora.

Beans also take on special flavors in the region. *Charra* or *ranchero* preparations add hearty seasonings such as chiles, onions, and garlic. *Frijoles borrachos* (drunken beans) are popular in Nuevo León, spiked usually with one of the beers from the Cervecería Cuauhtémoc in Monterrey, Mexico's biggest and most important brewery.

Throughout Nuevo León and into Coahuila and Tamaulipas, cooks may serve their beans with *cabrito al pastor*, spit-roasted suckling kid. Goats from Spanish stock thrive better than cattle in the most arid reaches of the north, and they land on the table as regularly as beef in those areas.

The taste for cabrito spills across the border into Texas, forming one of the elements of Tex-Mex cooking that's totally unknown to the fast-food chains that have spread an inferior version of the food around the United States. Like cabrito, most other Tex-Mex dishes also come originally from northern Mexico, but a long residency in the Lone Star State has modified them in distinctive ways.

One change that shocks many Mexicans is the Texas notion of a combination plate, where enchiladas, tamales, and tacos are served together in a single course along with beans and rice. Food writers protest that no cook in Mexico would offer such *antojitos* (snacks or street foods) side by side or make them a full meal. An indignant authority from Mexico City once claimed that after this kind of dinner, she would insist on bicarbonate of soda for dessert.

The combination plate is purely Texan in origin—a form of convenience packaging devised by Tex-Mex restaurants almost a century ago—but the critics ignore both its Mexican roots and its abiding appeal. *Antojitos* form the core of the diet for many poor people in northern Mexico, the ones who immigrated the most readily, and they are in fact combined to some degree in such a popular Mexican dish as *carne asada a la tampiqueña*, of Tamaulipas inspiration.

The Mexican connections don't create the charisma, though. That comes from Texas chili sauce, the special ingredient in any good Tex-Mex combination or enchilada plate and the most common failing in weak renditions. The fabled chili queens of San Antonio, who operated street stands on the old Military Plaza around the turn of the century, turned a makeshift frontier meal into the Texas chili of today. Made traditionally with ancho chiles, cumin, and beef, it became an instant favorite in the state, and cooks began ladling a gravy version over Mexican food. The sauce transformed the taste and, when it was done well, added a layer of lusty intensity.

Tex-Mex cooking continues to evolve, often following the established pattern of adopting and then adapting ideas and ingredients from Mexico. When Texans imported jalapeños from the Veracruz area a few decades ago, they ate them in customary ways initially and then ended up putting them in everything from jam to cornbread. *Arracheras* arrived across the border as fajitas and rapidly mutated from a strictly beef dish into chicken and other variations.

In Arizona, similar experimentation led to the chimichanga, the state's most notable contribution to border cooking. Roughly translatable as "thingamajig," it's a deep-fried burrito, usually stuffed with meat or beans, cheese, and mild chiles. The crunchy surface enhances the texture, providing contrast with the molten interior.

In most other respects the best local food in southern Arizona remains true to its roots, bedded deeply in the soil of Sonora directly across the border. The Spanish never settled the state extensively and eventually abandoned everything except two tiny outposts in Tucson and Tubac. Unlike the other Southwestern territories, the small colony didn't develop a distinct culinary approach of its own.

Arizona's Mexican cooking migrated north intact, mostly in the past century, although it is increasingly influenced by commercial trends in other nearby states. Apart from the chimichanga, Sonoran specialties are the most characteristic fare, from *carne seca* and *machaca* to burritos made with large flour tortillas. As in Sonora, dairy products figure prominently in preparations, and chiles take a back seat.

New Mexico food couldn't be more different and still be so closely related. Chiles are the core of the cooking, often in fiery forms, pork becomes more important than beef, and corn replaces wheat as the main grain. Truly indigenous to the upper Rio Grande, the style derives as much from Pueblo influences as from contact with other areas of the New Spain frontier. Strong relationships exist with Mexican cuisine, but they are remote in time and place, not the continuing interaction seen in Arizona and Texas.

The Pueblos probably cooked with chiles to a limited degree in pre-conquest days—using wild chiltepíns or dried pods traded from central Mexico—but Spanish settlers introduced extensive cultivation and made chiles a staple of the diet. Over time they began specializing in one variety, a long green pod that turns red as it dries. The New Mexican chile, as it's now generally known, flavors most of the traditional dishes of the state, including *carne adovada*, tamales, and many kinds of enchiladas.

Chile even finds its way into squash and hominy preparations such as calabacitas and *pozole*, the local versions of which likely date to the Pueblos in an embryonic form. The Rio Grande Natives also passed along their special blue corn, one of several varieties they used for tortillas, *atoles*, and more. The Spanish brought the wheat that went into fried breads, most notably sopaipillas, but the grain didn't catch up with corn in popularity until the era of modern grocery stores.

New Mexican food developed its unique cast because of extreme isolation. Among all the remote areas in northern New Spain, Santa Fe and its satellite settlements were the most detached, difficult to reach and largely out of touch with the world for more than two hundred years until the nineteenth century. That fostered not only a singular culinary style, but also a strong sense of self-preservation and great stability in the cooking up to the present.

In California, by contrast, another distinctive version of frontier food died out decades ago, at least as a whole tradition. The Californias, both Baja and Alta, were as distant as Santa Fe from the rest of New Spain except by ship. Colonists came relatively late in the empire's history and their heritage was ultimately overwhelmed by a range of outside influences, from Anglo to Chinese.

The original mission and rancho cooking benefited from a natural abundance found nowhere else in the Hispanic north. Native peoples introduced the Spanish to unfamiliar wild greens, roots, nuts, and berries. The padres discovered to their delight that grapes grew well, offering opportunities to make ample wine and brandy. The settlers also planted olive trees, and added both the fruit and the oil to their pantry. Their chile of choice, among the many they raised, was the Anaheim, similar in appearance to the New Mexican but milder.

The Californians reaped the bounty of the sea as well as the land. Spanish pioneers tended to avoid the steamy coastlines in Texas and Sonora, and they seldom relished fishing for sustenance, but in California the Native inhabitants knew the waters well and they showed the Europeans how to enjoy abalone, clams, mussels, and more.

The old rancho cuisine disappeared as an entity after the missions folded, but important elements survive. The vineyards started by the padres inaugurated wine industries in California and Baja California that are still the largest in their respective nations. Fresh produce, fish, and seafood have become more prominent in border cooking everywhere, largely due to contemporary leadership from the Californias. From the famous Baja lobsters of Puerto Nuevo to brimming fish-and-salsa tacos in Santa Barbara, the spirit of California cornucopia thrives.

None of these branches of border cooking is better or more authentic than the others. Good Tex-Mex enchiladas are as tasty and true to their source as *diablo* shrimp from Guaymas, the *arracheras* in Monterrey match Tucson's *carne seca* in both bona fides and hearty flavor, and the chile dishes of New Mexico reach the same pinnacles of success as Chihuahua cheese. Styles and specializations vary in the vast border region, but the food everywhere shares a common heritage and an uncommon ability to delight.

BORDER BASICS

Ingredients,
preparation techniques,
and equipment

Border cooking is not daunting or exotic, but it does have its own individual characteristics, like any other regional or national style. We cover many of the specific features in the recipe chapters, in a broad range of "Technique Tips," "Regional Variations," and other observations on the food. Before dealing with the nuances, though, we should review the fundamentals, to introduce the basic elements of the cooking style and the major keys to success.

INGREDIENTS

Cheese and Crema

CHEESE plays a prominent role in border cooking, as a principal ingredient in some dishes and a supporting flavor in many more. Our recipes usually provide choices among some of the following cheeses, all popular in the region, but we also suggest substitutes readily available anywhere. An increasing number of cooks on both sides of the border favor the distinctive and specialized tastes of the Mexican quesos, which are gaining much broader distribution throughout the United States.

ASADERO, northern Mexico's favorite cheese, is white and semisoft, with a slightly tangy taste made by souring a portion of the milk used in its production. Asadero melts in luscious, gooey strings, an asset in everything from enchiladas to *queso flameado*. The usual substitute is Monterey jack, but mozzarella, provolone, or a combination of these cheeses works well too.

CHEDDAR, mild in flavor and made to melt, blankets most Tex-Mex dishes and many other Southwestern favorites. Border cooks normally prefer inexpensive, yellow varieties, sometimes called "longhorn" after the famous cattle of the Lone Star State.

CHIHUAHUA comes from the northern Mexican state of the same name. The creamy, off-white, semisoft cheese was created by Mennonites, who brought European cheese-making skills to the border region almost a century ago. The religious sect still produces the finest version of the cheese, *queso menonita*. Slightly spongy in texture and buttery in flavor, all Chihuahua melts well, making it especially suited to foods such as soups and chiles rellenos. Muenster is the best substitute, though a mild white cheddar can also be used.

COTIJA (the most common name in the United States) and AÑEJO (a broader, generic name) are aged cheeses with dry, crumbly textures and salty, somewhat sharp flavors. They don't melt, so cooks use them mainly as toppings, adding them to tacos, enchiladas, and beans just before serving. Some authorities suggest grated Romano or Parmesan (not the canned type) or aged Asiago as substitutes. All are acceptable, but they usually have harder textures than Cotija or añejo. We prefer feta as a replacement, drained of any storage liquid and blotted with paper towels before crumbling. If you have time, let it dry further by sitting out uncovered for thirty minutes.

FRESCO (sometimes marketed as *queso caribe*) is the most common cheese in Mexico. Like the tangier, drier Cotija or añejo, it is sprinkled on top of hot dishes just before serving. As a substitute, use crumbled farmer cheese or feta. We favor feta, preparing it as suggested above for the Cotija substitute, but with the additional step of rinsing and draining it a second time to eliminate some of the salty tang.

MONTEREY JACK originated in Monterey, California, and remains a favorite on the West Coast. Now well known throughout the United States, its repute comes from a mild, buttery flavor and easy melting. Jalapeño-laced versions heat up many Southwestern dishes.

PANELA is a slightly salty, milky-tasting white cheese that holds its shape when melted. Typically sold in rounds or blocks, it is often sliced thick and broiled or baked. Substitute the milder, stringier Monterey jack.

CREMA, a thickened and soured cream, garnishes many Mexican dishes. It is easy and inexpensive to make (see page 63), though commercial crème fraîche also substitutes well. The most common American replacement, sour cream, lacks the richness, is more acidic, and doesn't melt as well on top of warm dishes.

Chiles Botanists consider chile a berry in the nightshade family, horticulturists call it a fruit, and almost everyone else thinks of it as a vegetable—except perhaps when it's dried and ground, at which point they may call it a spice. Even the spelling causes confusion, with some people insisting the word should end in an *i* instead of an *e*, a protocol we follow only for chili con carne and related products. The single broadly agreed fact is that chile is the hottest thing in Mexican cooking, on the border and beyond, and has been since the Aztecs gave us the original name.

Some chiles—primarily young green ones—are eaten fresh, often sliced in strips or chopped. Many need to be roasted first, a process we describe in the following section, "Preparation Techniques and Equipment." If allowed to mature to red, chiles mellow in flavor and turn sweeter, but the heat level remains the same. At that stage most pods are dried to use in a whole, crushed, or ground form. Our recipes generally call for the ground version, the most widespread option, except in cases where whole pods make a major difference in a dish.

All except the tiniest chiles should be stemmed and seeded unless a recipe specifies otherwise. Removing the seeds helps eliminate any potential bitterness and tones down the heat. If you wish to tame more of the firepower, slice or break out the lighter-colored veins that run the length of the pods.

In working with any chiles, but especially with the hottest ones, wear rubber gloves if your skin irritates easily. Always refrain from touching your eyes, contact lenses, lips, or other sensitive body parts.

Variations in names and fluctuations in availability can be frustrating even to chile aficionados, but there are more commonalities than differences among the pods. We divide the most common border favorites into mild, medium, and hot varieties, which provides a good guide to appropriate substitutions.

ANCHO, a dried, red, heart-shaped pod, should feel heavy for its size. Most are several inches long and almost as wide through their "shoulders." The flavor is earthy and a little reminiscent of chocolate. Like all mild chiles, it is often used in relatively large quantities, providing depth of chile taste without scorching heat.

ANAHEIM is a common name given to some of the mildest long green or red New Mexican pods, particularly ones that come from southern California.

GUAJILLO is almost always marketed in a dried form. Unlike most red chiles, it dries smooth rather than wrinkled. About four to five inches long, rather thin, and tough-skinned, guajillos offer rich chocolate and berry flavors.

NEW MEXICAN chiles, favored for robust full flavor, are so common in border cooking that some people simply refer to them as long greens and reds. Others in the Southwest use the Anaheim name, and south of the border, the pods may be called *colorado* in Sonora, *cascabel* near Tampico, *chilaca* around Monterrey, and *de la tierra* or *colorín* in Chihuahua. Valleys in southern New Mexico, near Hatch, produce some of the best-known green pods, large and meaty, and the state's northern village of Chimayó grows the most sought-after reds, small, thin-walled pods with incomparable flavor and sweetness. If you purchase fresh green pods, they usually should be roasted to peel off the tough skin, as described later in "Preparation Techniques and Equipment." Frozen and dried green chiles are the best alternatives to fresh pods, and both are increasingly available throughout the United States. Forget canned chiles. If they are your only option locally, get your New Mexican greens from one of the businesses listed in "Mail-Order Sources," which also sell the dried red chile, both ground and in whole pods.

POBLANO, the fresh chile known as ancho when dried, is plump, heart-shaped, and deep green in hue. Often called a pasilla in California, it's especially popular for stuffing. Like the New Mexican pod, the poblano is usually roasted before using.

CASCABEL, an inch-around dried red chile, takes its name from the Spanish word for sleigh bell because the loose seeds inside rattle melodiously. Like

most chiles in the medium heat range, it's used in small to moderate amounts as a flavor and heat accent in salsas, sauces, or other dishes. Deep and woodsy in taste, cascabel pairs especially well with red wine.

CHIPOTLE, a name that combines the Aztec words for chile and smoke, is properly a generic term for any smoked chile. Normally the variety is a ripe jalapeño, dried originally through slow smoking because other drying techniques don't work well with the chile. The process produces a wrinkled, rusty-brown pod that resembles a dried mushroom. Some chipotles are pickled and canned in adobo sauce, a vinegar-based brew laced with onion, garlic, tomato, seasonings, and sometimes other chiles. We prefer them in that form, considering the sauce a bonus, though dried versions are equally good. Chile authorities make distinctions between chipotles, *mecos*, *moras*, and more, but all these smoked pods taste similar.

GÜERO and GÜERITO are distinguished by their yellow-green to bright yellow color. A güero is usually about three inches long, and the diminutive, slightly hotter güerito about half that size. Often pickled, the yellow chiles are particularly popular around El Paso.

JALAPEÑO, a pungent dark green pod, is the most common fresh chile in the United States, widely used on nachos and in salsas as well as in main dishes. In recent generations, it acquired a strong association with Tex-Mex cooking, but the chile has a much longer history south of the border. Many Mexicans know only the pickled version as a jalapeño. Fresh pods are often called *cuaresmeños*, or Lenten chiles, because cooks like to serve them as a red-meat substitute, fried with fillings of cheese or fish. If you can't find fresh jalapeños, substitute the pickled variety, rinsed well. In the late summer and fall, look for scarlet jalapeños, allowed to mature on the vine. They taste similar but add extra color to dishes.

SERRANO sits on the top end of the medium-heat scale. A bullet-shaped, blunt-pointed fresh pod of one to two inches, it packs a more intense zing than the jalapeño, the closest substitute. Most serranos are deep shiny green, but look for red ones too.

CHILE PEQUÍN is a tiny, bud-shaped pod with a bit of a point at one end. Normally sold in the dried red form, pequín offers deep intense heat, although the fire doesn't linger as long as it does with some other pods. Like all small hot chiles, use pequín sparingly, to add pizzazz to salsas, sauces, or other dishes. Substitute either of the chiles below, or cayenne in a pinch.

CHILTEPÍN, unlike other chiles, still grows wild in northern Mexico, Arizona, and Texas. People who can't get enough spice in their lives add the tiny pea-shaped pods to everything from beans to vodka. Often used fresh and green at their source, chiltepíns are usually dried to a red-orange state for commercial distribution. Substitute pequín, the domesticated cousin, or chile de árbol or cayenne.

CHILE DE ÁRBOL, a slim, sharp-pointed dried red pod, often comes from Chihuahua. About one-and-a-half inches long, it's sold and used whole, crushed, or ground. For its searing heat, cayenne makes the best substitute.

LARD, still the most common cooking fat in Mexico, doesn't entirely deserve its dangerous reputation. The food police have put it at the top of their most wanted list, but it's no worse than other saturated fats, all of which should be used sparingly and only in ways that truly enhance food. Lard adds tenderness to baked goods, richness to refried beans, and lightness to some types of tamales. Nothing can really replace it well in those situations.

Most of the lard on the U.S. market is processed to remove its naturally strong taste, leaving a mild nuttiness. Depending on the technique used, grocers may stock it beside the vegetable shortening, which it resembles in consistency, or in the refrigerated section near the butter. Keep lard tightly wrapped in the refrigerator since it absorbs other flavors readily.

OILS now replace lard in most Southwestern kitchens when animal fat isn't needed for taste or texture. If a dish benefits from a neutral taste, our recipes don't usually specify a particular kind of vegetable oil, though canola is our personal favorite. Olive oil never gained a major foothold in the border region, or farther south in Mexico, because the Spanish Crown prohibited its production in the colonial period, to protect established suppliers in the mother country.

When the recipes call for olive oil, we often recommend extra-virgin, the first pressing, for fullest taste. We shop for Spanish brands for a combination of flavor and value, but we also like Loriva, which originates in Morocco, and Consorzio, from California.

Flours   HIGH- and LOW-GLUTEN FLOURS are made from different types of wheat, and ALL-PURPOSE FLOUR combines both. Each finds important applications along the border, where flour plays as large a role in the cooking as corn, the primary Mexican staple in other areas. The standard all-purpose variety is designed to cover a broad range of culinary needs. Although it works well in some dishes, it seldom excels for baking. High-gluten flours, often labeled as bread flours, form strong elastic doughs excellent for large thin tortillas and for yeast breads. Other styles of thicker, flakier tortillas and tender baked goods fare best with a low-gluten or pastry flour, which absorbs less liquid.

MASA, the generic word in Spanish for dough, almost always refers in Mexico and the Southwest to the corn dough that forms the backbone of Mexican cookery. Processors boil the kernels of starchy field corn with slaked lime, which loosens the hull, makes the grain more glutinous, and increases the accessibility of the corn's protein. The treated damp corn, or *nixtamal*, is then ground into masa and used to make tortillas, tamales, gorditas, and other dishes. (If the corn is dried whole for later use, it becomes *posole*.) Fresh masa can be purchased from tortilla factories and from some Mexican markets, especially around Christmas. It freezes well but otherwise must be used within a day's time because it loses elasticity and then sours. For that reason and the limited access, our recipes call for dried masa harina rather than fresh masa.

MASA HARINA is the ground dried form of the corn used in masa. Quaker and Maseca brands, which get broad national distribution in the United States, are found in supermarkets either with other flours or in the Mexican foods section. Both do a satisfactory job, but if you plan to make tortillas, tamales, or other masa dishes with frequency, look for local stone-ground masa harina milled in different grinds. Typically, coarser grinds are used for tamales and finer grinds for tortillas. If you don't have a local source, many of the

Southwestern businesses listed in "Mail-Order Sources" stock superior masa harinas.

CORNMEAL, an Anglo frontier favorite used in cornbread, appears in some border dishes, but never as a replacement for masa harina. Stone-ground varieties from small mills provide the best texture and flavor, though they usually need to be refrigerated or frozen because of a relatively short shelf life.

AVOCADOS add buttery voluptuousness to many border dishes. Our recipes always specify the Haas variety, the avocados with pebbly black-brown skins. Other types taste watery in comparison. If you plan to use them immediately, buy avocados that yield easily to pressure. Otherwise, let them sit at room temperature for a few days, inside a paper sack if you're in a rush. Refrigerate avocados only when they are soft and you won't be able to use them by the next day.

Fruits and Vegetables

CACTUS, particularly the prickly-pear variety, is a versatile plant for border cooking. People eat both the vegetable-like pads, or nopales, and the sweet fruits, usually called *tunas*.

NOPALES is a generic name for any cactus pad, but on the border it usually refers to the flat, "beaver-tail" pads of the prickly pear. Usually boiled or grilled, cooked nopales resemble green beans in flavor and okra in texture. Our recipes specify prepared nopales, the pre-cooked style, available in jars in stores with a well-stocked Mexican or Southwest food section. The mucilaginous juice should be rinsed off before using. If you find fresh cactus pads in U.S. produce sections, the stickers have normally been removed. The most desirable pads are the tenderest, harvested in the spring and early summer. Boil them in two changes of heavily salted water for about thirty minutes total, or grill them over a hot fire until softened. Slice the nopales before using them in a recipe, or dice them into nopalitos.

TUNAS are the knobby prickly-pear fruits that sprout around the edges of the pads in summer and early fall. They turn from green to ruby red, encasing a magenta juice of neon intensity. The exotic flavor seems to mate pomegranates, cherries, and strawberries. If you come across fresh *tunas*, be careful of their fine, nearly invisible stickers. You're most likely to find the fruit cooked down to a superb syrup, which keeps indefinitely in the pantry. We call for the syrup in several recipes, but suggest substitutes as well.

JÍCAMA, a homely brown-skinned root vegetable, has a creamy, crunchy flesh usually eaten raw. The sweetness and texture resemble a mix of water chestnuts and apples. Some jícamas get as large as a football, but many are smaller, and some are sold already cut in chunks. Choose firm, relatively smooth-skinned specimens, store in the refrigerator for up to two weeks, and peel before using in recipes. Where diced jícama is specified, water chestnuts can be substituted.

LIMÓNES, LIMES, and LEMONS all sound alike but each offers a different tang. Small Mexican limes, *limónes* are a part of nearly every meal south of the border, served sliced on a plate alongside beverages and foods. The juicy little fruits are known as key limes in the United States, and much prized for their tart, tasty juice, but hardly ever available commercially. Persian limes, the common American variety, and lemons rarely appear in Mexican cooking, though they are popular with Southwestern cooks, who use lemon when the flavor should blend in and lime when it should call attention to itself. Avoid anything but fresh juices.

OLIVES, both green and black, are especially popular in Tamaulipas and the Californias. When using the ripe black variety, try to avoid the canned, water-packed versions in favor of the ones in brine-filled jars, such as those from the Santa Barbara Olive Company, a widely available brand. As much as we enjoy the pungent olives found in Mediterranean cooking, their flavor is too assertive for border dishes.

TOMATILLOS get called green tomatoes, *tomates verde*, and husk tomatoes, but they are actually more closely related to the kiwi fruit than to tomatoes. Their refreshing, citrus-like flavor enhances sauces and salsas, and fish and seafood, in particular. When mature, tomatillos are deep green, sometimes with a purple blush. Tight papery husks signify freshness, which can be maintained for several weeks when the fruit is refrigerated in a paper sack. Many cooks boil or roast fresh tomatillos before using them, as described in the following section, "Preparation Techniques and Equipment." Canned varieties can substitute, though we prefer to limit their application to recipes in which theirs is one of several strong flavors.

TOMATOES are featured prominently in our recipes, particularly the small, pear-shaped Roma or Italian plum tomatoes. Both varieties have a high percentage of flesh to liquid, which concentrates their flavor and gives them more time to mature on the vine without undercutting their shipping potential. Store tomatoes at room temperature, refrigerating only ripe ones you can't use immediately. In some recipes, we prefer canned tomatoes, usually the crushed style. For best flavor and consistency, search out the many brands that contain "extra purée," always specified on the label.

Herbs and Spices

You don't find as many different herbs and spices on the border as you do in southern Mexico—largely because of lack of availability in the frontier past—but the use of seasonings is equally important to success. Buy all herbs and spices in small quantities for the freshest flavor. Though leading American brands distribute most of the seasonings needed in border cooking, it's worth seeking out the best, most aromatic spices available. Two excellent mail-order suppliers are Penzeys Ltd. Spice House (414-574-0277) and Vanns Spice Ltd. (410-583-1643, fax 410-583-1783), both of which have catalogs.

CANELA, the Mexican cinnamon, is also called true or Ceylon cinnamon. It's softer in texture and flavor than the most common American cinnamon, which comes from the cassia bark. When canela is used whole, our recipes call for sticks about two to three inches long, the size found most often north of the border, rather than the giant-size sticks more common in Mexico. Canela can be a challenge to find in the United States, but it's worth the effort. If you have to substitute the harsher cassia bark, experiment with reducing the amount by about one-third to get the most authentic taste possible.

CILANTRO, the green leafy herb with a slightly anise-like flavor, has its fans and detractors. Some consider it soapy and others think it's divine. Much more common today than even a few years ago, cilantro might be labeled Chinese parsley because of its equal prominence in Asian cooking. Store cilantro in the refrigerator with the roots in a cup of water and the leaves covered with a plas-

A legacy from Spain, the aged vinegar has some of the qualities of a fine Italian balsamic vinegar.

Nuts and Seeds   Compared to their use in traditional American cooking, nuts and seeds play a broad, important role in the borderlands, serving as protein sources and flavoring agents in many dishes. Pumpkin and other squash seeds are actually among the oldest known foods in the hemisphere, and they're still well loved in the region. Shelled, green-colored pumpkin seeds, pepitas give crunch to salads and toppings and, when ground, add body to sauces such as pipiáns. Border cooks also like oil-laden sesame seeds, particularly the tan variety, which should be bought in small quantities because they can go rancid quickly. Both kinds of seeds are found in health food stores as well as in Mexican food sections and markets.

Pecans, walnuts, pistachios, and peanuts are all popular in the region, but piñon nuts make more distinctive contributions to the cooking. Tiny hard-shelled nuts from the cones of certain species of high-altitude pines, the rich, buttery nuggets enjoy almost legendary repute in some areas of northern Mexico, New Mexico, and to a more limited extent, Arizona. If you can't find Southwestern piñon nuts, Italian pine nuts (*pignoli*) have a similar flavor and are preferable to the less expensive Chinese variety.

Store nuts and seeds in the refrigerator or freezer for the longest shelf life, and toast them before using to bring out their flavor. Large nuts like pecans can be baked in a moderate oven for ten minutes, and smaller nuts and seeds can be toasted in a small dry skillet over medium heat until fragrant.

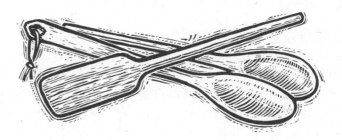

PREPARATION TECHNIQUES AND EQUIPMENT

Outdoor
Cookery

One cookbook claims flat-out that you can't cook traditional border fare on a stove indoors. We're more pragmatic in our approach, but outdoor flavor and preparations are certainly chief characteristics of regional food. In the dishes that rely on high-heat grilling and slow, indirect cooking with wood smoke, we gear most of our recipes toward the use of charcoal grills, the most common kind of outdoor equipment. In many cases, gas grills, water smokers, log-burning pits, and other devices work just as well and sometimes better.

Roasting
Tomatoes,
Garlic, Chiles,
and More

Advance roasting of ingredients before their addition to a dish is a venerable Mexican method of enriching flavor and complexity. Many of our recipes call for the step, a simple but essential part of their success.

Countless cooks on both sides of the border still use an asador for the process. A wire-mesh stovetop grill, it was designed originally for use over an outdoor fire, though today most people employ it inside on a range. Sold in Mexican markets and some cookware shops, and through many of the businesses listed in "Mail-Order Sources," it's fast and easy to master, and normally retails for less than twenty dollars.

To approximate the results in an oven, broil whole tomatoes for eighteen to twenty minutes, tomatillos for ten to fifteen minutes, and halved onions for eight to ten minutes. Turn them a time or two to ensure even cooking. Often the charred skins are used in dishes too, helping to deepen the flavor.

Smaller ingredients, such as individual garlic cloves and fresh serranos or jalapeños, can be roasted with the asador or in a small dry skillet over high heat until darkened and soft. Dried chiles often get a similar but briefer treatment. To bring out their natural oils, toast them over the asador or in the dry skillet just long enough to release their fragrance.

Fresh green poblano and New Mexican chiles are almost always roasted to remove their tough skins before eating. Put the whole chiles in a single layer on a grill, or on a baking sheet beneath a broiler, and heat them until they are blistered and uniformly darkened. Some authorities recommend dunking chiles in hot oil to blister the skin instead. The technique works, but doesn't develop as much flavor in the pod as roasting.

Transfer the chiles to a sturdy plastic bag to steam, which loosens the skin and makes it easier to peel after the chiles are cool enough to handle. (If you want to freeze the chiles, a fine way to store them, don't bother to peel them. The skin slips off more easily after the pods have been frozen and thawed.) Use the chiles whole or remove the stems and seeds and cut the pods into strips or bite-size chunks.

Grinding, Blending, Mashing, and Smashing

Used to grind dried chiles and other spices, and to make salsas and guacamole, the *molcajete* hasn't changed much in the last three thousand years. The volcanic rock mortar and its accompanying pestle, the *tejolote*, provide an ideal rough surface and weight for their job, and the *molcajete* doubles well as a ready-made serving bowl for dishes mixed inside. When new, both pieces are filled with dirt and grit. Before using, rinse them multiple times, and grind small batches of rice or light-colored dried beans, a handful at a time, until the grain no longer picks up gray particles. The process takes a while, but you'll have a tool that should last a lifetime. Alternatives include other kinds of mortars as well as spice mills and coffee grinders.

Metates are sometimes confused with *molcajetes*. The flatter, slightly concave *metate* is the old Native American utensil for grinding corn. Some people keep them in the kitchen for decoration, but you don't want to try it to make masa, a back-breaking job. Traditional wooden bean mashers, which may be just as ancient, remain useful, though similar potato mashers work just as well.

Today the blender, or *licuadora*, common throughout the borderlands, is the primary tool for puréeing sauces and other mixtures. For some tasks, when all the ingredients are moderately soft, a food processor can substitute, but it won't make much headway on seed- or grain-based blends.

Ollas and Other Cooking Pots

In Mexico, cooks still favor earthenware pots, terra cotta pieces typically glazed on the inside only. They are inexpensive and offer a seductive air of rusticity, but unfortunately, the glaze often contains dangerous lead. Cautious people seldom if ever cook or serve in earthenware, and no one should store food in it.

Ollas are the most common Mexican pot, tall and tapered inward on the top, shaped especially for cooking beans. Stockpots and large saucepans substitute fine, just as skillets, shallow saucepans, and baking dishes can take the place of cazuelas, casserole-style pans.

Long prominent in cowboy cooking on both sides of the border, cast iron is still a superior cooking material, particularly for Dutch ovens, skillets, and griddles. If you're working with new cast iron, start by seasoning it. Rub the pan inside and out with lard, Crisco, or canola oil, and bake it in a 350° F oven for around an hour. Over the next few days, as time allows, repeat the process. After you start using a pan, clean it mainly with water and a sponge. Avoid using soap, which can undermine the effect of the seasoning. To guard against rust, always dry the pan with heat, either on the burner of the stove or in a warm oven.

Both flour and corn tortillas figure prominently in border cooking. You don't need to make your own to succeed in the kitchen, particularly if you have a good commercial source, but you should understand the principles and you may want to master the process for some special meals.

Tortilla Cookery

Although small differences exist in the size of corn tortillas, the vast majority of them are about five inches in diameter and one-sixteenth to one-eighth inch in thickness. Our recipes assume those dimensions for corn tortillas, but they state preferences for the size and thickness of flour tortillas, which differ considerably in style. Only a few dishes—such as chimichangas and cheese crisps—require a certain type of flour tortilla, but we always provide guidance on what works best.

For making corn tortillas, nothing beats a tortilla hand press. Spend enough to get a cast-iron press with the heft to flatten the masa evenly, to at least one-eighth inch, an investment that should still leave you plenty of change from a twenty-dollar bill. You may come across a larger, blockier wooden press, especially if shopping in Mexico. They feel a little awkward to use and take up extra counter space, but they are functional and eccentrically charming. Electric presses, which cost four times more, allow you to press and cook a tortilla in one step. Many people love them, but the actual time and energy saved seems negligible to us given the premium in price.

To make corn tortillas without a press, it's easiest to roll out the dough between pieces of waxed paper. Roll from the center outward, turning the masa a bit after each stroke to get it as round as possible. Trim off any ragged edges. You also can pat out tortillas by hand, slapping the dough back and forth between the bases of your palms, but the process is harder than it looks.

Making flour tortillas requires a rolling pin of some sort. Though you can use the standard large pin designed for pastry and cookies, a smaller tortilla roller works better. Nothing more than a five- to six-inch length of broomstick, it's inexpensive to buy and also easy to cut for yourself. The tool puts less pressure on the dough, yielding lighter tortillas.

We prefer to cook our homemade tortillas, both corn and flour, on a *comal*, or griddle, or in a large shallow cast-iron skillet. The surface should be well seasoned but requires no oil.

For keeping tortillas warm and for serving, invest in a small tortilla basket in the traditional reed style, which works well for muffins and other breads too. Place a dishtowel or cloth napkin in the bottom of the basket, and cover the tortillas loosely with it before closing the lid. Ceramic tortilla warmers hold in more moisture, a significant disadvantage.

BURRITOS, ENCHILADAS, TACOS, AND OTHER COMMON DISHES

Many people in the United States think of border cooking in terms of *tipico* dishes, particularly the ones that wrap favorite ingredients in tortillas. Tacos, enchiladas, and burritos, along with tamales and salsas, led the way when Mexican food spread in popularity across the country.

In classic Mexican cuisine, the tortilla treats are *antojitos*, literally "little whims," served as appetizers, snacks, or street food. For a sophisticated cook in central or southern Mexico, they rank on about the same level as hot dogs or hamburgers in American culinary circles.

The fare assumed greater importance in the borderlands, however, from an early period. The scarcity and simplicity of frontier life kept the basic dishes closer to the core of the diet, and for the poorer people who were most likely to move to the American Southwest, they were everyday essentials. Over the years, northern cooks from Sonora to New Mexico to Texas embellished the simple *antojitos* with local products and ideas, making them into hearty, satisfying meals. They are not the essence of Mexican food anywhere, but they are a proper part of the soul in the Hispanic borderlands.

We include recipes for many regional versions of tortilla and other *tipico* dishes, presented according to their principal ingredient. Rather than put them together in a single chapter, as many authors do, we attempt to reflect their role in border cooking by integrating them into various chapters. You can find cheese enchiladas with other cheese appetizers and entrées, and beef tacos alongside fajitas and steaks. Since the recipes don't appear together, we list them here to facilitate a search.

THE RECIPES

SALSAS, SAUCES, AND SAVORY CONDIMENTS

In 1922, the Presbyterian Ladies Aid Society in Santa Barbara published a cookbook that set out to explain Mexican food to Anglo cooks in southern California. The good ladies pointed out that chile sauce was the foundation of the cuisine and "when made properly, has a peculiar but delicious flavor."

By the 1990s, "delicious" triumphed over "peculiar" in the United States, as Mexican salsas passed ketchup as the best-selling condiment in the country. The commercial products that carried the day are mainly border creations from Southwestern states, but they don't begin to represent the full range of fresh salsas, cooked sauces, and spicy condiments found in the region. As those Presbyterian ladies knew long ago, to cook with authentic Mexican and Southwestern relish, you make your own at home.

Many of the best border sauces share a distinguishing characteristic, the roasting or broiling of the tomatoes or other ingredients. The resulting flavor, almost smoky, adds depth and complexity to simple mixtures, the reason contemporary Southwestern chefs have adopted the old technique recently with such fervor. This Salsa del Norte is sometimes called *molcajete*, because traditionally home cooks used the hand tool of that name to combine the ingredients.

Makes about 2 cups

1 1/2 pounds whole small tomatoes, preferably Roma or Italian plum, unpeeled
1/2 medium onion, chunked
1/4 cup chopped fresh cilantro
2 to 3 fresh jalapeños or canned chipotles in adobo sauce
2 garlic cloves
1 1/2 teaspoons salt
2 to 3 tablespoons vinegar, preferably cider or cane
Pinch of sugar (optional)

Heat the broiler.

Place the tomatoes on a small baking sheet, covered with foil for easier cleaning. Broil the tomatoes for 15 to 18 minutes, turning occasionally, until the tomatoes are soft and the skins split and turn dark in spots. Cool the tomatoes briefly.

In a blender, purée the tomatoes and their skins and cores with the rest of the ingredients.

You can serve the salsa warm or refrigerate it for use later. Like most salsas, it can be served as an accompaniment to chips, but it really shines in tortilla and masa dishes such as Machaca Breakfast Burros and Bean Gorditas.

Technique Tip: For a chunkier salsa, leave one tomato unbroiled, chop it, and stir it and the onion—chopped rather than chunked—in at the end.

In Spanish, any kind of sauce is a "salsa." In colloquial American English, on the other hand, that term is often reserved for what Mexicans would call salsa *cruda*, or fresca, a condiment made of raw or mostly raw ingredients, served cold on the side. Some elements may be cooked, but the mixture tastes fresh on the whole.

A chile "sauce" in the Southwest is usually cooked, a concoction of spooning consistency that's integral to dishes such as enchiladas. "Hot sauces" are thinner, often vinegar-based blends. Whether molten or mellow, they tend to be used sparingly, sprinkled over tacos or other finished dishes.

The terminology gets all the knottier the further back you go in the past. Some turn-of-the-century Southwestern cookbooks talked about "chili-salyas," and before then in California, sauces were known as "sarsas."

Regional Variations: In Sonora and Arizona in particular, most people prefer a milder version of this kind of salsa. They would replace the jalapeño or chipotle with a few tablespoons of chopped roasted mild green chile, such as New Mexican or Anaheim.

CHIPOTLE-TOMATILLO SALSA

The American practice of serving salsas primarily with tortilla chips, as a snack or hors d'oeuvre, doesn't do justice to their original purpose or culinary potency. As the recipes in later chapters show, salsas developed as a way of flavoring all kinds of food, either as an accompaniment or as a core part of the cooking. As good as most of them taste with chips, they are even better in the regular dishes they were designed to enhance.

Tomatillos look like green tomatoes but they are actually more closely related to the gooseberry. Roasting mellows the citrus-like bite, making it even more refreshing in a salsa, particularly when paired with the smoked jalapeños known as chipotles.

Makes about 2 cups

1 pound whole tomatillos, husked
1 tablespoon extra-virgin olive oil
1 small red or sweet onion, chopped fine
1/2 cup minced fresh cilantro
2 canned chipotle chiles, minced, or more to taste
1 tablespoon vinegar, preferably white or cane
1 teaspoon dried oregano, preferably Mexican
1/2 teaspoon salt, or more to taste

Heat the broiler.

Place the tomatillos on a small baking sheet, covered with foil for easier cleaning. Broil the tomatillos for 15 to 18 minutes, turning occasionally, until the tomatillos are soft and dark in spots. Cool the tomatillos briefly.

Warm the oil in a small skillet. Add the onion and sauté until just softened. Transfer the onion to a medium bowl.

Chop the tomatillos fine and add them to the onion. Stir in the remaining ingredients.

The salsa can be served warm or refrigerated, depending on the occasion and dish.

Technique Tip: Canned chipotles are increasingly easy to find across the country, but some of the best versions don't make it beyond the borderlands. Our favorite brand is Chile Bravo, from Phoenix (1103 West

Marconi Avenue, Phoenix, Arizona 85023, 602-866-8393). Angel Sustaeta and her staff smoke jalapeños in underground pits in a traditional pre-Columbian fashion, then age the chiles in cider vinegar before adding spices and bottling the blend. The chipotles have a slightly sweeter flavor than most.

Regional Variations: Tomatillo salsas come in plenty of guises. We like chipotle versions for the smoke and sass, but many people would substitute an equal number of fresh jalapeños or a single serrano. Some cooks boil the tomatillos rather than roast them, or use them raw for a more assertive taste. Others would purée the tomatillos, or even the whole salsa.

PICO DE GALLO

In northern Mexico, this kind of fresh relish would be known usually as salsa méxicana or salsa *cruda*. Ours is a Texas version, perfect paired with fajitas, so we stick with the Lone Star name, pico de gallo.

Makes approximately 2 ¹/2 cups

1 pound small tomatoes, preferably Roma or Italian plum, chopped
4 to 5 fresh jalapeños, minced
3 green onions, sliced
1/4 cup chopped white onion
1/4 cup chopped fresh cilantro
Juice of 1/2 lime
Salt to taste

Mix all the ingredients together in a bowl. Refrigerate for at least 30 minutes.

Serve chilled, as an accompaniment to meat and cheese dishes. Pico de gallo is best the day it's made.

Technique Tip: To brighten the dish in late summer, substitute small yellow tomatoes for a couple of the reds, or mix red and green jalapeños.

The term *pico de gallo* is a linguistic mystery, which is probably the real reason we prefer it as a name. Literally, it means "rooster's beak," a translation that makes little metaphorical sense. The most common explanations claim that the chiles in the salsa resemble bird beaks or that the mixture is chopped almost as fine as chicken feed.

In the high hills and plateaus of northern New Mexico, the short growing season and cool summer nights curtail the crop of fresh tomatoes. Salsa lovers learned to rely on canned varieties, flavoring them with lots of garlic and oregano in addition to chile.

Makes approximately 3 1/2 cups

28-ounce can crushed tomatoes
2 tablespoons minced white onion
2 to 3 fresh jalapeños, minced
5 garlic cloves, roasted and mashed
2 to 3 teaspoons crushed chile caribe or 1 to 2 teaspoons crushed chile
    de árbol or cayenne
1 1/2 teaspoons dried oregano, preferably Mexican
1/2 teaspoon salt

Mix all the ingredients together in a bowl. Refrigerate for at least 30 minutes.

The salsa adds bold flavor to lightly seasoned dishes.

SALSA COCIDA DE CHILES GÜEROS

Sonoran in style, this cooked but fresh-tasting salsa gets its zip from small, hot güeros. Boiling the chiles mellows their bite and softens the texture.

Makes approximately 2 cups

8 to 9 güero chiles, preferably fresh
Water
3 small tomatoes, preferably Roma or Italian plum, chunked
3 garlic cloves
1 teaspoon dried oregano, preferably Mexican
1/2 teaspoon salt
Juice of 1/2 lemon

Place the güeros in a saucepan with enough water to cover them by an inch. Bring the chiles to a boil over high heat and boil them for 5 minutes. Drain the chiles, reserving several tablespoons of the cooking liquid.

When the chiles are cool enough to handle, discard the stems and seeds. Purée the chiles with the tomatoes, garlic, oregano, salt, and half of the lemon juice, adding the reserved cooking liquid if needed to get a sauce-like consistency. Taste and add more lemon juice if needed for a slightly tart but not sour finish. Chill for 30 minutes and serve as an accompaniment, particularly with roasted meats or poultry.

In his masterpiece about the Sonoran Desert, *Gathering the Desert* (University of Arizona Press, 1985), Gary Paul Nabhan cites a Native American creation myth to illustrate the importance of chiles in pre-Hispanic Mexico. According to the Cora Indians, among the first people created by the Maker was a man, anointed as the patron of chile, mescal, and salt. At the world's first fiesta, held in the middle of the earth, the man arrived at the dinner table late, naked and covered with salt. He took salt from his face and sprinkled it on the food, and then reached down for his testes, where chile pods sprouted, and he added their spice to the feast. The other guests scolded the man for his crudeness, but he answered that nothing was as necessary to life as his gifts of salt and chile, and when the others tasted the food, they knew he was right.

The creamy avocado soothes some of the fire from the serranos in this partially cooked, partially fresh salsa.

Makes about 2 cups

12 ounces whole tomatillos, husked
4 to 6 fresh serranos
Water
1 large avocado, peeled and seeded
3/4 cup chopped fresh cilantro
4 green onions, chopped
2 garlic cloves
Salt to taste
Pinch of sugar (optional)

Place the tomatillos and the serranos in a saucepan. Pour in water to cover them. Bring the mixture to a boil and boil for 5 minutes. Drain.

When the chiles are cool enough to handle, discard the stems and seeds. Transfer the chiles and tomatillos to a blender. Add about two-thirds of the avocado to the blender along with the cilantro, green onions, and garlic. Purée until smooth. Taste and add salt and, if you wish, sugar. Blend briefly.

Spoon the salsa into a decorative bowl. Chop the remaining third of the avocado and stir it into the salsa.

The salsa is best eaten within a couple of hours. It goes great with Homemade Tostadas or other chips, though you might also want to try it with grilled seafood or chicken.

GREEN CHILE SALSA

Another green salsa, this one takes its color from mild New Mexican or Anaheim chiles, the type favored in Sonora, Arizona, and southern New Mexico.

Makes 2 cups

1 tablespoon vegetable oil
1/2 medium onion, minced
2 garlic cloves, roasted and mashed
1 teaspoon cumin seeds, toasted and ground
1 cup chopped roasted mild green chile, preferably New Mexican or
    Anaheim, fresh or frozen
1 cup water
1/2 teaspoon salt, plus more to taste

In a saucepan, warm the oil over medium heat. Add the onion and sauté until limp. Stir in the garlic and cumin, and sauté for another minute. Add the chile, water, and salt, and reduce the heat to low. Simmer for 10 minutes. Spoon the salsa into a decorative bowl and refrigerate for at least 2 hours before serving.

Green chile salsa on apple fritters, mint-scented rice, savory shortbreads with cheese and chile, green chile mayonnaise: They sound like items from a contemporary Southwestern restaurant menu, but they're just a sampling of the recipes in Bertha Haffner-Ginger's 1914 *California Mexican-Spanish Cook Book*. A high school math teacher by profession, the author was also an inventive home cook who supplemented her salary by giving classes in kitchen arts and hospitality.

SALSA DE CHILTEPÍN

People ate wild chiltepíns in Tamaulipas at least eight thousand years ago. Today in northern Mexico, harvesters take off from other jobs for a few weeks in late summer to gather the wild chiles, collecting a couple of dozen metric tons in good years, much of which is exported to the States. In southern Arizona, nonprofit organizations like Native Seeds/SEARCH worked with the U.S. Forest Service to establish the first U.S. *in situ* conservation area for the chiltepín and other wild crops in the Coronado National Forest, south of Tucson. The Santa Cruz Chili and Spice Company (listed in "Mail-Order Sources") has the lease to harvest the chiltepíns and has set up a demo garden and orientation center at its nearby store.

When one of the early Jesuit missionaries in the Sonoran Desert first tried a tiny pea-shaped chiltepín, he swore he had "hellfire in my mouth." This Baja California creation may give you an equally intimate experience with the diabolical. If you can't find chiltepíns, substitute chiles pequíns.

Makes about 2 cups

2 small tomatoes, preferably Roma or Italian plum, chunked
1 heaping tablespoon dried chiltepíns
2 garlic cloves
3 tablespoons vinegar, preferably white or cane
1 1/2 teaspoons dried oregano, preferably Mexican
1 teaspoon salt
1 cup water

Place all the ingredients in a blender and purée until smooth. Let the mixture sit at room temperature for 30 minutes before serving. Spoon into a decorative bowl.

Refrigerate the salsa if you don't plan to use it within 1 or 2 hours. In a covered jar, it keeps for weeks. Shake well before using.

SALSA DE ÁRBOL

Chiles de árbol, similar to cayennes, don't pack as much wallop as chiltepíns, but their concentration in this salsa gives it a devilish kick.

Makes 1 1/4 cups

3 whole small tomatoes, preferably Roma or Italian plum, unpeeled
12 chiles de árbol
1/2 small white onion, chunked
3 garlic cloves
1/2 cup water
2 tablespoons vinegar, preferably cider or cane
2 tablespoons vegetable oil
1/2 teaspoon salt

Heat the broiler.

Place the tomatoes on a small baking sheet, covered with foil for easier cleaning. Broil the tomatoes for 15 to 18 minutes, turning occasionally, until the tomatoes are soft and the skins split and turn dark in spots. Cool the tomatoes briefly.

While the tomatoes broil, simmer the chiles, onion, and garlic in the water in a small pan until softened, about 5 minutes. Drain the mixture, reserving 1/4 cup of the cooking liquid. Transfer the mixture, the reserved cooking liquid, the roasted tomatoes (with peels and cores), and remaining ingredients to a blender. Purée briefly until semismooth. Chill for at least 1 hour.

The salsa pairs particularly well with Tucson Cheese Crisps and Tied-Up Beans.

Some people believe that all Mexican food is spicy hot, but it isn't really the case. With the notable exception of northern New Mexico, where locals freely admit to a chile addiction, salsa is almost always the fieriest item on the table in the borderlands. Traditionally, cooks provide a choice of salsas—perhaps a red and green, or a fresh and bottled—and diners tailor the heat of dishes to their own taste.

Slices or small chunks of young, tender pads from the prickly-pear cactus, nopales or nopalitos provide flavor to a salsa that goes wonderfully with grilled or boiled shrimp, among other dishes.

Makes about 2 cups

1 1/4 cups prepared nopales, rinsed and diced fine
3 small tomatoes, preferably Roma or Italian plum, diced
2 pickled jalapeños, minced, plus liquid from a jar of pickled jalapeños
    to taste (optional)
3 garlic cloves, minced
1 teaspoon cumin seeds, toasted and ground
1 teaspoon vinegar, preferably white or cider
Salt to taste
2 tablespoons minced fresh cilantro

In a bowl, combine all the ingredients except the cilantro. Refrigerate for 30 minutes or up to several hours. Stir in the cilantro just before serving.

Regional Variations: Southwestern master chef and cookbook author Mark Miller makes one of the most elaborate and tasty cactus salsas, mixing tiny strips of nopales with tomatillos, bell peppers, roasted corn, serranos, prickly-pear syrup, adobo sauce, cilantro, and mint.

SALSA SHOYU

This contemporary twist on a salsa for fish comes from the Pacific coast of Mexico.

Makes about 1 cup

3/4 cup soy sauce
3 tablespoons fresh lime juice
2 tablespoons minced red onion
2 to 3 garlic cloves, roasted and mashed
1/2 to 1 teaspoon chile caribe, or 1/4 to 3/4 teaspoon crushed chile de
    árbol or cayenne, or more to taste
2 tablespoons minced fresh cilantro

Combine all the ingredients in a bowl. Let the mixture sit at room temperature for at least 15 minutes.

Serve as an accompaniment to mild white fish fillets, atop meaty fresh tuna or salmon steaks, or spooned over scallops.

APPLE SALSA

Contemporary fruit salsas usually eliminate tomatoes but keep other classic ingredients.

Makes about 2 cups

1 large, tart apple, such as Granny Smith, peeled, cored, and diced fine
1/4 cup finely diced red bell pepper
1/4 cup finely diced red onion
1 heaping tablespoon minced fresh mint
1 heaping tablespoon minced fresh cilantro
1 tablespoon tequila
1 canned chipotle chile plus 1 teaspoon adobo sauce, or more to taste
1/4 teaspoon salt
1/4 teaspoon ground coriander
Juice of 1/2 to 1 lemon

Tucson abounds in great specialty salsas. Margaret Audilet reworked pioneer recipes to establish her line of Territorial Gourmet condiments, sold by mail (P.O. Box 228, Cortaro, Arizona 85652, 800-798-7328 or 602-297-9646). Nearly two decades ago, Desert Rose Foods started making its products with a forty-four-gallon barrel and a canoe oar. The company now offers a half-dozen salsas and hot sauces (P.O. Box 5391, Tucson, Arizona 85703, 800-937-2572 or 602-620-6227). Donna Nordin's popular contemporary Southwestern restaurant, Cafe Terra Cotta, developed its own line of salsas, dip mixes, and condiments. Contact them at 4310 North Campbell Avenue, Tucson, Arizona 85718, 800-550-0013 or 602-577-8100.

Within an hour of serving, combine all the ingredients, except the lemon juice, in a bowl. Stir in the smaller quantity of lemon juice and let the salsa sit for 10 minutes. Taste and add more juice if needed for a balance of tart-sweet flavor.

Serve with grilled or roast chicken, quail, pork, or lamb, or top a small round of goat cheese with the salsa and present it with bread or crackers.

Regional Variations: Different cooks experiment with a wide range of fruit in salsas, without much reference today to whether the ingredients are local or not. Many fruits combine gracefully with one or more chiles. Melons pair well with fresh serranos and jalapeños, peaches with chipotles, and tropical fruits like papayas and pineapples with habaneros. Citrus mates with cayennes and chiles de árbol, and apples also go nicely with chiltepíns.

JALAPEÑO HOT SAUCE

Inspired by a Tucson creation, this fiery green elixir keeps for weeks bottled.

Makes about 1 3/4 cups

8 fresh jalapeños, stemmed
1 dried or fresh mild green chile, preferably New Mexican or Anaheim, stemmed
1 cup vinegar, preferably white or cane
1/2 cup water
2 tablespoons pepitas (shelled pumpkin seeds), toasted
2 tablespoons chopped onion
6 garlic cloves
1 1/2 teaspoons salt
1/2 teaspoon dry mustard
1/2 teaspoon cumin seeds, toasted

Place all the ingredients in a blender and purée for 2 minutes, until the sauce is smooth but still a little grainy. Refrigerate the sauce for at least 8 hours. Reblend the sauce for 30 seconds and strain it into a bottle.

The sauce can be served immediately or refrigerated for later use. Shake well before using.

GUAJILLO MILD SAUCE

The berry tones of the guajillo mix marvelously with tomato.

Makes 2 cups

3 whole small tomatoes, preferably Roma or Italian plum, unpeeled
6 to 7 dried guajillos
Water
1/3 medium onion, chunked
5 garlic cloves
1 1/2 tablespoons extra-virgin olive oil
1 tablespoon vinegar, preferably white
1 tablespoon tequila
1/2 teaspoon salt, plus more to taste
1 tablespoon minced fresh cilantro (optional)

Heat the broiler.

Place the tomatoes on a small baking sheet, covered with foil for eas-ier cleaning. Broil the tomatoes for 15 to 18 minutes, turning occasion-ally, until the tomatoes are soft and the skins split and turn dark in spots. Cool the tomatoes briefly.

While the tomatoes broil, prepare the guajillos. Toast them in a hot dry skillet just until they become fragrant and a little pliable. Discard the stems and seeds. Place the chiles in a bowl, cover them with boiling water, and let them sit for 15 minutes or until soft.

Peel the tomatoes and transfer them to a blender. Drain the chiles and add them and the remaining ingredients, except the cilantro, to the blender. Purée the mixture. Pour the sauce into a small saucepan and cook for 15 minutes over low heat. Cool the salsa to room temperature, stir in the cilantro, if you wish, and serve. Refrigerate the salsa if you don't plan to use it within 1 or 2 hours.

We particularly like this sauce with grilled or broiled fish or shrimp.

Throughout New Mexico, southern Arizona, and parts of northern Mexico, some green chiles are allowed to ripen to red on the vine and made into *ristras,* or strings. While still fresh and flexible, several are tied together at the stem and then fastened in clusters that measure one to six feet in length. Traditionally, people hung the *ristras* to dry in a place with good air circulation, often outdoors under the eaves of a house. Before the days of blenders and food processors, and the wide availability of ground chile, cooks picked the crimson pods off the strings, soaked the chiles in water, and pulverized them in some way—with a sieve, a knife, or even their fingers.

The red chiles from Chimayó in northern New Mexico develop more slowly and stay smaller than most varieties, concentrating their sweet yet mellow heat. Try to find them for optimum flavor in this cooked sauce, though any dried New Mexican or Anaheim chiles can be substituted. You can find Chimayó chile, always labeled as such, in some well-stocked groceries, or you can order from the New Mexican suppliers in "Mail-Order Sources."

Makes approximately 4 cups

2 tablespoons vegetable oil
1 medium onion, minced
3 garlic cloves, minced
3/4 cup ground dried mild red chile, preferably Chimayó
4 cups water or beef stock
1 teaspoon dried oregano, preferably Mexican
1 teaspoon salt

Warm the oil in a heavy saucepan over medium heat. Add the onion and garlic, and sauté until the onion is limp. Stir in the chile and then the water, a cup at a time. Add the oregano and salt, and bring the sauce just to a boil. Reduce the heat to a low simmer and cook for 20 to 25 minutes. The completed sauce should coat a spoon thickly but still drop off it easily.

Serve warm with enchiladas, burritos, tamales, and other dishes. The sauce keeps, refrigerated, for 5 to 6 days and freezes well.

Regional Variations: A few decades ago, most New Mexico cooks liked to add pork to the sauce when they could afford it. The present generation prefers beef, either ground or chunked, when it uses meat at all. Some people think a little cumin contributes to the flavor, but others would say the idea is a Texas heresy.

ARIZONA CHILE COLORADO

Arizonans usually like a thinner and less pungent red chile sauce than New Mexicans, but in a similar style.

Makes approximately 4 cups

2 tablespoons vegetable oil
1 medium onion, minced
2 garlic cloves, minced
2 tablespoons all-purpose flour
6 tablespoons ground dried mild red chile, preferably Anaheim or New Mexican
2 cups water
2 cups tomato juice
1 teaspoon dried oregano, preferably Mexican
1 teaspoon salt

Warm the oil in a heavy saucepan over medium heat. Add the onion and garlic, and sauté until the onion is limp. Mix in the flour, eliminating any lumps. Stir in the chile and then the water, a cup at a time. Add the tomato juice, oregano, and salt and bring the sauce just to a boil. Reduce the heat to a low simmer and cook for 20 to 25 minutes. The completed sauce should coat a spoon thinly and drop off it easily.

Serve warm with enchiladas, burros, chimichangas, and other dishes. The sauce keeps, refrigerated, for 5 to 6 days and freezes well.

The californios, the original Spanish settlers in California, made a sauce like this, using vinegar to cut the chile heat.

Makes approximately 4 cups

3 tablespoons vegetable oil

3 tablespoons fine-textured dried breadcrumbs

2 garlic cloves, minced

1 1/2 teaspoons dried oregano, preferably Mexican

1/2 cup ground dried mild red chile, preferably Anaheim or New Mexican

5 cups water

2 tablespoons vinegar, preferably cider

1 1/2 teaspoons salt

In a large, heavy saucepan, warm the oil over medium heat. Sprinkle in the breadcrumbs and brown briefly. Add the garlic, oregano, and chile. Stir in the water slowly to avoid lumps, and add the vinegar and salt. Bring the sauce to a boil, then reduce the heat to a simmer. Cook the sauce for 20 to 25 minutes.

Serve the sauce warm with enchiladas or other dishes. The sauce keeps, refrigerated, for about 5 days and freezes well.

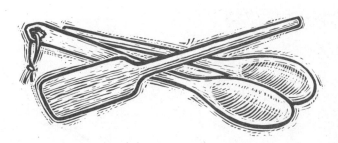

HATCH GREEN CHILE SAUCE

This sauce comes from Hatch in southern New Mexico, home of some of the best green chiles raised in the United States.

Makes approximately 4 cups

3 tablespoons vegetable oil
1 large onion, chopped
3 garlic cloves, minced
2 tablespoons all-purpose flour
2 cups chopped roasted mild green chile, preferably New Mexican or
    Anaheim, fresh or frozen
2 cups chicken stock
1 teaspoon salt
1 teaspoon ground coriander

In a heavy saucepan, warm the oil over medium heat. Add the onion and sauté until well softened, about 5 minutes. Stir in the garlic and sauté for an additional minute, then add the flour and continue cooking for another 1 or 2 minutes. Mix in the chile. Pour in the stock and add the seasonings. Bring the mixture to a boil. Reduce the heat to a low simmer and cook for about 15 minutes, until thickened but still very pourable.

Serve warm with enchiladas or other dishes. The sauce keeps, refrigerated, for about 5 days and freezes well.

The El Paso chapter of the United Daughters of the Confederacy presented some unusual approaches to regional food in their 1926 book *How We Cook in El Paso*. They offered good instructions for making green and red sauces, but also suggested such oddities as green chili sandwiches—chopped pods mixed with mayo and spread on bread—and baked tamale pudding—featuring canned tamales mixed with canned corn, ketchup, and Worcestershire sauce.

Near the Arizona–Sonora border, in towns like Tubac, you find two related styles of green chile sauces, both relatively mild. Some cooks tame the chile heat with tomatillos, the Mexican way, and others take more of an Anglo angle, accomplishing the same end with tomatoes.

Makes approximately 4 cups

3 tablespoons vegetable oil
1 large onion, chopped
3 garlic cloves, minced
2 tablespoons all-purpose flour
1 1/2 cups chopped roasted mild green chile, preferably New Mexican or Anaheim, fresh or frozen
1 cup canned crushed tomatoes or 8 ounces husked tomatillos, boiled in water until soft, drained, and chopped
1 1/2 cups chicken stock
1 teaspoon salt, or more to taste

In a heavy saucepan, warm the oil over medium heat. Add the onion and sauté until well softened, about 5 minutes. Stir in the garlic and sauté for an additional minute, then add the flour and continue cooking for another 1 or 2 minutes. Mix in the chile and tomatoes or tomatillos. Pour in the stock and add the salt. Bring the mixture to a boil. Reduce the heat to a low simmer and cook for about 15 minutes, until thickened but still very pourable.

Serve warm with enchiladas or other dishes. The sauce keeps, refrigerated, for about 5 days and freezes well.

TEX-MEX CHILI GRAVY

The key to a true Tex-Mex combination plate, this chili con carne gravy covers enchiladas, tamales, and in some kitchen at some time somewhere, almost anything else with a Lone Star soul.

Makes approximately 6 cups

3 ounces dried red chiles, about 12, preferably a combination of 8 ancho and 4 New Mexican
4 cups beef stock
1 pound chili-grind ground beef
1 medium onion, chopped fine
2 garlic cloves, minced
2 tablespoons bacon drippings (optional)
2 teaspoons cumin seeds, toasted and ground
1/2 teaspoon dried oregano, preferably Mexican
1/2 teaspoon salt
1 tablespoon masa harina

Many Texans take a reasonable shortcut in their gravy, starting with chili powder (about 1/2 cup in this recipe) rather than dried chiles, and reducing the cumin and oregano by half. The favorite powder for more than a century has been Gebhardt's, probably the model for all others. German-born William Gebhardt, a New Braunfels resident, developed his blend in 1896 to emulate the famous fare of San Antonio's chili queens.

Preheat the oven to 300° F. Break the stems off the chile pods and discard the seeds.

Place the pods in a single layer on a baking sheet and roast them for about 5 minutes. Watch the pods closely because they can scorch easily. Break each chile into several pieces.

In a blender, purée the pods with the stock. You should be able to see tiny pieces of chile pulp, but they should be bound in a smooth, thick liquid. Set the purée aside.

In a medium saucepan or skillet, brown the meat with the onion and garlic. Drain the meat mixture of excess fat. Add the bacon drippings, if you like, and return the pan to the heat. When the bacon drippings have melted, add the cumin, oregano, salt, and puréed chiles. Simmer the mixture for about 50 minutes, until the meat is tender and the liquid has thickened slightly. In a small bowl mix the masa harina with 2 tablespoons of the cooking liquid, and stir the mixture back into the gravy. Simmer the gravy for an additional 10 minutes.

Serve with Tex-Mex enchiladas, tamales, or other dishes.

From the heart of Mexican ranching country, this chunky tomato-based sauce is best known for its leading role in huevos rancheros, but it's much more versatile.

Makes approximately 3 cups

1 tablespoon vegetable oil
1 medium onion, chopped
2 garlic cloves, minced
3/4 cup chopped roasted mild green chile, preferably
   New Mexican or poblano
2 cups canned crushed tomatoes
1 tablespoon vinegar, preferably white
1 to 2 teaspoons sugar
1/2 teaspoon cumin seeds, toasted and ground
1/2 teaspoon salt, or more to taste
1/3 cup chopped fresh cilantro
1 tablespoon fresh lime juice

Warm the oil in a skillet over medium heat. Add the onion and garlic and cook until softened. Mix in the chile, tomatoes, vinegar, sugar, cumin, and salt and simmer over low heat, covered, for about 15 minutes. If the mixture gets dry, add a little water. The sauce can be made a day ahead to this point and rewarmed. Add the cilantro and lime juice in the last 1 or 2 minutes of cooking.

Technique Tip: If you have a smoker, try substituting 1 pound of fresh tomatoes for canned and smoking them before cooking them down with the other sauce ingredients. Smoke the tomatoes whole until the skins split, chop them, and then add them to the skillet to simmer with everything else.

DIABLO SAUCE

Because of the emphasis in Mexican cuisine on roasting tomatoes, garlic, and other vegetables and then cooking them a second time by frying, many quick sauces have a depth of flavor that would take hours of conventional American or European simmering to accomplish. *Diablo* sauce, a classic with shrimp and other seafood, is a prime example. Be aware that this is a hot one, called a devil's brew for good reason.

Makes approximately 3 cups

2 whole small tomatoes, preferably Roma or Italian plum, unpeeled
2 canned chipotles or dried chipotles soaked in hot water to soften
8 garlic cloves, roasted
1 tablespoon plus 1 teaspoon ground dried mild red chile, preferably
    ancho, guajillo, or New Mexican
1 teaspoon Worcestershire sauce
2 bay leaves
1/2 teaspoon salt, plus more to taste
1/2 teaspoon dried oregano, preferably Mexican
1/8 teaspoon ground cloves
2 cups stock, either seafood, chicken, or a combination
1/4 cup vegetable oil

Heat the broiler.

Place the tomatoes on a small baking sheet, covered with foil for easier cleaning. Broil the tomatoes for 15 to 18 minutes, turning them occasionally, until they are soft and the skins split and turn dark in spots. Cool the tomatoes briefly.

In a blender, purée the tomatoes and their skins and cores with the rest of the ingredients except the oil.

In a heavy skillet or large saucepan, warm the oil over high heat. Pour in the sauce, being careful to avoid splatters as the liquid hits the hot oil. When the mixture stops its most insistent sputtering, reduce the heat to medium-low and simmer for about 15 minutes, until the sauce thickens but still spoons easily.

The sauce can be made a day ahead and rewarmed. We like to poach shrimp in it or serve it over grilled shrimp or fish fillets.

The hottest club of all is Don Alfonso Foods' Fresh Chiles of the Month Club. José Marmalejo's Austin-based company will send you a variety of pungent pods, including exotic varieties. The company also sells frozen New Mexican greens and poblanos, the chiles called for most often in our recipes. A portion of the proceeds goes to the protection of Mexican rain forests. See "Mail-Order Sources" for additional information.

Not all Mexican and Southwestern sauces are chock full of chile. Like this one, a few contain nothing in the least fiery.

Makes approximately 2 1/2 cups

1 1/2 pounds whole small tomatoes, preferably Roma or Italian plum
1/2 medium onion, sliced thick and rubbed with vegetable oil
2 garlic cloves, unpeeled, rubbed with vegetable oil
3/4 teaspoon salt
2 bay leaves

Heat the broiler.

Place the tomatoes, onion, and garlic on a baking sheet, covered with foil for easy cleanup. Broil for 10 minutes, then remove the garlic and turn the tomatoes and the onion slices. Continue broiling the remaining vegetables for another 8 to 10 minutes.

Peel the garlic and place it in a blender. Add the unskinned tomatoes, the onion, and the salt to the blender and purée. Pour the mixture into a saucepan and add the bay leaves. Simmer the sauce over medium heat for 10 minutes.

Use the sauce for Nogales Entomatadas, as an accompaniment to any chiles rellenos, or over an omelet or grilled vegetables.

ROASTED GARLIC–PIÑON SAUCE

Makes approximately 2 cups

3 whole heads of garlic, unpeeled
2 cups chicken stock
4 medium shallots, minced
1/4 teaspoon dried rosemary, crumbled
1/4 teaspoon ground chile de árbol or cayenne
1/3 cup piñon (pine) nuts, toasted
1/2 cup Crema (page 63) or crème fraîche
Salt to taste

Preheat the oven to 400° F. Place the garlic in a small baking dish and bake until the skin is browned and the cloves are very soft, about 35 to 40 minutes.

When cool enough to handle, peel and mash the garlic. Transfer the garlic to a heavy saucepan and add the stock, shallots, rosemary, and chile. Simmer over medium heat for 25 minutes to reduce.

Transfer the mixture to a blender, add the piñon nuts, and purée until smooth. Return the mixture to the saucepan, stir in the crema and salt, and heat through.

Serve the sauce with grilled fish, squash, or eggplant, or substitute it for more robust chile sauces on cheese enchiladas or on tamales, such as Cheddar and Piñon or Green Corn.

CILANTRO CREAM SAUCE

Makes approximately 2 cups

2 teaspoons vegetable oil
1 tablespoon minced onion
1 cup whipping cream

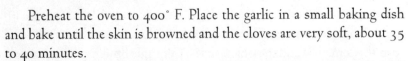

Politics gets really heated when the subject is chile. Even the spelling of the capsicum can be a hot topic, so important to New Mexicans that Senator Pete Domenici felt compelled to declare "chile" (rather than "chili") the official name in the *Congressional Record*. Back in Santa Fe, the legislature got into the act as well, making the fruit the official state vegetable. Meanwhile in Arizona, Flagstaff legislator Tony Gabaldon proposed an improvement to the criminal code that would outlaw sales of inauthentic Mexican food. Suggesting his recipes as the standard, he wanted to prohibit an offender from enjoying local cooking again for several years. Gabaldon ultimately withdrew the bill as "too hot to handle."

1 cup half-and-half
1/2 cup white wine
1/4 teaspoon salt
2 tablespoons mayonnaise
2 tablespoons minced fresh cilantro

In a saucepan, warm the oil over medium heat. Add the onion and sauté briefly until limp. Add the cream, half-and-half, wine, and salt. Reduce the heat to medium-low and simmer the sauce for 20 to 25 minutes, until reduced by about one-quarter. Strain the sauce. Stir in the mayonnaise and the cilantro. Rewarm if necessary.

The sauce makes a particularly good match with vegetables, such as Red Pepper–Piñon Enchiladas, and with roasted or grilled chicken or turkey. Leftover sauce can be used in place of mayonnaise as a binder in vegetable or chicken salads with a Southwestern flair.

CALIFORNIA SALAD VINEGAR

Inventive salad toppings are not new in California. Versions of this vinegar for greens appear in several turn-of-the-century cookbooks.

Makes 1 quart

1 small cucumber, peeled, seeded, and sliced
1/2 small red onion, sliced in rings
1/2 small bunch of parsley, with stems trimmed to 2 to 3 inches
3 medium sprigs of tarragon
4 garlic cloves, halved
3 cups white wine vinegar

Arrange the vegetables and herbs decoratively in a sterilized quart bottle or jar, using a skewer or the handle of a wooden spoon to help position the ingredients.

In a saucepan, bring the vinegar to a boil. Pour as much of it over the vegetables and herbs as will fit in the bottle or jar. Cool to room temperature, cover, and store in a dark pantry for at least 5 days before using.

VOLCANIC VINEGAR

Makes 1 quart

8 to 10 chiles de árbol
6 to 8 cascabel chiles
1/2 small bunch of fresh cilantro, with stems trimmed to 2 to 3 inches
  (optional)
2 green onions, trimmed of any drooping green tops
3 garlic cloves, halved
3 3/4 cups vinegar, preferably cider or white wine

In a dry skillet, toast the chiles briefly over medium heat, just until they begin to release their fragrance. Place the chiles in a quart bottle or jar. Add the cilantro, if you wish, green onions, and garlic, using a skewer or the handle of a wooden spoon to help position the ingredients.

In a saucepan, bring the vinegar to a boil, and pour as much of it over the chiles, vegetables, and herbs as will fit in the bottle or jar. Cool to room temperature, cover, and store in a dark pantry for at least 5 days before using.

Sprinkle the vinegar over Drunken Beans or Quelites, or use it in salsas and hot sauces to kick up their heat quotient.

Regional Variations: All kinds of chiles are used in Southwestern vinegars today. The most colorful versions employ a variety of fresh pods picked for their multiple hues. The hottest entries, found most often in Texas and Arizona, rely on chiltepíns, which grow wild in the arid southern areas of those states.

Sylvia Vergara's orchards in Montecito, New Mexico, just outside Dixon, contain some of the oldest apple trees in the United States, planted by the Spanish in the early years of settlement. The venerable trees produce fruit for her small line of La Carreta vinegars and preserves. The cider vinegars are superlative, scented with chiles de árbol and local garlic. Several of the New Mexico companies listed in "Mail-Order Sources" carry her products, or you can order direct from Box 70, Dixon, New Mexico 87527, 505-579-4358.

CREMA

This tangy thickened cream works much better on border dishes than sour cream, the usual American substitute. The same as French crème fraîche, it tops everything from quesadillas to *carne adovada* in Mexico and parts of the Southwest.

Makes about 1 cup

1 cup whipping cream (preferably not ultra-pasteurized)
2 tablespoons buttermilk

In a small, nonreactive bowl, combine both ingredients. Cover the bowl loosely, and let it stand at room temperature for 8 to 24 hours, until the cream is thickened and tart. Stir the crema well, cover it, and refrigerate it. Use it as needed. Crema keeps for up to 10 days.

BORDER ESCABECHE

Jalapeños and vegetables *en escabeche*, or "pickled," are an old favorite on border tables. Store-bought versions don't compare in flavor or beauty to what you can prepare easily at home.

Makes 1 quart

16 to 18 medium fresh jalapeños, preferably a mix of red and green, or
    a mix of jalapeños with güeros, roasted and peeled
1 medium carrot, sliced in rounds and blanched
3 ounces jícama, cut in fat matchsticks
1/4 cup extra-virgin olive oil
3/4 cup pearl onions, preferably purple, peeled
3 garlic cloves, halved
1 cup white vinegar
1/2 cup water
2 teaspoons salt
1 teaspoon dried oregano, preferably Mexican
2 bay leaves

Place the chiles in a quart jar, interspersed decoratively with the carrot and jícama.

Warm the oil in a heavy, nonreactive saucepan over medium heat. Add the onions and sauté for a couple of minutes until they begin to soften. Stir in the garlic and sauté for another minute. Mix in the vinegar, water, salt, oregano, and bay leaves. Pour the hot liquid over the jalapeños and vegetables. Cool the mixture to room temperature, cover, and chill for at least 3 days.

The vegetables keep, refrigerated, for 2 months or longer.

PICKLED ONIONS

Makes approximately 1 1/2 cups

1 medium red onion, sliced into thin rings
Hot water
1/2 cup red wine vinegar
3 ounces frozen orange juice concentrate (half a 6-ounce can)
2 garlic cloves, minced
1/2 teaspoon dried oregano, preferably Mexican
1/4 teaspoon cumin seeds, toasted and ground
Pinch of salt

Place the onion slices in a medium bowl. Pour enough hot water over the onions to cover them by about 1 inch. Let the onions sit for 15 minutes, then pour off the water to eliminate some of the strong flavor.

Add the remaining ingredients to the onions and stir to combine. Refrigerate the mixture, covered, for at least 24 hours.

Serve the onions with Elemental Arracheras, Slow-Grilled Pork al Pastor, soft tacos, or on chicken-topped nachos. The onions keep well, refrigerated, for a couple of weeks.

This "coastal pickle" comes from a preservation technique favored by a California mission.

Makes 1 quart

1 pound small to medium tomatillos, husked and halved
1 whole mild green chile, preferably Anaheim or New Mexican, fresh or frozen, roasted and sliced in several fat strips
1 whole mild red chile, preferably Anaheim or New Mexican, fresh or frozen, roasted and sliced in several fat strips, or an additional roasted green chile
2 whole fresh chiles güero, 4 güeritos, or 2 fresh jalapeños
6 garlic cloves, halved
1 cup vinegar, preferably white wine
1/4 cup water
1 teaspoon salt
1 teaspoon brown sugar
1/2 teaspoon cumin seeds
1/2 teaspoon dried oregano, preferably Mexican

Arrange the tomatillos, chiles, and garlic decoratively in a quart jar.

Combine the remaining ingredients in a saucepan and bring to a boil over high heat. Pour into the jar as much of the liquid as will fit. Cool the mixture to room temperature, cover, and chill for at least 5 days.

Pair the refreshingly tart tomatillos with grilled fish or boiled shrimp. The vegetables keep, refrigerated, for 2 months or longer.

In a heavy saucepan, melt the butter over medium heat. Add the blender mixture and then stir in the remaining ingredients. Reduce the heat to low and cook for about 50 minutes, or until the mixture is reduced and very thick, but still spoonable. Stir often toward the end. Pour into a jar and refrigerate the ketchup overnight.

Use the ketchup on hamburgers, French fries, cold roast pork, meatloaf, grilled fish sandwiches, or anything else that seems appealing. The ketchup keeps, refrigerated, for several weeks.

Technique Tip: Be very careful when working with the habanero, a chile with thirty to fifty times the firepower of a jalapeño. Jeff Campbell of the Stonewall Chili Pepper Company in central Texas, one of the few commercial habanero operations in the States (see "Mail-Order Sources"), dresses like a beekeeper and wears a respirator with an air tank when he grinds the chiles. He also closes his retail shop so visitors don't breathe the dust. You don't have to take that many precautions when you're working with a single habanero, but be sure to wear rubber gloves and avoid standing directly over equipment in which you mince, purée, or cook the chiles.

Major national companies were caught off guard when salsa passed ketchup as America's most popular condiment. They are playing catch-up with a variety of spicy ketchups and salsas, but according to researchers at *Fiery Foods* magazine, small regional brands controlled 70 percent of the market in 1994.

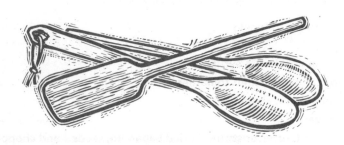

The scion of a family that made maple syrup and jellies, the late David Pace of San Antonio led the way in bottling Southwestern salsas. His first batch of Pace Picante Sauce, released in 1947, literally exploded on the shelves, but eventually the jalapeño brew exploded only in popularity instead. Now the Texas company makes half a million pounds of the salsa daily.

Jalapeño mustards are among Texas's liveliest contributions to the condiment scene. This south Valley version demonstrates why.

Makes approximately 1 cup

1/3 cup dry mustard, preferably Colman's
1/3 cup vinegar, preferably cider
2 teaspoons yellow mustard seeds
2 eggs
1/2 cup beer or water
2 tablespoons minced pickled jalapeños, or more to taste, plus 2 tablespoons jalapeño pickling liquid
1 1/2 tablespoons molasses
1 tablespoon minced onion
1/2 teaspoon salt

In a small bowl, mix together the dry mustard and vinegar until a smooth paste forms. Stir in the mustard seeds, cover, and let the mixture sit at room temperature for several hours.

Transfer the mustard mixture to a small, heavy saucepan. Add the remaining ingredients and warm over medium-low heat. Cook the mixture slowly, stirring frequently, until thick, about 30 minutes. Cool to room temperature. Transfer the mustard to a small jar and refrigerate for later use.

The mustard keeps for up to 2 weeks and tastes great on sausage or a grilled cheese sandwich, or mixed into salad dressings.

Technique Tip: If you're in a rush, you can whip up a simpler version of jalapeño mustard by adding the same amounts of pickled jalapeño and onion in the recipe to 3/4 cup prepared yellow mustard.

DATE-ONION RELISH

Makes about 1 1/2 cups

1 large onion, chopped
Hot water
1 pound dates, chopped
1/2 cup red wine vinegar
1/2 cup red wine
3 tablespoons brown sugar
3/4 teaspoon salt
2 tablespoons brandy

Place the onion in a bowl and cover it with the water. Let the mixture stand for 15 minutes, then drain the liquid.

In a small, heavy saucepan, combine the onions with the vinegar, wine, sugar, and salt and bring the mixture to a boil over high heat for 15 minutes, or until the consistency is like jam. Stir in the brandy. Let the relish cool briefly, then cover and refrigerate it overnight. The relish will keep for several weeks.

Serve it with grilled or smoked pork or lamb chops or on a sandwich of thin-sliced pork roast.

The Tarahumara people in northern Mexico use chiles in curing ceremonies to ward off witchcraft. They distrust people who don't eat chiles, even suspecting them of sorcery.

Makes about 2 cups

1 cup vinegar, preferably cane or cider
1 cup brown sugar
6 ounces tomatillos, husked and chopped
1 medium onion, minced
3/4 cup chopped roasted mild green chile, preferably New Mexican or Anaheim, fresh or frozen
1/2 teaspoon cumin seeds, toasted and ground
1/2 teaspoon salt

Combine all the ingredients in a heavy saucepan. Simmer over medium heat until cooked down and thick, about 35 to 45 minutes. The chutney can be used warm immediately or transferred to a jar, chilled, and kept for up to 2 weeks.

Try it on cornbread or biscuits, as a glaze for grilled salmon or steamed carrots, spooned over cream cheese and served with crackers, or on a turkey and cheddar sandwich.

Regional Variations: Border cooks routinely add chile to down-home American condiments. We've particularly enjoyed chutneys of apricots with chiles de árbol and peaches paired with chipotles. Pickle relish perks up when laced with fresh New Mexican pods, and sweet pickles sizzle with chiles pequíns. Chile jellies and jams are getting as common as cactus in the Southwest.

BREAKFAST BOUNTY

You have to love a culture that believed in two breakfasts. Traditionally along the border, as well as farther south in Mexico, people ate an early *desayuno*—maybe coffee or chocolate and warm tortillas—and then enjoyed a larger *almuerzo* in the mid-morning. Identical in derivation to the English word *breakfast*, the *desayuno* would break the fast (*ayuno*) of the night and the *almuerzo* would prepare you for a day of labor.

Hardly anyone on the border follows the custom fully now, but it remains alive in a fondness for big morning meals. Breakfasts are sometimes more bountiful than dinners, and often involve similar foods and styles of preparation. From hearty burros and burritos to snappy combinations of eggs and jalapeños, the regional specialties today accomplish the purposes of two meals in one. They send you away ready for a full day and they really blast the fast.

MACHACA BREAKFAST BURROS

The *ito* in *burrito* implies something small. That's why people call it a "burro" in Arizona, where the dish is hardly diminutive. This version, with a mildly spicy *machaca* filling, comes from the Phoenix area. We usually prepare the beef a day or two ahead, using chuck instead of the short ribs, flank, or brisket that some cooks prefer. Leftover *machaca* makes superb tacos and flautas.

Serves 6 generously

3-pound boneless shoulder chuck roast
Salt and fresh-ground black pepper to taste
1/4 cup bacon drippings or vegetable oil
1 cup beef stock
1 medium onion, chopped
2 garlic cloves, minced
3 small tomatoes, preferably Roma or Italian plum, chopped
1/2 cup chopped roasted mild green chiles, preferably New Mexican or
     poblano
1 tablespoon fresh lime juice
2 to 3 eggs, lightly beaten (optional)
6 thin flour tortillas, preferably at least 8 inches in diameter, warmed

Salsa del Norte (page 38) or other salsa

Rub the roast with sprinklings of salt and pepper.

Warm 2 tablespoons of the oil or, for more flavor, the bacon drippings in a heavy, lidded skillet or Dutch oven over medium-high heat. Brown the meat on all sides.

Reduce the heat to low. Pour the beef stock over the meat and add half of the onion and half of the garlic to the pan. Cover the dish and simmer until the meat is very tender, about 1 to 1 1/4 hours. Let the meat sit in the cooking liquid until cool enough to handle. Drain the meat, reserving the cooking liquid. Shred the meat with your fingers or two forks, or in a food processor in several small batches. (If your processor has a plastic blade for dough, use it for the nicest shreds.)

In a heavy skillet, warm the remaining bacon drippings or oil over

Machaca originally referred to meat (usually beef) that was seasoned, dried for preservation, and later tenderized by pulverizing and cooking. The word comes from the verb *machacar,* meaning to pound or crush. Ranchers and cowboys refined the technique in the cattle country of northern Mexico, and it became as vital to their lives as jerky was to western American pioneers. After refrigeration arrived in the region, and dehydration was no longer needed for preservation, *machaca* took on a different connotation. Many people now use the term to describe any beef cooked well-done with seasonings and then shredded. For a taste closer to the original dish, see the recipe for Tucson Carne Seca.

medium heat. Sauté the remaining onion and garlic in the fat until the onion softens. Add the meat and sauté until well browned, 10 to 12 minutes. Scrape the meat up from the bottom every few minutes. It should get brown and, in spots, crusty, but it shouldn't burn. Stir in the reserved cooking liquid, tomatoes, chile, and lime juice. Cook over low heat for about 25 minutes, until most of the liquid has evaporated and the meat remains a little moist. Add more salt and pepper if you wish. (The meat can be made ahead to this point and refrigerated for several days. Warm the meat before proceeding.)

If you are using eggs, continue cooking the meat over medium heat. Stir in the eggs, mixing them well with the meat until the eggs have cooked through.

Spoon the mixture into warm tortillas, rolling each into a cylinder. Arrange the burros on plates, seam side down, and offer salsa on the side.

Regional Variations: Phoenix's funky, down-home El Norteño food stand serves a great version of this burro, without the egg but with fried cubed potatoes added to the filling. South of the Gila River in Arizona, the beef inside would likely be a drier, more intense preparation similar to our Tucson Carne Seca. In Ciudad Juárez at Julio's Casa Corona restaurant, customers choose whether they want the meat dry, soupy, or *medio*. In the San Diego area, the popular Roberto's chain favors a *medio* version with the egg and calls the dish a burrito, despite its considerable heft.

GREEN CHILE BREAKFAST BURRITOS

In contrast to burros in Arizona and Sonora, New Mexico burritos usually come smothered in a red or green chile sauce. This potato-and-bacon combo is our favorite of several popular styles.

Serves 4 generously

1/4 cup vegetable oil

1 medium onion, chopped

1 garlic clove, minced

4 medium baking potatoes, peeled or unpeeled, parboiled and grated on the largest holes of your grater (at room temperature or warm)

1/2 teaspoon salt

Fresh-ground black pepper to taste

4 flour tortillas, preferably medium-thick and 7 to 8 inches in diameter, warmed

8 to 12 slices bacon, cooked until crisp

3 to 4 cups Hatch Green Chile Sauce (page 54), warmed

6 to 8 ounces mild cheddar cheese, grated

A number of dishes in other chapters can be adapted for breakfast fare. Take a look at the Sweet Tamales and the Baked Apples with Cajeta in "Cross-Cultural Desserts," and the Tostónes and the Mama's Papas in "Versatile Vegetables." Also consider new twists on old ideas—for example, topping biscuits with a green chile sauce instead of gravy.

Preheat the oven to 400° F.

In a heavy skillet, warm the oil over medium-high heat. Add the onion and garlic, and sauté for a minute. Stir in the potatoes, salt, and as much pepper as you wish. Pat the mixture down evenly, cook for 1 or 2 minutes, and scrape it up from the bottom of the skillet. Repeat the process until the potatoes are cooked through, are somewhat browned, and have some crisp edges, about 8 to 10 minutes.

Spoon one-fourth of the potatoes onto a tortilla. Top it with 2 to 3 slices of bacon. Roll up into a loose cylinder, and place the burrito, seam side down, on a heat-proof plate. Spoon one-fourth of the chile sauce over the burrito and sprinkle it generously with cheese. Repeat with the remaining ingredients.

Bake the burritos until the cheese is melted and gooey, about 5 minutes. Serve immediately.

Regional Variations: Everyone in the Land of Enchantment seems to hold a different notion about what constitutes a breakfast burrito. Unlike this version, most contain scrambled eggs, along with chile and maybe meat or potatoes. Some people substitute fried sausage for the bacon, and others get their crunch from onions. Outside New Mexico, similar ideas appear with various local twists. In Corpus Christi, Texas, we found a whole omelet wrapped in a flour tortilla and called an omelet a la taquito; it came topped with melted cheddar cheese and fresh tomato salsa rather than a cooked chile sauce.

COAHUILA CHILAQUILES

Mexican cooks developed chilaquiles as an appetizing way to use up left-over corn tortillas and sauces. Colloquially, the word means "broken-up old sombreros," definitely a reference to the appearance rather than the taste. This version migrated to us via Múzquiz, Coahuila, a ranching area in north central Mexico, where they use as much as twice the amount of chorizo as we do.

Serves 6

SAUCE
2 cups chopped husked tomatillos, preferably fresh
1/2 cup chopped roasted mild green chile, preferably poblano or New Mexican, fresh or frozen
1 fresh serrano, chopped (optional)
1/4 cup minced onion
2 garlic cloves, chopped
3/4 cup chicken stock
1/4 cup whipping cream
3 tablespoons minced fresh cilantro
Salt and fresh-ground black pepper to taste

12 stale corn tortillas (thicker tortillas are best—add a couple of extra tortillas if yours are on the slim side)
Vegetable oil for pan-frying

1 cup cooked chorizo, crumbled

1/2 medium onion, sliced in very thin rings
2 cups grated asadero or Monterey jack cheese
**Crema (page 63), crème fraîche, or sour cream thinned slightly with
    milk, for garnish**

Mix together the tomatillos, green chile, serrano if you want more firepower, onion, garlic, stock, and cream in a saucepan over medium-high heat. Bring the sauce to a boil, then lower the heat and simmer for 10 minutes, until reduced slightly. Add the cilantro, and salt and pepper to taste. Spoon the sauce into a blender and purée. Pour the sauce into a shallow dish.

Preheat the oven to 350° F. Grease a shallow baking dish. Cut the tortillas into sixths.

Heat about 1/2 inch of oil in a skillet over medium heat. Add some of the tortilla wedges, frying briefly until golden and chewy, not as crisp as a chip. Drain the wedges on paper towels. Repeat until all the wedges are fried.

Dip the wedges in the tomatillo sauce and layer all of them in the bottom of the baking dish. Sprinkle the chorizo, onion, and cheese over the tortillas. Top the dish with the remaining tomatillo sauce. Bake the chilaquiles for 20 to 25 minutes until bubbly. Drizzle the crema, crème fraîche, or diluted sour cream over the chilaquiles and serve immediately.

To simplify the last-minute tasks, you can make the tomatillo sauce and fry the tortilla wedges the night before. Don't assemble the chilaquiles, though, until shortly before baking or the tortillas will become soggy.

Regional Variations: In most of Mexico, including some border areas, shredded chicken is more common in chilaquiles than chorizo. Some cooks eliminate the meat entirely in favor of eggs, adding perhaps two to the sauce. Cochita Ybarra created a satisfying California version in the 1960s, topping the fried tortillas and cheese with a red sauce like our Californio Colorado, chopped onions, and a scattering of black olives. Texans also favor a red sauce—usually based on ancho chiles simmered with beef stock or beer, tomatoes, and cumin—and maybe a dollop of sour cream. Stephan Pyles, the acclaimed chef at Star Canyon in Dallas, reinvented chilaquiles with contemporary flair, using a yellow squash custard rather than sauce, and baking the custard with crisp tortilla chips.

You can order chilaquiles all day and evening at La Hacienda in El Paso, but even at dinner they'll be served morning-style with orange juice, coffee, and *pan dulce* (sweet rolls). An amazing place, full of border character, the restaurant occupies a historic nineteenth-century home on the grounds of the original Fort Bliss, just barely on the U.S. side of the Rio Grande.

A Tex-Mex classic, *migas* takes its name from the Spanish word for crumbs, a reference to the tortilla chips mixed in with the scrambled eggs. In other areas, the dish may be called *huevos con tostaditos.*

Serves 2 (easily doubled or tripled)

4 eggs
1 tablespoon water
1 tablespoon tomato-based salsa
1 tablespoon bacon drippings or vegetable oil
1/4 cup chopped red bell pepper
1/4 cup chopped onion
1/2 to 1 fresh jalapeño, minced
12 to 16 tostada chips, broken into bite-size pieces
3 ounces mild cheddar or Monterey jack cheese, grated

Flour tortillas, warmed
Tomato-based salsa

In a small bowl, beat the eggs lightly with the water and salsa. Set aside.

In a heavy skillet, warm the bacon drippings or oil over medium heat. Add the bell pepper, onion, and jalapeño and sauté until limp. Pour in the eggs and stir them up from the bottom of the skillet as they cook to your desired doneness. About a minute before the eggs are done, add the chips, stirring in well. Remove the eggs from the heat and stir in the cheese, reserving a little to scatter over the top.

Serve the *migas* immediately with warm flour tortillas and more salsa.

Regional Variations: Some Texans make *migas* with fresh corn tortillas instead of chips, cutting the tortillas into thin strips and sautéing them along with the bell pepper, jalapeño, and onion, which yields a chewy rather than crisp texture. Other people start with a ranchero sauce, rather than a base of sautéed vegetables, and then cook the scrambled eggs and chips in the warm sauce. At the morning bakery branch of Fort Worth's legendary Joe T. Garcia's restaurant, the kitchen adds shredded chicken to the tangle of chips, cheese, and eggs.

JOE'S BREAKFAST NACHOS

Joe's Bakery and Coffee Shop in Austin makes a style of *migas* very different from most, loaded with cheese and other toppings. It's so distinctive we call our version of the dish breakfast nachos.

Serves 2 to 4

1/4 pound bulk chorizo
Vegetable oil as needed
1 small onion, chopped
1 tablespoon butter
3 eggs
1 tablespoon water
Salt to taste
Salted tortilla chips
6 to 8 ounces mild cheddar cheese, grated
1 small tomato, preferably Roma or Italian plum, chopped
1 to 2 fresh or pickled jalapeños, sliced

Preheat the oven to 350° F.

In a skillet, sauté the chorizo over medium heat. Remove the chorizo from the skillet with a slotted spoon and drain it. Add a little oil to the skillet if the chorizo drippings don't lightly cover the surface. Reduce the heat to medium-low and add the onion. Sauté the onion for about 10 minutes, until soft. Reserve the onion.

Place the butter in a shallow, medium baking dish and melt it in the oven.

In a bowl, whisk the eggs with the chorizo, water, and salt. Remove the baking dish from the oven and pour the eggs into the warm dish. Top the eggs with enough chips to make a single dense layer. Scatter the onions and cheese over the chips. Bake for 5 to 8 minutes, or until the eggs are set lightly and the cheese is melted. Top with the tomato and jalapeño and serve immediately.

Many people love to wake in the morning to the smell of coffee or frying bacon. For Lucy M. Garza, growing up in Santa Monica, Texas, near Harlingen, the aroma was breakfast tacos. A home economist, teacher, and author of the fascinating *South Texas Mexican Cookbook* (Eakin Press, 1982), she fondly recalls her mother warming flour tortillas and wrapping them around eggs, beans, chorizo, or *machacado,* a version of dried beef found most commonly in the lower Rio Grande Valley and northeastern Mexico.

Simple in concept and execution, a breakfast taco is a tortilla (usually flour) folded or wrapped around almost anything on the stove. Most common in Texas, the tacos may make use of leftovers—perhaps *carne guisada,* chili con carne, or refried beans—or they can be just a tasty, invigorating way of eating basic morning foods such as scrambled eggs and sausage. When we want to do something special with the idea, we often opt for this combination.

Serves 4

FILLING
12 ounces chorizo
1 medium onion, chopped
3 garlic cloves, minced
1/2 green bell pepper, chopped
1 small waxy red potato, boiled, peeled, and diced
1/2 teaspoon dried sage
1/2 cup corn kernels, fresh or frozen
1/2 cup beef stock
Salt to taste

12 flour tortillas, preferably medium-thick and about 6 inches in diameter, warmed
Melted butter

4 ounces mild cheddar cheese, grated
4 ounces pepper jack or Monterey jack cheese, grated
Pico de Gallo (page 40) or other favorite salsa
Chopped fresh cilantro (optional)

Heat the broiler. Grease a baking sheet.

In a heavy skillet, crumble the chorizo and cook it over medium heat until browned. Add the onion, garlic, bell pepper, potato, and sage and continue sautéing until the vegetables are soft. Mix in the corn and stock, add salt to taste, and cover the skillet. Reduce the heat to low and cook for 5 minutes, until the corn is just tender.

Top the tortillas with spoonfuls of filling and fold them in half. Brush the tacos lightly with butter and transfer them to the baking sheet. Pop the tacos under the broiler for 2 minutes, until lightly crisp on top.

Serve immediately, accompanied with bowls of the cheese and salsa, plus cilantro if you wish.

TAMALE HASH

Serves 2

2 tablespoons butter
1 to 2 tablespoons vegetable oil
1/2 medium onion, chopped
1/2 cup corn kernels, fresh or frozen (optional)
3 to 4 tamales (depending on size), pork, green corn, or other, husked and cut into bite-size chunks
2 eggs
Your favorite red or green chile sauce, warmed
Chopped tomato and green onions
Crema (page 63), crème fraîche, or sour cream
Grated cheddar cheese, or crumbled Cotija cheese or queso fresco

In a heavy skillet, warm the butter and oil over medium heat. Use the larger amount of oil if the tamales are relatively dry. Add the onion and sauté until very soft. Mix in the corn, if you like. Add the tamale pieces and stir them in gently. It's fine for some of the tamale pieces to disintegrate, but you want to keep a good portion of them in recognizable chunks. Cover the skillet for 2 to 3 minutes to let the mixture steam and heat through, developing a little crust on a few pieces.

Keep the mixture warm while preparing the 2 eggs in your favorite simple style. For this dish, we favor them scrambled or fried sunny-side up.

Spoon the tamale mixture neatly onto two plates. Arrange an egg over each and add a generous ladling of sauce. Top with the tomato and green onions, crema, crème fraîche, or sour cream, and the cheese. Serve immediately.

Tamale hash is the kind of homey dish you seldom see in restaurants, even in the numerous borderlands cafés that specialize in home cooking. La Pila in downtown Phoenix is a notable exception, in this and many other ways. Chef-owner Norman Fierros takes basic regional foods and elegantly refines them without redefining them. The result is some of the best cooking we've sampled in many years of grazing the Southwest.

Whether you call it the Río Grande, as it's known in the United States, or the Río Bravo, the Mexican name, the river is no barrier to food ideas. This kind of hearty cowboy hash could show up on either side of the water.

Serves 4

2 tablespoons vegetable oil
1 tablespoon butter
2 1/2 cups diced waxy red potatoes, peeled or unpeeled
1 1/2 cups diced onions
1 cup diced red bell pepper
1 fresh jalapeño, minced
4 cups shredded brisket, cooked as for Brisket Burritos (page 207) or
    other baked or smoked brisket
1 cup beef stock
1 tablespoon prepared yellow mustard
1 tablespoon tomato-based salsa, such as Salsa del Norte (page 38)
1 teaspoon fresh-ground black pepper
Salt to taste

Warm the oil and butter together in a heavy skillet over medium heat. Add the potatoes, onion, bell pepper, and jalapeño and sauté for 10 minutes. Mix in the remaining ingredients. Simmer, covered, for 15 minutes, stirring the mixture up from the bottom once after about 10 minutes and patting it back down. Uncover the skillet and continue cooking for another few minutes until the liquid is absorbed and the mixture just begins to get crusty on the bottom.

Serve hot.

Josefina Velazquez de Leon included a recipe for this norteño-style egg dish—named for its appearance—in her bilingual *Libro de Cocina Mexicana para el Hogar Americano*. Published by the Culinary Arts Institute in Mexico City in 1956, and distributed in the United States as well, the book was among the most ambitious of its era, certainly worth seeking out today in libraries or used bookstores.

Serves 6 generously

1 whole small tomato, preferably Roma or Italian plum
1-pound pork loin
1 large onion, chopped
1 bay leaf
1 canned chipotle chile plus 1 teaspoon adobo sauce
1/2 teaspoon salt, plus more to taste
1/4 teaspoon dried thyme
1/2 cup water

Vegetable oil for pan-frying
6 corn tortillas
1 tablespoon cream
1 to 2 fresh serranos, chunked
2 medium Haas avocados
1 tablespoon minced fresh cilantro
12 eggs

Red radish slivers and crumbled queso fresco or grated Monterey jack cheese, for garnish

Heat the broiler. Place the tomato on a small baking sheet and broil for about 15 minutes, turning once or twice. Set the tomato aside to cool and reduce the oven heat to 350° F.

Place the pork loin in a small baking dish and add half the onion, the bay leaf, the chipotle and adobo sauce, 1/2 teaspoon of salt, and the thyme. Pour the water over the meat. Cover the pork and bake until it's tender and pulls apart easily, about 1 hour. Let the meat sit in the cooking liquid until cool enough to handle. Remove the meat and reserve the liquid.

Heat $1/2$ to 1 inch of oil in a skillet until the oil ripples. With tongs, dunk a tortilla in the oil long enough for it to turn crisp. Repeat with the remaining tortillas and drain them. Reserve a few tablespoons of the oil for frying the eggs.

Shred the meat with your fingers, with two forks, or in a food processor in several small batches. (If your processor has a plastic blade for dough, use it for the nicest shreds.) To the pork, add the cream and about 1 tablespoon of the cooking liquid, enough to make the pork moist but not soupy. (The meat can be made ahead to this point and refrigerated for several days. Warm the meat before proceeding.)

In a blender, combine the broiled tomato with the reserved onion and the serranos. Mash the avocados in a bowl and add the tomato mixture. Sprinkle in the cilantro. Stir to combine.

Spoon a thin layer of pork over a tortilla and place it in the center of a plate. Repeat with the remaining meat and tortillas. Keep the plates warm.

In the skillet used for softening the tortillas, fry the eggs to your desired doneness, salting them if you wish. Add a little of the reserved oil when the pan becomes dry. As the eggs are done, position two on each plate, at opposite sides of the tortilla, overlapping it some as necessary to fit on the plate. Spoon equal portions of the avocado mixture atop the pork and eggs. Sprinkle the plates with radish slivers and cheese. Serve immediately.

Serves 4

Vegetable oil for pan-frying
8 corn tortillas
8 eggs
2 ounces Monterey jack or mild cheddar cheese, grated
Ranchero Sauce (page 57), warmed

Crema (page 63), crème fraîche, or sour cream, and cilantro sprigs, for
     garnish (optional)

Heat about $1/2$ inch of oil in a skillet. Dip the tortillas into the oil, one or two at a time, and cook for a few seconds until soft and pliable. Drain the tortillas. Arrange 2 tortillas overlapping on each of 4 plates.

Pour out of the skillet all but enough oil to generously coat its surface. Reserve the extra oil.

Place the skillet back on the stove and heat the oil over low heat. Fry the eggs, in batches, adding a little of the reserved oil when the pan becomes dry. Top each tortilla with a fried egg. Alternatively, the eggs can be poached in the simmering ranchero sauce.

Sprinkle a couple of tablespoons of the cheese over each serving of eggs, and top with equal portions of the sauce.

Serve the eggs immediately with crema, crème fraîche, or sour cream, and cilantro if you wish. Huevos rancheros are almost always accompanied with refried beans, and often with chorizo.

Regional Variations: Californian Jacqueline Higuera McMahan uses a quesadilla base with her huevos rancheros, an idea she picked up in Saltillo, Mexico. To duplicate the technique, sprinkle asadero or Monterey jack cheese between two corn tortillas and fry with a small amount of oil until the cheese is melted but the tortillas are chewy rather than crisp.

Other south-of-the-border twists might include sprigs of fresh epazote in the classic ranchero sauce, or extra heat from minced fresh serranos or dried chiles de árbol. In Arizona we've seen a version that used an uncooked salsa, or pico de gallo, on the eggs, and flour tortillas underneath rather than corn.

Texas versions may double the amount of cumin in the sauce, and are often spicier than those elsewhere, including in Mexico. The sauce likely gets its punch from a combination of jalapeños and New Mexican green chiles, as it does in Juan Rubio's recipe for his Rubio's café in El Paso. Farther south in Texas, sliced avocado may garnish the eggs, and in southern California both avocado and black olives might top the dish.

BREAKFAST CORNBREAD

This idea, adapted from Los Angeles chef Roger Hayot's creation, takes its inspiration from huevos rancheros but ends up in a much different place. It's no surprise that the cornbread works so well in the dish, because on the Anglo frontier, cornbread was the equivalent of corn tortillas.

Serves 6

6 big squares or wedges of your favorite cornbread
Butter
Vegetable oil for frying
6 eggs
Salt to taste
Diablo Sauce (page 58)

Split the cornbread horizontally. Toast and butter the bread and keep it warm.

Warm a thin film of oil in a heavy skillet over medium-high heat. Fry the eggs to your desired doneness, salting them as you wish.

Arrange 2 pieces of cornbread on each plate. Top with a fried egg and spoonfuls of sauce. Serve with grilled or fried mild-flavored sausage—chorizo doesn't offer enough flavor contrast.

New Mexicans eat an unusual cornmeal dish called *chauquehue.* More popular in the past than today, the breakfast porridge is made with a special toasted blue or yellow cornmeal. Some cooks thicken the gruel, fry it into a cake, and top it with red chile sauce. Soupy or crusty, it's a form of *atole,* one of the most pervasive Native American foods in New Spain before and after the conquest.

TORTA TEX-ICANA

The Mexican influence rises to the top in this strata, a type of layered casserole loved in Texas.

Serves 4 to 6

1 tablespoon vegetable oil
3/4 cup chopped roasted mild green chile, preferably New Mexican or poblano, fresh or frozen
1/2 red bell pepper, diced
1/2 cup grated zucchini
1/4 cup chopped onion
4 green onions, sliced
1 garlic clove, minced
4 eggs
1/4 cup milk
1/4 teaspoon cumin seeds, toasted and ground
Salt and fresh-ground black pepper to taste
3 flour tortillas, preferably thick and 6 to 7 inches in diameter
2 to 3 tablespoons grated mild cheddar cheese

Preheat the oven to 350° F. Grease a medium baking dish. A 1 1/2-quart soufflé dish or other deep round dish works perfectly for this.

In a sauté pan or skillet, warm the oil over medium-low heat. Sauté the chile, bell pepper, zucchini, onion, green onions, and garlic for about 12 to 15 minutes, until the vegetables are soft and most of the liquid has evaporated. Cool the mixture briefly.

In a medium bowl, whisk together the eggs and milk and add the cumin, salt, and pepper.

Place a tortilla in the bottom of the baking dish. Top it with one-third of the vegetable mixture, then pour one-third of the egg mixture over it. Repeat with the remaining tortillas, vegetable mixture, and egg mixture. Sprinkle the cheese over the top.

Bake the torta for 30 minutes, or until puffed, golden brown, and lightly set in the center. Allow the torta to sit for 10 to 15 minutes before slicing it into wedges. Eat it hot or warm.

THE BORDER COOKBOOK

Serves 1

2 extra-large eggs
1 tablespoon water
Salt to taste
1/8 teaspoon fresh-ground black pepper
1 tablespoon butter
3 tablespoons grated mild cheddar cheese
3/4 cup Hatch Green Chile Sauce (page 54) or other mild green chile
    sauce, warmed

Grated mild cheddar cheese, for garnish

In a bowl, briefly whisk together the eggs, water, salt, and pepper, just enough to combine the yolks and whites.

Over high heat, warm a 7- to 8-inch omelet pan or skillet, preferably nonstick. Add the butter to the pan, swirling it to coat thoroughly the entire surface. Just when the butter begins to color, add the egg mixture and swirl it to coat the entire pan as well. Let the pan sit directly over the heat for a few seconds, until the eggs firm in the bottom on the pan. Sprinkle the cheese over the eggs. Pull the pan sharply toward you several times, and then tilt the pan so that the front half of the omelet begins to roll over the back portion. Use a spatula to help shape the eggs into a loose cylinder. Tip the omelet out onto a warm serving plate, neatening it with the spatula, if needed. Pour the chile sauce over the omelet and sprinkle it with cheese. Serve immediately.

Technique Tip: While you can make only one omelet at a time, the preparation goes fast enough to serve several guests at one seating. Pre-measure the amounts of butter, cheese, and sauce needed for the number of omelets required, and have them handy. Mix up each batch of eggs separately for best results. Just wipe out the pan between omelets.

An old favorite along the border, these poached eggs appeared in cook-books at least as early as 1898, when an El Paso cook raved about them as "very fine." The taste varies across the region according to local styles in sauces, but we like the balance in this California version.

Serves 3 or 6

2 cups Californio Colorado (page 53)
2 to 3 tablespoons water (optional)
6 eggs
Salt (optional)

Thin flour tortillas, warmed
Minced chives, sliced black olives, and shredded lettuce, for garnish

In a heavy pan or skillet, bring the sauce to a hearty simmer over medium-high heat. Add the water if the sauce doesn't stir easily.

Break an egg into a cup. Stir a small indentation in the sauce and slip the egg neatly into the indentation. Repeat quickly with the remaining eggs and sauce. Cover the pan, reduce the heat to medium-low, and cook the eggs until poached to your desired doneness. Sprinkle the eggs with salt if you wish.

With a large spoon, transfer the eggs to serving plates, either 1 or 2 eggs to a serving. Spoon the chile sauce in pools around the eggs. Serve immediately, on or accompanied with the tortillas, and garnished with the chives, olives, and lettuce.

Jacqueline Higuera McMahan says that the Spanish fondness for chile at breakfast shocked early Anglo settlers in California. Some Bostonians tried to explain the practice by claiming that the *californios* had the digestive system of ostriches. If you're not afraid of a similar reputation, check out Jacquie's *Mexican Breakfast Cookbook* (The Olive Press, 1992), a delightful collection of recipes and reminiscences. She captures the mood of the borderlands when she says, "Have breakfast like a king, lunch like a prince, and dinner like a pauper."

Just seven miles from the Mexico border, and not much farther from the fabled town of Tombstone, Bisbee roared through the turn of the century as a copper-mining boomtown. Built into the side of a mountain, the town climbs up timeworn stone steps in a way that reminds some people of a medieval European village, which it has portrayed in several Hollywood sagas. Artists, writers, and other escapees from civilization moved into Bisbee when the copper company moved out, creating a sophisticated and lively community in a truly remote corner of the Southwest.

The most common scrambled egg dishes in Mexico sparkle with salsa or burst with chorizo, though seldom at the same time. At the historic Copper Queen Hotel in Bisbee, Arizona, the kitchen combined both elements to create the original model for this modern scramble.

Serves 4

8 eggs
2 tablespoons water
2 tablespoons New Mexico Salsa Picante (page 41) or other tomato-based salsa
Salt to taste
1/2 pound bulk chorizo
2 medium onions, preferably sweet, sliced in thin strips

New Mexico Salsa Picante or other tomato-based salsa

In a bowl, whisk the eggs lightly with the water, salsa, and salt. Set the bowl aside.

Crumble the chorizo into a heavy skillet and cook it over medium heat until browned. Chorizo generally renders a fair bit of fat. If you have what appears to be more than 2 tablespoons of drippings, pour off any extra. Add the onions and continue cooking until the chorizo is a little crispy and the onions are soft.

Pour in the eggs and stir them up from the bottom as they cook to your desired doneness. Serve immediately, accompanied with additional salsa.

Regional Variations: Salsa ingredients are such a common addition to scrambled eggs in Mexico that the dish is called huevos a la méxicana. Sometimes the salsa goes on top of the eggs, instead of being cooked with them, perhaps with a little chorizo too. Creative cooks on both sides of the border today may be more inclined to mix in squash or even yucca blossoms, or in New Mexico maybe such local favorites as sage and piñon nuts. Traditionally, beans accompany eggs, but Helen C. Duran goes further, putting whole pintos inside a scramble in her *Blonde Chicana Bride's Mexican Cookbook* (Filter Press, 1981).

Though the term is used somewhat differently elsewhere, in northern New Mexico *torrejas* usually refers to these light, crispy egg fritters. We first discovered them in the village of Chimayó, paired with the town's incomparable red chile sauce. Sometimes called a *torta tradicional*, the *torrejas* serve as a meat substitute during Lent, though we find them no sacrifice. The methodology in the recipe comes from lifelong cook Genoveva Martínez, who makes delicately delicious fritters.

Makes 2 to 3 main-dish servings

3 eggs
3 tablespoons all-purpose flour
Scant 1/4 teaspoon baking powder
Pinch of salt
Vegetable oil for pan-frying

Chimayó Red Chile Sauce (page 51), warmed
Minced green onion tops

Separate the eggs, dropping the whites into a medium-size nonplastic mixing bowl and placing the yolks in another bowl. Whisk the yolks lightly, stir in the flour, baking powder, and salt, and set aside.

Beat the egg whites with a mixer at high speed until they are stiff. Gently fold the egg yolk mixture into the egg whites.

Pour enough oil to measure about 1 inch into a heavy skillet. Heat the oil to 370° F. Drop a large spoonful of the batter gently into the oil. Within seconds the *torreja* should puff up by about 50 percent or more. Turn the fritter at least once while cooking. Fry it until it is deep golden brown and crisp.

Remove the first *torreja* and drain it. Cut into the fritter to see if it is cooked through. The interior should be lightly moist with a melting tenderness. Adjust the oil temperature if necessary. Drop in the remaining batter, a few spoonfuls at a time. Avoid overcrowding the fritters as they cook.

Transfer the *torrejas* to a platter and top with the chile sauce, or offer the sauce on the side. Sprinkle the green onion over the platter. Serve immediately.

Regional Variations: In parts of northern Mexico, similar fritters contain dried shrimp, sometimes mixed in the best versions with fresh shrimp. To the yolk mixture in this recipe, you add 1 or 2 teaspoons of dried shrimp—purchased in small cellophane packages in Mexican or Asian markets—pulverized to breadcrumb texture, and 3 or 4 chopped peeled, boiled shrimp.

JALAPEÑO PIE

Early California ranchers started the day in a big way. In *The California Dons* (Appleton-Century-Crofts, 1962), Edna Deu Pree Nelson describes an 1842 Spanish breakfast that consisted of "stewed beef, beans, fowl, tongue cooked with hot peppers and garlic, and rice, pumpkin, and cabbage." Mostly Sonoran soldiers originally, sent north to protect the California missions, the dons became land and cattle barons of enormous influence before the U.S. Army arrived and claimed the state in 1846.

Named a pie because you cut and serve it in slices, this modern Texas treat is really more of a cross between a casserole and a frittata. It's guaranteed to stir your morning juices.

Makes one 12-inch skillet, enough for 6 to 8 main-dish servings

2 tablespoons butter
1 1/2 cups chopped onions
2 garlic cloves, minced
4 to 6 fresh jalapeños, halved vertically, veins removed, and sliced in very thin half-moon rings
1 teaspoon ground dried mild red chile, preferably ancho or New Mexican
1 1/4 teaspoons cumin seeds, toasted and ground
1 teaspoon fresh-ground black pepper
1/2 teaspoon salt, or more to taste
8 eggs
8 ounces mild cheddar cheese, grated

Additional rings or slices of jalapeños, for garnish (optional)

Preheat the oven to 350° F.

In a heavy skillet, warm the butter over medium heat. Add the onions and garlic, cooking until softened. Add the jalapeños, red chile, cumin, black pepper, and salt and cook for 5 minutes more. Remove the skillet from the heat, patting the jalapeños down in an even layer.

In a medium bowl, whisk the eggs together until foamy and stir the cheese into the eggs. Pour the eggs and cheese over the jalapeño mixture.

Scatter the optional jalapeño slices over the pie if you wish.

Bake the pie for 25 to 30 minutes, or until lightly puffed and golden. Cool for 10 to 15 minutes.

Slice the pie in wedges and serve. Leftovers can be reheated or served cold.

BROWNSVILLE BABY CACTUS PIE

Many border residents enjoy eggs with nopales. In the lower Rio Grande Valley, near the Gulf of Mexico, some cooks also add shrimp to the combination.

Serves 6 to 8

2 tablespoons vegetable oil
1/2 medium onion, chopped
2 garlic cloves, minced
1 red bell pepper, chopped
1/2 cup chopped peeled raw shrimp
8 eggs
2 tablespoons water
1 canned chipotle chile, minced
1/4 teaspoon salt, or more to taste
Fresh-ground black pepper
1 cup prepared nopales, diced
2 tablespoons crumbled queso añejo, Cotija, or feta cheese
2 rings of red bell pepper

If you're determined to do something different for breakfast, consider the "Nidos de Golondrinas" (Swallows' Nest) eggs suggested in a 1926 El Paso cookbook. You wrap hard-boiled eggs in thin strips of filet, bread the beefy balls, and fry them. The author served the dish topped with gravy.

Preheat the oven to 350° F. Grease a medium baking dish, preferably shallow.

In a heavy skillet, warm the oil over medium heat. Add the onion, garlic, and bell pepper and sauté until the onion is limp. Add the shrimp and cook through briefly. Remove the skillet from the heat.

In a large bowl, beat the eggs lightly with the water. Add the chipotle, salt, and pepper.

Stir the sautéed mixture and the nopalitos into the eggs and pour the mixture into the prepared dish. Sprinkle the cheese over the eggs and top with the rings of bell pepper overlapping in the pie's center.

Bake the eggs for 25 to 30 minutes, or until lightly puffed and golden. Cool for 10 to 15 minutes.

Slice the pie in wedges and serve. Leftovers can be reheated or served cold.

TAMPICO SHRIMP AND SPINACH TORTA

Serves 6

SALSA
1/2 cup chopped fresh spinach
1/2 cup chopped fresh parsley
2 green onions, chopped
2 garlic cloves, roasted
1 tablespoon dried breadcrumbs
2 teaspoons vinegar, preferably white
1 fresh serrano, minced
1/2 teaspoon dried thyme
1/2 teaspoon salt
1/2 cup extra-virgin olive oil

OMELET
8 eggs
2 tablespoons water
3 tablespoons extra-virgin olive oil
1 medium red bell pepper, chopped
1/2 cup thin-sliced green onions
2 fresh serranos, minced
1 garlic clove, roasted and mashed
1 teaspoon dried oregano, preferably Mexican
1/2 teaspoon dried thyme
3/4 teaspoon salt
1/2 cup sliced hearts of palm (optional) (see "Technique Tip")
6 ounces fresh spinach, chopped
1/2 pound small-to-medium shrimp, boiled, peeled, and halved

Combine all the salsa ingredients except the oil in a food processor and purée together. With the machine running, add the oil in a steady stream and process until combined. (The salsa can be made ahead several hours and refrigerated if you wish.)

Heat the broiler.

In a bowl, whisk together the eggs and water.

In a heavy, 10-inch, ovenproof skillet, warm the oil over medium heat. Add the bell pepper, green onions, serranos, garlic, oregano, thyme, salt, and, if you wish, the hearts of palm and sauté until the vegetables are soft. Stir in the spinach and sauté until it is limp. Stir in the shrimp quickly and pat the mixture down evenly in the skillet.

Pour the eggs evenly over the mixture and reduce the heat to low. Cook the mixture briefly, until it is just set around the edges, tilting it from side to side a bit if necessary for even cooking.

Transfer the skillet to the broiler and cook for 3 to 4 minutes, until the center is set and the top is lightly browned. Let the torta cool for 5 to 10 minutes before cutting it into wedges.

Serve warm with the salsa.

Technique Tip: Hearts of palm are rarely found fresh in the United States, but well-stocked groceries, gourmet shops, and Hispanic or Latino markets often carry cans of the tender shoots from the cabbage palm tree. They resemble artichoke hearts in flavor and use.

PIÑON PANCAKES WITH APPLE CIDER SYRUP

The Pueblo people of New Mexico taught Spanish settlers to love the *piñones*, or pine nuts, of the area. Among other uses, the Pueblos ground the rich nuggets into a meal or flour, a technique we borrow here. We prefer to make the pancakes with blue cornmeal, also originally from the same people, because it adds another element of nutty flavor.

Serves 4 to 6

SYRUP
2 cups apple cider, preferably unfiltered
2 tablespoons light corn syrup
1 canela stick, or other cinnamon stick
1 tablespoon butter

PANCAKES
1 1/4 cups piñon (pine) nuts
3/4 cup all-purpose flour
1/2 cup cornmeal, preferably blue
1 tablespoon sugar
3/4 teaspoon baking powder
3/4 teaspoon salt
2 eggs
1 1/4 cups milk
2 tablespoons melted butter
2 drops almond extract
Vegetable oil for pan-frying

Toasted piñon (pine) nuts, for garnish (optional)

In a heavy saucepan combine the cider, corn syrup, and canela. Bring the mixture to a boil over medium-high heat, and continue boiling until reduced by about one-fourth. Remove the syrup from the heat and stir in the butter until it melts. Keep the syrup warm or reheat it before serving.

In a food processor, process 3/4 cup of the nuts briefly until ground. Avoid processing them so long that they turn to butter. Add the flour, cornmeal, sugar, baking powder, and salt and process just until a coarse

Piñones from New Mexico and elsewhere are expensive, but for good reason. The gnarled pines that produce the nuts yield a good crop only once every few years. Farmers won't bother with such a fickle and slow-growing tree, so harvesters have to gather the little kernels in the wild by hand. They can pick some loose nuts off the ground, but they must shake or beat most of them out of their cones. Cracking the shells is tough work too, most commonly accomplished with needle-nose pliers. Despite the difficulties, New Mexicans approach the harvest with enthusiasm. In a big year some families still camp in piñon forests and make a weekend out of gathering the nuts, an old tradition that Fabiola Cabeza de Baca Gilbert described fondly in *The Good Life* (Museum of New Mexico Press reprint, 1982), her fascinating 1949 memoir. Today the Navajo nation is turning the pastime into a growing commercial operation.

meal forms. Transfer the mixture into a large bowl and stir in the eggs, milk, butter, almond extract, and remaining nuts. Chill the batter, covered, for 20 to 30 minutes.

Heat a griddle or heavy skillet. Pour a thin film of oil into the skillet. Fry the pancakes a few at a time, about 1 minute per side, adding more oil as needed to keep the pancakes cooking evenly.

Serve the pancakes, garnished with more pine nuts if you wish, accompanied with the warm syrup.

A homey on-the-run Mexican breakfast, particularly popular in the northern states, a *mollete* is a toasted open-faced sandwich filled with refried beans and cheese. It's a brawny border combo, simple and robust.

Serves 4

4 bolillos or other crusty rolls, split (see "Technique Tip")
Vegetable oil
2 tablespoons Guajillo Mild Sauce (page 50) or other
tomato-based salsa
1 cup Refried Beans (page 378) or other mashed leftover beans,
warmed
2 tablespoons minced onion
1 to 2 tablespoons chopped pickled jalapeño (optional)
3 ounces asadero or Monterey jack cheese, sliced thin

Heat the broiler. Brush the cut sides of the bolillos or other rolls with the oil. Place the roll halves, cut side up, on a baking sheet. Broil the split rolls for 2 or 3 minutes, until the slices just begin to color.

Remove the split rolls from the oven and spread each half with a portion of the salsa and beans. Sprinkle with onion and jalapeño and top with cheese slices.

Return the open-faced *molletes* to the broiler and cook until the cheese melts, another 2 to 3 minutes. Serve hot.

Technique Tip: Yeast rolls that often replace tortillas at formal meals in Mexico, bolillos can be found in supermarkets and bakeries on both sides of the border. Usually light-crusted with a slightly sweet dough, they are trim and rectangular in shape, with tapered ends. If you can't locate them in your area, substitute any similar homemade or bakery roll.

Regional Variations: Some cooks add leftover meat to *molletes* to increase the dish's heartiness. Chicken would be the most common choice in southern Mexico, but in the beef-raising states you're just as likely to find thin-sliced pieces of *carne asada* or fajitas. For other norteños, fried bacon or chorizo may spike the taste even more, a goal that Texans might accomplish with a sprinkling of jalapeños instead.

FRITADA WITH WINE FRUIT SYRUP

In old *californio* mission and rancho cooking, a *fritada* resembled what we call French toast today. Early recipes used olive oil for frying, but a mixture of butter and a neutral vegetable oil works better for both cooking and flavor.

Serves 4

SYRUP
1 cup sugar
1 cup fruity, somewhat sweet wine, white or red
1 tablespoon butter
1 teaspoon citrus zest, preferably lemon with white wine or orange with red wine
Pinch of cinnamon
Pinch of nutmeg

8 bolillos (see "Technique Tip" on page 99) or a medium loaf of French bread, slightly stale
3 eggs
1/2 cup half-and-half or whole milk
1 teaspoon sugar
Pinch of cinnamon
Pinch of nutmeg
Butter and vegetable oil, for pan-frying

Orange or lemon slices, for garnish (optional)

Border residents don't make fine distinctions between morning and evening foods: they frequently use leftover dishes and ingredients from the day before at breakfast. Last night's enchiladas might reappear freshened with a fried egg over the top, an approach that goes back at least as far as California mission cooking. New Mexicans might mix their chile sauce into fresh fried potatoes, or serve the rest of the trout from dinner. Ocean fish appear on the plate along the coasts of the Pacific and the Sea of Cortés, and in Chihuahua, Sonora, and Texas, breakfast steak is common, with or without eggs.

Combine all the syrup ingredients in a small saucepan. Simmer over medium-low heat for 8 to 10 minutes, stirring occasionally to dissolve the sugar evenly. Keep the syrup warm.

Slice the bolillos or the bread into fat finger-length pieces about 1/2 inch thick.

In a medium bowl whisk together the eggs, half-and-half or milk, sugar, and spices. Dip the bread slices into the mixture, soaking both sides well.

Heat a griddle or heavy skillet. Add 1 tablespoon each of butter and oil to the skillet. Fry the bread in batches until golden brown, adding more butter and oil as needed to keep the bread browning evenly.

Serve the *fritada*, garnished perhaps with the optional orange or lemon slices, accompanied with the warm syrup.

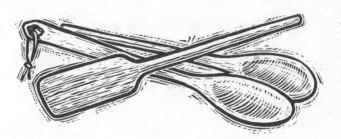

SOUPS AND SALADS

*S*outh of the border, cooks are much more likely to start a meal with a soup than with a salad. They often excel in the domain, taking justifiable pride in flavorful stocks, creative combinations of ingredients, and the resourceful use of leftovers. The tradition spills into Southwestern cooking, but it has gotten diluted over time, sometimes in a literal way. Indicative of American attitudes in the region, one of the top Texas cookbooks ever published called its soup chapter "Crybaby Feed."

In the U.S. borderlands, salads are the most common appetizers, partially as a result of contemporary influences from the rest of the country. Mexicans invented such wonderful salads as guacamole and *noche buena*, but most of the time they eat raw vegetables as salsas, other condiments, and garnishes alongside main dishes. When these foods cross into the Southwest, cooks often expand the ingredients, heighten the flavor, and make them separate salad courses. They also add new notions from their own heritage and the broader national culture, displaying the same imagination with salads that Mexicans apply to soups. Whichever of the two you prefer as a starter, or even as a full meal, the borderlands brim with bright ideas.

CALDO DE QUESO

Filling and flexible in ingredients, depending on what is available, this hearty cheese soup has been a cowhand favorite on northern Mexico ranches for generations. The cheese changes from one area to another, varying with local styles and preferences, but many types work.

Serves 6 to 8

2 tablespoons vegetable oil

1 1/2 medium onions, minced

1 carrot, grated

1 pound red waxy potatoes, peeled and chunked

6 cups chicken stock

3/4 teaspoon dried epazote or marjoram

3/4 teaspoon dried rosemary

1 bay leaf

1/2 teaspoon salt, or more to taste

1/2 cup chopped roasted mild green chile, preferably New Mexican or Anaheim, fresh or frozen

2 small tomatoes, preferably Roma or Italian plum, minced, or 1/2 cup canned crushed tomatoes

1/2 cup half-and-half

3/4 pound Chihuahua, Muenster, Monterey jack, or mild cheddar cheese, grated

3 tablespoons crumbled queso añejo or Cotija, feta, or other aged cheese, for garnish (optional)

In a large saucepan, warm the oil over medium heat. Sauté the onions and carrot and cook until soft. Add the potatoes, stock, epazote, rosemary, bay leaf, and salt and simmer for 10 to 12 minutes, until the potatoes are tender but still hold their shape. Stir in the green chile, tomatoes, and half-and-half and simmer the soup over low heat for 10 minutes. Stir in half of the grated cheese and remove from the heat.

Arrange the remaining grated cheese in bowls and ladle the steaming soup over it. Scatter the crumbled aged cheese over the soup, if you wish. Serve immediately.

Technique Tip: The quality of stock is the most important difference between average and great soup. Many people, particularly north of the border, have given up the old tradition of keeping a stockpot simmering on the back of the stove, but that pot's long-cooked elixir is essential to soup success and an advantage in lots of other dishes as well. Store-bought cans and cubes of mystery substances are weak substitutes, usually long on salt, short on taste, and stiff on price.

Making your own stock is easy and can be done in advance in large quantities. You don't need a precise recipe because depth of flavor does not depend on exact measurements. Start by saving your own ingredients and maybe begging scraps from your meat cutter. Keep trimmings and bones from raw or cooked beef, poultry, and seafood in separate plastic bags, and collect carrot trimmings, onion skins, and maybe celery tops (more common in the United States than Mexico) together to use in all stocks. Stash the ingredients in the freezer until you've got several pounds for a particular stock.

Before beginning the stock, we like to roast and brown the meat and vegetables in a hot oven for about 45 minutes, to amplify their flavor, but that's not a necessary step or even common south of the border. To proceed, put the roasted or frozen ingredients into a stockpot or large saucepan, along with a few chopped garlic cloves and whole peppercorns. Some cooks also toss in a bay leaf, a little parsley, or a touch of thyme or rosemary. Don't add salt; save it for the dish you make with the stock. Cover the trimmings with double their volume in water, bring the pot to a boil, and then reduce the heat to low. Leave the pot uncovered, to evaporate the liquid and intensify the taste.

Seafood stocks need only 1 hour to develop maximum flavor, but chicken and beef welcome several hours or even a full day of slow, low simmering. Cook the stock until about one-third of the original liquid remains. When it reaches that point, strain it, let it cool, and if you wish, degrease it. Bag the stock in small containers, for easy use later, and freeze it. If your freezer space is limited, cook the stock down even further, until thick and gelatinous, and pour it into ice cube trays. When frozen, transfer the cubes to freezer bags. As you need stock, add water to a cube or two to thaw and thin to stock consistency.

A meaty beef and vegetable soup, *cocido* easily makes a full meal. In some parts of Arizona and Sonora, in fact, the term refers to a dish that's closer to a boiled dinner, what others would call *puchero*.

Serves 8

1 1/2 pounds beef short ribs

6 cups water

4 cups beef stock

2 cups peeled, cubed winter squash, such as pumpkin or butternut

15-ounce can garbanzo beans, drained and rinsed

2 cups chopped cabbage

2 medium onions, chopped

1 baking potato, peeled and cubed

2 carrots, diced

1/3 cup ground dried mild red chile, preferably Anaheim or New
    Mexican

5 garlic cloves, minced

1 tablespoon salt

2 bay leaves

1 teaspoon dried thyme

1/2 pound link or bulk chorizo, sliced or crumbled

1/2 cup minced fresh cilantro

Soups have always been a way of extending a little to feed many. In her 1942 cookbook, *The Genuine New Mexico Tasty Recipes,* Cleofas M. Jaramillo recalls Depression-era families passing a soup bone from house to house to flavor the pot. At the time, she said, even lard was a delicacy reserved for the rich.

In a stockpot, simmer the ribs with the water over medium-low heat for about 1 hour, skimming any gray foam from the top.

To the stockpot, add all of the ingredients except the chorizo and cilantro. Simmer for another hour, until the vegetables are quite soft and the rib meat pulls easily from the bone. Remove the ribs from the pot with a slotted spoon and set them aside to cool.

With a slotted spoon, drain 1 to 2 cups of the vegetables from the pot and purée them in a food processor. Return the mixture to the pot. Pick the meat from the ribs and return it to the pot.

In a skillet, fry the chorizo over medium-low heat until browned and crisp. Add it and, if you wish, any rendered fat to the pot. Simmer the soup an additional 15 minutes. Remove the soup from the heat and stir in the cilantro.

Serve warm.

NORTEÑO TORTILLA SOUP

Developed originally as a way to use old tortillas and other leftovers, this soup grew into one of the classics of Mexican cuisine. In most of the country, chicken stock serves as the base, but in the north, beef stock frequently gives the dish a deeper, stouter tone.

Serves 6

8 cups beef stock
6 garlic cloves, roasted
1/2 cup canned crushed tomatoes
1 large onion, half chopped and half sliced into thin rings
1 to 2 chipotles (use whole if dried, or minced if canned)
1 teaspoon dried oregano, preferably Mexican
Juice of 1 lime
Salt to taste
4 corn tortillas, sliced in thin strips and toasted or broiled until crisp
4 ounces asadero or Monterey jack cheese, grated
1 Haas avocado, cubed

In a large, heavy saucepan, bring the stock to a boil. Reduce the heat and simmer until the stock is reduced to approximately 6 cups.

Add the garlic, the tomatoes, the chopped half of the onion, the chipotle, and oregano to the stock. Continue to cook over medium-low heat for another 30 minutes.

While the soup cooks, place the sliced onion on a greased baking sheet and broil until softened and a little brown around the edges.

Add the broiled onions, lime juice, and salt to the soup and just heat through. If you used 1 or 2 dried chipotles, remove the chile and either mince it and return it to the pan or discard it, depending on how spicy you want the soup.

To serve, divide the tortilla strips, cheese, and avocado among the bowls and ladle the soup over. Serve immediately.

Regional Variations: With the beef stock in this recipe, we use twice the amount of onions that many people do, partially as a replacement for meat. When cooks make the soup with chicken stock, they usually add shreds of chicken as well. Dallas chef Dean Fearing does that in his delicious adaptation, and puts in epazote, cumin, chili powder, and bay leaves for seasoning, topping it all with cheddar cheese. We've come across versions in both Arizona and New Mexico that use mild red chile sauce in the stock rather than chipotles or chili powder, and many norteño cooks would eschew all those forms of heat and add minced jalapeño or serrano. A Sonoran variation called *caldo fraile* (priest's soup) substitutes pieces of flour tortillas for the corn tortilla strips.

ALBÓNDIGAS SOUP

Some American cooks like to pair meatballs with spaghetti, but in Mexico and the Southwest, similar *albóndigas* are more closely associated with a popular soup. This version adds a little pork to the region's beefy meatballs, and cuts the potential greasiness by partially cooking them before adding them to the stock.

Serves 6

SOUP
1 tablespoon vegetable oil
1/2 medium onion, chopped
3 garlic cloves, minced
1/2 teaspoon dried oregano, preferably Mexican
1/4 teaspoon cumin seeds, toasted and ground
6 cups beef stock
2 cups canned crushed tomatoes
1 canned chipotle chile plus 1 to 2 teaspoons adobo sauce
2 carrots, grated
1 teaspoon salt

1/2 cup grated zucchini
1/4 cup uncooked rice

ALBÓNDIGAS
1/2 pound ground beef
1/4 pound bulk chorizo or ground pork
1/4 cup grated zucchini
1 egg
1 garlic clove, minced
1 stale small corn tortilla, minced or processed to crumbs
    in a food processor
1 tablespoon minced fresh cilantro
1/2 teaspoon salt
1/4 teaspoon cumin seeds, toasted and ground
1/4 teaspoon dried oregano, preferably Mexican

Water
Chopped fresh cilantro and fresh mint, for garnish

In a large, heavy saucepan or stockpot, warm the oil over medium heat and sauté the onion and garlic with the oregano and cumin until the onion is softened. Pour in the stock and add the tomatoes, chipotle, carrots, and salt. (The zucchini and rice will be added later.) Reduce the heat to medium-low and simmer the soup for 20 minutes while you form the *albóndigas*.

In a bowl, combine all the meatball ingredients and mix well. Form into small balls, about 3/4 inch in diameter. In a large saucepan, bring to a boil enough water to cover the meatballs and add them. Boil for 3 to 4 minutes to eliminate some of the grease. Drain the *albóndigas*, discarding the cooking water.

Add the *albóndigas*, along with the reserved zucchini and rice, to the soup. Continue simmering for 30 minutes.

Ladle the soup into bowls and top with generous sprinklings of cilantro and mint before serving.

Regional Variations: Some cooks replace the rice in the soup with a handful of macaroni, while others add more rice by using it as the binding for the meatballs rather than the tortilla crumbs. Masa harina is another popular binding agent, and north of the border you find advocates for cornmeal and breadcrumbs. California variations sometimes call for forming the *albóndigas* around pitted green olives, or using ground chicken instead of beef.

SEAFOOD ALBÓNDIGAS SOUP

Albóndigas soup is an entirely different dish when nuggets of fish and seafood replace the meatballs, as they often do along the coasts of Baja California and Sonora.

Serves 4

ALBÓNDIGAS
1/2 pound shrimp, peeled
1/4 pound marlin, swordfish, or other meaty fish steak or fillet, cut in several pieces
1/2 medium onion, minced
2 ounces tomatillos, husked and minced
2 teaspoons minced fresh cilantro
1 teaspoon adobo sauce from canned chipotles
1/2 teaspoon ground coriander
1/4 teaspoon salt
1 egg
1/4 cup masa harina

SOUP
2 tablespoons extra-virgin olive oil
3 garlic cloves, minced
4 small tomatoes, preferably Roma or Italian plum, chopped
1 to 2 canned chipotle chiles, minced
3 cups seafood stock or bottled clam juice
3 cups chicken stock

Minced fresh cilantro, for garnish

The same areas of Baja California and Sonora that specialize in seafood *albóndigas* used to feature another soup made with *caguama,* or sea turtle. Concerted conservation efforts protect the turtle today, but in the past the meat was popular in everything from stews to tamales.

In a food processor, purée the shrimp until pasty. Add the fish, 1 tablespoon of the onion, and the tomatillos, cilantro, adobo sauce, coriander, salt, and egg. Pulse to combine, leaving a little texture to the fish. Add as much of the masa harina, a tablespoon at a time, as needed to make a thick paste. Refrigerate the mixture.

In a large saucepan or Dutch oven, warm the oil over medium heat. Sauté the remaining onion and the garlic until very soft but not colored. Stir in the tomatoes and chipotles, cover, and cook for an additional 5 minutes. Pour in both stocks, reduce the heat to medium-low, and simmer 10 minutes.

Form the seafood mixture into 3/4-inch balls. Add the seafood balls to the soup and poach them gently until cooked through, about 2 to 3 minutes. Do not let the soup come to a rolling boil or the balls may disintegrate.

Serve the soup hot, ladled into bowls, and topped with cilantro.

TAMAULIPAS BLUE CRAB CHIMPACHOLE

Also spelled "chilpachole," particularly outside Tamaulipas, this spicy, rich crab stew is a Tampico favorite.

Serves 4 to 6

3 garlic cloves, with skin on
1/2 medium onion, skinned but attached to stem end
4 whole small tomatoes, preferably Roma or Italian plum, roasted
1 1/2 tablespoons extra-virgin olive oil
6 cups seafood stock, bottled clam juice, or a combination
1 bay leaf
1 to 2 canned chipotle chiles plus 1 to 2 teaspoons adobo sauce
1 teaspoon dried epazote
Salt to taste
1 tablespoon masa harina
1 1/2 pounds crabmeat, fresh or frozen, picked over well to remove
    any shells

Lime wedges, for garnish

Warm a small, heavy skillet over high heat. Dry-roast the whole garlic cloves, browning them evenly. Remove them and add the onion half, letting its exterior turn brown and the interior get semisoft. When the garlic is cool enough to handle, remove its skin. Transfer the garlic and onion to a blender, add the tomatoes, and purée the mixture.

In a large, heavy saucepan, warm the oil over high heat. Pour in the tomato mixture, being cautious as it sputters and spatters. When the sputtering becomes minimal, reduce the heat to low and simmer for about 5 minutes, until thickened but not dried out. Add the stock, bay leaf, chipotle and adobo sauce, epazote, and salt. Cover the pan and simmer for 20 minutes.

Sprinkle the masa harina into a small bowl. Spoon out $^1/_4$ cup of stock and mix it with the masa. Stir the mixture back into the pan and simmer, uncovered, for about 10 minutes. Add the crabmeat and heat just until it is warmed through. Spoon into individual bowls and garnish with lime wedges. Try it accompanied by split, toasted bolillos or other crusty rolls spread with garlic butter.

Technique Tip: In Tamaulipas, chimpachole is often made with fresh crabs in their shells. If you're fortunate enough to be able to get whole crabs, such as the relatively small blue crabs found in the Gulf of Mexico, you'll find they work particularly well in the soup. For this recipe, use 10 small live blue crabs or other whole crab(s) to equal about 2 1/2 pounds.

You can make fresh stock for the recipe while you cook the crabs. Combine 1 teaspoon salt, a chopped onion, and a minced garlic clove with 2 quarts of water. Bring the water to a boil over high heat and boil for 5 minutes. Plunge the crabs into the water, reduce the heat to medium, and cover. Simmer for 5 minutes, until the crabs turn from blue to scarlet. With tongs or a slotted spoon, remove the crabs and set the cooking liquid aside.

As soon as the crabs are cool enough to handle, remove the meat from the shells. Break off the legs, remove the shells, and pick out as much meat as possible from the bodies and legs. Save any yellow-orange roe but pull off and discard the white gills. Throw away tiny bits of shell or cartilage, but put other parts of the shell back in the cooking liquid. Bring the liquid to a simmer again over medium heat and cook for 20 minutes to make stock.

Strain the stock before using it in the recipe along with the fresh crabmeat and roe.

Cypress-lined rivers in Coahuila ranching country traditionally provided ample catfish for sustenance during Lent, when meat was avoided. This remains a tasty way to prepare the fish. Snapper also works well in the soup.

Serves 6 to 8

2 tablespoons vegetable oil
1 tablespoon butter
1 1/2 to 1 3/4 pounds catfish fillets
1 1/2 medium onions, chopped
2 garlic cloves, minced
3 cups chicken stock
2 cups seafood or fish stock or bottled clam juice
1 large baking potato, peeled and diced
1/2 red bell pepper, diced
2 medium carrots, grated
2 teaspoons dried oregano, preferably Mexican
1 teaspoon salt, or more to taste
3/4 teaspoon dried rosemary
1 bay leaf
Generous grinding of black pepper
2 chiltepíns, chiles pequíns, or other tiny hot red chiles, crushed
2 egg yolks

Minced fresh cilantro, for garnish

Warm the oil and butter in a large, heavy saucepan over medium-high heat. Add the catfish and sauté it for about 2 minutes. Flip the fillets over, add the onions and garlic, and continue cooking for another 2 minutes. Add the rest of the ingredients, except the egg yolks and cilantro, and cook for 25 to 30 minutes. Break the fish into bite-size flakes if any large chunks remain.

In a small bowl, beat the egg yolks lightly. Pour $^1/_2$ cup of stock slowly into the bowl, mixing well. Pour the mixture into the hot soup and heat through for a couple of additional minutes.

Ladle the soup into serving bowls and top with the cilantro.

Border cooks don't always simplify the classic Mexican soups when they bring them north. In San Antonio, Mary and Julian Treviño established a statewide reputation—which isn't easy in Texas—for formidable renditions of *caldo azteca,* a type of tortilla soup, and *caldo xóchitl,* made with garbanzos, rice, and many condiments. The Treviño kitchen at El Mirador restaurant makes the soups only on Saturdays, when waiting lines often extend down the block.

This dish may have evolved as a simplified border version of *caldo tlalpeño,* a complex soup from central Mexico that includes many additional ingredients.

Serves 6

1/4 cup butter
1 large onion, chopped
2 garlic cloves, minced
1 cup uncooked rice
8 cups chicken stock
1 bay leaf
15-ounce can garbanzo beans, drained
3/4 cup chopped roasted mild green chile, preferably New Mexican or Anaheim, fresh or frozen
1 cup cubed cooked chicken
1 teaspoon cumin seeds, toasted and ground
Salt and fresh-ground black pepper to taste

In a heavy saucepan or Dutch oven, warm the butter over low heat. When melted, add the onion and garlic. Cover the pan and cook for 5 minutes. Stir in the rice and sauté it briefly until the grains become opaque.

Pour in the stock, add the remaining ingredients, and simmer for 25 to 30 minutes, until the rice is very soft.

Serve hot.

Regional Variations: Huntley Dent, author of *The Feast of Santa Fe* (Simon and Schuster, 1985), often makes his version of this soup with leftover turkey rather than chicken. He loads bowls with Monterey jack cheese before pouring the hot soup over, and tops it with a sprinkling of cilantro. Some Mexican cooks might add a cup of chopped calabacita, a zucchini-like summer squash. Farther south, around Mexico City, the more elaborate *caldo tlalpeño* would contain other vegetables, chipotle, avocado, and lime juice.

EL PASO GREEN CHILE SOUP

Serves 4 to 6

1/4 cup butter
1 1/2 medium onions, chopped
3 garlic cloves, minced
4 cups chicken stock
2 baking potatoes, peeled and diced
1 1/2 cups chopped roasted mild green chile, preferably New Mexican
    or Anaheim, fresh or frozen
1 teaspoon dried oregano, preferably Mexican
1 teaspoon salt
1/2 cup half-and-half
4 ounces Monterey jack cheese, grated

Minced fresh cilantro, for garnish (optional)
Toasted thin corn tortilla strips, for garnish (optional)

In a large saucepan or Dutch oven, warm the butter over medium heat. Stir in the onions and garlic and sauté until translucent. Add the stock, potatoes, chile, oregano, and salt and bring the mixture to a boil. Reduce the heat to a simmer and cook for about 30 minutes, until the potatoes are very soft.

Transfer the soup to a food processor (or blender in batches) and purée until smooth. (The soup can be made ahead to this point and refrigerated for a day. Warm the soup before proceeding.) Pour the soup back into the pan, add the half-and-half, and heat through.

Divide the cheese among the serving bowls. Ladle the soup into each bowl. If you wish, top the soup with cilantro or tortilla strips, or both. Serve immediately.

Regional Variations: South of El Paso in Chihuahua, a similar soup might be based on red chile instead of green. To make it in that fashion, substitute $^1/_4$ to $^1/_3$ cup of ground dried ancho or New Mexican chiles for the fresh green pods, use beef stock instead of chicken, and garnish with Chihuahua, Muenster, or mild cheddar cheese. Over in Tucson, Consuelo Flores at El Parador makes her green chile soup without cream and adds tomatoes, green onions, and cilantro to the blend.

SONORAN SOPA DE MILPAS

The "soup of the cornfields" takes its name from the mix of vegetables grown on the typical Sonoran farm. A robust harvest dish, it appears most commonly in its birthplace in the late summer, after the seasonal rains have worked their garden miracles.

Serves 6 to 8

1 pound ham hocks, cut into several chunks by your butcher
1 cup whole unprocessed wheat kernels, rinsed (see "Technique Tip")
8 cups water
3 cups corn kernels, fresh or frozen
8 ounces zucchini or summer squash, cut in small dice
3 ounces greens, such as spinach, chard, or purslane, chopped
1 cup diced green beans, fresh or frozen
1 large onion, diced
2 garlic cloves, minced
3/4 teaspoon salt, or more to taste
1/2 teaspoon dried thyme
1 cup peas, fresh or frozen

In a large saucepan or Dutch oven, simmer the ham hocks and wheat with the water over medium heat for about 1 hour.

Add the corn, zucchini, greens, green beans, onion, garlic, salt, and thyme to the stock. Simmer the soup for another 30 minutes. Remove the hocks with a slotted spoon. We like to give the soup a little more body by puréeing about 1 1/2 cups of it in the food processor or blender at this point.

When the meat is cool enough to handle, pick the meat from the hocks and return it to the soup. Add the peas and simmer for 5 minutes.

Serve warm.

Technique Tip: The wheat kernels needed in the recipe are a staple in health food stores and whole foods groceries. If the place you shop has a bulk foods department, check there first for the small quantity required. You may find the wheat kernels marketed as "wheat berries."

GARLIC SOUP

Few soups are more satisfying than this Mexican treasure. The long roasting and then the simmering of the garlic mellow its sharpness but enhance the underlying sweetness.

Serves 6 to 8

3 whole heads of garlic
2 tablespoons vegetable oil, preferably peanut
1 medium onion, sliced thin
8 cups chicken stock
1 to 2 dried or canned chipotle chiles
1/2 teaspoon salt, or more to taste
1/2 teaspoon cumin seeds, toasted and ground
Juice of 1/2 to 1 lime

Toasted thin flour tortilla strips and sliced avocado, for garnish
   (optional)

Preheat the oven to 400° F.

Coat the garlic with a thin film of the oil, reserving the remaining oil. Place the garlic in a shallow pan and bake it until very soft, for about 45 minutes. When the garlic is cool enough to handle, peel all the cloves and reserve them.

Pour 1 tablespoon of the oil into a large saucepan or Dutch oven and warm over medium heat. Add the onion to the oil and sauté until it's softened and lightly colored. Transfer the mixture to a blender and add the reserved garlic. Purée, adding a little stock if necessary to blend the mixture.

Add the remaining oil to the saucepan and warm it over medium-

California is the garlic capital of the United States, home of the famed Gilroy Garlic Festival and of most of the ten thousand acres of bulbs harvested annually in the country. Arizona and New Mexico farmers share in the bounty to a lesser degree. In Dixon, New Mexico, Stan and Rose Mary Crawford win laurels for their garlic, just as Stan has for his marvelous books on farming the upper Rio Grande, *Mayordomo* and *A Garlic Testament*. Charles Onion, another bulb grower, started Arizona's Own Garlic Festival in 1991 in Camp Verde, north of Phoenix. Celebrants drink garlic shooters—garlic minced up in a shot glass with lemon or lime juice. The citrus is supposed to help keep your breath fresh, but you might want to keep in mind that a Mr. Onion is hosting the day.

high heat. Pour in the blender mixture, being careful of any splatters, and sauté it until it just begins to dry out and color. Add the rest of the stock, the chipotle, salt, and cumin, and reduce the heat to medium. Simmer the soup for 25 to 30 minutes, remove it from the heat, and add the lime juice.

Divide the tortilla strips and avocado between the bowls and pour the hot soup over them. Serve immediately.

Regional Variations: Barbara Pool Fenzl includes a creamy western Arizona version of this soup in her truly beautiful *Southwest The Beautiful Cookbook* (Collins Publishers, 1994). She starts with a similar garlic-and-chicken-stock base, adds diced snowy flour tortillas and half-and-half for the creaminess, and mixes in mustard, cumin, and butter for extra flavor.

This garden soup thrives on fresh ingredients, particularly juicy-ripe tomatoes and shiny red chiles.

Serves 6

3 1/2 pounds whole small tomatoes, preferably Roma or Italian plum
Vegetable oil
1 1/2 tablespoons extra-virgin olive oil
1 1/2 tablespoons butter
2 medium celery stalks, chopped
1 carrot, chopped
1/2 small onion, chopped
1 roasted fresh mild red chile, preferably New Mexican or Anaheim, or
    2 to 3 teaspoons ground dried red chile
3 to 4 cups chicken stock
Salt and fresh-ground black pepper to taste

Sliced green onion tops, minced fresh cilantro, or chopped avocado,
    for garnish

Preheat the oven to 400° F. Cover a baking sheet with foil, making a small lip with the foil if your baking sheet lacks sides.

Cut the tomatoes in half and squeeze out their seeds and liquid. Rub a thin coat of vegetable oil on the tomatoes' skins and transfer them to the baking sheet, cut side down. Roast the tomatoes for 45 to 50 minutes, until the skins are dark. Check the tomatoes halfway through the roasting time, pouring off any liquid that might have accumulated (which will stew the tomatoes rather than allow them to roast). Set the tomatoes aside until cool enough to handle.

In a skillet, warm the olive oil and butter over medium-low heat. Sauté the celery, carrot, onion, and the fresh chile pod. Cook until the vegetables are soft, for about 10 minutes. If you are using ground dried chile, add it to the mixture now. Pour in the stock and simmer for 30 minutes.

Pull the skins off the tomatoes and discard them. Transfer the tomatoes to a blender and add the stock mixture, in batches if necessary. Purée the soup and add salt and pepper to taste.

Serve the soup immediately or keep warm over very low heat. Garnish individual bowls with green onions, cilantro, or avocado, as you wish.

CHILLED AVOCADO-TOMATILLO SOUP

We found this cooling soup on a hot July day in Monterrey, where the tomatillos that enhance its refreshing quality are called *fresadillas*. It's certainly no sweat to prepare.

Serves 4

3 chopped roasted mild green chiles, preferably poblano or New
    Mexican, fresh or frozen
10 to 12 ounces tomatillos, husked, roasted, and chunked
2 Haas avocados, chunked
1 teaspoon salt, or more to taste
1 garlic clove, minced
Generous grinding of black pepper
3 cups chilled defatted chicken stock
1 to 2 tablespoons Crema (page 63), crème fraîche, or sour cream
Juice of 1 lime

Sliced green onions and slivered red radishes, for garnish

In a blender, combine all the ingredients except the lime juice and purée until smooth. Taste the mixture, adding more salt or pepper if you like and as much lime juice as is needed to heighten the soup's fresh citrus flavor without making it sour.

The soup is ready to serve but can be refrigerated for 1 hour or longer without losing its sprightly green color. Garnish individual bowls of soup with green onions and radish slices.

Technique Tip: Be sure the chicken stock is skimmed of all fat before using it in this soup or the following gazpacho recipe. Since the soups are served cold, any remaining fat will be unappealingly congealed.

Serves 6 to 8

2 cups defatted chicken stock

2 cups chopped watercress

2 medium cucumbers, peeled and seeded, 1 1/2 roughly chopped, 1/2 diced

6 green onions, tops sliced thin, white portions chunked

3 tablespoons sour cream

3 tablespoons mayonnaise

1 tablespoon minced dried dill

3 tablespoons fresh lime juice

1 tablespoon extra-virgin olive oil

1 1/2 teaspoons salt, or more to taste

2 garlic cloves, chopped

1/8 teaspoon ground white pepper

1/2 medium green bell pepper, diced

1/2 small red bell pepper, diced

1 fresh jalapeño, minced

In a blender, purée together the stock, watercress, roughly chopped cucumbers, white portions of the green onions, sour cream, mayonnaise, dill, lime juice, oil, salt, garlic, and white pepper. Pour the mixture into a large bowl. Stir in the bell peppers, jalapeño, green onion tops, and the reserved cucumber. Chill the mixture for at least 2 hours.

Before serving, taste and adjust the seasoning. Spoon into soup bowls and serve chilled.

Regional Variations: Making the most of voluptuous summer tomatoes, cooling traditional gazpachos appear more often in southern California and Arizona kitchens than elsewhere in the Southwest. Today, contemporary cooks use the basic idea as a springboard to other preparations, including our green variation. Food writer Mary Anita Loos came up with one of the most imaginative ideas. Celebrating the Mexican tastes of her southern California childhood in *Gourmet* magazine, she created a refreshing salad out of the gazpacho vegetables—bell peppers, cucumbers, tomatoes, and onions—by combining them with lettuce and a red-wine vinaigrette, and topping it all with slivered almonds and garlic croutons.

GUACAMOLE

A 1926 El Paso cookbook provided an overly pragmatic recipe for avocado salad. It called for flavoring the fruit with bits of tomato, green chile, onion, and olives, but then said that if avocados weren't in season, you could just eliminate them from the recipe.

You can't make superior guacamole from mediocre avocados; when you start with good fruit, the only way to fail is by spoiling your blessing with a heavy hand. One of Mexico's greatest culinary contributions, guacamole is also one of the world's simplest foods. It should practically make itself, relying on the flavor and texture of the avocados. It's always best freshly prepared at the table, which you can do with brilliant flair in a *molcajete*, an oversized volcanic rock mortar with pestle.

Makes about 1 1/2 cups

2 perfectly ripe Haas avocados
2 tablespoons minced onion
1 fresh serrano or jalapeño, minced
1/2 teaspoon salt
Juice of 1/2 lemon or lime

In a bowl, mash the avocados roughly, leaving some small chunks. Stir in the remaining ingredients.

Serve within 30 minutes with chips, or as a garnish with other dishes.

Technique Tip: Throughout the book, our recipes specify Haas avocados—the variety with the pebbly black-brown skin and a full, buttery, almost nutty flavor. Avocados ripen best off the tree, so it's fine to buy a rock-hard one at the supermarket. When ripe, an avocado should yield to gentle pressure. Don't refrigerate one until it's reached that stage, but then it can be chilled for 2 or 3 days. Once it's cut open, lime or lemon juice helps prolong the color briefly, but there's no truth to the notion that replacing the pit salvages the fleeting emerald intensity.

Regional Variations: While *simple* translates to *superior* in guacamole lingo, the versatility of the avocado encourages alternatives, from the silly to the sublime. On the former side, we've seen the dish dulled with peas, Worcestershire sauce, and sour cream. On the other end of the flavor prospect, some people enjoy the addition of crisp bits of *chicharrones*, or bacon, especially when combined with garlic, an idea we picked up from a Sonoran cook who attributed the inspiration to Baja California. Another norteño supplement, a few ounces of grated zucchini, helps extend a small amount of avocado tastily. For a thinner but still sprightly guacamole that works best as a sauce, add about $^{1}/_{2}$ pound of puréed boiled tomatillos.

ENSALADA CAESAR

You can stump anyone except real foodies in a quiz contest by asking the origin of the famous Caesar salad. It's from Tijuana rather than Milan, Naples, or New York City, served first in Caesar's Bar & Grill in the Baja California burg one Fourth of July night in the 1920s. An Italian chef created it, mainly for an American clientele escaping Prohibition, but it remains a standard in many norteño kitchens. This version is as close to the original as we can reconstruct it. For the best results, make sure the romaine is quite chilled and crisp.

Serves 3 to 4 as a main course, 6 to 8 as an appetizer

1 cup extra-virgin olive oil
4 garlic cloves
1 1/2 cups day-old French bread cut into 1/2-inch cubes
1 egg, unshelled
2 tablespoons fresh lemon juice
Salt and fresh-ground black pepper to taste
1/2 teaspoon Worcestershire sauce
3 small heads of romaine, all outer less-than-totally-crisp leaves saved
    for another recipe
1/4 cup fresh-grated Parmesan cheese

Chef Caesar Cardini gave his name to the famous salad, but no less an authority than Diana Kennedy maintains that his brother Alex deserves at least equal credit. We know for sure that crowds swamped their restaurant on that holiday evening in the 1920s, the kitchen ran short of everything, and the tableside preparation was meant to distract from the lack of ingredients. Some people claim the original salad came with a raw egg and the now common anchovies, but most believe the egg was coddled and that the only anchovies were those in the Worcestershire sauce. Patrons ate the treat as finger food, the reason for the use of whole uncut romaine hearts. Caesar and Alex are long gone, but you can still enjoy the salad in Tijuana at the source of inspiration.

Preheat the oven to 350° F.

In a heavy ovenproof skillet, warm 1/4 cup of the oil over medium heat. Sliver 1 garlic clove, add it to the oil, and sauté about 1 minute. Stir in the bread cubes, tossing them to coat well with the oil. Transfer the skillet to the oven and bake the bread cubes for 15 minutes, stirring occasionally, until browned and crisp.

In a small saucepan, bring 2 to 3 inches of water to a boil. Slip the egg into the water and boil, or "coddle," for exactly 1 minute. (When broken, the egg will be viscous but still runny.)

In a food processor or blender, purée the remaining garlic with the rest of oil and pour the mixture through a strainer into a large bowl. Break the egg into the oil and, with a fork, blend in the lemon juice, salt, pepper, and Worcestershire sauce. Add the romaine leaves, all lying the same direction in the bowl. Toss the romaine gently with the dressing, scatter the cheese over the salad, and serve immediately.

Technique Tip: The 1 minute of cooking time for the egg is not enough to kill any salmonella bacteria that could possibly be present. If that concerns you, eliminate the egg in the recipe or mash the yolk of a hard-boiled egg into the dressing.

Regional Variations: In northern Mexico, Caesar salad usually stays close to its roots, with seldom more than minor additions such as avocado slices, bacon, or a bit of mustard in the dressing. James Peyton, author of *El Norte* (Red Crane Books, 1990), did find a Chihuahua version, however, topped with green olives and artichoke hearts. This works well, and so does a scattering of toasted piñon (pine) nuts, the substitution of a good aged Mexican cheese like Cotija for the Parmesan, or a light dusting of ground red chile over the croutons. We would eschew the trendier supplements sometimes seen north of the border, which can include anything from eggplant to enoki mushrooms.

ENSALADA DE NOCHE BUENA

In Mexico and the Southwest, Christmas Eve is known as *noche buena*, the good night. Traditionally, families ate the salad of the same name that evening, adding ingredients like placing ornaments on a tree to suit their sense of celebration. In different preparations, you can find walnuts, apples, cheese, bell peppers, beets, coconut, and all manner of contrasting flavors. This version is our household favorite.

Serves 6

DRESSING
Juice and zest from 1 lime
2 tablespoons mayonnaise
2 tablespoons Crema (page 63) or crème fraîche or additional
    mayonnaise
2 tablespoons honey
1 tablespoon vinegar, preferably cider or cane
1 teaspoon ground dried red chile, preferably New Mexican or ancho
1 garlic clove, minced
Salt to taste

4 oranges, peeled, sectioned, and cut into bite-size pieces
3/4 pound jícama, peeled and cut in slim matchsticks
2 bananas
1/4 cup chopped fresh cilantro
4 red radishes, slivered
Romaine or other lettuce leaves
1/4 cup roasted salted peanuts, chopped
Seeds of 1 pomegranate

In a blender, purée all the dressing ingredients. Refrigerate until ready to use. The dressing can be prepared 1 day ahead.

In a medium bowl, toss together the oranges and jícama and refrigerate for at least 45 minutes. Shortly before serving time, peel and slice the bananas. Add the bananas, cilantro, and radishes to the orange-and-jícama mixture. Toss with the salad dressing.

Line a serving bowl or platter with lettuce leaves. Turn the salad mixture out onto the platter. Scatter peanuts and pomegranate seeds over the salad and serve.

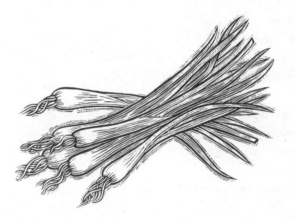

PAINTED DESERT ROASTED CHILE SALAD

Serves 4 to 6

DRESSING
1/2 cup extra-virgin olive oil
1/4 cup vegetable oil
2 garlic cloves
1 tablespoon chopped onion
1/4 cup vinegar, preferably cider or another fruit variety
1/2 teaspoon salt
1/2 teaspoon sugar
1/8 teaspoon dried oregano, preferably Mexican
Fresh-ground black pepper to taste

4 fresh mild green chiles, preferably a combination of poblano and
    New Mexican or Anaheim, roasted
1 fresh mild red chile, preferably New Mexican or Anaheim, or red bell
    pepper, roasted
1 yellow or orange bell pepper, roasted

Crumbled Cotija or aged Monterey jack cheese or grated Monterey
    jack cheese
Romaine or other sturdy lettuce leaves, for garnish (optional)

To make the dressing, purée the oils with the garlic and onion in a blender. Pour the mixture through a strainer into a large lidded jar. Combine with the rest of the dressing ingredients and shake well. For the best flavor, refrigerate the dressing for 30 minutes.

Slice the chiles and bell pepper into ribbons about $1/2$ inch thick. Arrange them decoratively on a serving platter. Pour the dressing over the chiles and scatter the cheese on top. Garnish with lettuce around the plate's edge if you wish.

A starchy, slightly sweet tuber, jícama looks like a football in the produce market. The other ingredients in the salad help highlight the refreshing taste.

Serves 6

1 small jícama (about 1 pound), peeled and diced
1/2 cup fresh orange juice
2 tablespoons fresh lime juice
1/4 teaspoon salt
Barest pinch of ground cloves
2 medium oranges, peeled, membranes removed, and
    sections sliced in half
8 ounces cantaloupe, honeydew, or other melon, or fresh
    pineapple, diced
1 large cucumber, peeled, seeded, and diced
2 teaspoons vegetable oil
1/2 to 1 teaspoon chile caribe or other dried red chile flakes
Pinch of sugar (optional)
2 tablespoons minced fresh cilantro

In a large bowl, combine the jícama with the fruit juices and salt. Refrigerate for 30 to 60 minutes.

Add the remaining ingredients, except the cilantro, to the jícama and juices and toss well. The salad can be refrigerated for several hours, if you wish, before serving. Stir the cilantro into the salad before serving.

Serves 6

Shredded lettuce

DRESSING
6 tablespoons extra-virgin olive oil
2 tablespoons sherry vinegar
1 garlic clove, roasted and mashed
1/4 teaspoon salt
1/4 teaspoon dried thyme
1/4 teaspoon dried rosemary

3 large or 6 medium beefsteak-style tomatoes, peeled and sliced thick
1/2 cup chopped roasted mild green chile, preferably poblano or
**   Anaheim, fresh or frozen**
4 to 6 ounces asadero or Monterey jack cheese, grated

Heat the broiler. Grease a heat-proof baking sheet. Arrange a bed of lettuce on individual salad plates.

In a lidded jar, combine the dressing ingredients.

Arrange the tomatoes in a single layer on the baking sheet. Top the tomatoes with equal portions of the chile and sprinkle the cheese over the chile.

Broil the tomatoes for 1 or 2 minutes, until the cheese is melted and bubbly. Transfer the tomato slices to the plates and drizzle the dressing over them. Serve immediately.

Cumin, or *comino*, appears in copious quantities in Tex-Mex cooking, contributing its earthy redolence to classics like chili con carne. It pairs just as successfully with sweet summer corn and rice.

Serves 4 to 6

SALAD

3 cups cooked corn kernels, preferably fresh

1 1/2 cups cooked rice

1 to 2 pickled jalapeños, minced

1/4 cup thin-sliced green onions

1/4 cup sliced black olives, preferably brine-packed

3 tablespoons diced red onion

DRESSING

1/4 cup vegetable oil, preferably unrefined corn

1 tablespoon fresh lime juice

1 1/2 teaspoons cider vinegar

1 teaspoon molasses

1/2 teaspoon ground dried mild red chile, preferably New Mexican or ancho, or chili powder

1/2 teaspoon salt

1/2 teaspoon cumin seeds, toasted and ground

Lime slices, for garnish

In a bowl, combine the salad ingredients.

In a lidded jar, shake together the dressing ingredients. Pour the dressing over the salad and toss gently. Refrigerate the salad for at least 1 hour and at most overnight.

Serve chilled, garnished with lime slices.

ENSALADA DE DOS FRIJOLES

Spanish settlers brought garbanzos to the borderlands from Europe, and their descendants eventually established them as a major crop. Black beans didn't migrate north until a more recent period, but they are gaining a strong foothold in the region. This contemporary Southwestern salad blends the two beans and much more in a compelling combination.

Serves 6

DRESSING
6 tablespoons extra-virgin olive oil
2 tablespoons vinegar, preferably sherry or red wine
1 canned chipotle chile, chopped, plus 1 to 2 teaspoons adobo sauce
1/2 teaspoon prepared Dijon mustard
Pinch of brown sugar
1/4 teaspoon cumin seeds, toasted and ground
1/4 teaspoon dried sage
Salt and fresh-ground black pepper to taste

SALAD
2 cups cooked garbanzo beans, drained, or a 15-ounce can garbanzo
    beans, rinsed and drained
2 cups cooked black beans, drained, or a 15-ounce can black beans,
    rinsed and drained
3 ounces cheddar cheese, diced fine
1/2 medium red onion, minced
2 small tomatoes, preferably Roma or Italian plum, seeded and diced
1 small green or red bell pepper, diced
2 to 3 tablespoons minced fresh cilantro

In a lidded jar, combine the dressing ingredients.

In a bowl, mix together the salad ingredients except the cilantro and toss with the dressing. Refrigerate for at least 1 hour or overnight.

Stir in the cilantro just before serving.

Native Americans introduced Spanish settlers to both nopales and *tunas*—the cacti's succulent ruby fruits—even bringing them as special offerings to Padre Junípero Serra when he first arrived in California. The indigenous peoples not only ate the prickly-pear cactus but also used it medicinally. The Pimas placed warmed nopales on the breasts of new mothers to stimulate milk flow, and other groups bound wounds with split pads.

Mexicans learned to make mortar from the mucilaginous juice, adapting it for construction purposes in the same way that islanders employed molasses in the Caribbean. Ranchers in the region were equally inventive, making the cacti into a natural fence to corral their livestock and, in more recent drought years, blow-torching the pads to singe the stickers so that cattle could eat them.

The cooked pads of the prickly-pear cactus—called nopales or, when chopped, nopalitos—give salads a mild vegetable crunch reminiscent of green beans. Preparations similar to ours are common from Baja to the Brazos River in Texas, though the presentation in a tomato cup is an unusual twist.

Serves 6

6 round, well-shaped tomatoes, red or yellow or a combination of both, about 6 to 7 ounces each
2 cups prepared nopales, diced (see "Technique Tip")
3 tablespoons minced onion
2 garlic cloves, roasted and minced
1 fresh serrano or jalapeño, minced
Juice of 1/2 lime
1 tablespoon Crema (page 63), crème fraîche, or sour cream (optional)
1 to 2 tablespoons extra-virgin olive oil
3 tablespoons minced fresh cilantro
3 tablespoons crumbled queso fresco or Cotija or aged Monterey jack cheese

Slice the tops from the tomatoes and, with a melon baller or spoon, scoop out their pulp. Leave the sides of the tomatoes intact. Discard the watery pulp, but dice any meaty portions that were scooped out of the tomatoes.

Toss together the diced tomatoes, nopalitos, onion, garlic, and chile with the lime juice in a medium bowl. Add the crema, crème fraîche, or sour cream if you wish, and just enough olive oil to bind the mixture together.

The salad can be served immediately or chilled for several hours. Stir in the cilantro shortly before serving. Spoon the salad into the prepared tomatoes. Transfer the tomatoes to a serving platter and scatter the cheese over the top of each.

Technique Tip: In the Southwest, prickly-pear cactus pads are frequently sold fresh, with stickers removed, especially at Hispanic or Latino markets. To prepare them for the salad, either grill the pads or boil them for 15 minutes in two changes of lightly salted water. In other areas look for nopales or nopalitos in Mexican food sections, either canned or in jars. Rinse the vinegary solution from the cactus before using.

BAJA POTATO SALAD

Potato salads appear regularly in home-style cookbooks on both sides of the border. Most are standard preparations, perhaps adding a little chile or cilantro for local flavor. This one evolved from a more creative Baja recipe developed originally by Mirna Meza de Barajas.

Serves 6 to 8

1/2 cup rice vinegar, or 6 tablespoons white wine vinegar diluted with
    2 tablespoons water
10 peppercorns
4 whole cloves
1 bay leaf
1/2 cup vegetable oil
1 large onion, chopped
1 small head of garlic, minced
3 ounces tomatillos, husked and chopped
4 carrots, grated
4 medium baking potatoes, boiled in salted water until tender, peeled,
    and chunked
5 to 6 fresh or pickled güeritos, or 1 to 2 fresh or pickled güeros or
    jalapeños, minced
1/4 cup chopped fresh parsley, preferably the flat-leaf variety
3/4 teaspoon dried oregano, preferably Mexican
Salt and fresh-ground black pepper to taste

In a small saucepan, bring the vinegar, peppercorns, cloves, and bay leaf to a boil. Remove the mixture from the heat and set it aside to steep.

In a heavy skillet, warm the oil over medium heat. Add the onion and garlic and cook for several minutes until softened. Stir in the tomatillos and cook for 5 minutes more. Add the carrots and cook for another 1 or 2 minutes, just until the carrots wilt.

Place the potatoes in a large bowl. Spoon the sautéed vegetable mixture over the potatoes and pour the vinegar through a strainer over the vegetables. Add the güeritos, parsley, and oregano and mix again. Taste and add salt and pepper, as you wish. Refrigerate the salad, covered, for at least 2 hours. It keeps well for several days.

Serve the salad chilled.

ENSALADA DE COL

The Spanish spread cabbage throughout Mexico and the Southwest, but later immigrants influenced its uses in the border region. Germans who settled in central Texas in the mid-nineteenth century probably introduced the idea of topping tacos with cabbage. In Coahuila, Lebanese and Syrian merchant families imported the stuffed cabbage preparations of their homeland, now known locally as Arabian tamales.

Here's a slightly dressed-up version of the slaw-style garnish that accompanies many border dishes, particularly on the Mexican side. If you use red cabbage with green, plan to eat the salad within an hour or two. The acid in the vinegar will cause the red to bleed so that all the cabbage turns pink.

Makes about 2 cups

2 1/2 cups shredded green cabbage, or a mixture of green and red
1/2 small red onion, sliced thin in rings and rings halved
1 carrot, grated
1/4 cup vegetable oil
2 tablespoons vinegar, preferably white
1 teaspoon fresh-ground black pepper
3/4 teaspoon salt
1/2 to 1 teaspoon chile caribe or dried red chile flakes (optional)
1/4 teaspoon sugar

Place the cabbage in a large bowl. In a small bowl, stir together the remaining ingredients, and when the sugar has dissolved, pour the mixture over the cabbage. Toss the cabbage with the dressing and refrigerate for 30 minutes before serving.

Regional Variations: Norteño and Southwestern cooks elaborate basic cabbage salads in numerous ways, adding a few tablespoons of minced mint, sliced bell peppers in a profusion of colors, or matchsticks of jícama, cucumber, or fresh chiles. Creamy slaws, made with a couple of tablespoons of mayonnaise, are found mostly north of the border. If you want a creamy version with some contrasting heat, flavor the mayo in the way chef Mark Miller recommends in *Coyote Pantry* (Ten Speed Press, 1993), lacing it with minced blackened serranos and fresh cilantro.

WATERCRESS SALAD WITH TEQUILA-TANGERINE DRESSING

In the United States, watercress usually plays a tertiary role in meals, maybe as a single sprig garnishing the side of a plate. It's more highly prized south of the border, under the name *berro*, for the fresh peppery flavor. We like to combine it with other vegetables and fruits and top the salad with a dressing brightened by border citrus and the fire of tequila.

Serves 4 to 6

DRESSING
1/4 cup fresh tangerine or orange juice
1/4 cup vegetable oil
2 tablespoons tequila, preferably gold
2 tablespoons fresh lime juice
2 teaspoons honey
1 garlic clove
Salt and fresh-ground black pepper to taste

SALAD
3 large bunches watercress, tough stems removed
2 tangerines or 1 small orange, sectioned, membranes removed, and
    sections halved
3/4 cup diced jícama
1/2 cup thin-sliced mild red radishes
1/4 cup sliced green onions

As in the States, there is increasing emphasis in Mexico today on healthy eating. Bookstores feature a variety of vegetable and vegetarian cookbooks, even in the meat-loving north, and newspapers regularly include articles on lighter fare. This salad was partially inspired by a recipe from nutritionist Alma Laura Zendejas that appeared in the Monterrey newspaper *El Norte*.

To make the dressing, combine the ingredients in a blender or food processor until smooth. (The dressing can be made a day ahead, but shake well before using.)

In a serving bowl, toss the watercress with enough dressing to coat well. Toss with the remaining salad ingredients. Serve immediately with additional dressing on the side.

VEGETABLES VERDE WITH CILANTRO VINAIGRETTE

Makes approximately 3/4 cup dressing, enough to top vegetables for 4 to 6

1/2 cup extra-virgin olive oil
1/4 cup chopped fresh cilantro
2 garlic cloves
1/2 fresh serrano (optional)
3 tablespoons vinegar, preferably white wine
1/2 teaspoon salt

Peeled, seeded, and sliced cucumber
Butter lettuce or other leaf lettuce
Sliced Haas avocado
Sliced green bell pepper
Toasted pepitas (shelled pumpkin seeds) (optional)

Combine the oil, cilantro, garlic, and, if you wish, the serrano in a blender or food processor. Add the vinegar and salt and combine again. Strain the dressing through a sieve and discard the remaining solids. The dressing keeps well, refrigerated, for several days.

When ready to serve, mix the cucumber slices with enough dressing to coat them well, and let them sit for 10 minutes. In a bowl, toss the lettuce with enough dressing to coat lightly and turn it out onto a platter. Top the lettuce with the cucumber, avocado, and bell pepper slices, arranged decoratively. If you wish, scatter pepitas over all for a contrasting crunch. Drizzle additional dressing over the vegetables or serve it accompanying the salad.

CHEESE COURSES FOR ALL OCCASIONS

erhaps more than anything else, cheese is the telltale sign of border cooking, the easiest and quickest way to distinguish it from other forms of Mexican cuisine. Many of the regional specialties are based on cheese, and an extraordinary range of other dishes rely on it for flavor and texture. When the food shines, it's often due to the skillful use of cheese, and when it disappoints, the problem may be too much of a good thing. Except for chile, no other ingredient is so likely to make or break a border cook.

Simple and ethereal, "flamed" cheese epitomizes border cooking. It developed as a fireside preparation, typically baked over dying embers after the meat was done. The cheese of choice is asadero, which melts in gooey strings and derives its name from the word *asar*, meaning "suitable for roasting over a flame." In most of the nation, Mexicans call the dish *queso fundido*, or "melted cheese," but the northern term *flameado* better reflects the roots.

Serves 4 to 6

8 ounces asadero, Chihuahua, Monterey jack, or Muenster cheese,
    coarse-grated
4 ounces panela cheese or additional asadero, Chihuahua, Monterey
    jack, or Muenster cheese, coarse-grated
1 to 2 fresh serranos or jalapeños, chopped (optional)
1/4 pound cooked chorizo (optional)

Flour or corn tortillas, warmed
One or two favorite salsas, such as Salsa del Norte (page 38) and
    Chipotle-Tomatillo Salsa (page 39)

Preheat the oven to 375° F or fire up enough charcoal in your outdoor grill to make a single layer of coals. Place a baking dish, preferably shallow and about 8 to 9 inches in diameter, in the oven to warm for about 5 minutes.

Remove the heated dish from the oven. Sprinkle the cheese evenly in the dish, and top it with the chile, chorizo, or both, if you wish.

Place the dish in the oven, or on the grill after the coals have died down to the point that they are covered in gray-and-white ash. Bake for about 10 minutes, or until the cheese is melted through and bubbly. Set the dish on a trivet and serve immediately, accompanied with the tortillas and salsa.

Queso flameado is often served before a meal of broiled or roasted meat, but given its heartiness we usually prefer it with something lighter, like a soup or salad.

Thousands of Mennonites moved from Canada to Chihuahua around the turn of the century in search of a religious haven, a place where they could practice their strict beliefs in freedom and isolation. They settled on 650,000 acres near Cuauhtémoc, about 250 miles south of El Paso, and turned the arid scrubland into very productive soil. Along with farming expertise, the Mennonites brought with them cheese-making skills that date back to the origins of their religion in sixteenth-century Holland. They soon developed a famed cheese sold today throughout Mexico, a buttery white product that resembles a good Muenster. The style came to be known as Chihuahua, and it's now produced in a generic form in factories that churn out up to a ton of cheese a day. The best specialty version is still *queso menonita*, made by the creators themselves in small *queserias*.

Technique Tip: American-made versions of asadero are spreading across the country. The most common brand is Cacique, made by a California company that also distributes the Nochebuena label, which has a slightly saltier flavor that we like. We prefer to mix in some panela too, another Mexican white cheese with a mild tang. Cacique and La Vaca Rica sell panela nationally, though it's less common than asadero.

Regional Variations: Chihuahua residents often substitute their local cheese for the asadero or panela in *flameado*. North of the border, where bacon may pinch-hit for the chorizo, the queso is usually Monterey jack, less rich and less stringy but still tasty. From Monterrey, Nuevo León, to Monterey, California, some cooks prefer *rajas* (strips) of fresh green poblano or New Mexican chile to the hotter serrano or jalapeño used in this recipe. We sometimes skip both meat and chile, baking the cheese instead with a drizzle of the adobo sauce from canned chipotles. A delightful small California café, Taco Auctioneers in Cardiff-by-the-Sea, replaces the standard toppings with toasted sesame seeds.

CLASSIC CHILE CON QUESO

Ersatz versions of chile con queso, usually made with processed American cheese or canned cheese soup, have sullied the reputation of a fine dish. This rendition goes back to the original inspiration, using the cheese as a supporting flavor to green chiles.

Serves 4 to 6 as an appetizer

2 tablespoons butter
1 medium onion, chopped
1 garlic clove, minced
4 small tomatoes, preferably Roma or Italian plum, chopped
2 to 3 mild green chiles, preferably poblano, New Mexican, or
　　Anaheim, roasted and sliced into thin strips about 1 inch long
1/4 cup plus 2 tablespoons Crema (page 63) or crème fraîche
1/4 cup water
8 ounces asadero or Monterey jack cheese, cut in small, thin slices
Salt to taste

Tortilla chips, warmed

Melt the butter in a heavy saucepan over medium heat. Add the onion and garlic and sauté for a couple of minutes. Stir in the tomatoes and poblanos, cover the pan, and reduce the heat to low. Cook for about 5 minutes. Mix in the crema or crème fraîche and the water and bring to a boil, uncovered. Sprinkle in the cheese, stir quickly, cover the pan, and remove it from the heat.

Let the mixture stand for 5 minutes. Uncover, stir again if needed to help the cheese melt evenly, and add salt to taste.

Chile con queso is best served immediately, or kept heated over a warming tray or in a chafing dish for more leisurely munching. Accompany with the tortilla chips.

Although the dish gained popularity as an appetizer, try it also as a side dish with grilled meats or chicken, served with warm flour or corn tortillas, or spooned over simple vegetables like steamed summer squash or cauliflower.

The British dish rarebit probably undermined authentic chile con queso in the United States. Anglo cooks, even in the Southwest, tended to blur the distinctions between the two cheese preparations from the beginning, substantially reducing the chile content in the process. In an early Arizona cookbook, for example, chile con queso contains only "cayenne pepper to taste," and it's served like rarebit, on toast.

In Bell Mondragón's northern New Mexico homeland, cheese-making was as common a chore as bread-baking up through the Second World War. Historically, goats were more common in the area than dairy cattle and served as the primary source for cheese. Farmers added rennet from an animal's stomach to warm goat's milk, which then coagulated quickly. They separated the curd and whey, and patted the drained curds into a mold, perhaps a coffee can in the later years.

We got our favorite Southwestern-style chile con queso from one of our favorite New Mexico cooks, Bell Mondragón.

Serves 4 to 6 as an appetizer

3/4 cup Hatch Green Chile Sauce (page 54) or other mild green chile sauce
3/4 cup chicken stock
6 ounces mild cheddar or a combination of cheddar and Monterey jack cheese, grated
Salt to taste

Tortilla chips, warmed

In a heavy saucepan, bring the chile sauce and the stock to a boil. Sprinkle in the cheese, stir quickly, cover the pan, and remove it from the heat.

Let the mixture stand for 5 minutes. Uncover, stir again if needed to help the cheese melt evenly, and add salt to taste.

Chile con queso is best served immediately, or kept heated over a warming tray or in a chafing dish for more leisurely munching. Accompany the dish with the tortilla chips.

NACHOS EL NORTE

Several cafés along the Texas-Mexico border, as far apart as El Paso and Piedras Negras, claim credit for concocting the nacho. All that's certain is a Rio Grande origin about fifty years ago—and an inventor blessed with insight into the elemental.

Serves 4 to 6

5 ounces tortilla chips, about 3 dozen chips
1 cup Refried Beans (page 378), warmed
6 ounces cheddar, Monterey jack, or asadero cheese, or a combination
  of two of the three cheeses, grated
2 to 3 minced fresh jalapeños or sliced pickled jalapeños

Pico de Gallo (page 40) (optional)
Border Escabeche (page 63) (optional)
Guacamole (page 123) (optional)

Preheat the oven to 400° F.

Spread each chip with a thin layer of beans. Place the chips on a heat-proof baking dish or platter. Top the chips with equal portions of the cheese and sprinkle jalapeños over all.

Bake the nachos for about 5 to 7 minutes until the cheese is melted and a little bubbly. Serve the nachos immediately, accompanied, if you wish, with pico de gallo, escabeche, guacamole, or all three.

Regional Variations: Nachos bear some affinity to chilaquiles, but they probably popped into existence in some snacker's fantasy rather than evolved from another dish. The treat is made for tinkering, as the range of toppings shows. At its most basic, a nacho consists of a crisp corn chip capped with melted cheese and chile, usually pickled jalapeños. From that starting point, anything is possible. Some change the chile—we prefer fresh jalapeños—and others change the cheese, even substituting artificial orange glop in ballpark versions. Beans are a common supplement, as in this recipe, but big meat eaters are more likely to add chorizo or drained Texas chili. Among vegetarian variations, we liked one from Tucson that came crowned with avocado chunks and sliced green olives.

After its introduction about the time of the Second World War, the nacho spread rapidly around Texas. By the time it reached debutante age, the snack made its first big splash at the state fair in Dallas. In the 1970s the Texas Rangers' ballpark started serving gooey nachos of an indeterminate food group, kicking off a baseball revolution almost as big and controversial as AstroTurf, another Lone Star contribution to the game. When some people outside the border region resisted the treat because of the jalapeño heat, Texas growers developed a mild new variety specifically for the national nacho market. Today, you find the gloppy ballpark version even in Mexico, at least in Monterrey, home of the Mexican Baseball Hall of Fame.

Serves 6

6 ounces cream cheese, at room temperature

4 ounces asadero or Monterey jack cheese, grated

1/4 cup sour cream

1 pickled jalapeño, minced, plus 1 to 2 tablespoons of pickling liquid from a jar of pickled jalapeños

1 garlic clove, minced

1/4 teaspoon cumin seeds, toasted and ground

8 ounces crabmeat, fresh or frozen, picked over well to remove any shells

1/2 cup sliced artichoke hearts (optional)

5 ounces tortilla chips, about 3 dozen chips

1 pickled jalapeño, sliced thin

Minced green onion tops, for garnish

Preheat the oven to 400° F.

In a bowl, mix together the cheeses, sour cream, jalapeño and pickling liquid, garlic, and cumin until well blended. Fold in the crabmeat and, if you wish, the artichokes. (The mixture can be made ahead and refrigerated for several hours. Return it to cool room temperature before proceeding.)

Spread each chip with a layer of the topping mixture. Place the chips on a heat-proof baking dish or platter. Sprinkle the sliced jalapeño over everything.

Bake the nachos for about 5 minutes, until the cheese is melted and a little bubbly. Scatter the green onion tops over the nachos and serve immediately.

TUCSON CHEESE CRISPS

Cheese crisps are the Arizona equivalent of nachos, another popular twentieth-century creation utilizing the old border basics of cheese and tortillas. They work best with the local Sonoran-style tortillas, as large and thin as you can find or make.

Serves 2 as an appetizer

SALAD TOPPING (OPTIONAL)
2 small tomatoes, preferably Roma or Italian plum, chopped
2 to 3 tablespoons chopped roasted mild green chile, preferably New Mexican or poblano
2 green onions, sliced
1 tablespoon minced fresh cilantro
Splash of vegetable oil and vinegar

1 large, thin flour tortilla, 12 inches or larger, or 2 medium, thin flour tortillas of 7 to 8 inches
4 ounces cheddar cheese, grated
4 ounces Monterey jack cheese, grated

Preheat the oven to 400° F.

Combine the salad topping ingredients in a small bowl, if you plan to use the topping.

Bake the tortilla for 4 to 5 minutes directly on the oven rack. Remove the tortilla from the oven and place it on a baking sheet or pizza stone. Sprinkle the cheeses on and return the tortilla to the oven. Bake until the cheese melts completely, another 4 to 5 minutes.

Transfer the tortilla to a platter and spoon on the salad topping if you wish. Serve the crisp immediately, breaking off pieces of the tortilla to eat it. To add heat, accompany with Salsa de Árbol.

Most early Southwestern cookbooks included a section on border dishes, usually called "Spanish," but few American publications from outside the region dealt with Mexican cooking at all. One of the first exceptions was Elinor Burt's 1938 *Olla Podrida: Piquant Spanish Dishes from the Old Clay Pot,* which covered both Old World and New World cuisines.

A regular guest at New Mexico's Rancho de Chimayó, Mark Burrell used to place special orders for this ingenious dish, one of his home treats. At first, the restaurant just obliged the good customer, but the staff soon discovered that it had a hot idea. When they decided to add the appetizer to the menu, they named it for Mr. Burrell.

Makes 1 appetizer tortilla, enough for 2 appetizer portions

1 flour tortilla, preferably medium-thick and 7 to 8 inches in diameter
1/2 cup Hatch Green Chile Sauce (page 54) or other mild green chile sauce
3 ounces mild cheddar cheese, grated

Preheat the oven to 350° F.

Cut the tortilla into 6 wedges with a sharp knife or pizza cutter. Place the tortilla wedges back in a circle on a heat-proof platter or baking sheet. Spoon the chile sauce evenly over the reassembled tortilla and sprinkle the cheese over all.

Bake for 5 to 6 minutes, until the cheese is melted and a little bubbly. If the tortilla was cooked on a baking sheet, transfer the wedges to a decorative plate. Serve while piping hot with lots of napkins.

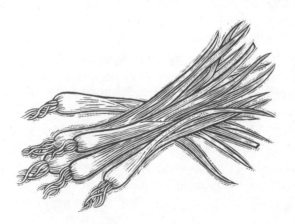

CAZUELITAS

This recipe comes from Nuevo León, but you can adapt it for a range of local or individual tastes by filling the "pot-shaped" shells with anything you wish. The bite-size tidbits are great for parties.

Makes 24 cazuelitas, enough for 6 appetizer servings

DOUGH
1 cup masa harina
1/4 pound small red waxy potatoes, boiled in salted water,
    peeled, and mashed
3 ounces Chihuahua, Muenster, Monterey jack, or mild cheddar
    cheese, grated
1/2 teaspoon salt
1/2 cup water, or more as needed

Vegetable oil for pan-frying

FILLING
3/4 cup drained Frijoles de Olla (page 374) or other well-seasoned
    cooked whole beans
3/4 cup Tucson Carne Seca (see page 209) or fried crumbled chorizo,
    warmed
6 ounces Chihuahua, Muenster, Monterey jack, or
    cheddar cheese, grated
Diced tomato, for garnish

    In a food processor or bowl, combine the dough ingredients. If the mixture is not pliable enough to shape easily, add a little more water. Form the dough into 24 balls, covering them as you work. Using the cupped palm of one hand and the thumb of the other, shape a ball of dough into a low-sided cup, or *cazuelita*, with sides about $^1/_4$ inch thick. Keep the edge of the *cazuelita* equal in thickness to its bottom and sides, using your thumb and fingers to smooth it. Repeat with the remaining dough.

    Warm about 1 $^1/_2$ inches of oil in a heavy skillet to 350° F. Fry the dough in batches, flared side down, for about 1 minute. Turn over and fry for an additional minute, or until the dough is crisp and golden. (Sometimes the cooking dough puffs up in a way that begins to fill the cup's hollow. Immediately after removing the cooked shell from the oil, push the dough back down with a paper towel–covered thumb to reshape it, if needed.) Drain the *cazuelitas*. They can be kept at room temperature for a couple of hours.

Heat the broiler.

Fill the *cazuelitas* with the beans and meat, and top with the cheese. Transfer the *cazuelitas* to a baking sheet. Broil 1 minute, or just until the cheese melts through. Serve immediately, topped with bits of tomato.

Regional Variations: In Sonora, a similar preparation might be called a "gordita," and in other areas the terminology could range from "chalupa" to "sope." Some doughs are lightened with wheat flour rather than potatoes, and they would be less likely to contain cheese farther south in Mexico. Meat or even vegetable leftovers often end up as the filling, perhaps *carne guisada*, *carne adovada*, or summer calabacitas in place of the *carne seca* or chorizo.

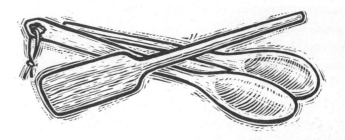

STUFFED SQUASH BLOSSOMS

Fried squash blossoms are wonderful on their own, but a cheese filling broadens the taste further.

Serves 4 to 6

FILLING
4 ounces fresh goat cheese, crumbled, at room temperature
4 ounces Monterey jack cheese, grated, at room temperature
1/2 teaspoon dried oregano, preferably Mexican

10 to 12 squash blossoms

BATTER
1 cup all-purpose flour
1 tablespoon ground dried mild red chile, preferably New Mexican or ancho
1 teaspoon baking powder
1 teaspoon salt
1 teaspoon cumin seeds, toasted and ground
3/4 teaspoon cinnamon
3/4 teaspoon ground coriander
1/2 teaspoon sugar
1 egg, lightly beaten
1 cup beer

Vegetable oil for deep-frying

All types of squash produce blossoms, but the zucchini and yellow summer varieties are the Southwest favorites for eating. The golden blossoms appear after the plant sprouts and before the squash forms, and they taste best when young. Abiquiu, New Mexico, vegetable farmer Elizabeth Berry, who supplies many fine restaurants, plants one type of squash just for the blossoms alone.

Prepare the filling, combining the ingredients in a small bowl. Gently stuff each blossom with a portion of the filling and wrap the blossom snugly around the filling.

Prepare the batter, stirring together the dry ingredients in a medium bowl. Mix in the egg and beer.

Fill a heavy pan with at least 2 inches of oil. Heat the oil to 350° F.

Dip the blossoms in the batter, coating them lightly but thoroughly. Fry the blossoms in batches for about 1 minute, until crisp and golden, turning them as needed. Drain the blossoms. Serve warm.

THE BORDER COOKBOOK

Technique Tip: Look for squash blossoms at farmers' markets, specialty produce stores, and Hispanic, Italian, or Filipino markets, or harvest them from your own garden in the morning when they are fully open. They always look a little limp, but try to make sure they are fresh. Extremely perishable, the blossoms are best the day they are picked. If you gather or buy them with some stem attached, you can keep them in water to prolong their lives another day.

QUINTESSENTIAL QUESADILLAS NORTEÑAS

Named for their queso filling, quesadillas are the border equivalent of the grilled cheese sandwich, except maybe even more soul-satisfying.

Serves 8 as an appetizer or 4 as an entrée

1 1/2 cups shredded cabbage, preferably red for color
1 1/2 teaspoons vegetable oil
1/2 teaspoon vinegar, preferably cider
1/4 teaspoon dried oregano, preferably Mexican
Pinch of salt

3/4 pound asadero, Chihuahua, Monterey jack, or Muenster cheese, grated
1/2 teaspoon dried epazote (optional)
1/2 teaspoon ground dried red chile, preferably New Mexican or ancho (optional)

Vegetable oil for pan-frying
8 flour tortillas, preferably thin and 7 to 8 inches in diameter
Green Chile Salsa (page 44) or other salsa

In a small bowl, toss the cabbage with the oil, vinegar, oregano, and salt. Refrigerate the mixture until you are ready to serve the quesadillas.

Preheat the oven to 275° F.

If you are using the epazote or chile or both, sprinkle them into the cheese and mix together.

On a griddle or in a large, heavy skillet, warm just enough oil to coat the surface, over medium heat. Cover the first tortilla with about 1/3 cup of cheese. Transfer it to the skillet and cook just until the cheese begins to melt. Fold the tortilla in half, turnover style, and continue cooking for a couple of minutes until lightly colored and crispy. Flip the tortilla over on its other side and continue cooking until lightly colored and crispy too. Drain. Place the tortilla on a heat-proof plate in the oven to keep warm.

Repeat the assembly and cooking process with the remaining tortillas and filling. When the quesadillas are cooked, slice them into manageable wedges and serve immediately, garnished with the cabbage and accompanied with salsa.

Regional Variations: Mexican cooks often supplement the cheese in quesadillas with other ingredients. The extras can be as simple as thin-sliced grilled or fried onions, as hearty as shredded chicken, or as elegant as steamed or sautéed squash blossoms cooked with a bit of garlic or green chile. A double-decker quesadilla called a *sincronizada*, particularly popular in Monterrey, allows for a wide range of additions. One version we've enjoyed combined asadero cheese, refried beans, fried chorizo, sliced green onion, and salsa, all sandwiched between two whole flour tortillas. In recent years, Southwestern restaurant chefs have begun treating the quesadilla as a blank canvas, worthy of embellishments such as brie cheese with lobster and mango or smoked gouda with Peking duck and pineapple.

CORN QUESADILLAS

Santa Fe cooking instructor Kathi Long introduced us to these corn tortilla quesadillas. They feature meaty wild mushrooms, which are reminiscent of *huitlacoche*, a corn fungus delicacy more common in central Mexico than along the border.

Serves 8 as an appetizer or 4 as an entrée

1 tablespoon vegetable oil

2 tablespoons minced onion

1 garlic clove, minced

1 cup corn kernels, fresh or frozen

4 ounces mushrooms, preferably a wild variety such as portobello,
     sliced thin

1/2 teaspoon salt

2 canned chipotle chiles, minced, plus 2 to 3 teaspoons adobo sauce

Vegetable oil, preferably corn, for pan-frying

8 corn tortillas

6 to 8 ounces asadero or Monterey jack cheese, grated

2 to 3 tablespoons minced fresh cilantro

Chipotle-Tomatillo Salsa (page 39) or other chipotle salsa (optional)

Preheat the oven to 275° F.

In a small skillet, warm the tablespoon of oil over medium heat. Add the onion and garlic and sauté for 1 minute. Stir in the corn, mushrooms, salt, and chipotles and continue cooking for about 5 minutes, until the vegetables are cooked through.

On a griddle or in a large, heavy skillet, warm just enough oil to coat the surface, over medium heat. Cover the first tortilla with about one-quarter of the vegetable mixture, a similar amount of cheese, and 1 or 2 teaspoons of cilantro. Top with a second tortilla. Transfer the quesadilla to the skillet and cook until the cheese is melted and the tortillas are lightly browned and chewy-crispy, about a minute per side. Drain. Place the tortilla on a heat-proof plate in the oven to keep warm.

Repeat the assembly and cooking process with the remaining tortillas and filling, adding as many to the skillet as will fit comfortably at one time. Slice the quesadillas into wedges and serve hot, accompanied with salsa if you wish.

QUESADILLAS CAMPESINAS

The original quesadilla, before the shortcut of pre-made tortillas, was this little corn pocket. Lard enhances the crust, but unlike in the past, we fry the turnovers in vegetable oil.

Serves 8 to 12 as an appetizer or 4 to 6 as an entrée

FILLING

2/3 cup grated zucchini or chopped squash blossoms, steamed and drained
1 small tomato, preferably Roma or Italian plum, chopped
2 green onions, minced
1 garlic clove, minced
2 fresh serranos, minced

DOUGH

2 cups masa harina
6 tablespoons all-purpose flour
1 teaspoon baking powder
1 teaspoon salt
3 tablespoons lard or vegetable shortening
1 cup plus 2 tablespoons warm water, or more as needed

12 ounces asadero, panela, or Monterey jack cheese, grated
Vegetable oil for pan-frying
Serrano Salsa Verde (page 43) or other salsa

In a small bowl, mix together the zucchini or squash blossoms, tomato, green onions, garlic, and serranos and reserve.

For the dough, combine the masa harina, flour, baking powder, and salt in a food processor. Mix in the lard just until combined. Add the water and continue processing just until the dough forms a smooth ball. The dough should be quite moist but should hold its shape. Add a little more water, if needed, to achieve the proper consistency. Form the dough into 16 equal balls and cover them tightly with plastic wrap. Let the balls sit for about 20 minutes.

Form the *campesinas*, using a tortilla press. (If you do not have a

press, see the chapter "Border Basics" for instructions about rolling out dough.) Flatten a ball of dough to about $1/8$-inch thickness. Spoon about $1 \, 1/2$ tablespoons of cheese and $1/2$ tablespoon of the vegetable mixture onto the center of the dough. Using the bottom piece of plastic from the tortilla press for support, fold the tortilla in half, turnover style. Seal the edge, being sure to enclose all the filling. Using the tines of a fork, crimp the edge of the dough. Transfer the *campesina* to a platter and cover with plastic wrap. Repeat with the remaining dough and filling.

In a heavy saucepan or skillet, pour enough oil to come halfway up the side of the quesadillas. Heat the oil to 375° F. Pan-fry the *campesinas*, two or three at a time, until golden brown, about $1 \, 1/2$ minutes per side. Drain and serve hot.

STACKED BLUE CORN AND
RED CHILE ENCHILADAS

The word *enchilada* comes from the way the dish is made, by dipping or drenching tortillas "en chile." How appropriate, then, that the chile lovers of New Mexico created these perfect but simple enchiladas. A stacked "flat" style, they pair the state's special blue corn tortillas with a robust red sauce and cooling cheese. You lose a little nutty flavor by substituting yellow or white corn tortillas, but the dish still satisfies. Multiply the recipe by the number of people you plan to serve.

Makes 1 serving

Vegetable oil for pan-frying
3 blue corn tortillas
2 teaspoons minced onion
3/4 cup Chimayó Red Chile Sauce (page 51), warmed
4 ounces mild cheddar cheese, grated

The Shed in Santa Fe serves the world's best restaurant version of these stacked blue corn, red chile enchiladas. Just across the New Mexico state line in El Paso, next to the cemetery where John Wesley Hardin lies, the funky L & J Cafe comes close in results using yellow corn tortillas. Both places offer a fried egg on top as a popular option.

Heat the broiler.

Heat $^1/_2$ to 1 inch of oil in a small skillet until the oil ripples. With tongs, dunk a tortilla in the oil long enough for it to go limp, a matter of seconds. Don't let the tortilla turn crisp. Repeat with the remaining tortillas and drain them.

On a heat-proof plate, layer the first tortilla with half of the onion and one-third of the chile sauce and cheese. Repeat for the second layer. Top with the third tortilla, then add the remaining chile sauce and sprinkle the rest of the cheese over all.

Broil the enchilada until the cheese melts. Serve hot.

Regional Variations: As recently as the 1950s and '60s, many New Mexicans would have made these enchiladas with fresh goat cheese rather than the cheddar and Monterey jack common today. Some people still prefer the dish with *queso de cabra*, because the tanginess of the cheese balances the richness of the red chile sauce. A half-and-half blend of the goat cheese with Monterey jack gives you the best of both possibilities.

In *Recipes of the Ranchos* (Ward Ritchie Press, 1964), Mildred Yorba MacArthur says that early Anglo settlers in California called enchiladas "Spanish Cakes with Chile Frosting." Under whatever name, they must have seemed daunting in the days before store-bought tortillas, because a 1902 *Los Angeles Times* cookbook felt the need to encourage novices by saying that with practice enchiladas "would be as easy to prepare as some Yankee dishes."

California rancho cooks developed a delightfully different style of red cheese enchiladas, unlike all others in the border region past or present. The long cooking of the onions is the key to their mild yet grand flavor.

Serves 6

3 tablespoons extra-virgin olive oil
4 cups diced onions

12 thin flour tortillas, preferably 10 to 12 inches in diameter
3 cups Californio Colorado (page 53) or other mild red chile sauce, warmed
3/4 pound sharp cheddar cheese, grated
3/4 cup sliced pitted, brine-packed black olives

Preheat the oven to 350° F. Grease a medium baking dish, one that is at least as wide as your tortillas.

In a large, heavy skillet, warm the olive oil over medium-low heat. Add the onions and sauté for 30 minutes, stirring occasionally. The onions should become translucent and very soft, but not brown. Reduce the heat if needed to achieve the desired texture.

Dip a tortilla into the chile sauce and place it on a plate. Sprinkle about 3 tablespoons of the cheese and 2 tablespoons of the onions down the center of the tortilla. Scatter a couple of teaspoons of olive slices over the onions. Fold the tortilla in half and, with a spatula, transfer the enchilada to the baking dish. Repeat with the remaining tortillas and filling ingredients, placing each enchilada so that it overlaps the previous one. Spoon the remaining sauce over the top of the enchiladas and then sprinkle on the remaining filling ingredients.

Bake the enchiladas for 20 minutes, until the cheese is melted and bubbly. Some tortillas will puff a bit as they cook. Serve the enchiladas piping hot.

GREEN CHILE ENCHILADAS

Serves 4 to 6

FILLING
1 1/2 pounds Monterey jack, grated
4 green onions, minced

Vegetable oil for pan-frying
12 to 16 corn tortillas
**Tubac Chile Verde (tomato version, page 55) or other mild green chile
    sauce, warmed**
**Grated Monterey jack cheese, chopped tomato, sliced green onions,
    sour cream, and minced fresh cilantro, for garnish**

Preheat the oven to 350° F. Grease a medium baking dish.

In a bowl, mix the cheese with the onions.

Heat $1/2$ to 1 inch of oil in a small skillet until the oil ripples. With tongs, dunk a tortilla in the oil long enough for it to go limp, a matter of seconds. Don't let the tortilla turn crisp. Repeat with the remaining tortillas and drain them.

With tongs, dip a tortilla in the sauce to coat it lightly. Lay the tortilla on a plate, sprinkle about $1/4$ cup of filling over it, and roll it up snugly. Transfer the enchilada to the baking dish. Repeat with the remaining tortillas and filling. Top the enchiladas with the remaining sauce, seeing that each enchilada is submerged in the sauce. Bake for 15 to 18 minutes, until the enchiladas are heated through and the sauce is bubbly.

Remove the dish from the oven and sprinkle immediately with generous amounts of cheese, tomato, onions, sour cream, and cilantro.

Regional Variations: Our mild green chile enchiladas are Arizonan in style, but less embellished than many versions in the state. Some cooks would dip the tortillas in the chile sauce and then top the dish with another sauce, perhaps onion sautéed in olive oil with Ro-Tel canned tomatoes with green chiles, a perennial Southwest favorite. Most New Mexicans would make a hotter, more robust chile sauce, and would scorn

On the early California ranchos, cheese-making was a daily task. Settlers used rennet from a calf's stomach to curdle a cow's milk and made a simple farmer cheese out of the curd, which they ate with bread, in place of butter. From that legacy, later California cheese makers developed Monterey jack, one of the state's most notable contributions to Southwestern cooking.

any toppings other than a shred or two of lettuce and perhaps a bit of chopped tomato. West Texans might use the same New Mexico green chiles but create a creamier, more mellow sauce by adding milk and maybe even avocado. South of the border, cooks commonly start with roasted or boiled tomatillos to form the base of the blend, and spike it up with jalapeños or serranos. They would ordinarily serve a red sauce on cheese enchiladas, though, reserving the green variety to pair with chicken.

ENCHILADAS EN CHIPOTLE

Smoky and spicy, these enchiladas rev up the heat.

Serves 4 to 6

SAUCE
2 tablespoons vegetable oil
2 tablespoons bacon drippings, or additional vegetable oil
3 tablespoons all-purpose flour
2 garlic cloves, minced
2 tablespoons ground dried ancho chile or chili powder, preferably Gebhardt's
3 cups beef stock
2 to 3 canned chipotle chiles, minced, plus 3 to 4 tablespoons adobo sauce
1 1/2 teaspoons dried oregano, preferably Mexican
Salt to taste

FILLING
1 1/2 pounds asadero, Monterey jack, or mild cheddar cheese, grated
1/2 medium onion, minced

Vegetable oil for pan-frying
12 to 16 corn tortillas
4 ounces fresh goat cheese or queso fresco, crumbled

In a saucepan, warm the oil and bacon drippings over medium heat. Sprinkle in the flour and cook until a golden-brown roux forms, about 5 to 8 minutes. Add the garlic and the ground chile. Stir in the stock slowly to avoid lumps and add the chipotle chiles, adobo sauce, oregano, and salt. Bring the sauce to a boil, then reduce the heat to a simmer. Cook the sauce for 20 to 25 minutes.

Prepare the filling by mixing the cheese with the onion in a bowl.

Preheat the oven to 350° F. Grease a medium baking dish.

Heat $1/2$ to 1 inch of oil in a small skillet until the oil ripples. With tongs, dunk a tortilla in the oil long enough for it to go limp, a matter of seconds. Don't let the tortilla turn crisp. Repeat with the remaining tortillas and drain them.

With tongs, dip a tortilla in the sauce to coat it lightly. Lay the tortilla on a plate, sprinkle about 1/3 cup of filling over it, and roll it up snug. Transfer the enchilada to the baking dish. Repeat with the remaining tortillas and filling. Top the enchiladas with the remaining sauce, seeing that each enchilada is submerged in the sauce. Sprinkle any remaining grated cheese over the enchiladas.

Bake for 15 to 18 minutes, until the enchiladas are heated through and the sauce is bubbly. Immediately scatter the goat cheese or queso fresco over the dish.

Serve hot.

A 1936 San Antonio cookbook, *Gebhardt's Mexican Cookery for American Homes,* says the difference in Mexican and American enchiladas is meat. Produced by a well-regarded chili powder company, the book claims Mexican versions are based on cheese and American versions always contain beef in the form of chili con carne. The self-serving case has some basis in truth in Tex-Mex cooking, but not elsewhere in the borderlands.

OLD-FASHIONED SONORAN-STYLE RED ENCHILADAS

A south Arizona favorite, this dish originated in Sonora. It features a mild red chile topping and fat, flat corn tortillas used as a pedestal for building the enchilada upward. If you want extra punch, add a few crushed dried chiltepíns to the sauce.

Serves 4 generously

2 cups masa harina
2 ounces mild cheddar cheese, grated
1 small baking potato, cooked, peeled, and grated
1 teaspoon baking powder
1 teaspoon salt
1 cup water, or more as needed

Vegetable oil for deep-frying
1 recipe Arizona Chile Colorado (page 52) or other mild red
    chile sauce, warmed
12 ounces queso blanco or Monterey jack cheese, or a combination of
    Monterey jack and cheddar cheese, grated

4 green onions, sliced
Shredded lettuce tossed with a splash of vegetable oil and vinegar,
    to coat lightly
1/2 cup sliced green olives (optional)

Preheat the oven to 400° F.

In a medium bowl, stir together the masa harina, cheese, potato, baking powder, and salt. Mix in the water until the dough is smooth and moist but not sticky. Shape the dough into 8 balls about 2 to 2 $^{1}/_{2}$ inches in diameter. Between sheets of waxed paper, roll the balls into tortillas about 4 inches in diameter.

Heat 1 to 2 inches of oil in a small skillet until the oil ripples. Dunk a tortilla in the oil and fry until lightly brown and crisped but still chewy. Repeat with the remaining tortillas and drain them.

Transfer 2 tortillas per serving to heat-proof plates. Spoon equal portions of sauce over the tortillas and top with the cheese. Bake 4 to 5 minutes, or until the cheese melts and becomes bubbly. Top each serving with green onions, lettuce, and, if you wish, olives. Serve immediately, 2 to a serving.

NOGALES ENTOMATADAS

The usual description of entomatadas as chile-less enchiladas left us less-than-convinced until we tried a good version once in Nogales, Sonora.

Serves 4 to 6

FILLING
1 1/4 pounds crumbled queso fresco or grated Chihuahua, Muenster, or Monterey jack cheese
2 ounces Cotija or feta cheese, crumbled
1/2 medium onion, minced

Vegetable oil for pan-frying
12 to 16 corn tortillas
Roasted Tomato Sauce (page 59)

Crema (page 63) or crème fraîche, for garnish

Preheat the oven to 350° F.

To prepare the filling, mix the cheeses and the onion in a bowl.

Heat $^1/_2$ to 1 inch of oil in a small skillet until the oil ripples. With tongs, dunk a tortilla in the oil long enough for it to go limp, a matter of seconds. Don't let the tortilla turn crisp. Repeat with the remaining tortillas and drain them.

With tongs, dip a tortilla in the sauce to coat it lightly. Lay the tortilla on a plate, sprinkle about $^1/_4$ cup of filling over it, and roll it up snug. Transfer the entomatada to the baking dish. Repeat with the remaining tortillas and filling. Top the entomatadas with the remaining sauce, seeing that each is submerged in the sauce. Sprinkle the remaining cheese over the entomatadas.

Bake for 15 to 18 minutes, until the entomatadas are heated through and the sauce is bubbly.

Serve hot, topped with crema or crème fraîche.

In the days of subsistence agriculture, which dominated the borderlands until this century, cheese was a highly sustainable product. Instead of the limited meat from one butchering, families could make cheese from the same cows or goats for years. The Tejanos, the early Spanish-speaking residents of Texas, sometimes clabbered cow's milk with juice from a wild plant called *santa pera*, making rough versions of asadero and panela. They placed the cheese in cloth and hung it high in trees to dry.

Regional Variations: Texas cooks, especially in the Rio Grande Valley, make *envuelos* with tortillas dipped in a tomato-based sauce and then wrapped, envelope-fashion, around a filling. The sauce might have a hint of serrano, or even be a ranchero preparation, but as with entomatadas, tomato plays a bigger flavoring role than chile.

COAHUILA BAKED TACO CAZUELA

If you know tacos in only the fast-food, ground-beef version, this one will shock as well as delight. A deeply flavored cheese-and-vegetable dish, it resembles a double-decker enchilada but is called a taco instead because the tortillas aren't dipped "en chile."

Serves 6

FILLING
1 pound whole small tomatoes, preferably Roma or Italian plum
3 tablespoons vegetable oil
1 medium onion, sliced in very thin strips
4 mild green chiles, preferably poblano, fresh or frozen, roasted and
    cut into *rajas* (thin strips)
1/4 teaspoon salt, or more to taste

Vegetable oil for pan-frying
12 corn tortillas
3/4 cup Crema (page 63) or crème fraîche
1 cup grated or crumbled queso fresco, queso blanco, or Chihuahua or
    Muenster cheese
1 tablespoon minced fresh cilantro, for garnish (optional)

    Preheat the broiler.
    Place the tomatoes on a small baking sheet, covered with foil for easier cleaning. Broil the tomatoes for 12 to 15 minutes, turning occasionally, until the tomatoes are soft and the skins split and turn dark in spots. Cool the tomatoes briefly. Reduce the oven temperature to 350° F.

In a blender, purée the tomatoes with their skins and cores. Set the mixture aside.

In a large, heavy skillet, warm the oil over medium heat. Sauté the onion in the oil briefly until softened. Add the chiles and the salt and sauté for another couple of minutes. Raise the heat to medium-high. Stir in the tomato purée, being careful to avoid splatters from the mixture as it hits the hot oil. When the most-insistent splattering dies down, reduce the heat to medium-low and simmer the filling for another 5 minutes, until somewhat thickened. (The filling can be made ahead and refrigerated for a day. Warm the filling before continuing.)

Heat $^1/_2$ to 1 inch of oil in a small skillet until the oil ripples. With tongs, dunk a tortilla in the oil long enough for it to go limp, a matter of seconds. Don't let the tortilla turn crisp. Repeat with the remaining tortillas and drain them.

Spoon about 2 tablespoons of the filling onto a tortilla. Roll it up loose and place it in a baking dish. The baking dish should be deep enough to hold two layers of the rolled tacos but should fit the tortillas closely on their sides, if possible. (The 7-inch-square, 1 $^1/_2$-quart Corning Ware casserole works perfectly.) Repeat with half the tortillas, filling the bottom of the dish. Top the rolled tacos with about half of the crema and half of the cheese. Repeat with the remaining tortillas and filling, placing them on top of the cheese in a second layer. Top the second layer of rolled tacos with the remaining crema and cheese.

Cover the dish and bake the tacos for 12 to 15 minutes, until the cheese is melted and the tortillas are soft. Garnish with the remaining crema, which will melt over the surface, and sprinkle cilantro on top, if you wish. Serve immediately.

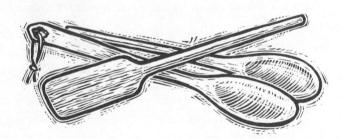

Californian Laura Chenel, whose business takes her name, and Paula Lambert of Dallas's Mozzarella Company led the way in re-establishing goat cheese in the Southwest in recent decades. Now smaller producers are excelling with farmstead cheeses, raising their own goats for the milk they use. In New Mexico, for example, Coon Ridge in tiny Pie Town makes wonderful cheeses marinated in olive oil and spices, and the Harrison-Inglis family at Sweetwoods Dairy create luscious fresh cheeses coated with herbs.

These tacos look more like the commonplace version than the ones in the previous recipe, but they still taste much different. Goat cheese flourished in the borderlands until recent generations, particularly in areas that lacked dairy cattle, and now it's experiencing a welcome renaissance.

Serves 4

8 flour tortillas, preferably medium-thick and 7 to 8 inches in diameter, warmed
4 ounces creamy fresh goat cheese, at room temperature
1 cup Refried Beans (page 378) or other well-seasoned mashed beans, warmed
4 ounces Monterey jack cheese, grated
2 to 3 pickled jalapeños, sliced thin
Melted butter

Guacamole (page 123) or avocado slices
Pico de Gallo (page 40)

Preheat the oven to 400° F.

Spread the tortillas with equal portions of the goat cheese. Add spoonfuls of beans and sprinklings of jack cheese and jalapeños. Fold the tortillas in half and transfer them to a baking sheet. Brush the tops of the tortillas generously with butter and bake them 5 to 8 minutes, or until the cheese is melted and the tortillas are crisp. Serve immediately with guacamole and pico de gallo.

CHEDDAR AND PIÑON TAMALES

Makes 36 medium tamales, about 8 to 12 main-dish servings

6-ounce package dried corn husks

FILLING
1 cup corn kernels, fresh or frozen
5 garlic cloves, minced
3 to 4 fresh serranos, minced
1 cup piñon (pine) nuts, toasted
1 pound mild cheddar cheese, grated
1/2 teaspoon salt

MASA
6 cups masa harina
1 tablespoon salt
1 3/4 cups vegetable oil
1/4 cup garlic-flavored oil, or additional vegetable oil plus 1 teaspoon
    garlic powder
4 1/2 cups chicken stock, or more as needed

Hatch Green Chile Sauce (page 54) or other mild green chile sauce,
    warmed (optional)
Grated mild cheddar cheese and toasted piñon (pine) nuts,
    for garnish (optional)

To prepare the corn husks, soak them covered by hot water in a deep bowl or pan. After 30 minutes the husks should be softened and pliable. Separate the husks and rinse them under warm running water to wash away any grit or brown silks. Soak them in more warm water until they are ready to use.

In a bowl, mix the filling ingredients together.

To prepare the dough, measure the masa harina and salt into a large bowl. Add the oil or oils, the garlic powder if you are using it, and the stock. Mix with a sturdy spoon, a powerful electric mixer, or your hands until smooth. When well blended, the masa should have the consistency of a moist cookie dough. Add more stock if needed for your preferred consistency. Keep the dough loosely covered while working.

To assemble the tamales, use approximately equal amounts of masa and filling. To make 3 dozen 3-ounce tamales, use 2 tablespoons of masa and 2 heaping tablespoons of filling for each tamale.

Hold a corn husk flat on one hand, smooth side up. (You may, depending on the size of the corn husks, need to overlap two husks to form one tamale. Spread the dough over the husks together, just as if they were one.) With a rubber spatula, spread a thin layer of masa across the husk, but not to the edges. Top with filling spread more thickly through the dough's center, stopping short of the dough's edges. Make sure that the dough's edges meet to enclose all of the filling. Secure the tamale by folding the wrapper over or tying it. Repeat the procedure until all the filling and masa are used.

Place the tamales in a steamer, packing them loosely in crisscross directions or standing them on end. Allow enough space between them for the steam to rise effectively. Cover the pot and cook over simmering water for about 45 minutes, until the masa is firm and no longer sticks to the corn husk. Unwrap one tamale to check its consistency.

The tamales should be eaten warm. When the tamales are served unadorned, the corn husks are usually left on, to be removed by each guest before eating. If you choose to top the tamales with sauce or other garnishes, the husks should be removed first. Add spoonfuls of sauce or a sprinkling of cheese and more piñon nuts, if you wish, before serving.

Technique Tip: Because of the multiple steps involved in preparing tamales, the work flows better with two or more people. Consider hosting a *tamalero*, a tamale-making party, to expedite the process. You can assemble dozens at a time, plenty for everyone, because they freeze well and the more you do at once, the less labor-intensive each one becomes.

Whether you're making tamales alone or with assistance, clear off a table for your workspace and line up the bowls of corn husks for wrapping, dough, and filling, and have a towel and scissors handy. You'll need a large bowl or plate for the finished product.

The wrapped tamales can be plump or thin, and shaped as long cylinders, square packages, or rounded pouches. They can be tied with extra strips of corn husk at both ends or at the top of a pouch, or the wrapper can simply be folded over at one end. To ensure that they cook fully, tamales should not be made any larger in weight than described in a recipe, but they can be made smaller for appetizers.

To cook the tamales, a Dutch oven, a large saucepan, or a small stockpot all work well. There are also pots with inserts made specifically for steaming tamales, available in areas with Hispanic or Latino populations. If you need a source, check with the suppliers listed in "Mail-Order Sources." If you're improvising, use a metal vegetable steamer or colander over a couple of inches of water.

BIG JIM CHILES RELLENOS

Although you can use most New Mexican, Anaheim, and poblano chiles for rellenos, the best one for stuffing is the mild, meaty, green variety called the Big Jim. Commonly eight or more inches long, the gentle giant takes its name from the Hatch, New Mexico, farmer who developed it in cooperation with state university scientists. The late Jim Lytle's family still farms the pods today and ships them to chile lovers nationwide through their Hatch Chile Express (505-267-3226). If you use smaller chiles in the recipe, increase the number of pods, allowing three per serving.

Serves 4

8 ounces mild cheddar cheese, grated
2 teaspoons dried oregano, preferably Mexican, or dried marjoram
8 whole large green chiles, preferably New Mexican Big Jims or Anaheims, or 12 smaller similar green chiles, roasted and slit from end to end

BATTER
1 1/4 cups all-purpose flour
3/4 teaspoon salt
4 eggs, separated
1/2 cup beer or water

Hardly a snooty culinary event, the Hatch Chile Festival on Labor Day weekend resembles a county fair. A parade kicks off the festivities, winding through the diminutive downtown, where the local health center may display the message, "Rx: Chile. Eat three times a day in generous amounts." Later, the celebrants get serious in contests for the tastiest recipes, the prettiest pods, and even the chile best dressed in doll clothes.

Vegetable oil for deep-frying
**Hatch Green Chile Sauce (page 54) or other mild green chile sauce,
  warmed**

In a bowl, combine the cheese with the oregano or marjoram. With your fingers, stuff each chile with cheese, filling them full but not to overflowing.

In a large bowl, combine the flour and salt with the egg yolks. Stir in the beer or water slowly, mixing well.

In a bowl, preferably copper, beat the egg whites until medium-stiff peaks form. Mix the egg whites into the batter thoroughly. The batter should seem pourable but thick enough to coat the chiles.

Heat 4 inches of oil in a large, heavy pan to 350° F.

Lay the first chile in the batter and spoon more batter over it. When evenly coated, pull it from the batter by its stem and let any excess batter drip back into the bowl. No cheese should show—the batter should be thick enough to seal the chile's slit. Fry each chile for about 4 to 5 minutes, turning as needed to fry them until evenly golden and lightly crispy. Drain the chiles.

Transfer the chiles to a platter or individual plates, top with chile sauce, and serve immediately.

Regional Variations: At the Hatch Chile Festival, an annual September celebration, vendors cut the sauce and wrap rellenos in flour tortillas to make them finger food. Just a skip farther south, the Delicious Mexican Food café in El Paso adds a layer of beans to that concoction to make a relleno burrito. Elsewhere in Texas, we once found the flour tortilla placed around an unbattered relleno, with the whole combo then batter-dipped and deep-fried, something like a glorified Arizona chimichanga. We haven't seen that in the home of the chimi, but we've come across a fine standard version in Tucson with a light, beer-less crust and a topping of grated cheddar cheese rather than sauce. In Mexico, cooks commonly stuff the fatter poblano chile, and usually simmer the battered and fried pods in a mild tomato sauce, which makes the texture less desirable to us.

BLUE CORN POBLANOS RELLENOS

Los Angeles chef Roger Hayot cooks with a sophisticated culinary sense, but his dishes have a homey authenticity that many restaurant chefs don't have the sense to try to achieve. Roger's lively Authentic Cafe serves food from around the world, including a range of inspired Mexican favorites. His zesty relleno with a crunchy coating, creamy filling, and smoky sauce inspired this one.

Serves 6

SAUCE (OPTIONAL)
2 dried mora or chipotle chiles

1 1/2 cups chicken stock

1 whole small tomato, preferably Roma or Italian plum, roasted

1/3 medium onion, chunked

1 garlic clove

1/2 teaspoon cumin seeds, toasted

1/4 teaspoon dried thyme

1/4 teaspoon salt, or more to taste

1/8 teaspoon dried epazote

1 tablespoon extra-virgin olive oil

1 tablespoon butter

FILLING
4 ounces Chihuahua or Muenster cheese, grated

4 ounces Monterey jack cheese, grated

4 ounces fresh creamy goat cheese or cream cheese, at room
   temperature

2 tablespoons minced red onion

1 garlic clove, minced

1/4 teaspoon dried epazote

6 poblano chiles or other fresh mild green chiles, roasted and
   slit from end to end

COATING

1/2 cup all-purpose flour
2 eggs
1/4 cup cream
1 cup stone-ground blue cornmeal
1/3 cup stone-ground yellow cornmeal
1/2 teaspoon cumin seeds, toasted and ground
1/2 teaspoon salt

Vegetable oil for deep-frying

To prepare the optional sauce, simmer the chiles with half of the stock for 20 minutes, or until very soft. Transfer the chiles and stock to a blender. Add the tomato, onion, garlic, cumin, thyme, salt, and epazote and purée.

In a heavy saucepan, warm the oil and butter over medium-high heat. Pour the sauce into the pan, being careful to avoid splatters as the liquid hits the hot oil. Reduce the heat to medium-low and simmer until reduced and somewhat thick. Stir in the remaining stock and heat through. Taste the sauce and add more salt if you wish. Keep the sauce warm. (The sauce can be made a day ahead and refrigerated. Warm the sauce before proceeding.)

To prepare the chiles' filling, mix together the ingredients in a bowl. Stuff the mixture equally into the chiles, bringing the slit edges of each chile back together tightly.

Place the flour in a shallow dish, whisk the eggs and cream together in another, and stir together the cornmeals, cumin, and salt in another.

Pour at least 4 inches of oil into a heavy skillet or saucepan. Heat the oil to 350° F.

Coat each chile in flour, dunk it in the egg mixture, and then into the cornmeal. Fry the chiles a few at a time for about 2 1/2 to 3 minutes, until lightly browned and crisped. Drain and serve immediately, on pools of the sauce if you wish.

CALIFORNIA POBLANOS RELLENOS

Although rich, these refreshing, contemporary rellenos are lighter and quicker to prepare than our other cheese versions because they lack a batter coating.

Serves 4

MANGO SALSA
3/4 cup diced mango
1/4 cup diced red onion
1/4 cup diced bell pepper, preferably a combination of red and yellow
1 tablespoon minced fresh cilantro
1 tablespoon fresh lime juice

FILLING
3 ounces Monterey jack cheese, grated
3 ounces asadero or additional Monterey jack cheese, grated
1/3 cup crumbled Cotija cheese (optional)
1 tablespoon minced onion
1 tablespoon minced fresh cilantro

**4 poblano chiles or other fresh mild green chiles, roasted and slit from
    end to end**

In a small bowl, combine all the salsa ingredients. Refrigerate until ready to serve.

Heat the broiler. Grease a shallow, heat-proof serving dish.

In a bowl, combine the cheeses, onion, and cilantro. With your fingers, stuff each chile with the cheese mixture, filling them full but not to overflowing. Transfer the chiles to the prepared serving dish.

Broil the chiles for 3 to 5 minutes, until the cheese is bubbly. Serve immediately with the salsa spooned over the chiles.

Regional Variations: Southwestern cooks have stuffed rellenos with all manner of fillings. In *An Army Wife's Cookbook*, researched in the 1870s and '80s, Alice Kirk Grierson recommended macaroni and cheese, with the pasta cooked first in sherry-flavored water. A few decades later, a Tucson cookbook author championed chopped olives and onions in a cheese medley, with the chile fried in hot lard "as you would for oysters." Today, professional restaurant chefs lead the way in new relleno combinations. John Rivera Sedlar, of the Abiquiu restaurants in Santa Monica and San Francisco, concocted a favorite of ours years ago, stuffing the pods with a mushroom duxelle mixture and serving them in a pool of garlic goat cheese sauce. In Phoenix at Vincent's on Camelback, Vincent Guerithault uses wild mushrooms in his filling and a blue cheese topping.

RANCH-COUNTRY BEEF

*F*or more than a century now, beef has been the preferred meat for special meals in both Mexico and the United States. In each country, the border region stimulated the national interest and served as the original supply source. Texas ranchers led the way in the States, enticing Americans away from pork after they launched the long trail drives that took their cattle to railroad centers and distant markets. In Mexico, the northern states of Chihuahua, Coahuila, and Sonora played a similar role, introducing other areas to beef and converting tastes to their regional specialty.

The borderlands were cattle country from the early years of Spanish settlement, when the first exploratory expeditions brought the animals along for food. Strays wandered off and formed wild herds, thriving on the grass and scrub of the plains. Colonists rounded up the cattle, and introduced stock of their own, to create ranches large and small throughout the region. While the eastern half of the United States and most of Mexico depended primarily on pork for domesticated meat, beef became a mainstay in the local diet in the borderlands, and eventually a major commercial product after the railroad provided a way to ship it from the frontier to booming industrial cities.

When that happened in the last decades of the nineteenth century, the ranchers exported more than cattle. They also sent along their well-established ideas about cooking the meat, notions that spread across both countries and continue to influence some of the most popular preparations. As the recent American craze for fajitas shows, the border remains the bastion of beef.

Texans like to take credit for fajitas, but they were only the popularizers, not the creators. The thought of eating the diaphragm muscle—a cut now known as skirt steak—would have horrified Houston until recently. The roots of the dish go back to wood-fire cookouts on northern Mexico ranches, where *vaqueros* originally tamed the naturally tough but flavorful meat, which they called *arracheras*. This is how some descendants of the developers prepare one of their favorite foods today on modern charcoal grills.

Serves 6 generously

2 skirt steaks, 1 to 1 1/4 pounds each, trimmed of membrane and fat

MARINADE
Juice of 6 to 7 limes
2 to 3 pickled jalapeños, minced
6 garlic cloves, minced

Salt to taste
1 to 2 medium onions, sliced thick
Vegetable oil

Flour tortillas, preferably thick, warmed

Place the meat in a shallow, nonreactive dish. Combine all the marinade ingredients in a bowl, mix them well, and pour over the meat. Refrigerate for at least 6 to 8 hours, turning the meat occasionally. Remove the meat from the refrigerator and drain it. Salt the meat and let it sit at room temperature for about 45 minutes.

Coat the onions well with oil.

On an outdoor grill, fire up enough charcoal to form a single layer of coals beneath the meat. When the coals are covered with gray ash, place the *arracheras* directly over the fire and the onions a little to the side, where they'll get a bit less heat. Grill the meat medium-rare, about 5 to 6 minutes per side. Turn the onions occasionally, taking them off when soft and some edges are browned and crispy.

Maybe all of us should use the Mexican term *arracheras* for charbroiled skirt steak. The American equivalent, *fajitas,* has completely lost its original meaning and is now applied to any kind of grilled fare meant to be eaten as a soft taco. Bemoaning the problem recently, food writer John Mariani said that the proliferation of fajitas made with everything from turkey to tofu was like "calling anything baked with a hole in it a bagel."

Allow the steaks to sit for 5 minutes before slicing. Sometimes whole sections of *arracheras* are brought to the table, to be cut by the diners. We prefer to slice the *arracheras* before serving, so that all the meat is cut across the grain diagonally into finger-length strips, for greatest tenderness.

To serve, pile a platter high with the meat and the grilled onions, garnished with lime wedges, and with tortillas on the side. Save any leftovers for Poblanos Rellenos con Carne.

Technique Tip: To get a little more of the original outdoor flavor of *arracheras,* put presoaked chips or chunks of hardwood on the charcoal fire. Charcoal alone won't provide the true taste of wood smoke because the carbonization process used in its manufacturing burns that away. Some contemporary cooks like to add fresh herbs such as sage or oregano instead of wood, for a new dimension in flavor, but unless you have copious amounts from your own garden, it'll be mainly your money that goes up in smoke in a short grilling process. Several heads of unpeeled garlic cloves make a more successful substitute.

Regional Variations: Charcoal-grilled *arracheras* frequently form the basis of the norteño specialty called tacos *al carbon,* though other cuts of beef are also used. Sometimes marinated but usually not, the meat is grilled, sliced thin or chopped, and wrapped in fluffy flour tortillas. Typically, the soft tacos come with salsa and a little lime juice squeezed on top, and may be accompanied with chile-laced *charra* beans. The combination distills the essence of traditional border fare.

RED CALDWELL'S SOUTH TEXAS FAJITAS

Today even a Dallas debutante may wax with some authority on fixing fajitas, but no one is more passionate about the preparation than south Texas cooks. Mexican-American cowboys in the area brought the dish into the state several generations ago, when they were sometimes paid partially with skirt steak and other unwanted beef cuts. Their simple open-fire cooking methods have evolved over time into more elaborate grilling recipes, such as this one that Red Caldwell provided in his delightful *Pit, Pot, and Skillet* (Corona Publishing Company, 1990). Like many home cooks today, Red relies on store-bought salad dressing and dried spices, but his tasty results reinforce the old chestnut about the whole being greater than the sum of the parts.

Serves 6 generously

2 skirt steaks, 1 to 1 1/4 pounds each, trimmed of membrane and fat

MARINADE
1 cup bottled herb-and-garlic or Italian salad dressing
12 ounces beer
1 large onion, minced
Juice of 3 to 4 limes, preferably the small key-type *limónes*
3 tablespoons chili powder
2 tablespoons minced fresh cilantro
2 tablespoons lemon pepper seasoning
1 tablespoon Worcestershire sauce
2 teaspoons ground cumin
1 1/2 teaspoons garlic powder
1 teaspoon cayenne
1 bay leaf

16 to 20 flour tortillas, preferably thick and 6 to 7 inches in diameter, warmed
Pico de Gallo (page 40)
Guacamole (page 123)

Fajitas broke through their humble origins into big-time popularity in the 1970s, primarily through the efforts of two food pros who learned their secrets in deep south Texas. Ninfa Rodriguez Laurenzo made fajitas a mainstay on the menu when she opened her Ninfa's restaurant chain in Houston in 1973, and around the same time Sonny Falcon began serving them at his Fajita King food stands on the state's fairs-and-festivals circuit. Texans are still spreading the dish's repute. Football guru John Madden was so impressed with Chuy Uranga's fajitas in the tiny town of Van Horn that he inducted the cook into his "Haul of Fame" and recommended Chuy's café on national television as his favorite Mexican restaurant.

Place the meat in a shallow, nonreactive dish.

Combine all the marinade ingredients in a bowl, mix them well, and pour over the steaks. Refrigerate the meat for at least 6 to 8 hours, turning it occasionally. Remove the meat from the refrigerator and drain it. Bring the steaks to room temperature.

On an outdoor grill, fire up enough charcoal to form a single layer of coals beneath the meat. When the coals are covered with gray ash, place the steaks directly over the fire. Grill the meat medium-rare, about 5 to 6 minutes per side.

Cut the steaks across the grain diagonally into finger-length strips.

To serve, pile a platter high with the meat, and accompany the platter with the tortillas, pico de gallo, and guacamole. Let everyone help themselves by filling tortillas with some of the meat and portions of the garnishes.

Technique Tip: Standard charcoal briquettes contain industrial binders and fillers that may pollute the air and your taste buds too. Look for brands that contain only "all-natural" vegetable-starch binders or for lump hardwood charcoal, which is left in irregular shapes instead of being compressed into briquettes.

Regional Variations: Some Texans, including Sonny "Fajita King" Falcon, don't marinate fajitas, but others experiment with everything from pickles to pop. It's hard to beat the beer base that Red Caldwell suggests, but many people prefer to get their meat soused on tequila or red wine. On the sober side, other popular choices include pineapple juice, Coke, soy sauce, and the liquid from jars of pickled jalapeños. California food writer Linda Lau Anusasananan straddles the fence, using orange and lemon juices with tequila.

Drying strips of venison and buffalo was a common preservation method in the arid borderlands well before the Spanish arrived, but the new settlers brought their own similar technology along with domesticated cattle. To keep beef beyond the day of butchering, the pioneers dehydrated it in thin slices (*carne seca*, or dried meat), which they later pounded and cooked back to tenderness to eat as *machaca*. Now that preservation is no longer an issue, some people make the dish with stewed rather than dried beef, a tasty but different preparation featured in our Machaca Breakfast Burros. This boiled, dry-baked, and pulverized version comes much closer to replicating the original, which still appears with frequency in northern Mexico, usually under the name *machaca*, and in Tucson as *carne seca*.

Serves 8 to 10

DRIED BEEF
3-pound eye of round or boneless shoulder chuck roast

3 tablespoons vinegar, preferably white

1 tablespoon salt

2 teaspoons fresh-ground black pepper

10 garlic cloves, sliced

1 tablespoon ground dried mild red chile, preferably ancho, New
    Mexican, or Anaheim

8 cups water

Juice of 2 limes

DRIED SEASONING BLEND
1 tablespoon ground dried mild red chile, preferably ancho, New
    Mexican, or Anaheim

1 teaspoon salt

1 teaspoon fresh-ground black pepper

1/4 cup vegetable oil

1 medium onion, chopped

3/4 cup chopped roasted mild green chiles, preferably poblano, New
    Mexican, or Anaheim, fresh or frozen

2 small tomatoes, preferably Roma or Italian plum, chopped
4 garlic cloves, minced
1 teaspoon dried oregano, preferably Mexican
Salt to taste (optional)

Lime wedges, for garnish

In a Dutch oven or large, heavy saucepan, combine all of the dried beef ingredients except the lime juice. Bring the meat mixture to a boil, skim off any foam, reduce the heat to a low simmer, and cover. Cook for about 2 to 2 ^{1}/4 hours, until the meat is very tender. Cool the meat in its cooking liquid for 30 minutes. Strain the cooking liquid, reserving 1 cup. (The remaining liquid can be used as a soup stock or to enrich vegetable dishes.)

Preheat the oven to 275° F.

Tear the meat into thin shreds and transfer it back to the Dutch oven or saucepan. Add the reserved cooking liquid and simmer over medium heat until the liquid is absorbed. Pour the lime juice over the meat and toss together.

Transfer the meat to 1 or 2 baking sheets, spreading it thin. In a small bowl, combine the dried seasonings and sprinkle about half of the mixture over the meat. Bake the meat for 20 minutes, stir it well, and sprinkle with as much of the remaining dried seasonings as you wish. Bake an additional 30 to 40 minutes, until browned and dry. (The meat can be prepared ahead to this point and refrigerated for 1 or 2 days. This method does *not* preserve the meat, so do not leave it at room temperature.)

Transfer the meat to a blender, a handful at a time, and purée briefly, in little bursts, until the meat is reduced to fine threads. Don't overdo it or the meat can end up resembling sawdust.

In a heavy skillet, warm the oil over medium heat. Add the onion and sauté until softened. Stir in the chiles, tomatoes, garlic, and oregano and cook for another couple of minutes, covered. Add the browned meat and heat through, cooking uncovered until all the liquid is evaporated. Add salt to taste if you wish.

Serve the *carne seca* with lime wedges.

Technique Tip: The dish still tastes best when made from authentic *carne seca*, or dried beef. If you live in an arid, desert climate, you can air-dry the meat yourself outdoors by methods akin to the traditional. Salt thin strips of beef, coat them in chile, drape them loosely with cheese-cloth, and hang them on a clothesline or something similar in the full sun for several days, bringing the meat inside at night. Most commercial versions of *carne seca* sold in Southwestern stores are mediocre, but La Parrilla in Del Mar, California (619-299-8743), produces an excellent one. Smokehouse jerky (such as that made by the New Braunfels Smokehouse in Texas, 800-537-6932) is a flavorful alternative, though much smokier than the original.

CARNE ASADA

The name is simple, meaning "flame-cooked meat," and the dish is deliciously simple as well, just tender beef sliced very thin and seared quickly over high heat.

Serves 4

1 1/2-pound top sirloin or tenderloin, trimmed of surface fat
2 garlic cloves, minced
1/2 teaspoon fresh-ground black pepper, or more to taste
1/2 teaspoon cumin seeds, toasted and ground
Salt to taste

Place the meat in the freezer for 20 to 30 minutes to make it easier to slice thin. Cut the meat into strips about $1/8$ inch thick. Toss the meat strips with the remaining ingredients and let sit covered at room temperature.

On an outdoor grill, fire up enough charcoal to form a single layer of coals beneath the meat. When the coals are covered with gray ash, place the meat directly over the fire. To make sure the thin slices don't fall into the fire, we use a small-holed grate, such as those made by Griffo Grill or Oscarware, or a grill basket like the one Brinkmann sells. Grill the meat medium-rare, about $1 \ 1/2$ minutes per side.

Carne asada serves as the centerpiece of one of the most popular restaurant dishes in all of Mexico, the *tampiqueña* plate. The name suggests an origin in the city of Tampico, but only the creator came from there. When José Luis Loredo moved from the Tamaulipas port to Mexico City and opened the Tampico Club around 1940, he wanted to serve food from his native region. His signature dish became the *tampiqueña* combination of *carne asada,* cheese enchiladas, *rajas,* salsa méxicana, *charra* beans, and a square of grilled white panela cheese. In various permutations today, it remains the only major combination plate found in Mexico.

Serve it immediately, preferably with Grilled Green Onions and Rajas or accompaniments that go on a *tampiqueña* plate (see the sidebar).

Technique Tip: If you don't want to fire up charcoal to cook *carne asada,* you can sear the meat in a wok. Mexican street vendors often use similar equipment, either concave round grill pans or an inverted version of the same tool that allows them to cook on the dome and keep food warm below on the sides.

Regional Variations: In the *South Texas Mexican Cookbook* (Eakin Press, 1982), Lucy M. Garza recalls how proud she felt when her mother decided she was old enough to grind garlic, black peppercorns, and *comino,* or cumin seeds, in the family's *molcajete.* Those are common seasonings for *carne asada* in the borderlands, as are oregano, Worcestershire sauce, güero or güerito chile, and lemon or lime juice. Most cooks tread lightly with the spices, however, relying on the flavor of tender beef, any cut of which will shine when sliced thin and grilled over hot coals. The cowboys and ranchers who developed the dish probably cooked the meat over fiery-red mesquite embers, but in California cattle country they used orange, eucalyptus, or walnut to get similar levels of heat.

PAN-FRIED T-BONES PIMENTÓN

Serves 4

Four 1-pound T-bone steaks, each 1 1/2 inches thick
2 garlic cloves, halved vertically
Fresh-ground black pepper to taste
2 large red bell peppers
1 fresh serrano (optional)
Salt to taste
Salted butter

Rub the steaks well with the garlic and pepper and allow them to come to room temperature.

Roast the peppers and the serrano as you would other chiles. Use a stovetop grill or the broiler to blacken the skin of the peppers and, if you wish, the serrano. Transfer the bell peppers and serrano to a plastic bag and let them steam until cool enough to handle. Strip off the charred skin off (you may want to wear rubber gloves for the fiery serrano). If any bits of skin are particularly stubborn, hold the pepper under running water just long enough to loosen it. Cut the bell peppers into strips and mince the serrano. Toss together in a bowl with any accumulated juice, salt lightly, and keep warm.

Warm a cast-iron skillet over high heat. When the skillet is very hot, place the steaks in it.

Cook the steaks to the desired doneness, about 4 to 5 minutes per side for medium-rare. After removing the steaks, top each with thick pats of butter and let them sit for about 5 minutes. Mix any accumulated meat juices into the peppers. Serve the steaks with the peppers on the side.

Most cattle raised in the United States eat corn in feedlots, but in northern Mexico they graze on the range, making the meat a bit chewier and gamier. The tradeoff is more robust flavor, especially in the less expensive cuts often preferred south of the border. Experts agree that the best Sonoran beef rates among the world's finest, but, ironically, some Mexican restaurants frequented by Americans in border towns and resorts import U.S. meat to satisfy customer expectations.

Serves 4

2 tablespoons prepared yellow mustard

2 tablespoons vegetable oil

6 garlic cloves, roasted

1/2 teaspoon Worcestershire sauce

1/2 teaspoon dried sage

Two 18-ounce to 20-ounce boneless top sirloin strip steaks, each about
 1 inch thick

Mesquite chips or beans

8 green onions, limp ends trimmed

Salt to taste

Fresh-ground black pepper

4 fresh serranos, halved lengthwise

In a food processor or blender, combine the mustard, oil, garlic, Worcestershire sauce, and sage. Rub the mixture into the meat and onions, salt and pepper both, and let them sit at room temperature for 45 minutes.

On an outdoor grill, fire up enough charcoal to form a single layer of coals beneath the meat. At the same time, put a few handfuls of mesquite chips or beans in water to soak.

When the charcoal is covered with gray ash, scatter the wood chips or beans over it and place the steaks directly over the fire. Place the tops of the onions, along with the serranos, on a small piece of foil, a little off to the side of the fire, where the heat is lower. Grill the steaks for about 4 to 5 minutes, partially covered with the grill's lid (dampers open), to trap some of the mesquite smoke. Turn the meat, re-cover the grill partially, and cook to the desired doneness, about 4 more minutes for medium-rare. Turn the onions and serranos when you turn the meat, removing them when soft.

Serve the steaks immediately, accompanied with the onions and serranos.

THE MYSTIQUE OF MESQUITE

Ranchers hate it, environmentalists miss it, and grillers love it. The mystique wood of the past decade, mesquite used to thrive throughout the arid borderlands, symbolizing and even sustaining life in the region. A tenacious survivor, at least before the advent of commercial charcoal, the trees sink taproots as deep as a desert well in search of water, and ward off people and other predators with nasty thorns, making them a nuisance on the range. At the same time, their firm grip on the dry soil prevents erosion, and their meager shade is an ecological blessing for small animals and plants.

The mesquite beans in the droopy seedpods provided food for Native Americans and, in a later period, many hungry pioneers. In the early sixteenth century, Álvar Núñez Cabeza de Vaca compared them to carob beans and described how Texas Natives ate them ground into a meal. Most Spanish and Anglo settlers were less impressed, but they understood the nutritional value in a pinch. J. Frank Dobie told a story of some stranded Mexicans who lived on prickly-pear cactus and mesquite beans until they were rescued. According to Dobie, they claimed, "With prickly pears alone one can live, but with prickly pears and mesquite beans, a person will get fat."

Early Southwesterners and Mexicans used the tree in other ways as well. The sap soothed sore throats, the root made a salve for cuts, the leaves brightened the laundry, and gum from the bark both glued broken pottery and dyed hair black. When cowboys ran out of coffee, they made a substitute from the beans.

Mesquite surged to a peak of popularity only recently, however, as a charcoal wood for grilling. Contemporary chefs found that mesquite briquettes produced a high, even heat and could be promoted as a special Southwestern accent in their cooking. As Gary Paul Nabhan says in *Gathering the Desert* (University of Arizona Press, 1985), "The Wild West is now shipped off to East Coast restaurants that advertise mesquite-broiled, smoky-flavored Marlboro Country meat. Even though charcoal gives off little of the mesquite wood scent, the whole pitch is lucrative as hell."

Most mesquite charcoal comes from Sonora, where it's inexpensive to make and much easier to ship than wood because of its condensed size. Crews stack logs in giant pits, cover them with straw, burlap, and soil, and burn them down to coals, a two-week carbonization process that eliminates most of the original flavor. The business has been so profitable that mesquite is on the verge of disappearing. Environmental groups urge cooks to substitute the beans in grilling, soaked like wood chips, for a greater tang that doesn't sacrifice the slow-growing trees. Look for them in ecologically minded supermarkets and outdoor-cooking supply stores.

In Mexico, these "tips" may be made with almost any variety of boneless beef, but they're best when a premium cut is used. Here we combine them with a buttery ranchero sauce.

Serves 4

2 tablespoons vegetable oil
1 1/2 pounds tenderloin, top sirloin, or other tender boneless beef, diced in 1-inch cubes
2 tablespoons butter
1 medium onion, diced
2 to 3 fresh serranos, minced
2 garlic cloves, minced
3 cups canned crushed tomatoes
1 cup beef stock
1 bay leaf
Salt to taste

Minced fresh cilantro, for garnish (optional)

In a Dutch oven or large saucepan, warm the oil over high heat. Brown the meat in the oil, turning it frequently, for 4 to 5 minutes. With a slotted spoon, remove the meat and reserve it.

Reduce the heat under the pan to medium and add the butter. When the butter is melted, stir in the onion and sauté until soft. Mix in the serranos and garlic and sauté for an additional couple of minutes. Add the tomatoes, stock, bay leaf, and salt. Simmer the sauce for 10 to 15 minutes. Stir the meat into the sauce and heat through.

Serve hot with rice or *fideos*.

Santa Fe's historic central plaza is a busy place almost any hour, but the crowds really swarm to the corner of Palace and Washington at lunchtime. From April through October, Roque Garcia and his partner Mona Cavalli operate a street stand at the intersection, serving flour tortillas brimming with little bits of succulent beef and a tangle of onions and chile. *Gourmet* raved about the treat, and so has a passel of major newspapers, but Roque remains a down-to-earth ambassador for the best of old Santa Fe. This is how he recommends that home cooks duplicate his *carnitas*, which he based on a recipe from his mother.

Serves 4

1 1/2-pound boneless sirloin or top round steak, cut across the grain
    into 1/8-inch strips

MARINADE
6 tablespoons vegetable oil
6 tablespoons soy sauce
2 tablespoons dried oregano, preferably Mexican
4 garlic cloves, minced

MONA'S SALSA
2 medium tomatoes, diced
1 small onion, chopped
2 to 6 fresh jalapeños, minced
2 tablespoons minced fresh cilantro (optional)
2 garlic cloves, minced

1 tablespoon vegetable oil
1 large onion, sliced thin
5 fresh mild green chiles, preferably New Mexican or Anaheim, sliced
    into very thin rounds
4 flour tortillas, preferably thick and 7 to 8 inches in diameter, warmed

The night before you plan to cook the meat, place it in a shallow, nonreactive dish. Combine the marinade ingredients in a bowl and pour the marinade over the meat. Refrigerate, covered, for at least 12 hours and preferably 24.

Prepare the salsa by combining all the ingredients in a bowl. Refrigerate until ready to serve.

Drain the meat and discard the marinade.

In a large, heavy skillet or wok, warm the oil over high heat until it just begins to smoke. Sauté the beef in two batches, tossing almost constantly, until browned well, about 2 minutes per batch. Transfer the beef pieces to a plate as they brown.

Reduce the heat to medium and add the onion and chiles to the skillet. Cook until softened, stirring almost constantly. Return the beef to the skillet and toss with the vegetables.

Using tongs, lift about one-quarter of the beef mixture from the skillet, allowing any excess juices to drip back into the skillet, and fill a tortilla. Repeat with the remaining beef mixture and tortillas. For stand-up eating, Roque bunches aluminum foil around the tortillas.

Serve immediately, topped with salsa.

Regional Variations: Roque Garcia's *carnitas* bear a resemblance to a venerable northern Mexico dish called *cortadillo*, which is also sold in street stands, partially as a hangover cure. The beef usually isn't marinated, and it's likely to be cooked in lard, but the rest of the preparation and ingredients are similar except for the addition of tomatoes. In Mexico and much of the Southwest, *carnitas* usually refers to morsels of pork (see page 228).

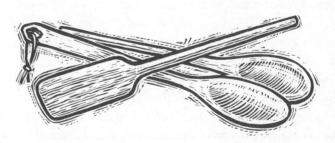

With an important twist or two, the classic Italian veal Milanese has become nearly as popular on northern Mexico tables as spaghetti is in the States. Italian immigrants to Mexico spread interest in the breaded and fried cutlet dish, and eventually acquiesced to making it with round steak rather than scarce veal. The resulting *milanesa*, curiously, comes close to the Texas favorite chicken-fried steak, widely regarded as the product of a different heritage. Some norteño restaurants today use veal or beef tenderloin, but most home cooks stick with round steak, which is tastier when properly tenderized.

Historically, veal rarely had a place in the borderlands. Cowboys might kill a calf to make their beloved sonofabitch stew, but most of the time beef on the hoof was valued by the pound. In *The Only Texas Cookbook* (Lone Star Books, 1981), a true daughter of the ranch country, Linda West Eckhardt, likened a desire for veal in the past "to cutting up hundred dollar bills and tossing them over your shoulder."

Serves 4 to 6

1 3/4-pound to 2-pound round steak, cut no more than 1/2 inch thick and tenderized by your butcher
Juice of 1 lime
1 teaspoon salt
1/2 teaspoon fresh-ground black pepper
2 eggs
3 tablespoons water
3/4 cup all-purpose flour
3 cups dried breadcrumbs
Vegetable oil for pan-frying

Lime wedges, for garnish

Cut the meat into 8 to 12 pieces. Pound the portions until each is about $1/8$ inch thick. Toss the steaks with the lime juice. Season each steak on both sides with salt and pepper, rubbing the seasonings into the meat.

Lightly beat the eggs with the water in a shallow bowl. One at a time, dip the steaks in the flour, then in the eggs, then in the breadcrumbs.

In a large, heavy skillet over medium heat, warm a couple of tablespoons of oil, enough to make a thick film of oil. Add several of the steaks and cook them, turning once, until the meat is cooked through and the coating is crisp and brown, about 4 minutes total. Keep the steaks warm while preparing the others. Repeat with the remaining steaks, adding more oil if needed.

Serve hot with lime wedges. Refried beans, *rajas* (strips of green chile), and summer squash or Classic Calabacitas typically accompany *milanesa*. For a change, we eat it chicken-fried-steak style, making a cream gravy out of the drippings and accompanying the *milanesa* with mashed potatoes and cooked greens like Charra's Chard.

CARNE MECHADA

Another norteño dish with a distinctly European past, *carne mechada* is an old Spanish preparation that remains a specialty in the Coahuila ranch country. Seldom seen today across the Rio Grande, it's better known farther south—where similar savory meat rolls might be called *malaya* in Chile or *matahambre* in Argentina.

Serves 6

1 3/4-pound to 2-pound flank steak, pounded to about 1/3-inch
    thickness

MARINADE
12 ounces beer
1 medium onion, chopped
1/4 cup vinegar, preferably cider
1 tablespoon Maggi seasoning or Worcestershire sauce
3 green onions, minced
3 garlic cloves, minced
1 teaspoon dried oregano, preferably Mexican
1/2 teaspoon cumin seeds, toasted and ground

Salt to taste
Fresh-ground black pepper to taste

FILLING
4 slices cooked bacon, crumbled
1 medium carrot, grated
1 small baking potato, parboiled, peeled, and grated
1/4 cup chopped fresh parsley, preferably the flat-leaf variety
1 to 2 fresh serranos, minced
2 green onions, sliced
2 garlic cloves, minced
1 teaspoon dried oregano, preferably Mexican
1/2 teaspoon cumin seeds, toasted and ground

Beef stock

Minced fresh parsley and sliced green onions, for garnish

The night before you plan to cook the meat, place the steak in a shallow, nonreactive dish. Combine the marinade ingredients and pour the marinade over the meat. Refrigerate overnight.

Drain the meat, reserving the marinade. Sprinkle salt and pepper lightly over the meat. In a bowl, combine the filling ingredients and spread the mixture evenly over the steak to within about $1/2$ inch of its edges. Roll up the steak from one of its longer edges, jellyroll fashion. Transfer the roll to a large piece of cheesecloth, wrap up the roll snug but not tight in the cloth, and tie the ends.

Transfer the roll to a Dutch oven or stockpot large enough to hold it. Pour the reserved marinade over it and then add enough stock to cover it by several inches. Bring the mixture to a boil over high heat, reduce the heat to a low simmer, and cover. Cook the roll for 2 to 2 $1/2$ hours, until the meat is very tender.

Remove the roll from the cooking liquid and let the meat cool for 15 to 20 minutes. Reserve $1/2$ cup of the liquid to pour over the meat if you wish, and save the rest of the flavorful liquid for soups or other dishes. Unwrap the meat, discard the cheesecloth, and slice the meat crosswise. Transfer the slices to a decorative platter, pour cooking liquid over them if you wish, and scatter parsley and green onions on top.

Serve warm. While it is not traditional, we like to accompany the *carne* with spicy McAllen Mustard or another prepared mustard.

JUÁREZ SALPICÓN

Salpicón means hodgepodge or hash in Spanish. Along the Ciudad Juárez–El Paso border, the word refers to this kind of hearty beef salad, a way to use brisket that rivals barbecuing. The meat can be prepared a day or two ahead.

Serves 8 to 10 as a main dish

3 1/2-pound to 4-pound fully trimmed beef brisket section
    (sometimes called the flat cut)
1 large onion, chopped
8 cups beef stock
2 bay leaves
3 garlic cloves, minced
2 canned chipotles
2 teaspoons salt
1 teaspoon black peppercorns

SALPICÓN DRESSING
1/3 cup canned chipotle chiles with adobo sauce
6 tablespoons extra-virgin olive oil
4 tablespoons fresh lime juice
2 tablespoons vinegar, preferably white
1 tablespoon ketchup
1 tablespoon minced onion
1 garlic clove, minced
Salt and coarse-ground black pepper to taste

SALPICÓN SALAD
4 small tomatoes, preferably Roma or Italian plum, diced
2 ripe Haas avocados, diced
1 medium red onion, diced
6 ounces asadero or Monterey jack cheese, in small cubes
1/2 cup chopped fresh cilantro

Radish roses, for garnish (optional)

In a Dutch oven or small stockpot, combine the brisket with the onion, stock, bay leaves, garlic, chipotles, salt, and peppercorns. Bring the mixture to a boil over high heat, skimming off any foam. Reduce the heat to low, cover, and simmer for 3 $^1/_2$ to 4 hours, or until the meat is falling-apart tender. Let the meat cool for 30 minutes in the cooking liquid. Reserve 2 tablespoons of the cooking liquid for the salad dressing and save the rest of the liquid for a soup or stew. Pull the meat apart into shreds. (The dish can be made ahead to this point and refrigerated for 1 or 2 days. Warm the meat wrapped in foil in the oven before proceeding.)

Combine all the dressing ingredients, plus the reserved cooking liquid, in a blender or food processor and purée.

In a bowl, mix the brisket with about three-fourths of the salad dressing. Transfer the brisket to a serving platter or bowl and toss it lightly with the remaining ingredients. Drizzle additional dressing over the top, enough to make the mixture moist, and serve warm or chilled as a main-dish salad. For a cocktail party, serve the *salpicón* with tostada chips for dipping.

Regional Variations: Some Chihuahua and Texas cooks favor flank steak, shredded with the grain, for their *salpicóns*, and others won't make the dish unless they have leftover roast beef. A nineteenth-century cookbook from the Salt River Valley in Arizona calls for tongue. We prefer brisket, but we like it best of all when the meat is barbecued Texas-pit style, which we describe in our book *Smoke & Spice* (Harvard Common Press, 1994).

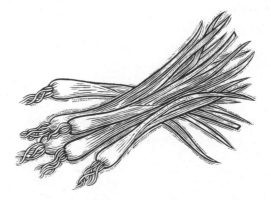

TERLINGUA BOWL OF RED

In the United States, no border dish is better known than Texas chili con carne. Norteños make meat and chile stews with similar roots, but the "bowl of red" as we know it today is a Lone Star invention, so foreign south of the border that one national authority labeled it "a detestable food with a false Mexican name." Christened after the Texas town that has hosted many fabled chili cookoffs, our version goes one step beyond most home preparations—cooking the meat initially over a mesquite fire. We think the extra effort is amply rewarded in flavor, but the recipe still works well if you skip the grilling.

Serves 8

1 whole head of garlic, peeled and crushed

2 teaspoons salt

4-pound chuck roast, at least 3 inches thick

1/2 cup ground dried mild red chile, preferably ancho, or chili powder, preferably Gebhardt's

Mesquite chips or beans

4 slices bacon, chopped

1 large onion, minced

2 cups beef stock, or more as necessary

1 tablespoon cumin seeds, toasted and ground

1 tablespoon *mole* paste (see page 296)

2 teaspoons dried oregano, preferably Mexican

1 teaspoon vinegar, preferably cider

1/2 teaspoon ground dried hot red chile, such as cayenne, chile de árbol, or chile pequín, or to taste

1 to 2 tablespoons masa harina, as necessary

Chopped onions, minced fresh or pickled jalapeños, and saltine crackers, for garnish (optional)

Two or 3 hours before you plan to begin making the chili, use a mortar and pestle to make a paste of 6 of the garlic cloves and 1 1/2 teaspoons of the salt. Rub the meat well with the paste and then sprinkle it with about 1 teaspoon of the mild red chile.

The Texas legislature made chili the official dish of the Lone Star State, but Arizona embraces the concoction with almost equal fervor. Some partisans claim, in fact, that Prescott's Juniper House hotel and restaurant featured bowls of red as early as 1864, almost two decades before the San Antonio chili queens popularized the dish in Texas. Though spirited in taste, the Arizona version is usually low to moderate in chile heat, with the firepower mellowed by tomatoes and beans. Barry Goldwater once won a U.S. Senate Chili Cookoff with just such a blend.

On an outdoor grill, fire up enough charcoal to form a single layer of coals beneath the meat. Soak a few handfuls of mesquite chips or beans in water. When the coals are covered with gray ash, spread them out evenly and scatter the mesquite on top. Place the meat directly over the coals. Cover the grill, but make sure the dampers are open. Let the meat cook for about 10 minutes on each side to flavor it. Remove the partially cooked meat from the grill and set it aside until cool enough to handle.

When the meat has cooled, trim away any fat or cartilage. With a sharp knife, cut the meat into $^1/_4$-inch to $^1/_2$-inch cubes, saving all the juices.

In a Dutch oven or small stockpot, cook the bacon over medium heat until browned. Remove the bacon from the drippings with a slotted spoon. Add the onion to the drippings and sauté briefly until softened. Mix in the remaining garlic and sauté until it turns translucent. Stir in the meat and all reserved meat juices, adding just enough beef stock to cover. Stir in the remaining salt and mild red chile, the reserved bacon, and the cumin, *mole* paste, oregano, vinegar, and hot red chile. Reduce the heat to very low.

Cook for about 3 hours, stirring every half hour or so and adjusting the seasoning as you wish. Add stock as needed to keep the mixture from getting dry, but keep in mind you're preparing a meat dish, not a soup. In the third hour of cooking, thicken the chili by adding the masa harina 1 or 2 teaspoons at a time.

The chili can be served immediately, but the flavor improves with a day's refrigeration and reheating. Serve steaming hot in bowls with the garnishes, if you wish.

Regional Variations: Several whole books are devoted to variations on chili, mostly from the Southwest. Cookoff contestants in particular contradict each other with gleeful passion, tinkering endlessly for the most special formula and fixings. Some swear by "chili-grind" rather than cubed beef, and others don't let beef in the pot, preferring venison, pork, or even rattlesnake. Cooks heat it up with all kinds and colors of chile, or commercial chili powder blends and sauces, and they differ about simmering the meat in stock, water, beer, or black coffee. Tomatoes are a controversial addition from recent generations, and among aficionados, beans can be a big bugaboo.

The only truly necessary ingredients are meat, chile, and imagination. Author C. W. Smith demonstrated the role of the latter in a 1994 *Texas Monthly* article that suggested how to age the magical potion. He said to cook the chili in an old pot over a backyard fire and then "lug it off into the closest mesquite thicket, where you let it sit, covered, overnight. You put the lid on tight enough to keep out bugs but loose enough to let it take on the natural tang that's riding on the air: crude oil vapors, a faint snatch of *corridos* or a whang of mariachi music, a whiff of saddle leather and horse apples. Then after a night out on the prairie, all it needs is for the cook to hold a jambox playing Bob Wills's 'I'm a Ding Dong Daddy (from Dumas)' over it for a minute or two."

DORA'S CARNE CON CHILE

In Texas it's chili con carne, but in New Mexico the related dish is carne con chile, a difference that's more substantial than it sounds. The dividing line gets blurred by the terminology, because despite the names, the Lone Star chili features meat and the Land of Enchantment *carne* brims with chile. Our version of the New Mexico bowl of red owes a big debt to Dora's Café in Hatch, where we got the inspiration for this recipe.

Serves 8

1/4 cup vegetable oil
2-pound chuck roast, cut into 1/2-inch cubes
2 medium onions, chopped
4 garlic cloves, minced
3/4 cup ground dried mild red chile, preferably New Mexican
1 tablespoon dried oregano, preferably Mexican
2 teaspoons salt
4 cups beef stock, or more as necessary
2 cups Frijoles de Olla (page 374), drained, or other well-cooked pinto
    beans
2 medium baking potatoes, parboiled, peeled, and chunked

Chopped onions and grated mild cheddar cheese, for garnish

In a Dutch oven or small stockpot, warm the oil over high heat and sear the meat. Add the onions and garlic and sauté until the onions turn translucent. Stir in the chile, oregano, salt, and stock, reduce the heat to very low, and cover.

Cook for 2 hours, stirring every half hour or so. Stir in the beans and potatoes, replace the cover, and continue cooking, stirring the mixture up from the bottom frequently, for an additional 45 minutes, or until both the meat and the potatoes are very tender. The consistency should be like a slightly soupy stew. The *carne* can be served immediately or refrigerated for a day before rewarming and serving. The flavor improves with age for 1 or 2 days.

Serve steaming hot in bowls with the garnishes.

Regional Variations: When you find chili-like stews in northern Mexico, they are usually closer to the New Mexican style than the Texan, though more limited in ingredients than either. One of the nearest relatives is *caldillo*, which seldom contains more than beef, chile, onion, and tomato. In Chihuahua and Nuevo León in particular, men often make the dish and take a macho pride in its heat level—one element that's closer to Texas chili.

Named for the big pot that it's cooked in, *puchero* is a boiled dinner in the style of the French pot-au-feu. This version comes from an early California rendition.

Serves 10 to 12

2 tablespoons extra-virgin olive oil
3 1/2-pound to 4-pound fully trimmed beef brisket section
    (sometimes called the flat cut)
2 medium onions, chopped
8 cups water
1 cup canned crushed tomatoes
2 bay leaves
1 tablespoon salt
1 teaspoon dried thyme
1/2 small cabbage head, in large shreds
2 medium baking potatoes, peeled and diced
1 medium sweet potato, peeled and diced
4 carrots, sliced
2 small turnips, sliced
3 leeks, sliced
1 cup thick-sliced summer squash
2 whole dried mild red chiles, preferably ancho or pasilla, stemmed
    and seeded
1 pound chorizo links, sliced in 1-inch to 2-inch sections
15 1/2-ounce can garbanzo beans, drained and rinsed
2 teaspoons sherry vinegar
Big pinch of saffron threads (optional)
Minced fresh parsley
Fresh-ground black pepper

In a stockpot, warm the oil over medium-high heat. Brown the brisket on both sides. Add the onions, water, tomatoes, bay leaves, salt, and thyme and bring the mixture to a boil. Reduce the heat to a low simmer, cover, and cook for about 2 hours.

When people traveled in the past, they often carried their own eating utensils. California ranchos welcomed visitors, but guests were expected to bring a knife for cutting beef and other meat. Such politeness didn't always reach Texas. Lone Star legend Big-Foot Wallace once encountered a dandy—"slick and as shiny all over as a newly varnished cupboard"— who brought his own silverware on a steamboat trip. Not to be outdone, the bombastic Big-Foot collected some wood at the next fuel stop, whittled a set of three-foot-long cutlery, and started carrying the pieces to the dining room in a gun case.

Add the cabbage, potatoes, sweet potato, carrots, turnips, leeks, squash, and chiles. Cover the pot again and simmer for another hour.

In a skillet, fry the chorizos over medium heat until cooked through. To the stockpot add the chorizos, garbanzos, vinegar, and saffron, if you wish, and cook for another 30 minutes or until the brisket is tender but still firm enough to slice.

Pour off the cooking liquid through a strainer and defat it. Remove the brisket from the pot and let it sit for 10 minutes.

Slice the brisket thin and arrange it at the center of a large rimmed platter. Remove the chorizo sections from the pot and arrange them around the brisket. Spoon the rest of the vegetables around the meat, placing them attractively, and top with 1 or 2 cups of the strained broth, a generous sprinkling of parsley, and a good grinding of pepper. Serve the platter of meats and vegetables with a large bowl of the broth to use like a gravy.

Technique Tip: Traditionally, bowls of the tasty strained broth are served as a first course. If you wish to do that, adjust the seasonings as needed and sprinkle each bowl with parsley. We prefer to use the broth liberally to flavor the meat and vegetables, and then if we have any leftovers, we serve it as a soup at a later meal.

CARNE GUISADA

Many *guisadas*, or stews, cook on top of the stove, but the meat will be more tender if it is slow-baked. In either case, the dish should be thick, without much liquid, as in this Texas version. *Guisada* can be served as is, or it can fill soft tacos.

Serves 3 to 4 as a main dish, or 4 to 6 in tacos

1 1/4 pounds beef tips cut from a chuck roast, in bite-size pieces
2 tablespoons all-purpose flour
1 tablespoon vegetable oil
3 celery stalks, chopped
1 medium onion, chopped
1 to 2 fresh jalapeños, minced
1 1/2 cups beef stock
1 tablespoon tomato paste
2 teaspoons cumin seeds, toasted and ground
1/2 teaspoon chili powder

Preheat the oven to 350° F.

Dust the meat cubes with the flour. Warm the oil over high heat in a heavy, ovenproof skillet or Dutch oven. Brown the meat quickly. Add the remaining ingredients and bring the *guisada* to a simmer on the stove. Cover the skillet and place it in the oven. Bake for about 2 $^1/_2$ hours, until the meat is falling-apart tender. Serve warm.

Regional Variations: You can tell this recipe probably hails from north of the border just because of the presence of celery. *Guisadas* or *guisados* are as popular in northern Mexico as in Texas, but Mexican cooks usually limit the vegetables to onion, tomato, and chile. Some Chihuahua versions are flavored only with anchos and tomatoes.

Susan Curtis's Santa Fe School of Cooking provides all the instruction you need to re-create Southwestern dishes at home, along with good food and good times. Six chefs offer demonstration classes in traditional and contemporary foods from New Mexico, the Southwest, and Mexico. Several hours each, the sessions feature technique and ingredient tips, insights into the area's culture and history, and a full lunch, all for reasonable rates. The school also arranges culinary tours and sells chiles, other local ingredients, Southwestern cookbooks, and cooking equipment. Call 505-983-4511 for a schedule or catalog.

In New Mexico, green chile stew warms both body and soul on cold winter nights. This version, based on one from the Santa Fe School of Cooking, requires neither the flour nor oil typical of most stews.

Serves 8

1 1/2 pounds beef stew meat
2 medium onions, diced
4 garlic cloves, minced
4 baking potatoes, peeled or unpeeled, and diced
1 tablespoon salt, or more to taste
5 cups chicken stock
3 cups chopped roasted mild green chiles, preferably New Mexican or Anaheim, fresh or frozen
1 red bell pepper, diced
3 tablespoons minced fresh cilantro (optional)

In a Dutch oven or large, heavy saucepan, cook the beef over medium heat until it browns and most of the liquid from the beef has evaporated. Stir in the onions and garlic and cook for a couple of minutes, until the onions become translucent. Add the potatoes, salt, and stock and raise the heat to bring the mixture to a boil. Reduce the heat to a low simmer and cook, uncovered, for about 1 hour.

Stir in the chiles and bell pepper and continue cooking for another 1 to 1 $^{1}/_{2}$ hours, until the beef is very tender.

Stir in the cilantro, if you wish, and serve hot. Accompany the stew with thick flour tortillas or wedges of golden cornbread.

SONORAN MENUDO BLANCO

Many cooks make menudo only on the weekend, partially because of the long preparation time but mainly because that's when demand swells for the famed hangover cure. Popular throughout the borderlands, the tripe stew has earned its reputation as "the breakfast of champions." This Sonoran rendition is white, or *blanco*, because the chile is sprinkled in at the table rather than cooked into the dish. A calf's foot is the most traditional meat for flavoring, but the other options listed may be easier to find.

Serves 6 to 8

2 pounds honeycomb tripe, cleaned (see "Technique Tip")
Water
2 tablespoons vegetable oil
2 large onions, chopped
8 garlic cloves, minced
6 cups chicken stock
1 small calf's foot, cut in several pieces by your butcher, or a ham
    hock, a pig's foot, or 3/4 pound oxtails
1 tablespoon dried oregano, preferably Mexican
1/4 teaspoon fresh-ground black pepper
Salt to taste
16-ounce can hominy, drained

Crushed chiles pequíns, chiltepíns, or chiles de árbol
Chopped onion, minced fresh cilantro, and lime wedges, for garnish

Slice the cleaned tripe thin into bite-size pieces and place in a stock-pot or large, heavy saucepan. Cover the meat with cold water and bring to a rapid boil over high heat. Boil the tripe for 30 minutes. Drain the water from the tripe, discard it, and reserve the tripe.

Rinse and dry the stockpot, return it to the stove, and add the oil. Warm the oil over medium heat and add the onions and garlic. Sauté until soft, about 3 to 5 minutes. Add the stock, reserved tripe, and calf's foot or other meat. Reduce the heat to a very low simmer, cover, and cook the menudo for 3 hours. Remove the pieces of calf's foot or other meat, discarding any bones or chunks of fat. Shred the meat and reserve

According to former resident Arnulfo D. Trejo, *menuderos* were the human equivalent of early-morning roosters in turn-of-the-century Tucson. Calling out "Menudooo! Menudooo!" they woke the neighborhood to sell their brew out of big pots hauled on hand-pushed carts. Even today the city has the roving El Buen Sonorense food truck, which serves tripe, tongue, *carne asada, carne al pastor,* and other norteño specialties. It doesn't arrive, like some of the *menuderos,* at five o'clock, but it may catch up with you later in the day.

it. Add the oregano, pepper, salt, and hominy. Simmer for another $^1\!/_2$ to 1 hour, until the stew is cooked down and the tripe is tender. Expect it to retain a little chewiness. Stir in the reserved meat and heat it through.

Serve steaming in large bowls, offering the chile and garnishes on the side so that the menudo can be customized to taste. Accompany menudo with thick or thin flour tortillas and icy Mexican beer or, for a late weekend breakfast, tequila Bloody Marys. The menudo will keep, refrigerated, for several days.

Technique Tip: The tripe used in menudo comes from the lining of one of the two beef stomach chambers. Try to get honeycomb tripe, the most tender of the varieties, which are all tough to varying degrees. In some supermarkets, tripe comes already cleaned and may even be cut for menudo in the border region. If that's not an option in your locale, clean the tripe as soon as possible because it perishes quickly otherwise. Start a day in advance of the cooking. Mix together 1 cup of kosher salt (its rough texture acts as an abrasive) and 1 cup of inexpensive vinegar. Pour about one-third of the mixture into a large bowl and add the tripe. Scrub the tripe vigorously with a brush for about 5 minutes. Chef Chris Schlesinger likens the process to washing a dirty shirt collar. Rinse the tripe under cold running water and repeat the process two more times. Transfer the tripe to a bowl and cover it with cold water. Chill, covered, at least 8 hours, or up to twice that long. Change the water once about halfway through.

Regional Variations: Menudo is brick red in most border areas, colored by the ample quantity of dried chile or chili powder cooked into it. At Rosita's in Phoenix, the kitchen is diplomatic, offering a choice of the white or red style. The café also leaves out the hominy but will serve you the hoof in the stew for a dollar extra. In Monterrey the choice of supplements could include onions, jalapeños, oregano, grated white cheese, and chips.

SOUTH VALLEY SWEETBREADS

Several generations ago, *mollejas*, or sweetbreads, enjoyed widespread appeal in the borderlands, making it into almost all regional cookbooks. The fans may be in the minority today but they're just as devoted, particularly in the lower Rio Grande Valley.

Serves 4 to 6

2 pounds veal sweetbreads
Water
3 tablespoons vegetable oil, plus more for pan-frying
1 to 2 tablespoons fresh lime juice
Salt to taste
1/2 medium onion, sliced thin
1/2 red bell pepper, sliced in matchsticks
1 fresh serrano, minced

Cilantro sprigs and lime wedges, for garnish (optional)

Soak the sweetbreads in very cold water for at least 4 hours or overnight, changing the water several times in the first hour. Drain the sweetbreads and transfer them to a saucepan. Add enough water to cover them and bring to a boil. Reduce the heat and simmer the sweetbreads for about 8 minutes. Don't overcook them or they will become tough. Drain the sweetbreads and plunge them into ice water.

When they are cool, peel off as much of the outer membrane as possible, taking care to keep the sweetbreads intact. Transfer them to a shallow, nonreactive dish. Mix together 3 tablespoons of the oil and 1 tablespoon of the lime juice and pour over the sweetbreads. Place a plate on top of the sweetbreads and weight them down (a couple of cans are good). Refrigerate for at least 2 hours and up to overnight.

Drain the sweetbreads and cut them into medallions. Salt lightly and reserve.

Warm $^{1}/_{2}$ inch of oil in a large skillet over medium-high heat and fry the sweetbreads until lightly crisped and colored. Remove the sweetbreads with a slotted spoon and transfer them to a baking sheet. Tent the sweetbreads with foil and keep them warm.

Variety and organ meats such as sweetbreads attract a bigger following along the border than in other areas of the United States. *Barbacoa* is one of the oldest and most widespread treats. A slowly cooked cow's head, the dish gets its name from the original ranch-style method of preparation, barbecuing over wood coals in an underground pit. It's still best that way, with lots of smoke flavor, but most contemporary versions are baked or steamed.

Heat the broiler.

Discard all but 2 tablespoons of the oil. Add the onion, bell pepper, and serrano to the oil and sauté for about 5 minutes, until well softened.

Place the sweetbreads under the broiler for 1 minute on each side. Watch the time carefully to avoid overcooking. The object is to just crisp the sweetbreads. Combine the sweetbreads with the sautéed vegetables and serve immediately, garnished with cilantro and limes if you wish.

Technique Tip: Some border cooks use the less expensive beef sweetbreads, but veal makes up for the difference in price with its delicacy. Select meat that is white, signifying its youth, rather than red. It should be firm and plump looking. Unprepared sweetbreads perish easily, so plan to begin their preparation the day you buy them.

BRISKET BURRITOS

Serves 6 to 8

FILLING
3 1/2-pound fully trimmed beef brisket section (sometimes called the flat cut)
Salt to taste
Fresh-ground black pepper to taste
1/4 cup bacon drippings or vegetable oil
1 cup beef stock
1 medium onion, chopped
2 garlic cloves, minced
3 small tomatoes, preferably Roma or Italian plum, chopped
1/2 cup chopped roasted mild green chiles, preferably New Mexican or poblano

6 to 8 flour tortillas, preferably thick and 7 to 8 inches in diameter
1 small onion, chopped
Hatch Green Chile Sauce (page 54) (optional)
Chopped tomato and Crema (page 63), crème fraîche, or sour cream, for garnish

Rub the brisket with generous sprinklings of salt and pepper.

Warm half of the bacon drippings (for more flavor) or oil in a heavy skillet or Dutch oven over medium-high heat. Brown the meat evenly.

Reduce the heat to low. Pour the beef stock over the meat and add half of the onion and half of the garlic to the pan. Cover the dish tightly and simmer until the brisket is very tender, about 3 hours. Let the meat sit in the cooking liquid until cool enough to handle. Strain the cooking liquid and reserve it. Shred the brisket with your fingers, with two forks, or in a food processor in several small batches. (If your processor has a plastic blade for dough, use it for the nicest shreds.)

In a heavy skillet, warm the remaining drippings or oil over medium heat. Add the remaining onion and garlic and sauté until the onion softens. Stir in the tomatoes, green chiles, and meat and heat through.

Over high heat, boil the reserved cooking liquid down to about 3 tablespoons. Pour the reduction into the meat and stir to combine. (The filling can be made ahead and refrigerated for 1 or 2 days. Rewarm the filling before proceeding.)

Spoon equal amounts of the filling on the tortillas and sprinkle with onion. If you plan to eat the burritos with your hands, spoon a little sauce, if you wish, in the tortilla and scatter the other garnishes over the filling before rolling up each tortilla with one end tucked in. If the burritos will be plate food, they can be formed as open tubes, with lots of sauce and garnishes spooned over the top.

Ranching has a long history in Arizona, going back to Father Kino's introduction of cattle in 1687. For a century afterward, large Spanish haciendas flourished, but Apache attacks eventually drove away many of the settlers. Only the most tenacious and successful ranchers, such as Sabino Otero, stayed on into the nineteenth century. By the time Otero sold his spread in 1884—for the then-fantastic sum of $35,000—Anglo cattle barons had moved into the state. Former Texas Ranger John Slaughter became a legendary leader among the clan. His San Bernadino Ranch, now a national historic landmark, had both a cowboy dining hall and a formal dining room decked out in crystal, silver, and fine china, where Slaughter served the kitchen's own homemade wine and brandy to guests that included Geronimo, Pancho Villa, and General John J. Pershing.

This hearty, all-in-one meal combines the best tastes of Tucson. Across the border in Sonora, it would be called a *chivichanga* and might be longer and thinner, and topped with more restraint.

Serves 4

5 cups beef prepared in the dried style of Tucson Carne Seca (see page 180) or like the *machaca* from Machaca Breakfast Burros (page 74), warmed
4 thin 10-inch to 12-inch flour tortillas, warmed
Vegetable oil for deep-frying

Arizona Chile Colorado (page 52), warmed (optional)
Grated Monterey jack or mild cheddar cheese, or both
Guacamole (page 123)
Sour cream, chopped tomato, and sliced green onion, for garnish
Sliced black olives, for garnish (optional)

Spoon equal amounts of the meat on the tortillas. Roll up each tortilla, tucking in the ends to make a secure fat package, resembling an overgrown egg roll. Secure the tortillas with toothpicks.

Warm at least 4 inches of oil in a Dutch oven or other large, heavy pan to 375° F. Fry the chimichangas one or two at a time until golden brown, about 3 minutes. Turn the chimis or use tongs to keep them submerged so that they fry evenly. Drain the chimis and place them on serving plates.

Spoon a pool of sauce around each chimi, if you wish, and top them all with cheese, spoonfuls of guacamole and sour cream, and the remaining garnishes. Serve immediately.

ARIZONA ENCHILADAS

These enchiladas employ the same basic ingredients as the previous chimichanga, but the result is distinctively different in tang and texture.

Serves 4

3 cups beef prepared in the dried style of Tucson Carne Seca (see page 180) or like the *machaca* from Machaca Breakfast Burros (page 74)
1/2 medium onion, minced
8 thin 8-inch to 10-inch flour tortillas
3 cups Arizona Chile Colorado (page 52), warmed
3 ounces Monterey jack cheese, grated
3 ounces mild cheddar cheese, grated

Preheat the oven to 350° F. Grease a baking dish.

In a bowl, combine the beef with the onion.

With tongs, dip a tortilla in the chile sauce to lightly coat it. Lay the tortilla on a plate, sprinkle about 6 tablespoons of the beef mixture down the center of it, and roll it up snugly. Transfer the enchilada to the baking dish. Repeat with the remaining tortillas and filling. Top the enchiladas with the remaining chile sauce and sprinkle the cheese over the sauce. Bake for 20 to 25 minutes, until the enchiladas are heated through and the sauce and cheese are bubbly. With a large spatula, serve 2 enchiladas per person.

TEX-MEX TRUCKSTOP ENCHILADAS

Nothing is more surely and purely Tex-Mex than these chili-crowned beef enchiladas.

Serves 4

FILLING
1 pound chili-grind lean ground beef

1/2 medium onion, minced
1/2 cup beef stock
1/3 cup corn kernels, fresh or frozen
1/3 cup chopped roasted mild green chile, preferably New Mexican or
**   poblano, fresh or frozen**
Salt to taste

1/2 recipe Tex-Mex Chili Gravy (page 56), warmed
Vegetable oil for pan-frying
12 to 16 corn tortillas
Grated mild cheddar cheese, chopped onion, and minced fresh
**   jalapeño or serrano, for garnish**

In a medium skillet, fry the ground beef with the onion until the meat is gray. Pour off any excess fat. Add the stock, corn, green chile, and salt and simmer, covered, for 10 minutes. (The filling can be made ahead and refrigerated for a day. Reheat the filling before proceeding.)

Preheat the oven to 350° F. Grease a medium baking dish.

Heat 1/2 to 1 inch of oil in a small skillet until the oil ripples. With tongs, dunk a tortilla in the oil long enough for it to go limp, a matter of seconds. Don't let the tortilla turn crisp. Repeat with the remaining tortillas and drain them.

With tongs, dip a tortilla in the gravy liquid to lightly coat it. Lay the tortilla on a plate, sprinkle 3 to 4 tablespoons of filling over it, and roll it up snug. Transfer the enchilada to the baking dish. Repeat with the remaining tortillas and filling.

Top the enchiladas with the remaining chili gravy, seeing that each enchilada is submerged in the sauce, and bake for 20 to 25 minutes, until the enchiladas are heated through and the sauce is bubbly. Remove the dish from the oven and sprinkle immediately with the cheese, onion, and jalapeño. Using a spatula, serve hot.

PICADILLO TACOS

Picadillo inspired the dreadful ground-beef mixture that goes into most North American fast-food tacos, but you shouldn't blame the model if you haven't tried a superior version. For the best results, ask your butcher to grind the meat fresh.

Serves 6

PICADILLO
3 tablespoons vegetable oil
1 large onion, minced
6 garlic cloves, minced
2-pound chuck roast, ground to order
1 tablespoon all-purpose flour
1 teaspoon dried oregano, preferably Mexican
1/2 teaspoon cayenne or chile de árbol
1 medium baking potato, parboiled, peeled, and diced fine
1/2 cup beef stock
1/2 teaspoon salt, or more to taste

Vegetable oil for pan-frying
18 corn tortillas
Shredded lettuce, chopped tomatoes, and grated mild cheddar or
    Monterey jack cheese, for garnish
Jalapeño Hot Sauce (page 49), Pico de Gallo (page 40), or other salsa
Crema (page 63), crème fraîche, or sour cream (optional)

In a heavy skillet, warm the oil over medium heat. Add the onion and garlic and sauté for a couple of minutes until softened. Add the meat and fry until it is gray. Stir in the flour, oregano, and chile. Then add the potato, stock, and salt and reduce the heat to low. Simmer the mixture for another 5 minutes, or until the potatoes are tender and most of the liquid has thickened but the picadillo remains moist.

Heat at least 1 inch of oil in another skillet until the oil ripples. With tongs, dunk a tortilla in the oil long enough for it to go limp, a matter of seconds. Don't let the tortilla turn crisp. Repeat with the remaining tortillas and drain them.

Next time you're driving through El Paso, stop for a picadillo plate and a car wash at the same time at H & H Car Wash & Coffee Shop. Near downtown, the timeworn institution features old-fashioned cleaning equipment, straightforward border cooking, and lines of fancy customers with flashy cars.

Fill a tortilla with about 3 tablespoons of picadillo, fold in half, and secure with a toothpick. Repeat with the remaining tortillas and picadillo.

Raise the temperature of the oil to 350° F. Fry the tacos, in batches, until lightly browned and crisp. Drain well. Remove the toothpicks and garnish with lettuce, tomatoes, and cheese. Serve the tacos immediately, accompanied with hot sauce and crema.

Regional Variations: Many cooks serve picadillo by itself as an entrée instead of in a taco. In that case they usually dress up the dish with additions such as tomatoes, raisins, almonds, green olives, and canela or even cloves for some extra spice. One San Antonio recipe reaches well beyond the border in calling for water chestnuts. A longtime Tucson family, who use picadillo to stuff their Thanksgiving turkey, like many of the common supplements just mentioned, plus celery, apples, and a splash of vinegar. In Texas, copious amounts of chili powder and cumin sometimes show up in the dish, though Dallas master cook Matt Martínez keeps it simple with pecans and raisins. Across the Rio Grande in Coahuila, cooks might accept a little of the cumin but would likely insist on fresh serranos for the chile zip.

Long before Texas gave the world the first fast-food taco, Tejanos made their tortilla fillings from shredded rather than ground beef and they used cuts of meat with real flavor. Many home cooks do the same today, preparing their beef tacos in this style.

Serves 6

1 1/2-pound to 1 3/4-pound eye of chuck

FILLING
4 tablespoons vegetable oil
2 tablespoons pickling liquid from a jar of pickled jalapeños
2 tablespoons fresh lime juice
1 1/2 teaspoons cumin seeds, toasted and ground
1 1/2 teaspoons chili powder
3 garlic cloves, minced
1 cup beef stock, if you choose to bake the meat
Salt to taste
Minced onion and fresh cilantro (optional)

18 taco shells
Chipotle-Tomatillo Salsa (page 39) or other salsa
Shredded lettuce, chopped tomatoes, sliced pickled jalapeños, and
    grated mild cheddar cheese or crumbled queso fresco, for garnish

You can choose one of two methods for cooking the meat. Charcoal grilling is faster and more flavorful. Baking gives a slightly moister meat and may be easier some times of the year.

If grilling the meat, cut it into slices about $1/2$ inch thick and place in one layer in a shallow pan. If you plan to bake the meat, it's not necessary to slice it thinner than 1 inch.

In a small bowl, combine the oil, pickling liquid, lime juice, cumin, chili powder, and garlic and pour the marinade over the meat. Cover and refrigerate for at least 4 hours, or overnight, turning occasionally if the meat isn't thoroughly submerged in the marinade. Drain the meat and bring it back to room temperature before proceeding. Save a tablespoon or two of the marinade if you plan to bake the meat.

Fire up the charcoal grill or preheat the oven to 350° F.

If you are grilling the meat outdoors, place it over the coals when they are covered with gray ash. Grill the meat until just cooked through, approximately 4 minutes per side, turning the meat once.

To bake the meat, place it in a small baking dish with the stock or water and the reserved marinade. Cover the dish and bake for approximately 1 $^1/_4$ hours, or until the meat is cooked through and pulls apart easily.

Let the grilled or baked meat cool for about 10 minutes and then shred it. A food processor equipped with a plastic blade takes care of this step in quick measure, or you can use your fingers or a pair of forks. Salt the meat and, if you like, add some onion, cilantro, or both. Serve immediately, or refrigerate the filling for later reheating.

Serve the taco filling with the shells, salsa, and garnishes heaped on a platter or in separate bowls. Let all the guests fill each of their taco shells with several tablespoons of filling, and top with the remaining ingredients.

Regional Variations: Mexico imports many products from the United States, but the fast-food taco is not leading anyone's list of choices. South of the border, the beef that usually goes into tacos resembles this filling, a long-cooked, flavorful cut that's shredded rather than ground. In Coahuila, for example, eye of round might be marinated in beer and vinegar with onion, garlic, and bay, then simmered in the liquid, covered, until it almost falls apart. Or the meat could be *machacado*, a jerky that's pounded into shreds and simmered in liquid. Instead of a North American taco shell, Mexicans wrap the beef in soft corn tortillas, perhaps first oil-dipped to make them pliable.

DOÑA ANA GORDITAS

These "little fat ones" from southern New Mexico are deep-fried corn pockets, overflowing with picadillo, beans, and toppings. They're a fun food for a casual party.

Serves 4

DOUGH
2 cups masa harina
1/3 cup all-purpose flour
1 teaspoon salt
1 teaspoon baking powder
3 tablespoons vegetable shortening
1 1/3 cups warm water, or more as needed

Vegetable oil for deep-frying

3/4 cup Refried Beans (page 378) or other well-seasoned mashed
    beans, warmed
2 to 3 cups Picadillo (see page 212), warmed
Shredded lettuce and grated mild cheddar cheese, for garnish

Guacamole (page 123)
Green Chile Salsa (page 44) or other salsa

In a food processor, combine the masa harina, flour, salt, and baking powder. Add the shortening and process just until mealy. Pour in the water and process until the dough becomes smooth and moist. Add a little more water, if needed, for the desired consistency. Take the dough out of the processor, form it into a ball, and cover it in plastic wrap. Let the dough sit for at least 20 minutes and up to 1 hour.

Divide the dough into 8 smaller balls and flatten each to about $1/2$-inch thickness, rounding any rough edges. Cover the dough rounds loosely with more plastic wrap.

In a Dutch oven or large, heavy saucepan, heat 3 to 4 inches of oil to 365° F. Fry the dough rounds in batches, cooking them for 4 to 5 minutes until golden and crisp. Turn them or hold them under the oil with tongs, if needed, for even cooking. Drain and repeat with the remaining dough.

Slice a *gordita* open on the edge, cutting about one-third of the way around it. Wrap a couple of thicknesses of paper towel around the *gordita* while you work if it's too hot to handle. With your fingers or a spoon, scrape out any uncooked dough from the center, leaving a hollow to fill later. Repeat with the remaining *gorditas*.

Coat the inside of each *gordita* with a generous tablespoon of beans, and then spoon in picadillo to fill the *gorditas* about two-thirds full. Top the picadillo with lettuce and cheese and serve immediately, accompanied with guacamole and salsa.

Regional Variations: In *Food from My Heart* (Macmillan, 1992), Zarela Martínez talks about the popularity of similar *gorditas* in Ciudad Juárez and how she later adapted the idea for her New York catering clients, using fillings such as potatoes and chorizo, red snapper hash, and savory shredded beef. An earlier pro, Pauline Wiley-Kleeman, took another inventive approach. An American who taught home economics in Mexico and wrote a food column in *El Universal* newspaper in the 1920s, she recommended cooking the fat corn tortillas on the griddle and filling them with green chile sauce, fresh goat cheese, and avocado slices.

Meat-filled chiles rellenos often come fried in a heavy batter coating and stuffed with picadillo. This approach from Santa Barbara is a fresher though still hearty take on that idea. Use leftover *arracheras* or fajitas, or make half a batch just for the rellenos.

Serves 6

1-pound to 1 1/4-pound grilled marinated skirt steak such as Elemental Arracheras (page 176) or Red Caldwell's South Texas Fajitas (page 178), sliced diagonally against the grain and sliced into bite-size pieces, warmed
1/3 cup raisins, soaked in brandy
3 green onions, minced
3 tablespoons minced fresh cilantro (optional)
5 ounces Monterey jack or asadero cheese, grated

6 fresh large poblano chiles or other mild green chiles, such as Anaheim, roasted and slit from end to end
Ground dried red chile or paprika
Californio Colorado (page 53) or other mild red chile sauce (optional)

Preheat the oven to 375° F. Grease a baking sheet.

In a bowl, mix together the meat, raisins, green onions, cilantro, if you wish, and half the cheese. Spoon the mixture into the chiles and transfer them to the baking sheet. Scatter the remaining cheese over the chiles. Dust the tops lightly with red chile.

Bake the chiles for 5 minutes, or until the cheese is melted and bubbly.

Serve hot, surrounded by pools of red chile sauce if you wish.

In *The Tejano Community, 1836–1900* (University of New Mexico Press, 1982), Arnoldo De León says that in nineteenth-century Texas, "Tamales matched any other delicacy. Tejanos cooked them regularly but invariably for festive occasions [and Anglos] eagerly endorsed [them] as a Mexican contribution to the totality of the Lone Star State." John C. Duval, hardly a cooking authority, was so impressed with his first tamale that he provided a recipe in his memoir, *Early Times in Texas:* "A quantity of fresh beef, venison or mutton is hashed very fine; this is seasoned with salt, red pepper and garlic (or onions) and then mixed thoroughly with an equal quantity of hominy beaten or ground into a paste. The mixture is made into rolls like small sausages and each wrapped in the inner shucks of corn husks, and boiled until done."

Tamales crossed ethnic food lines and won broad acceptance early in the borderlands. John C. Duval's experience was fairly typical among the Anglo pioneers. Around 1840 he and a traveling companion camped out near San Antonio. Their cook went to town to get corn and came back with rolls of husks he called "termarlers." The friend accused the cook of trying to feed them the roughage intended for the horses, but they later concluded that the strange dish was excellent. Like many border cooks today, we use vegetable oil in the masa rather than the traditional lard.

Makes 24 large tamales, about 12 main-dish servings

FILLING
1 1/2-pound chuck roast
1 medium onion, chopped
1 bay leaf
2 cups water
2 tablespoons vegetable oil
3 garlic cloves, minced
1 tablespoon all-purpose flour
1/2 cup chili powder, preferably Gebhardt's
3/4 teaspoon salt
1/4 teaspoon dried oregano, preferably Mexican
1 teaspoon cumin seeds, toasted and ground (optional)

6-ounce package dried corn husks

DOUGH
6 cups masa harina
2 cups vegetable oil
2 cups beef stock
2 1/2 cups water, or more as needed
2 tablespoons chili powder, preferably Gebhardt's
2 teaspoons salt

Tex-Mex Chili Gravy (page 56) (optional)
Grated mild cheddar cheese and minced onion, for garnish

Preheat the oven to 350° F.

Place the meat, onion, and bay leaf in a medium-size baking dish and cover with the water. Bake for approximately 1 1/2 hours, or until the meat is cooked through and pulls apart easily. Remove the beef from the broth. Set the meat aside to cool for a few minutes and refrigerate the broth. When the beef has cooled enough to handle, shred it fine, either with two forks or in a food processor. Strain the broth after any fat has solidified on its surface. If the broth doesn't measure 2 cups, add water to make 2 cups of liquid. Reserve the beef and the broth.

In a large, heavy skillet, warm the oil over medium heat and add the garlic and the meat. Sprinkle the flour over the mixture and stir constantly for about 1 minute as the flour begins to brown. Add the chili powder, broth, salt, oregano, and cumin, if you like. Continue cooking over medium heat for about 30 minutes, or until the mixture has thickened and is almost dry. Watch carefully toward the end of the cooking time, stirring frequently so as not to burn the mixture. The filling will be meltingly tender. Reserve the mixture. (The filling can be made ahead and refrigerated for a day.)

To prepare the corn husks, cover them with hot water in a deep bowl or pan. After 30 minutes the husks should be softened and pliable. Separate the husks and rinse them under warm running water to wash away any grit or brown silks. Soak them in fresh warm water until they are ready to use.

To prepare the dough, measure the masa harina into a large bowl. Add the oil, stock, water, chili powder, and salt. Mix with a sturdy spoon, a powerful electric mixer, or your hands until smooth. When well blended, the masa should have the consistency of a moist cookie dough. Add more water if needed for your preferred consistency. Keep the dough loosely covered while working.

To assemble the tamales, use approximately equal amounts of masa and filling. To make 2 dozen 4-ounce tamales, use 2 tablespoons each of masa and filling for each tamale.

Hold a corn husk flat on one hand, smooth side up. (You may, depending on the size of the corn husks, need to overlap two husks to form one tamale. Spread the dough over the husks together, just as if they were one.) With a rubber spatula, spread a thin layer of masa across the husk, but not to the edges. Top with filling spread more thickly through the dough's center, stopping short of the dough's edges. Make sure that the dough's edges meet to enclose all of the filling. Secure the tamale by folding the wrapper over or tying it. Repeat the procedure until all the filling and masa are used.

Place the tamales in a steamer, packing loosely in crisscross directions, or stand them on end. Allow enough space between them for the steam to rise effectively. Cover the pot and cook over simmering water for about 1 to 1 ^{1}/$_{4}$ hours until the masa is firm and no longer sticks to the corn husk. Unwrap one tamale to check its consistency.

The tamales should be eaten warm. When the tamales are served unadorned, the husks are usually left on, to be removed by each guest before eating. If the tamales will be topped with sauce, the husks should be removed before adding it. Sprinkle on cheese and onion before serving.

Regional Variations: Arizona cooks make red chile beef tamales called *colorados*, usually milder in seasoning than these and often with bigger chunks of meat. Sometimes they wrap the tamales in multiple corn husks spread with dough, so that when opened, several thin layers of masa can be eaten. Many early border versions called for meat from a *cabeza de vaca*, or cow's head, still considered a treat.

PORK, CABRITO, LAMB, AND GAME

*B*eef may be the most common meat of the borderlands, but it's never lacked company on the table. Native Americans and the first Spanish settlers in the region ate plenty of game before cattle became abundant, and many of their contemporaries still do, particularly in south Texas and northeastern Mexico. Sheep and goats from European stock gained an early foothold in large areas and provided plenty of meat in addition to other subsistence products. Mutton rivaled beef in prominence until this century, and cabrito, or kid, remains a major food in Nuevo León.

The Spanish brought pigs as well as the other domesticated animals, but the pigs' inability to digest grass made them less suited to the habitat than cattle. Still, they thrived in certain pockets, and at the same time that the borderlands began exporting beef to other areas of Mexico and the United States, the region began importing additional pork. Today, pork replaces mutton in some old preparations and stands on its own in other popular dishes. Now more than ever, the border abounds in meat.

SLOW-GRILLED PORK AL PASTOR

Cooking *al pastor* means to spit-roast meat in the style of the shepherds. Sheepherders in northern Mexico, often Basque in origin, perfected the technique over campfires with mutton, skewering or splaying the meat at a 45- to 75-degree angle over the coals to enhance the tenderness and flavor through slow, smoky cooking. The practice is still widespread in the north, particularly in Nuevo León and Tamaulipas, where the meat today is likely to be cabrito. It's difficult to emulate the method exactly without special equipment, but you can match the results on a standard charcoal grill by using a rotisserie attachment or the slow cooking process we describe. This pork *al pastor*, a popular adaptation of the shepherds' original meal, benefits from an array of robust country seasonings.

Serves 4

DRIED SEASONINGS
1 tablespoon ground dried mild red chile, preferably ancho or New Mexican

2 teaspoons ground dried chipotle chile or other medium-hot chile

2 teaspoons salt

1 teaspoon dried oregano, preferably Mexican

1 teaspoon garlic powder

1 teaspoon onion powder

1/2 teaspoon ground coriander

1/2 teaspoon cumin seeds, toasted and ground

1/2 teaspoon fresh-ground black pepper

1/2 teaspoon sugar

1/4 teaspoon dried sage

MARINADE
1 1/2 cups pineapple juice

2 tablespoons vegetable oil

4 garlic cloves, minced

1 3/4-pound to 2-pound pork loin

Pork was once much more popular than beef in the United States and it still is in much of Mexico. Pigs produce about twenty pounds of meat for each hundred pounds of feed, which is three times the norm for cattle. They are also great foragers in woodlands, rooting about for plants and nuts on their own, the reason they thrived in some of the first areas of European settlement in the New World. They couldn't compete with cattle in the borderlands, though, because the cud-chewing ruminants, unlike pigs, can digest the tough cellulose in grass.

Mesquite chips or beans
Flour tortillas, preferably thin and less than 8 inches in diameter
Salsa Cocida de Chiles Güeros (page 42) and Salsa de Árbol (page 46),
** or other salsas**

At least 6 hours before cooking and up to the night before, start preparations. In a small bowl, stir together the dried seasonings. Combine 1 1/2 tablespoons of the dried seasonings with the marinade ingredients and pour over the pork in a plastic bag. Refrigerate the pork.

Take the meat from the refrigerator 45 minutes before you plan to cook it. Drain the pork, discarding the marinade. Massage the remaining dried seasoning mixture evenly over the pork and let it sit at room temperature, uncovered.

On an outdoor grill, fire up about 30 or 35 charcoal briquettes, and put a few handfuls of mesquite chips or beans in water to soak. When the charcoal is totally covered in gray ash and begins to show tinges of white ash, spread the mesquite on top. Pile the coals loosely on one side of the grill. Place the pork on the other side of the grill, away from the coals.

Cover the grill, positioning the lid's damper immediately above the meat, and leaving all the dampers open. Insert a deep-fry or candy thermometer through the damper above the meat to monitor the temperature. The cooking time should be about 2 hours at a temperature averaging 300° F to 350° F. The cooking temperature should start at the higher end and drop gradually to the lower. If the temperature appears to be dropping rapidly, fire up another 10 to 15 coals and add them as needed to keep the temperature in the preferred range. The pork is done when the internal temperature taken on an instant-read thermometer measures 155° F to 160° F.

Let the meat stand for 5 to 10 minutes before slicing very thin. Toss th slices together so that each portion has some of the seasoned exterior meat mixed in with moister interior meat.

Serve warm with tortillas and salsas.

NEW MEXICO CARNE ADOVADA

You find versions of *carne adobada* or *adovada* in many places, but only northern New Mexico gives it great prominence in the cooking. Pork marinated and then slow-simmered in a thick red chile sauce, the dish represents the local style at its finest—simple, soulful, and spicy.

Serves 6 to 8

3 pounds pork Boston butt, trimmed of fat and cut into 1 1/2-inch cubes

SAUCE
8 ounces (about 20 to 25) whole dried red New Mexican chiles, preferably Chimayó, stemmed, seeded, and rinsed
2 cups chicken or beef stock
1 medium onion, chunked
4 garlic cloves
2 teaspoons vinegar, preferably sherry or cider
2 teaspoons dried oregano, preferably Mexican
1 teaspoon ground coriander
1 teaspoon salt, or more to taste

Shredded lettuce and chopped tomato, for garnish (optional)

Preheat the oven to 300° F. Oil a large, covered baking dish. Place the pork in the baking dish.

To prepare the sauce, begin by placing the damp chiles in one layer on a baking sheet and roast them in the oven for about 5 minutes. Watch the pods carefully so as not to burn them. The chiles can have a little remaining moisture. Remove them from the oven and let them cool. Break each chile into 2 or 3 pieces.

In a blender, purée half the pods with 1 cup of the stock. You still will be able to see tiny pieces of chile pulp, but they should be bound in a smooth, thick liquid. Pour the mixture into the baking dish. Repeat with the remaining pods and stock, adding the rest of the sauce ingredients to the blender. Pour this mixture into the baking dish and stir the sauce

Unlike some home-style dishes, *carne adovada* translates well to restaurant menus. Places in northern New Mexico that offer superior versions include Rancho de Chimayó, M. & J. Restaurant and Sanitary Tortilla Factory in downtown Albuquerque, Spic and Span in Las Vegas, and Jo Ann's Ranch O Casados on the main drag through Española.

together with the pork. (If you like, the pork can be prepared to this point and refrigerated overnight. Bring the mixture back to cool room temperature before proceeding.)

Cover the dish and bake at 300° F until the meat is quite tender and the sauce has cooked down, about 3 hours. If the sauce seems watery, return the dish to the oven, uncovered, and bake for an additional 15 to 30 minutes. Serve hot, garnished if you wish with lettuce and tomato. Reheated leftovers are outstanding.

Technique Tip: Any New Mexican red chile will work in *carne adovada*, but pods grown in Chimayó attain the best balance of sweet and heat. If you can't find the chiles in your area, see the list of suppliers in "Mail-Order Sources."

Regional Variations: New Mexicans eat their *carne adovada* plain as a meat entrée or, more commonly, wrapped between thick flour tortillas as burritos. The Arizona equivalent, the much milder *chile colorado*, also goes into burros. Early California cooks made an *adobada*, but the idea never got established in Texas, perhaps because chili con carne filled the gap. In Mexico, *adobada* takes many forms, though typically the proportion of vinegar is higher, making sharper-flavored dishes.

The same preparation works well with other meats. Even in New Mexico, some cooks use beef, particularly chuck. Cholesterol-conscious eaters may prefer turkey, which cooks about an hour less than pork or beef.

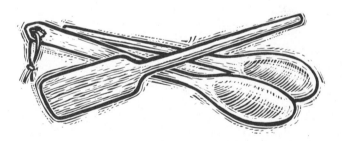

Hardly any dish is more beloved on the border, or farther south in Mexico, than the crispy morsels of pork called *carnitas*. Contemporary families usually consume a lot less of the rich nuggets than was the case a generation ago, but the taste is still treasured. An infrequent ingredient in the preparation, milk promotes deep browning and a crunchy surface. We got the idea for its addition from a lower Rio Grande Valley recipe.

Serves 6

4 garlic cloves
2 teaspoons cumin seeds, toasted
2 teaspoons dried oregano, preferably Mexican
1 teaspoon salt
1/2 teaspoon fresh-ground black pepper
2 chiles de árbol or cayennes
2 1/2 pounds pork Boston butt, cut into bite-size cubes
1/4 cup lard or vegetable shortening
1/4 cup milk

Salsa de Árbol (page 46) or Jalapeño Hot Sauce (page 49) or other
salsa or hot sauce
Corn or flour tortillas, warmed

In a mini–food processor or with a mortar and pestle, mash together the garlic, cumin, oregano, salt, pepper, and chiles. Spoon the mixture into a medium bowl. Add the pork cubes to the spices and toss to coat the cubes. Let the mixture sit at room temperature for 20 to 30 minutes.

Warm the lard in a Dutch oven or other deep, heavy pan over medium-high heat. Place the pork in the hot lard and sear the meat quickly. Reduce the heat to a bare simmer and cover the pan. Cook the pork for 1 hour, stirring the mixture at 20-minute intervals.

Uncover the pork and stir in the milk. Raise the heat to medium-high. Simmer the pork until most of the liquid has evaporated, scraping the mixture up from the bottom. After about 15 minutes the pork will be browned and lightly crisped, but tender and moist inside. Drain the pork.

Serve with salsa or hot sauce and warm, soft tortillas as make-your-own tacos, or reserve for enchiladas, burritos, or burros.

Farmers in Parras, several hours south of Laredo near Saltillo, feed their pigs discarded grape skins and lees from area vineyards. Local cooks concocted this preparation, laced with Spanish sherry, for the pork.

Serves 6

2 3/4-pound to 3-pound pork loin roast
3 tablespoons vegetable oil
3 garlic cloves, slivered
Salt and fresh-ground black pepper to taste
1 cup chicken stock
3/4 cup dry sherry
1/3 cup slivered almonds, toasted
1/2 medium onion
1 corn tortilla, torn into pieces
2 whole small tomatoes, preferably Roma or Italian plum, roasted
2 tablespoons sherry vinegar
1 tablespoon ground dried mild red chile, preferably ancho, guajillo, or New Mexican
1/4 teaspoon ground coriander
1/4 teaspoon dried thyme

Toasted sesame seeds, for garnish

Preheat the oven to 300° F. Oil a baking dish.

Rub the pork with 1 tablespoon of the oil. Make small slits in the roast's surface and insert approximately two-thirds of the garlic. Sprinkle the pork with salt and pepper.

In a heavy skillet over high heat, brown the pork. Transfer the roast to the baking dish, reserving the skillet, and spoon 1 tablespoon each of the oil, stock, and sherry over the meat.

Plan on a total baking time of about 2 1/2 hours. Bake the roast, covered, for 1 1/2 hours, basting once or twice.

Prepare the sauce while the pork cooks. In a blender, purée the remaining stock, sherry, and garlic with the almonds, onion, tortilla, tomatoes, vinegar, chile, coriander, and thyme. Warm the remaining oil in the reserved skillet over medium-high heat. Pour the blender mixture into the skillet, being careful to avoid splatters as the liquid hits the hot oil. When the most insistent sputtering dies down, reduce the heat to low and simmer for 5 minutes, stirring frequently and scraping up from the bottom.

Remove the pork from the oven, let the roast sit 5 minutes, and then slice the par-cooked meat. Return the meat to the baking dish and pan juices, overlapping the slices as needed to fit in the dish. Pour sauce over each slice. Cover and continue baking for 1 more hour, or until very tender.

Arrange the pork slices on a decorative platter and surround them with sauce. Sprinkle with toasted sesame seeds and serve, perhaps with refried beans and white rice or crusty hard rolls to soak up the sauce.

TENDERLOIN ASADA WITH SAGE AND SAVORY APPLES

Serves 4 to 6

2 pounds pork tenderloin, in 2 or 3 sections
1 1/2 cups apple cider or apple juice
3 tablespoons cider vinegar
2 tablespoons brandy
1 tablespoon vegetable oil
1 tablespoon prepared brown mustard
2 teaspoons dried sage
1 teaspoon ground dried chipotle or, for a milder flavor, ancho
**   or New Mexican chile**
1 teaspoon salt
1 teaspoon fresh-ground black pepper
1/2 teaspoon garlic powder

Mesquite chips or beans

3 tart apples, such as Granny Smith
2 tablespoons butter
Sage sprigs, for garnish (optional)

About 2 to 4 hours before you plan to grill the pork, place the tenderloins in a plastic bag. Add the cider, vinegar, brandy, oil, and mustard and refrigerate. Combine the sage, chile, salt, pepper, and garlic powder in a small bowl. About 30 minutes before grilling, take the pork from the refrigerator and drain the marinade into a small saucepan. Coat the pork with a thin layer of the mixed spices, reserving about 1 teaspoon of the mixture, and let the pork sit, covered, at room temperature.

Over high heat, boil the marinade vigorously for several minutes, until reduced by half. Keep the liquid warm.

On an outdoor grill, fire up enough charcoal to form a single layer of coals beneath the meat. At the same time, put a few handfuls of mesquite chips or beans in water to soak.

When the charcoal is covered with gray ash, scatter the wood chips or beans over it and place the meat directly over the fire. Grill the tenderloins, partially covered with the grill's lid (damper open), to trap some of the mesquite smoke. Turn the tenderloins once or twice to ensure even cooking. Grill until the tenderloins' internal temperature measures 155° F to 160° F on an instant-read thermometer, about 12 to 14 minutes. Let the meat sit at room temperature tented with foil.

Peel and slice the apples thin. Warm the butter in a skillet over medium heat and sauté the apples until softened. Add the reduced marinade and the remaining spice mixture and simmer until the apples are tender. Adjust the seasoning if needed.

Slice the pork into medallions and arrange it on a platter, surrounded by the apples and garnished, if you wish, with sage sprigs.

Crispy, tight tubes filled with meat, flautas take their name from their resemblance to flutes. This Nuevo León version, worthy of a celebration, is more elaborate than most border preparations of the dish.

Serves 5 to 6

FILLING

2 dried mild red chiles, preferably ancho or pasilla, seeded, covered with 2/3 cup boiling water, and soaked for 20 minutes
1 whole small tomato, preferably Roma or Italian plum
1/2 medium onion
2 garlic cloves
1/8 teaspoon ground canela or other cinnamon
2 tablespoons vegetable oil
1/3 cup slivered almonds
1 1/2 pounds shredded cooked pork, such as leftovers from Slow-Grilled Pork al Pastor (page 224) or Tenderloin Asada with Sage and Savory Apples (page 230)

Vegetable oil for deep-frying
18 thin corn tortillas
Chipotle-Tomatillo Salsa (page 39) or other salsa

In a blender, purée the chiles and their soaking liquid with the tomato, onion, garlic, and canela. In a saucepan or skillet, warm the oil over medium heat. Stir in the almonds and sauté until fragrant. Pour in the chile mixture, being careful to avoid splatters as the liquid hits the hot oil. When the sputtering stops, reduce the heat to medium-low and simmer for 10 minutes. Add the pork and heat through. The mixture should be moist but not soupy.

Pour enough oil in a heavy, high-sided skillet to measure at least 2 inches. Warm the oil over high heat until it ripples. With tongs, dip a tortilla in the hot oil, just until it becomes limp. Remove immediately and drain, repeating with the remaining tortillas. Turn off the heat under the oil while you fill the flautas.

Spoon 1 $^1/_2$ to 2 tablespoons of filling on a tortilla and roll up snug. Secure it with a toothpick. Set it aside and repeat with the remaining filling and tortillas.

Rewarm the oil in the skillet, raising the temperature to 375° F. Transfer 2 or 3 flautas to the oil and cook until golden and crisp. Drain. Repeat with the remaining flautas.

Remove the toothpicks and serve the flautas with salsa. Guacamole is good on the side as well.

Regional Variations: Pork flautas are more straightforward in New Mexico. Cooks frequently fill the tortillas with a shredded meat mixed only with a bit of onion or garlic. The spice is saved for the red chile sauce or salsa—such as New Mexico Salsa Picante—that goes on the side. Dallas chef Dean Fearing developed the most elaborate version we've seen for the famed Mansion on Turtle Creek. He fills the tortilla tubes with a smoky wild boar and chipotle mixture, and tops them with lime sour cream and pomegranate seeds.

PORK CHOPS VERDE

A Sonoran dish, this uses some of the least expensive pork chops you can find, which actually taste better than the finer cuts when prepared well.

Serves 4

8 ounces tomatillos, husked
Water
2 teaspoons Maggi seasoning or soy sauce
1 1/2 teaspoons sherry vinegar
2 garlic cloves
1 fresh serrano, chopped
2 slices bacon, chopped
4 pork chops cut from the shoulder, or as near the shoulder as your
    butcher can provide (sometimes called pork shoulder steaks)
1 medium onion, sliced and separated into rings
1 teaspoon dried oregano, preferably Mexican
1/2 cup chopped roasted mild green chile, preferably Anaheim
    or New Mexican
1/2 cup prepared nopales, diced

Cover the tomatillos with water and boil for 15 minutes, or until soft. Transfer the tomatillos and 1/2 cup of the cooking liquid to a blender. Add the Maggi, vinegar, garlic, and serrano and purée.

Fry the bacon over medium heat in a large (at least 10 inches) cast-iron skillet. Remove the bacon with a slotted spoon when it is brown and crisp, drain it, and reserve it.

Brown the chops in the bacon drippings, in batches if necessary. Arrange the 4 chops in the skillet, overlapping some if needed. Reduce the heat to low. Scatter the onion and oregano over the chops, and spoon in the chile, nopales, and tomatillo mixture evenly.

Cover the skillet and cook the chops over medium-low heat for about 1 1/2 hours, until they are cooked through and very tender. Check the dish a couple of times during the cooking, adding a little more water if the mixture appears to be getting dry. The finished sauce, though, should be cooked down and somewhat thick. Remove the skillet from the heat and let the dish sit, covered, for 10 to 20 minutes.

Serve the chops with spoonfuls of the sauce and topped with the bacon, accompanied perhaps by white rice flecked with green onion tops.

COSTILLAS DE PUERCO

Another inexpensive cut, pork spareribs claim plenty of fans all over Mexico and the United States. We think they reach their peak of perfection when bathed in smoke, as in this west Texas barbecue version. The instructions assume you are using a water smoker, the most common kind of smoker, but the recipe works with any kind of equipment.

Serves 6

3 full slabs of pork spareribs, trimmed of the chine bone and brisket flap (butchers often call this a St. Louis cut), preferably 3 pounds each or less
12 ounces beer
1/2 cup cider vinegar
3 tablespoons vegetable oil
2 tablespoons Worcestershire sauce
3 tablespoons chili powder
2 tablespoons brown sugar
1 tablespoon paprika
1 tablespoon fresh-ground black pepper
1 tablespoon salt
2 teaspoons Worcestershire powder (see "Technique Tip") (optional)
1 teaspoon cumin seeds, toasted and ground
1 teaspoon garlic powder
1 teaspoon dried oregano, preferably Mexican

Mesquite chunks, chips, or beans

Four to 8 hours before you plan to barbecue, place the ribs in a large plastic bag and pour the beer, vinegar, oil, and Worcestershire sauce over them. Chill the slabs, removing them from the refrigerator about 1 hour before you plan to begin cooking. Drain the ribs, reserving the marinade.

In a small bowl, combine the remaining ingredients. Rub the dry spice mixture over the ribs, coating them evenly.

At least 30 minutes before you plan to begin cooking, put a half-dozen handfuls of mesquite chunks, chips, or beans in water to soak. Prepare your smoker for barbecuing, following the manufacturer's instructions. When the smoker is ready, spread about one-quarter of the mesquite on the fire and pour the remaining marinade into the water pan, adding water to fill it.

Transfer the meat to the smoker. Cook the ribs for about 75 minutes per pound. Add wood to the fire as needed to keep a steady stream of smoke throughout the cooking time. When finished, the meat should be well-done and pull easily from the bones. If you wish, the ribs can be basted with a tomato-based barbecue sauce or salsa in the last 30 minutes of cooking. Allow the slabs to sit for 10 minutes before slicing them into individual ribs.

Technique Tip: A dehydrated version of Worcestershire sauce, Worcestershire powder adds a delicious tang to the "dry rubs" used on many slow-smoked barbecue meats. The powders we've seen, though, have a fairly high proportion of MSG among the ingredients, so you might want to skip it if you're sensitive to the flavor enhancer.

Regional Variations: Most Mexican cooks stew spareribs, usually in a chile-laced sauce. In Baja California, where Chinese culinary influences have been strong for a century, Josefina Castro de Inzuna developed a different approach with hints of Cantonese sweet and sour flavors. She cuts slabs into small sections of ribs, marinates them in soy sauce and garlic, dusts the meat with cornstarch and browns it, then bakes the ribs slowly around 300° F with onions, pineapple chunks, and pineapple juice until tender.

The Spanish, who brought pigs to Mexico, also introduced techniques for sausage-making. Today, both countries boast products called chorizo, but the resemblance ends with the name. The most common European influence on modern sausages in the borderlands is from Germany. Especially in Texas and the neighboring state of Chihuahua, cross-cultural currents produce some odd but authentic hybrids, such as chile-laced bratwurst.

Stained crimson with chile and redolent of garlic and herbs, a good chorizo ranks among the world's top sausages. Unfortunately, most commercial versions miss the mark. If you live in an area where a butcher makes first-rate chorizo, consider it a blessing and support the shop. If not, try this recipe, rich with the border's most common mild dried chiles.

Makes about 2 pounds

8 dried mild red chiles, preferably 4 ancho and 4 New Mexican
1 3/4 pounds pork Boston butt, with fat, ground once or twice by your butcher or with a meat grinder at home
1/2 cup minced onion
2 tablespoons vinegar, preferably white
10 garlic cloves, minced
2 teaspoons cumin seeds, toasted and ground
2 teaspoons dried oregano, preferably Mexican
1 1/2 teaspoons salt
1 1/2 teaspoons fresh-ground black pepper
1/2 teaspoon ground coriander
Pinch of ground canela or other cinnamon

Preheat the oven to 300° F. Break the stems off the chile pods and discard most of the seeds.

Place the pods in a single layer on a baking sheet and roast them for about 5 minutes. Watch the pods closely, because they can scorch easily. Break each chile into several pieces. Transfer the chiles to a blender and blend until they are evenly ground.

In a medium bowl, mix together the ground chiles with all the other ingredients. Cover the bowl and refrigerate it for at least 24 hours. Use the chorizo as needed. Form it into patties or fry it crumbled over medium-low heat until it is richly browned. The chorizo keeps, uncooked and refrigerated, at least a week and freezes well.

Regional Variations: In some areas along the border, especially in cattle country, chorizo may be made with a mixture of beef and pork. Substitute ground chuck (not the extra-lean variety) for half of the pork.

In southwest Texas and other deer-hunting areas, venison versions are common. Again use a half-and-half mixture of meats, but add 2 to 4 more ounces of pork fat to the recipe to compensate for the lean game.

On the border, the seasonings in chorizo are bold but not complex, relying on anchos, garlic, and cumin for most of the flavor. Farther south in Mexico, the makings expand. In his authoritative book *Authentic Mexican* (William Morrow and Company, 1987), Rick Bayless features a version with three kinds of red chiles and thirteen other ingredients, including ginger, canela, nutmeg, and cloves.

CHIHUAHUA GREEN CHILE CHORIZO

Makes about 2 pounds

1 3/4 pounds pork Boston butt, with fat, ground once or twice by your
    butcher or with a meat grinder at home
1 mild green chile, preferably New Mexican or poblano, fresh or
    frozen, roasted and puréed
1 cup minced fresh cilantro
1/2 cup minced onion
3 tablespoons vinegar, preferably cider
Tops of 8 green onions, minced
8 garlic cloves, minced
2 teaspoons dried oregano, preferably Mexican
1 teaspoon cumin seeds, toasted and ground
1 teaspoon salt
1/2 teaspoon ground coriander

In a bowl, mix together all the ingredients. Cover the bowl and refrigerate the mixture for at least 12 hours. Use the chorizo as needed. Form it into patties or fry it crumbled over medium-low heat until it is richly browned. The chorizo keeps, uncooked and refrigerated, at least a week, but the cilantro flavor fades after the first couple of days. Mix in a bit more of the fresh herb to add more sparkle.

Native Americans taught early Spanish settlers their technique for drying and preserving corn as *posole* or *pozole*, and the Europeans in turn added the pork, making the hearty stew that became a mainstay of the subsistence diet in the borderlands. The dish is simple, but be sure to allow plenty of time for the soaking and the cooking.

Serves 6

2 tablespoons bacon drippings or vegetable oil

1 pound pork Boston butt, trimmed of fat and cut into 3/4-inch cubes

2 large onions, chopped

8 garlic cloves, minced

2 cups dried *posole,* soaked for at least 4 hours or overnight and drained

8 cups chicken stock, or more as needed

1 tablespoon dried oregano, preferably Mexican

2 teaspoons salt, plus more to taste

2 bay leaves

1 teaspoon dried thyme

2 mild red chiles, preferably ancho or New Mexican

Lime wedges, sliced green onion tops, chopped fresh cilantro, and grated radish for garnish

Warm the bacon drippings in a large, heavy saucepan or stockpot over medium heat. Add the pork, onions, and garlic and sauté until the meat is lightly browned, about 10 minutes. Add the *posole*, stock, oregano, salt, bay leaves, and thyme and bring the mixture to a boil. Reduce the heat to medium-low and simmer, uncovered, for 1 hour. Add the chiles and continue simmering for another 1 to 1 $^1/_2$ hours, or until the corn is puffed and tender but still a little chewy. Add more stock if necessary to keep the mixture rather soupy.

Keep the *posole* warm for up to 1 hour, and serve ladled into bowls garnished with limes, green onions, cilantro, and radish.

Technique Tip: In making *posole*, starchy corn kernels are cut from the cob, treated with lime (the mineral, not the fruit) to loosen the hulls, and then rinsed and dried. The process creates corn that is chewy and glutinous when rehydrated. It resembles hominy, which can be substituted in a pinch without the soaking and lengthy cooking time, but with some loss in flavor and texture. Use two to three 14 $^1/_2$-ounce cans of drained hominy, about half the amount of chicken stock, and go light on the salt. Simmer all the ingredients together for just 30 minutes.

Regional Variations: In Sonora, traditional cooks are likely to add a cup or more of pinto beans to *posole*. On the contemporary side in California, one version mixes in puréed tomatillos and cilantro toward the end of the cooking time. The meat ranges from mutton, found in sheepherding areas, to pork ribs, suggested by Arizona cook Joe Burgoz in the *Arizona Highways Heritage Cookbook* (Arizona Department of Transportation, 1988). In New Mexico, *posole* is usually a vegetable side dish rather than a meaty stew entrée. To prepare it in that fashion, reduce the quantity of pork to about $^1/_4$ pound, just enough for flavoring, use only sufficient stock to keep the corn moist in the end, and skip the garnishes. A child once called this form of the dish "underwater popcorn."

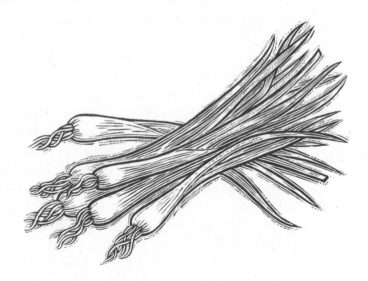

CHILE VERDE FROM THE VALLEY OF THE SUN

Modern real estate developers coined the term Valley of the Sun as a more marketable moniker for Phoenix's Salt River Valley. The original inhabitants, the Hohokam people, developed a sophisticated system of irrigation canals that enabled them to thrive in the desert environment. When the Swilling Irrigation Canal Company excavated the ruins after the Civil War, they brought the area back to life with an agricultural revival. The city of Phoenix, incorporated later in the nineteenth century, got its name by rising from the "ashes" of the Hohokam society.

As we described in the beef chapter, green chile stews in northern New Mexico can be fiery. Farther west in Arizona, similar dishes more often soothe than sizzle, like this pork version made with mild pods and tomatoes.

Serves 6

2 1/2 pounds pork Boston butt, trimmed of fat and cut into 3/4-inch cubes
1 cup chicken stock
1 medium onion, chopped
6 garlic cloves, minced
Two 14 1/2-ounce cans Mexican-style stewed tomatoes, undrained
2 cups chopped roasted mild green chile, preferably New Mexican or Anaheim, fresh or frozen
1 teaspoon dried oregano, preferably Mexican
1 teaspoon salt

In a large, heavy saucepan, combine the pork, $1/4$ cup of the stock, the onion, and the garlic. Cook over medium heat, stirring often, until the liquid evaporates and the meat is browned, about 20 to 25 minutes.

Add the remaining stock and scrape up any browned bits sticking to the bottom of the pan. Stir in the tomatoes, chiles, oregano, and salt. Reduce the heat to a simmer and cover the pan. Cook for 2 to 2 $1/2$ hours, stirring occasionally, until the meat is quite tender.

The chile can be served immediately, but the flavor improves with a day's refrigeration and reheating. Serve steaming hot in bowls.

CHILES EN NOGADA

Among all the classic dishes of Mexican cuisine, none is more inspired than *chiles en nogada*. The stuffed chiles originated in southern Mexico, in the city of Puebla, but they are so revered in the north that the leading Monterrey newspaper once ran an editorial in homage to the dish. In Monterrey and other border areas, the usual pork filling is often supplemented with beef or, even better we think, with veal. The jewel-like tones of *chiles en nogada* emulate the colors of the Mexican flag, making it a particularly festive favorite for Mexico's September 16 Independence Day and other holidays.

Serves 8

FILLING
1 pound ground pork
1 pound ground veal
1 small onion, chopped
4 garlic cloves, minced
1 cup canned crushed tomatoes
1 ripe pear, peeled and chopped
1/3 cup raisins
1/4 cup chopped candied citron
2 dried peaches, soaked in water and chopped
1 teaspoon salt
1 teaspoon cumin seeds, toasted and ground
1/2 teaspoon dried marjoram or Mexican oregano
1/4 teaspoon ground canela or other cinnamon
1 cup beef stock
2 teaspoons vinegar, preferably cider

SAUCE
1 cup walnuts, preferably from a new crop, toasted
1 cup half-and-half
1 garlic clove, roasted
8 ounces cream cheese, at room temperature
Pinch of ground canela or other cinnamon
Pinch of salt

8 large poblano chiles, roasted and peeled

Seeds from 2 pomegranates (see "Technique Tip")

In a large skillet, fry the pork and veal together over medium heat until gray. Add the onion and garlic and continue cooking for several minutes, until the onion has softened. Stir in the remaining filling ingredients, reduce the heat to low, and simmer, covered, for about 30 minutes, stirring occasionally. Uncover and continue simmering, until the mixture is no longer soupy but remains moist. (The filling can be made ahead and reheated if you wish.)

Preheat the oven to 350° F.

In a blender, purée the walnuts with the half-and-half and garlic. Add the cream cheese, canela, and salt and blend just until combined. Reserve the sauce at room temperature.

Slit the chiles lengthwise, down one side. Stuff the chiles generously with the filling and arrange on a heat-proof serving platter. Bake the chiles for 8 to 10 minutes, then let them cool for a similar amount of time.

Spoon the room-temperature sauce over the chiles and scatter the pomegranate seeds over the sauce. Serve immediately.

Technique Tip: Pomegranates from California can be found fresh in many markets in the fall and early winter. Refrigerated, they keep for weeks. Slice the orange-size fruits in half and pry out the seeds to use in *chiles en nogada.*

Regional Variations: In the original preparation of *chiles en nogada,* the poblanos are batter-dipped and fried. Though many cooks avoid the additional step today, you can duplicate it if you wish by using the batter and technique described in Big Jim Chiles Rellenos. Depending on the cook, apples, bananas, and pineapple might appear in the filling. Pecans, almonds, or cashews sometimes flavor the sauce, and occasionally cooks add a slice of bread to thicken it. Others might spike the sauce with sherry or enrich it with creamy fresh goat cheese.

RED CHILE PORK TAMALES, NUEVO LEÓN STYLE

Ancho and cascabel chiles marry with pork in these earthy tamales from northeast Mexico. The chiles turn up in both the filling and the dough, as is also commonly the case across the border in Texas.

Makes 30 medium tamales, about 10 to 12 main-dish servings

FILLING
1 1/4-pound pork loin
1/2 medium onion, chopped
2 cups water
2 ounces (about 4) whole dried anchos, stemmed, seeded, and rinsed
1 ounce (about 4 to 6) whole dried cascabel chiles, stemmed, seeded, and rinsed
2 garlic cloves
3/4 teaspoon cumin seeds, toasted and ground
3/4 teaspoon salt
1/2 teaspoon fresh-ground black pepper
1 tablespoon lard
1/2 cup sliced green olives
1/4 cup raisins

6-ounce package dried corn husks

DOUGH
1 cup lard
1 teaspoon salt
1 teaspoon baking powder
4 cups masa harina
3 1/2 cups water, or more as needed

Preheat the oven to 350° F.

To prepare the filling, place the pork and the onion in a medium-size baking dish and cover with the water. Bake for approximately 1 1/4 hours, or until the meat is cooked through and pulls apart easily. Remove the pork from the stock. Set the meat aside to cool for a few minutes and

refrigerate the stock. Reduce the oven temperature to 300° F.

When the pork has cooled enough to handle, shred it fine, either with two forks or in a food processor (the plastic dough blade on some models makes especially nice shreds) and transfer it to a medium bowl. Strain the stock, skimming any fat from the surface. If the stock doesn't measure 1 1/2 cups, add water to make 1 1/2 cups of liquid. Reserve the pork and the stock.

Place the damp chiles in one layer on a baking sheet and roast them in the oven for about 5 minutes. Watch the pods carefully so as not to burn them. The chiles can have a little remaining moisture. Remove them from the oven and transfer them to a blender. Add the garlic, cumin, salt, pepper, and reserved stock and purée the mixture. You will still be able to see tiny pieces of chile pulp, but they should be bound in a smooth, thick liquid. Strain the chile sauce.

Warm the lard in a heavy saucepan over high heat. When the lard has melted, add the chile sauce, being careful as it splutters and splatters. Stir continuously, until the most insistent sputtering subsides, reduce the heat to low, and simmer the sauce for about 15 minutes. Reserve 1/2 cup of chile sauce for the dough and pour the rest over the meat. Stir the olives and raisins into the meat. Reserve the mixture.

In a deep bowl or baking pan, soak the corn husks in hot water to cover. After 30 minutes the husks should be softened and pliable. Separate the husks and, if needed, rinse them under running water to wash away any grit or brown silks. Keep them covered with water until you are ready to use each one.

To prepare the dough, beat the lard in a large bowl with an electric mixer until it is light and fluffy. Pour in the reserved sauce, sprinkle in the salt and baking powder, and beat until combined. Mix in half of the masa harina and half of the water. If your mixer is powerful, continue using it to blend the dough. If not, switch to a sturdy spoon or your hands to avoid burning out the mixer's motor. Add the remaining masa and water and keep mixing until smooth. When well blended, the masa should have the consistency of thick cake batter. Add more water if needed for the preferred consistency. Keep the dough loosely covered while working.

To assemble the tamales, use approximately equal amounts of masa and filling. To make 2 1/2 dozen 3-ounce tamales, use 2 tablespoons of masa and 1 1/2 tablespoons of filling for each tamale.

Hold a corn husk flat on one hand, smooth side up. (You may, depending on the size of the corn husks, need to overlap two husks to form one tamale. Spread the dough over the husks together, just as if they were one.) With a rubber spatula, spread a thin layer of masa across the husk, but not to the edges. Top with filling spread more thickly through the dough's center, stopping short of the dough's edges. Make sure that the dough's edges meet to enclose all of the filling. Secure the tamale by folding the wrapper over or tying it. Repeat the procedure until all the filling and masa are used.

Place the tamales in a steamer, packing loosely in crisscross directions, or stand them on end. Allow enough space between them for the steam to rise effectively. Cover the pot and cook over simmering water for about 1 to 1 $^1/_4$ hours until the masa is firm and no longer sticks to the corn husk. Unwrap one tamale to check its consistency. If it is still doughy, rewrap it, return it to the pot, and continue steaming for a few more minutes.

Tamales should be eaten warm. The husks are usually left on when tamales are served without a sauce, to be removed by each guest before eating.

Regional Variations: These tamales come from Nuevo León, but they aren't the only style you find in northeast Mexico by any means. Another tasty version combines anchos and guajillos in a pork filling laced with cloves, allspice, and cinnamon. Other cooks mix the same ingredients into miniature cigar-shaped *tamalitos*. Tampico, Tamaulipas, produces gigantic ancho and pork tamales with fresh corn-studded masa, wrapped in banana leaves, that can measure nearly 3 feet in length.

A second exemplary version of pork tamales demonstrates how similar key ingredients and preparation techniques can yield very different but equally delicious results.

Makes 24 large tamales, about 12 main-dish servings

FILLING
1 1/2-pound pork loin
1 medium onion, chopped
2 cups water
2 tablespoons vegetable oil
2 garlic cloves, minced
1 tablespoon all-purpose flour
1/2 cup ground dried mild red chile, preferably New Mexican
3/4 teaspoon salt
1/2 teaspoon dried oregano, preferably Mexican

6-ounce package dried corn husks

DOUGH
6 cups masa harina
1 2/3 cups vegetable oil
5 cups water, or more as needed
2 teaspoons salt

Chimayó Red Chile Sauce (page 51) or other mild red chile sauce
    (optional)

Preheat the oven to 350° F.

To prepare the filling, place the pork and the onion in a medium-size baking dish and cover with the water. Bake for approximately 1 1/2 hours, or until the meat is cooked through and pulls apart easily. Remove the pork from the stock. Set the meat aside to cool for a few minutes and refrigerate the stock. When the pork has cooled enough to handle, shred it fine, either with two forks or in a food processor (the plastic dough blade on some models makes especially nice shreds). Strain the stock, skimming any fat from the surface. If the stock doesn't measure 2 cups, add water to make 2 cups of liquid. Reserve the pork and the stock.

In a heavy skillet, warm the oil over medium heat and add the garlic and the pork. Sprinkle the flour over the mixture and stir constantly for about 1 minute as the flour begins to brown. Add the chile, the reserved stock, the salt, and the oregano. Continue cooking over medium heat for 20 to 25 minutes, or until most of the liquid has evaporated and the meat is quite tender and a bit moist. Watch carefully toward the end of the cooking time, stirring frequently so as not to burn the mixture. Reserve the filling.

In a deep bowl or baking pan, soak the corn husks in hot water to cover. After 30 minutes the husks should be softened and pliable. Separate the husks and, if needed, rinse them under running water to wash away any grit or brown silks. Keep them covered with water until you are ready to use each one.

To prepare the dough, measure the masa harina into a large mixing bowl. Add the oil, water, and salt. Mix with a sturdy spoon, a powerful electric mixer, or your hands until smooth. When well blended, the masa should have the consistency of a moist cookie dough. Add more water if needed for the preferred consistency. Keep the dough loosely covered while working.

To assemble the tamales, use approximately equal amounts of masa and filling. To make 2 dozen 4-ounce tamales, use 2 tablespoons each of masa and filling for every tamale.

Hold a corn husk flat on one hand, smooth side up. (You may, depending on the size of the corn husks, need to overlap two husks to form one tamale. Spread the dough over the husks together, just as if they were one.) With a rubber spatula, spread a thin layer of masa across the husk, but not to the edges. Top with filling spread more thickly through the dough's center, stopping short of the dough's edges. Make sure that the dough's edges meet to enclose all of the filling. Secure the tamale by folding the wrapper over or tying it. Repeat the procedure until all the filling and masa are used.

Place the tamales in a steamer, packing loosely in crisscross directions, or stand them on end. Allow enough space between them for the steam to rise effectively. Cover the pot and cook over simmering water for

An old story tells how Cortés connived with his Aztec consort Malinche to get tamales to feed his army. After the Aztecs had realized that the Spaniards were not high priests from the court of Quetzalcoatl, they refused food to the invaders. Cortés appealed to Malinche for help, and according to the tale, she suggested a plan for the army to clamor at the gates of the palace on an agreed evening, when she would have the troops pelted with tamales from inside, ostensibly to make them go away.

about 1 to 1 $^1/_4$ hours until the masa is firm and no longer sticks to the corn husk. Unwrap one tamale to check its consistency. If it is still doughy, rewrap it, return it to the pot, and continue steaming for a few more minutes.

Tamales should be eaten warm. The husks are usually left on when tamales are served unadorned, to be removed by each guest before eating. These tamales are frequently served with a red sauce, in which case the husks should be removed before adding the sauce.

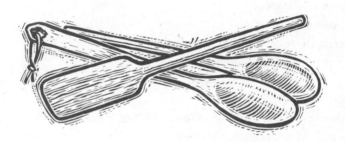

CREAMY CARNITAS ENCHILADAS

Houston restauranteur Ninfa Rodriguez Laurenzo, who grew up in Harlingen, Texas, gave us the idea for these hearty *carnitas* enchiladas.

Serves 4 to 6

SAUCE VERDE
2 medium-size green tomatoes, minced
12 ounces tomatillos, preferably fresh, husked and minced
2 fresh jalapeños, minced
4 garlic cloves, minced
1 teaspoon salt
1 cup chicken stock, preferably homemade
1/4 cup chopped fresh cilantro

FILLING
**1/2 recipe Lower Valley Carnitas (page 228) or 1 pound other
     prepared pork *carnitas*, warmed**
4 ounces cream cheese
3 tablespoons sliced green onions

Vegetable oil for pan-frying
12 corn tortillas
8 ounces Monterey jack cheese, grated

Chopped tomatoes and sliced green onions, for garnish

To prepare the sauce, place the tomatoes, tomatillos, jalapeños, garlic, and salt in a saucepan and pour the stock over them. Simmer over medium heat for about 15 to 20 minutes, until the mixture cooks down to a somewhat chunky sauce. Remove from the heat and stir in the cilantro. Reserve the sauce.

Preheat the oven to 350° F. Grease a 9-by-13-inch baking dish.

To prepare the filling, mix the *carnitas* with the cream cheese and green onions until combined.

Heat about $^1/_2$ inch of oil in a small skillet until the oil ripples. With tongs, dunk a tortilla in the oil just long enough for it to go limp, a matter of seconds. Don't let the tortilla turn crisp. Repeat with the remaining tortillas and drain them.

With tongs, dip a tortilla into the sauce to lightly coat it. Lay the tortilla on a plate, sprinkle about 3 tablespoons of filling on top, and roll it up snug. Transfer the enchilada to the baking dish. Repeat with the remaining tortillas and filling. Reserve the remaining sauce and keep it warm. Top the enchiladas with the cheese. Bake for 20 minutes, until the enchiladas are heated through and bubbly. Spoon the reserved sauce over the enchiladas. (Not baking the sauce into the enchiladas allows it to stay greener and fresher tasting.)

Garnish the enchiladas with tomatoes and green onions. Serve hot, using a spatula to scoop the enchiladas from the dish.

CHORIZO, ONION, AND OLIVE ENCHILADAS

Serves 4

SAUCE
6 dried mild red chiles, preferably ancho
3 cups water, or more as needed
1/2 medium onion, chopped
3 garlic cloves, chopped
3/4 teaspoon salt
1/2 teaspoon cumin seeds, toasted and ground

FILLING
3/4 pound bulk chorizo
3 medium waxy red potatoes, parboiled, peeled, and chopped
   (about 1 cup)
1 1/2 medium onions, chopped
1/2 cup sliced black olives, preferably brine-packed

Vegetable oil for pan-frying
12 corn tortillas
8 ounces asadero or Monterey jack cheese, grated

Whole black olives, preferably brine-packed, for garnish

To prepare the sauce, place the chiles in a medium saucepan and pour the water over them. Simmer over medium heat for 20 to 25 minutes, until the chiles become soft and supple.

Spoon the chiles out of the liquid and transfer them to a blender. Taste the chile cooking liquid. If the flavor is earthy and pleasant, measure 2 1/2 cups of the liquid and add it to the blender. If the liquid tastes bitter, discard it and add 2 1/2 cups of water to the blender. Add the remaining sauce ingredients to the blender and purée. Return the mixture to the saucepan and simmer over low heat for 25 to 30 minutes. If the sauce gets too thick to flow easily from a spoon, add a bit more water.

Preheat the oven to 350° F. Grease a 9-by-13-inch baking dish.

To prepare the filling, fry the chorizo in a medium skillet. As soon as the sausage begins to release oil, add the potatoes and onions and continue frying until the chorizo is cooked through and crisp and the vegetables are tender. Stir in the olives. Remove the mixture from the heat but keep it warm.

Heat about $1/2$ inch of oil in a small skillet until the oil ripples. With tongs, dunk a tortilla in the oil just long enough for it to go limp, a matter of seconds. Don't let the tortilla turn crisp. Repeat with the remaining tortillas and drain them.

With tongs, dip a tortilla into the sauce to lightly coat it. Lay the tortilla on a plate, sprinkle about 2 tablespoons of filling and 1 tablespoon of cheese over it, and roll it up snug. Transfer the enchilada to the baking dish. Repeat with the remaining tortillas and filling. Top the enchiladas with the remaining sauce and cheese. Bake for 20 minutes, until the enchiladas are heated through and the sauce is bubbly.

Garnish the enchiladas with whole black olives. Serve hot, using a spatula to scoop the enchiladas from the dish.

BELL'S GORDITAS

Parents in the borderlands used to tell unruly children: "Come y calla!"—"Eat and shut up!" Bell Mondragón and her son once used the familiar phrase as the name for a take-out restaurant in Santa Fe.

Eating too many of these treasures could turn anyone into a *gordita*, or "little fat one," but an occasional indulgence makes a super splurge. A great Santa Fe cook, Bell Mondragón, developed the dish, though we replace the *chicharrones* (fried pork rinds) in her original recipe with similar-tasting thick-sliced slab bacon, which is easier to find and may be easier to explain to your friends.

Serves 4 as a main dish, 8 as an appetizer

1 1/2 pounds slab bacon, cut at least 1/4 inch thick and preferably 1/2 inch
Vegetable oil for deep-frying
8 corn tortillas
1 cup Refried Beans (page 378) or other well-seasoned cooked, mashed pinto beans

Guacamole (page 123), chopped tomatoes or Pico de Gallo (page 40), and sour cream, for garnish

Cut the bacon into 1-inch slices. In a heavy skillet, fry the bacon over medium heat until browned and chewy-crispy. Drain the bacon.

Pour enough oil into a deep, heavy skillet to measure at least 3 inches in depth. Heat the oil to 375° F.

While the oil is warming, cut four evenly spaced 1-inch slits in the tortillas' edges. Fry the tortillas as described in the accompanying "Technique Tip" until crisp and golden, a matter of seconds. Drain the tortilla shells.

Spoon 2 tablespoons of beans onto each tortilla shell followed by equal portions of the bacon. Top each with a generous spoonful of guacamole, a sprinkling of tomatoes or pico de gallo, and a dab of sour cream. Eat immediately.

Technique Tip: To fry the tortillas in the proper upturned shape, you need some kind of round but flat-ended tool, perhaps a wooden flour tortilla roller or a cylindrical bean or potato masher. Place the tortilla into the hot oil and immediately press down on it with your chosen device. The hot oil will force the tortilla back up toward your tool, forming it into a cup. Use a slotted spoon in your other hand to help mold the cup shape uniformly. Have a few extra tortillas on hand when you first try the technique, but the process becomes simple with practice. Commercially available tools to mold tortilla cups take more effort to use.

Regional Variations: In her *gorditas*, Bell Mondragón uses a cut of skin and fat from the pork jaw to make *chicharrones* in a traditional New Mexico fashion. Unlike the puffy pork rinds eaten in other border areas and the Mexican interior as a chip-like snack, hers are thick, meaty chunks fried crisp like bacon.

Never miss a chance to sample cabrito in the region that specializes in it. In Nuevo Laredo, consistent good bets for restaurant versions are El Rincón del Viejo and Nuevo León. Across from Brownsville, in Matamoros, Los Norteños near the city market shouldn't disappoint. Farther west in Monterrey, the world capital of cabrito consumption, it's hard to turn a street corner without bumping into an option. All things considered, our favorite spot is the downtown El Rey del Cabrito, a big and bright legend of a restaurant loaded with memorabilia honoring *vaqueros* and *charros*. Austin, Texas, is about as far north and east as the meat travels in style. There, check out the colorful El Azteca café, where the Guerra family bakes the cabrito first and later deep-fries it for a wonderful contrast of textures.

One of the most common and distinctive sights of Monterrey is cabrito, or kid, roasting in the *al pastor* style described earlier in the chapter. Many cooks add little if any seasoning to the meat, though we like to start with a beer marinade, an approach we got from Jorge Mejía Prieto's *Gastronomía de las Fronteras* (Consejo Nacional para la Cultura y las Artes, 1989). As with pork *al pastor*, you can use a spit attachment for cooking the cabrito on a modern charcoal grill or the method we outline below.

Serves 6 to 8

1 cabrito hindquarter, about 4 to 5 pounds

MARINADE
12 ounces beer
1 medium onion, minced
1/4 cup vegetable oil
Juice of 2 limes
1 tablespoon Worcestershire sauce
1 tablespoon dried oregano, preferably Mexican
2 teaspoons cumin seeds, toasted and ground
2 teaspoons salt

Mesquite chips or beans

Pico de Gallo (page 40) and Serrano Salsa Verde (page 43), or
**   other salsas**
Guacamole (page 123)
Flour tortillas, warmed

The night before you plan to cook the cabrito, place the meat in a large plastic bag.

Combine the marinade ingredients. Pour the mixture over the cabrito and refrigerate overnight.

Take the meat from the refrigerator 1 hour before you plan to cook it. Drain the marinade from the cabrito, reserving the marinade. Loosely cover the cabrito and let it sit at room temperature. In a saucepan, boil the marinade vigorously over high heat for several minutes. Keep the marinade warm.

Prepare an outdoor grill for barbecuing. Put a half-dozen handfuls of mesquite chips or beans in water to soak, and fire up about 20 or 25 charcoal briquettes. When the charcoal is totally covered in gray ash and begins to show tinges of white ash, pile the coals loosely on one side of the grill. Spread about one-fourth of the mesquite on top. Place the cabrito on the other side of the grill, away from the coals.

Cover the grill, positioning the lid's damper immediately above the meat and leaving all the dampers open. Insert a deep-fry or candy thermometer through the damper above the meat to keep track of the temperature. The cooking time should be about 2 3/4 to 3 1/4 hours at a temperature averaging 300° F to 350° F. The cooking temperature should start at the higher end and drop gradually to the lower. After the cabrito has been cooking about 45 to 60 minutes, fire up another 20 coals and add them as needed to keep the temperature in the preferred range. Turn and baste the cabrito with the reserved marinade every 45 minutes or so, adding more mesquite at the same time as needed to continue producing smoke. The cabrito is done when the internal temperature taken on an instant-read thermometer measures 160° F.

Let the meat stand for 5 to 10 minutes before slicing it very thin. Toss the slices together so that each portion has some of the seasoned exterior meat mixed in with moister interior meat. Serve warm with the salsas, guacamole, and tortillas.

Technique Tip: Cabrito is a milk-fed kid, 30 to 40 days old and about 12 to 15 pounds in weight. It can be a challenge to find in areas without Hispanic or Greek populations, though many butchers who don't carry it do know of sources. In southwest Texas, it's widely available in supermarkets in cuts that include the shoulder, breast, head, and the popular hindquarter. In other places, be prepared to purchase a full quartered kid. The second hindquarter can be refrigerated or frozen for later use, and the forequarters stewed and shredded for tamales, burritos, or other dishes.

Texas legend J. Frank "Pancho" Dobie told a story about a barbecue dinner he made in 1929 for a *National Geographic* team that was researching an article on the Big Bend country. He and a Mexican friend, who were accompanying the group, tracked down a mountain lion, cooked it, and told the Easterners that it was the great local specialty, genuine cabrito. The writers and photographers, according to Dobie, declared it the best cabrito they could ever hope to eat.

Another classic way of cooking cabrito, *birria* preparations developed out of pit techniques for steam roasting. The marinating and long baking produce a succulent and tender result. The method can be applied to other meats as well, such as pork butt or veal breast.

Serves 6 to 8

1 cabrito hindquarter, about 4 to 5 pounds, cut into 2 pieces by your butcher or with a heavy cleaver
1 1/2 cups canned crushed tomatoes
1 medium onion, chopped
1 whole head of garlic, roasted
1/4 cup plus 1 teaspoon ground dried mild red chile, preferably ancho
1/4 cup vinegar, preferably cider
1 1/2 teaspoons salt, or more to taste
2 teaspoons dried oregano, preferably Mexican
1 teaspoon minced fresh ginger
1/2 teaspoon black peppercorns
1/2 teaspoon cumin seeds, toasted

Diced onion, minced fresh cilantro, and lime wedges, for garnish

The night before you plan to cook the *birria*, place the cabrito in a large plastic bag.

In a blender, purée 1 cup of the tomatoes, the onion, the garlic, and ¼ cup of the chile with the remaining ingredients. Spread the paste over the meat and refrigerate overnight. Take the cabrito from the refrigerator and let it sit at room temperature for 1 hour.

Preheat the oven to 325° F.

Pour 1 inch of water into the bottom of a roasting pan with a tight-fitting lid. Place a wire rack over the water, balancing it on custard cups if needed to keep it above the water's level. Transfer the paste-covered cabrito sections to the rack. Cover the cabrito and bake for 3 hours. Remove the pan, leaving the oven on, and set the meat aside until cool enough to handle. Remove the cabrito and the rack from the pan. Save about ½ cup of the broth and degrease it. Add the remaining tomatoes and chile to the broth and adjust the seasonings, if necessary.

Pull the meat away from the bones and fat in chunks. Combine the reserved broth with the cabrito in a smaller baking dish, cover it, and return it to the oven for 20 minutes.

Serve the meat topped with the onion, cilantro, and limes.

Regional Variations: Some Mexican preparations of cabrito don't find much favor north of the border. Both *fritada de cabrito* and *cabrito en su sangre* fry the meat and then simmer it in its blood with chile and spices such as thyme, cumin, and mint. *Machitos* combine goat meat, liver, and heart, wrapped in intestines and often grilled. On a recent trip to Monterrey, we had the dish wrapped in corn tortillas and steamed in a banana leaf. Over the Rio Grande in Texas, the styles may seem more familiar to Americans. You see Lone Star recipes for everything from cabrito burgers to pot pies, and we've even run across it served like corned beef, with cabbage.

GRILLED POMEGRANATE LAMB CHOPS

California rancho cooking authority Jacqueline Higuera McMahan remembers a leg of lamb prepared by her grandparents in this style. We substitute succulent chops for a faster but still elegant dish.

Serves 4

8 loin lamb chops, each weighing about 5 ounces and cut 1 inch thick

MARINADE
1 1/2 cups pomegranate juice (see "Technique Tip")
2 tablespoons extra-virgin olive oil
4 garlic cloves, minced
2 teaspoons dried rosemary, crushed
1/2 teaspoon salt

Fresh rosemary sprigs, for garnish (optional)

Even on the great cattle ranches of Sonora and Chihuahua, lamb was and is popular. In *Mexican Family Cooking* (Fawcett Columbine, 1986), Aída Gabilondo relates how she allowed her four daughters to select the meat for holiday celebrations. After giving them the choice of roast beef, filet mignon, ham, or leg of lamb, the girls would write the four choices on slips of paper and then draw one. When lamb seemed to win the little lottery year after year, Señora Gabilondo got curious and peeked at the slips. Each one said "lamb."

Place the chops in a shallow, nonreactive pan or plastic bag.

Combine the remaining ingredients and pour the marinade over the chops. Refrigerate for at least 2 hours and up to 4 hours, turning the meat at least once if it's not entirely submerged.

About 30 minutes before cooking, take the chops from the refrigerator and drain the marinade into a saucepan. Boil the marinade vigorously over high heat for several minutes.

On an outdoor grill, fire up enough charcoal to form a single layer of coals beneath the meat.

When the charcoal is covered with gray ash, place the meat directly over the fire. Grill the chops until done to your taste, about 6 to 7 minutes per side for medium-rare. Serve the chops immediately, with spoonfuls of the reduced marinade sauce, and garnished if you wish with the rosemary sprigs.

Technique Tip: To make pomegranate juice from fresh fruit, slice pomegranates in half and pry out the seeds. Press the seeds into a sieve to release the tart ruby juice. If that sounds like too much effort, or if the fruit is out of season, you can find bottled pomegranate juice in well-stocked supermarkets and health food stores.

LAMB SHANKS ADOBO

Serves 4

4 pounds lamb shanks, sliced in chunks by your butcher

1/2 cup ground dried red chile, preferably New Mexican or Anaheim

2 cups chicken or beef stock

2 cups canned crushed tomatoes

1 medium onion, chopped

1 canned chipotle chile, minced, plus 1 teaspoon adobo sauce (optional)

1 tablespoon vinegar, preferably sherry or cider

3 garlic cloves, minced

1 teaspoon dried oregano, preferably Mexican

1 teaspoon salt, or more to taste

2 bay leaves

Minced onion and fresh cilantro, for garnish (optional)

Preheat the oven to 300° F. Oil a large, covered baking dish. Place the lamb in the baking dish.

Mix together the remaining ingredients and combine with the lamb. (If you like, the lamb can be prepared to this point and refrigerated overnight. Bring the mixture back to cool room temperature before proceeding.)

Cover the dish and bake until the meat is quite tender and comes easily away from the bones and fat, about 3 to 3 1/4 hours. If the sauce seems watery, return the meat to the oven, uncovered, and bake for a few minutes longer.

Serve hot, garnished if you wish with onion and cilantro. Reheated leftovers are outstanding.

A hardy breed, known for rich-flavored meat and superior wool, churro sheep came to the New World with the Spanish. Early settlers in the Southwest, and later the Navajos, prized the wool for weaving because of its silky, relatively smooth texture, but the churro line was almost lost in the United States after the introduction of other breeds. Now the distinctive-looking sheep are making a regional comeback, due in large part to a northern New Mexico cooperative, Ganados del Valle. The group sells churro and other lambs whole, halved, in individual cuts, and in sausages laced with mint or chile through its Pastores Feed and General Store in Los Ojos, near Chama, or by mail order, frozen, from Ganados del Valle, P.O. Box 118, Los Ojos, New Mexico 87551, 505-588-7896. It's best to order in the fall or early winter, when the meat is first available, especially if you want churro lamb, the most popular breed.

South Texas has long been a destination for hunters. In addition to axis deer and antelope, the area offers rabbits, wild boar, javelina, and game birds. The hunting is just as good across the Rio Grande. For information on permits, guides, and outfitters in Mexico, contact the Mexican Hunting Association's U.S. office at 6840 El Salvador, Long Beach, California 90815, 310-421-1619.

While a resurgence of interest in game is sweeping the United States, venison's popularity in south Texas and northeast Mexico never really waned. The most tender cuts, like these scaloppine, are best prepared simply and then enhanced with a savory sauce. In this case the sauce stars the dried cascabel, a round, nutty chile named in Spanish for its rattling noise.

Serves 4

1 1/2 pounds venison scaloppine, cut against the grain in slices 1/3 inch thick

SAUCE
1 1/2 cups game or beef stock
1 1/2 cups fruity young red wine
3/4 cup inexpensive port
1 medium onion, minced
3 to 4 cascabel chiles, crumbled
2 tablespoons crème de cassis
1 teaspoon dried thyme
1 canela stick, splintered, or other cinnamon stick, broken in pieces
1/2 to 1 1/2 teaspoons brown sugar
Salt to taste
1 tablespoon butter

Salt and fresh-ground black pepper
1 tablespoon vegetable oil

4 whole well-shaped cascabel chiles, for garnish (optional)

If the venison is frozen, thaw it in red wine to keep the meat moist.

To prepare the sauce, combine the stock, wine, port, onion, chiles, crème de cassis, thyme, and canela in a heavy saucepan. Simmer the mixture over low heat for 30 minutes until the sauce has reduced by about one-third. Strain the sauce, extracting as much liquid as possible from the solids, and return it to the saucepan. Continue cooking the sauce until it has been reduced to about 1 1/2 cups. Taste the sauce and add just enough sugar to balance the acidity of the wine. Salt the sauce to taste and whisk in the butter until melted. Keep the sauce warm while preparing the venison.

Sprinkle the venison lightly with salt and pepper. Heat the oil in a heavy skillet until it is almost smoking. Add the venison and stir-fry it for 1 or 2 minutes, searing the meat on all sides.

Remove the meat to a warm serving platter. Scrape the remaining pan juices and any browned bits into the sauce and stir to combine.

Ladle the sauce over the meat. Garnish with the cascabel chiles, if you like. Serve the scaloppine immediately.

Technique Tip: The lack of fat in venison requires some adjustments in the way you normally handle and cook meat. If the venison is frozen, thaw it in a wine bath to keep it moist. When you sauté a premium cut like these scaloppine, cook the meat for less time than you allow for beef. You want to sear the outside while leaving the inside rare or medium-rare. Plan to eat the venison immediately because it will dry out quickly.

A cousin of *carne seca*, jerky developed as a way to preserve meat, but in this case the goal is flavor instead of long life. The preparation, from Coahuila originally, also works well with beef top round steak.

Serves 6 to 8 as a snack

1-pound venison backstrap (tenderloin)
12 ounces beer
Juice of 2 limes
2 tablespoons vegetable oil
2 teaspoons soy sauce
2 garlic cloves, minced
1 teaspoon ground dried mild red chile, preferably ancho or
　　New Mexican
1 teaspoon dried oregano, preferably Mexican

About 2 hours before you plan to cook the jerky, place the venison in the freezer to make slicing easier. After 30 to 40 minutes, remove the meat from the freezer and slice it as thin as you can with a good sharp knife. Trim the meat of any fat.

Combine the beer, lime juice, oil, soy sauce, and garlic and pour the mixture over the venison. Marinate, refrigerated, for about 1 hour.

Preheat the oven to 225° F. Grease a baking sheet.

Remove the meat from the refrigerator, drain it, and toss it with the chile and oregano. Cover the meat and let it sit at room temperature for 10 to 15 minutes. Transfer the meat to the baking sheet, separating and smoothing the pieces. Bake the jerky for 1 1/2 hours or until deeply colored and well dried. Let the jerky cool to room temperature before serving. Refrigerate any leftovers.

Lucy M. Garza's *South Texas Mexican Cookbook* (Eakin Press, 1982) paints a loving portrait of life in Santa Monica, Texas, deep in the Rio Grande Valley. In one of her childhood stories she tells about sharing fried rabbit, *conejo frito*, with the school principal. Her mother cooked it something like this.

Serves 4

3 cups buttermilk
1 tablespoon prepared yellow mustard
2 teaspoons chili powder
2 teaspoons salt
1 teaspoon fresh-ground black pepper
2 rabbits, about 2 pounds each, cut into 4 to 6 serving pieces each
1 1/2 cups all-purpose flour
1 1/2 pounds (3 cups) vegetable shortening
3 tablespoons bacon drippings

At least 2 hours (and up to 8 hours) before you plan to eat, mix the buttermilk, mustard, $1/2$ teaspoon of the chili powder and the salt, and $1/4$ teaspoon of the pepper in a shallow, nonreactive dish or heavy-duty plastic bag. Add the rabbit parts, turning to coat them well with the mixture. Cover or seal, and refrigerate the rabbit.

About 20 minutes before you plan to fry the rabbit, bring it to room temperature. Sprinkle the remaining chili powder, salt, and pepper into a medium-size paper bag and add the flour. Set the bag aside.

In a 10-inch to 12-inch cast-iron skillet, melt the shortening over high heat. Add the bacon drippings to the skillet. When small bubbles form on the surface, reduce the heat slightly.

Take a piece of rabbit out of the marinade, shake off the excess liquid, and drop it into the bag of seasoned flour. Shake the bag well so that the piece is coated thoroughly. Remove it from the bag and lower it gently into the skillet, skin side down. Repeat until all the pieces are in the skillet, arranged so that they cook evenly. Reduce the heat to medium and cover the skillet. Fry the rabbit until richly browned, about 12 to 15 minutes.

Lower the heat slightly, take off the cover, and turn the rabbit with tongs. Fry it, uncovered, for another 12 to 15 minutes, until richly browned on the second side. Drain the rabbit briefly and serve it piping hot.

Try the rabbit accompanied with mashed potatoes and cream gravy, just as you might serve fried chicken in Texas. If any leftovers remain, refrigerate them and serve them cold rather than reheated.

Technique Tip: Rabbit can be found in many well-stocked supermarkets, usually pre-cut into pieces and frozen. A well-connected butcher may be able to locate a fresh rabbit, particularly in the spring. Similar in taste to chicken, rabbit has virtually no fat and fewer calories per pound than almost any other meat. The buttermilk soak helps keep the lean meat moist and turns it a beautiful brown.

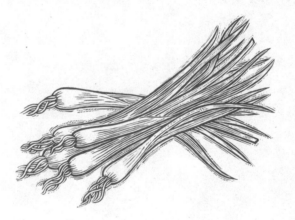

THE SIMPLE PLEASURES OF POULTRY

*H*istorically, border cooks have developed fewer distinctive regional dishes with chicken than almost any other primary food. They get a little more adventuresome with turkey and game birds, and recent generations are taking a fresh look at all fowl, but on the whole, people enjoy poultry in straightforward styles. Some of the most popular dishes are borrowed from other places, then often reduced to their essentials for ease of preparation, and others feature chicken or turkey as a foil for stronger flavors. That doesn't suggest a lack of interest, though, or a disregard for the culinary potentials. On the border, poultry is one of the simple pleasures.

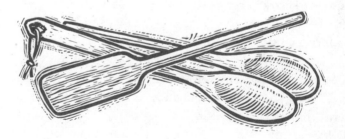

ARROZ CON POLLO PICANTE

Many New World versions of this Spanish classic lack depth and flavor. Our border rendition, spiced with chile and Mexican chorizo, sings with a robust voice.

Serves 6 to 8

3-pound chicken, cut into serving pieces and skinned

2 chicken legs, thighs, or small chicken breasts, skinned

5 tablespoons extra-virgin olive oil

2 teaspoons ground dried mild red chile, preferably ancho or New
    Mexican

2 teaspoons dried oregano, preferably Mexican

2 teaspoons cumin seeds, toasted and ground

1 teaspoon salt

1/2 teaspoon dried thyme

1 large onion, chopped

2 garlic cloves, minced

2 cups uncooked rice

3 cups chicken stock

3 small tomatoes, preferably Roma or Italian plum, chopped

1 bay leaf

3/4 pound link chorizo, cut in 1-inch sections

1 cup peas, fresh or frozen

1/3 cup sliced black olives, preferably brine-packed

Minced fresh parsley, for garnish

Coat the chicken pieces with 1 to 2 tablespoons of the oil. Combine the chile, oregano, cumin, salt, and thyme in a small bowl and rub the mixture lightly into the chicken.

Refrigerate the chicken for at least 1 hour and up to overnight. Let the chicken sit at room temperature for 30 minutes before continuing.

Preheat the oven to 350° F.

In a Dutch oven, warm the remaining oil over medium-high heat. Fry the chicken in the oil, in batches if necessary, just long enough to brown it. Transfer the chicken to a plate. Reduce the heat to medium, add the onion and garlic, and sauté for a couple of minutes until the onion begins to soften. Stir in the rice and sauté briefly until it becomes translucent.

Remove the Dutch oven from the heat. Transfer the chicken back to the Dutch oven, arranging it on top of the rice. Add the stock, tomatoes, and bay leaf. Cover and bake for 1 hour.

While the chicken and rice bake, fry the chorizo until well browned and cooked through. Drain the chorizo.

Take the chicken and rice from the oven and stir in the chorizo, peas, and black olives. Re-cover the pot and let it sit at room temperature for at least 10 minutes and up to 30 minutes. Spoon the rice on a platter and top it attractively with the chicken and chorizo. Scatter parsley over the platter and serve.

Regional Variations: The original Spanish *arroz con pollo* featured saffron, and some New Mexican versions maintain that tradition, substituting the local *azafrán* for the European product and dropping the chile and spicy chorizo. On the modern end of the scale, some Southwestern cooks transform the dish into an easy casserole, combining tender cubes of chicken breast with cooked rice, Monterey jack cheese, and a sauce like Hatch Green Chile Sauce.

CHIPOTLE-TOMATILLO CHICKEN

This recipe evolved from one that Elizabeth Borton de Treviño, a long-time Monterrey resident, gave to Diana Kennedy, who printed her own version in *The Art of Mexican Cooking* (Bantam Books, 1989). It's a case where simplicity shines.

Serves 6

6 bone-in, skin-on chicken breasts
4 cups unsalted or low-salt chicken stock
1 medium onion, chopped
2 to 3 dried or canned chipotles
2 garlic cloves, sliced
1 bay leaf
1 pound whole tomatillos, husked
1/3 cup chopped fresh cilantro
2 tablespoons vegetable oil
1 teaspoon sugar (optional)
Salt to taste

Minced fresh cilantro
Crema (page 63) or crème fraîche and Guacamole (page 123) or
avocado slices, for garnish

Place the chicken in a Dutch oven or large saucepan. Pour the stock over the chicken and add the onion, chipotles, garlic, and bay leaf. Bring the mixture to a boil, then reduce the heat to a low simmer and cover the pan. Poach the chicken 15 to 20 minutes, until just cooked through. Let it cool in the stock for 15 minutes.

Remove the chicken from the stock with a slotted spoon. While the chicken cools enough to handle, add the tomatillos to the stock, bring the mixture to a boil over medium-high heat, and boil the tomatillos, uncovered, for 10 minutes, or until soft. With a slotted spoon, transfer the tomatillos and the chipotles to a blender, add the cilantro, and purée. Pour the mixture back into the stock and mix well.

Pull the chicken from the bones in large pieces and reserve.

Warm the oil over high heat in a Dutch oven or large saucepan. Add

Boston-born journalist and author Elizabeth Borton de Treviño moved to Monterrey in the 1930s after marrying a public relations specialist for the local chamber of commerce. *My Heart Lies South* (Thomas Y. Crowell Company, 1972) chronicles her life in a provincial city much more foreign than modern Monterrey, now a bustling center of international commerce.

the stock mixture, being careful to avoid spatters as the liquid hits the oil. When the sputtering dies down, reduce the heat to medium-low and cook the sauce about 10 minutes, until somewhat reduced. Taste the sauce and add the sugar if the sauce seems too tart, and add as much salt as is needed to round out the flavor.

Slice the chicken into neat bite-size chunks. Stir the chicken into the sauce, reduce the heat to low, and cook, covered, an additional 10 to 15 minutes. Top with the minced cilantro.

Garnish the chicken with small dollops of crema and guacamole, or avocado slices, and serve hot.

ROAST CHICKEN GRANDE Y GORDITA

The original Sonoran version of this recipe calls for "one chicken, big and fat," which gave us our name for the citrus-bathed bird.

Serves 3 to 4

3 1/2-pound to 4-pound whole chicken
1 tablespoon vegetable oil, preferably peanut
1/2 tablespoon butter
Salt to taste
Fresh-ground black pepper to taste
1 small orange, quartered
1/2 medium onion, chunked
1 whole head of garlic, separated into cloves but unpeeled
1 cup chicken stock
1/2 cup orange juice
1 tablespoon fresh lime juice
1/4 teaspoon ground canela or other cinnamon

Pico de Gallo (page 40)
Lime wedges

Preheat the oven to 400° F. Grease the rack of a small roasting pan.

Slip your fingers under the chicken's skin and loosen it, being careful not to tear it. Massage the oil into the flesh and inside the cavity. Rub the butter over the chicken's skin. Salt and pepper generously inside and out. Fill the cavity with the orange and onion and half of the garlic. In a small bowl, mix the stock with the juices and the canela.

Place the chicken on the rack in a roasting pan, breast up, and roast for 15 minutes. Turn the chicken on one side, add the remaining garlic cloves to the pan, and baste the chicken with a little of the stock mixture. Reduce the heat to 350° F and cook the bird for 15 minutes more. Turn the chicken on its other side and baste again. Cook for 15 minutes longer, and turn the bird back side up. Baste again and roast for another 15 minutes. Turn the chicken breast side up again and baste with the pan juices and a little more stock. After 15 more minutes, the chicken should be golden brown with a crispy skin. The total cooking time is 1 1/4 hours.

Remove the chicken from the oven. Spoon out the orange, onion, and garlic from its cavity. Discard the orange but add the onion and garlic to the roasting pan. Transfer the chicken to a serving platter, cover it with a foil tent, and let it sit for 10 to 15 minutes before carving.

Pour the contents of the roasting pan, and the remaining stock, into a blender or food processor and purée. Strain the sauce, reheat it if needed, and serve it with the roast chicken. Accompany the chicken with pico de gallo and limes.

In his account of life in late eighteenth-century Sonora, Jesuit missionary Ignaz Pfefferkorn reported that the Native peoples in the area loved most meats, but wouldn't eat any kind of fowl. He said they raised chickens, after the Spaniards introduced them, but only to trade them and their eggs to the padres for tobacco, knives, and other items of more interest.

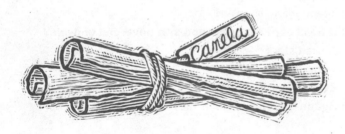

The similarity to stir-frying techniques in the Chicken Machaca is not just an odd coincidence. There has been a strong Chinese influence in southern California, Baja, and Arizona since the early railroad years. Pauline Wiley-Kleeman's fascinating 1929 cookbook, *Ramona's Spanish-Mexican Cookery: The First Complete and Authentic Spanish-Mexican Cook Book in English*, included a chop suey recipe among the Mexican dishes. Mexicali, the capital of Baja California Norte, has several dozen Chinese restaurants.

In this contemporary twist on beef *machaca*, chicken breasts are pounded thin, cut in slender strips, and then quick-fried in a manner that resembles stir-frying.

Serves 6

2 pounds boneless, skinless chicken breasts
2 tablespoons vegetable oil
1 medium onion, diced
2 small tomatoes, preferably Roma or Italian plum, chopped
1/2 red bell pepper, diced
1/2 green or yellow bell pepper, diced
1 to 2 fresh jalapeños, minced
2 garlic cloves, minced
1 tablespoon soy sauce
1 teaspoon vinegar, preferably white wine
1/2 teaspoon cumin seeds, toasted and ground
2 tablespoons minced fresh cilantro, for garnish

Pound the chicken breasts to $^1/_2$-inch thickness and slice them into ribbons about $^1/_2$ inch wide.

Warm a large, heavy skillet over high heat. Pour in the oil and swirl it around the pan. Add the chicken and cook it through quickly, stirring continuously. Remove the chicken with a slotted spoon and transfer it to a nearby plate. Add the onion, tomatoes, red and green bell peppers, and jalapeño to the skillet and cook for 1 to 2 minutes. Reduce the heat to medium and stir in the garlic, soy sauce, vinegar, and cumin. Cook another 1 or 2 minutes, then add the chicken back to the skillet and heat through.

Serve immediately, garnished with cilantro. The dish pairs well with Mexican Red Rice.

PIÑATA POLLO

This rolled chicken breast is stuffed with treats, like a party piñata.

Serves 6

6 boneless, skinless chicken breasts

MARINADE
4 tablespoons extra-virgin olive oil
1/4 cup chicken stock
3 tablespoons minced fresh cilantro
3 garlic cloves, minced
1 fresh or pickled serrano or jalapeño, minced
1/2 teaspoon salt

FILLING
1/4 pound bulk chorizo
1/4 pound spinach, chopped
1 fresh or pickled serrano or jalapeño, minced
4 ounces fresh creamy goat cheese
2 ounces asadero or Monterey jack cheese, grated
1 tablespoon minced fresh cilantro

Ground dried mild red chile, chili powder, or paprika
Vegetable oil for pan-frying
2 tablespoons chicken stock or water
Minced fresh cilantro, for garnish

Start the preparations for the chicken at least several hours before you plan to eat. Pound the breasts to about $1/4$-inch thickness and place them in a plastic bag. Combine the marinade ingredients and pour over the chicken. Transfer the breasts to the refrigerator and chill them for at least 2 hours or overnight.

To prepare the filling, fry the chorizo in a skillet over medium heat until browned. Pour off any accumulated grease and return the skillet to the stove. Add the spinach and chile and stir until the spinach wilts. Stir in the cheeses and cilantro and remove from the heat. There should be

Stuffed with candies, confetti, and small toys, whimsically shaped papier-mâché piñatas serve as a festive focus of birthday parties and other celebrations in Mexico and parts of the Southwest. A blind-folded child tries to get to the goodies by hitting the piñata with a bat or stick while someone else raises and lowers the target on a rope hung over a tree or ceiling beam.

The origin of the custom is clouded in the mists of prehistory, but we know that the Aztecs honored their war god by the ritual breaking of a feather-decorated clay pot full of trinkets. Marco Polo brought a similar tradition to Europe from China, where he found people scattering seeds over prepared fields during spring agricultural celebrations by striking hollow, seed-filled cones. Even today the practice retains religious significance in Spain, where families break open ceramic pineapples on the first Sunday of Lent, *domingo de piñata.*

enough accumulated heat to just melt the cheese. Spoon out the chorizo-spinach mixture onto a piece of waxed paper in six equal portions, shaped in rectangular mounds. Refrigerate the filling mounds for at least 1 hour.

Preheat the oven to 350° F. Grease a medium baking dish.

Drain the chicken and discard the marinade. Remove the chorizo-spinach mixture from the refrigerator and place one mound in the center of each chicken breast. Carefully roll the chicken up around the filling, tucking the ends in well and completely enclosing the filling. Secure with toothpicks. Dust the chicken rolls with red chile.

Warm 1/4 inch of oil in a skillet over medium-high heat. Sear the chicken rolls quickly on all sides. Transfer the chicken to the baking dish. Add the stock or water to the dish, cover, and bake for 25 minutes, or until cooked through and tender. Sprinkle cilantro over the chicken rolls and serve.

Regional Variations: Stuffed chicken breast dishes are popular in New Mexico, the original source of our Piñata Pollo. One recipe from several generations ago contained a filling of piñon (pine) nuts, raisins, and ground lamb, a common meat at the time. In a more contemporary vein, *Chile Pepper* magazine editor Nancy Gerlach created a version featuring ham, asadero cheese, sliced avocado, and minced cilantro. In *Just North of the Border* (Prima Publishing, 1992), written with Dave DeWitt, she calls for baking the rolls and then topping them with a simmered sauce of poblano chile, chopped walnuts, onion, cilantro, and chicken broth.

CHICKEN WITH GREEN PIPIÁN

The Aztecs taught the Spanish about *pipián* preparations, and a nun later made the idea into the base for *mole poblano*. This border version gets much of its tang from tomatillos.

Serves 6

1/2 pound whole tomatillos, husked
Water
1/4 cup slivered almonds
1/4 cup pepitas (shelled pumpkin seeds)
2 tablespoons sesame seeds
1/2 teaspoon cumin seeds
4 garlic cloves, unpeeled
2 to 3 fresh jalapeños
1 slice of toast, torn in several pieces
1/3 medium onion, chunked
1/4 cup minced fresh cilantro
1 teaspoon dried oregano, preferably Mexican
1/2 teaspoon salt
1/8 teaspoon ground canela or other cinnamon
1 cup chicken stock
3 tablespoons vegetable oil, preferably peanut or sesame
6 boneless, skinless chicken breasts
1/4 cup orange juice

Minced fresh cilantro and slivered almonds, for garnish

In a saucepan, cover the tomatillos with water and simmer for about 10 minutes until tender. Transfer the tomatillos to a blender and reserve.

In a small skillet, toast the almonds just until fragrant and transfer them to the blender. Repeat with the pepitas, sesame seeds, and cumin seeds. To the skillet, add the garlic cloves and the jalapeños. Roast the garlic until browned and softened and the chiles until somewhat blackened and blistered. Transfer the garlic to the blender, and seed the jalapeños and then transfer them to the blender. Add the toast, onion, cilantro, oregano, salt, canela, and stock to the blender. Purée the mixture for 1 to 2 minutes, until smooth but still a little grainy.

In a large skillet, warm the oil over medium-high heat and sauté the chicken just long enough to lightly brown it. Remove the chicken with a slotted spoon and reserve it.

Pour the blender mixture into the skillet, being careful to avoid splatters when the liquid hits the hot oil. When the most insistent sputtering dies down, reduce the heat to medium-low. Simmer the sauce for about 3 minutes, stirring frequently. Add the orange juice to the sauce and arrange the chicken on the sauce, submerging it partially. Cover, reduce the heat to low, and simmer for about 20 minutes, stirring once or twice, until the chicken is cooked through.

Transfer the chicken to a serving platter and surround it with the sauce. Top with a scattering of cilantro and almonds and serve.

Regional Variations: *Pipiáns* can be red or green, with much of the color coming from the choice of fresh or dried chiles. A number of border recipes call for peanuts rather than almonds, as James W. Peyton recommends in his *Cocina de la Frontera* (Red Crane Books, 1994). Some cooks add a couple of tablespoons of peanut butter to heighten the nutty flavor, or a similar quantity of sherry to increase the depth. In southern Mexico, many people use a sour orange to get the tomatillo tartness in this recipe.

ABUELITA'S ALMOND CHICKEN

Like *pipián* and *mole*, this dish relies on a sauce thickened by ground nuts, but in this case it also incorporates dairy products, found so commonly in border cooking. The results are fast enough for a weeknight but fancy enough for company. The original idea came to us from Maria de Cardenas of Los Angeles, who gave it the name of "grandmother's" chicken.

"Comiste gallo?" ("Did you eat a rooster?") is the border equivalent of asking someone if he got up on the wrong side of the bed.

Serves 6

1 cup Crema (page 63) or crème fraîche
1 cup chicken stock
1/2 cup whole milk
1/4 cup slivered almonds, toasted
3 dried mild red chiles, preferably ancho or pasilla, stemmed and
   seeded
1 garlic clove, sliced
Salt to taste
6 chicken leg-thigh sections, skinned
2 tablespoons vegetable oil, preferably peanut
Toasted sesame seeds, for garnish

In a saucepan, combine 3/4 cup of the crema with the stock, milk, almonds, 2 of the anchos, and garlic and bring the mixture just to a boil over medium heat. Let it sit for 5 minutes for the anchos to soften more. Transfer the mixture to a blender and purée. Add salt to the sauce to taste.

Salt the chicken lightly. Warm the oil in a large, heavy skillet over medium heat. Add the chicken and brown it on both sides. It may be easier to brown the chicken in batches, but return all the pieces to the skillet before proceeding. A snug fit is desirable.

Pour the sauce over the chicken, cover, reduce the heat to low, and simmer until the chicken is cooked through and tender, about 12 to 14 minutes. Stir up from the bottom at least once to make sure the sauce isn't sticking.

While the chicken cooks, cut the remaining chile into slivers with scissors.

Transfer the chicken to a serving plate. Top with dollops of the remaining crema, and scatter the chile slivers and sesame seeds over the dish. Serve hot.

YUMA SMOKED CHICKEN

The borderlands penchant for outdoor cooking surfaces in this dish, based on one that Emajean Jordan Buechner suggested in her *Mexican Cooking (Authentic Sonoran Style)* (Thunderbird Press, 1982). The chicken can be prepared in a dedicated smoker or using an indirect cooking method with a covered grill. The instructions assume you are using a water smoker, the most common kind of smoker, but the results will be similar on other equipment if you follow the manufacturer's guidelines.

Serves 3 to 4

MARINADE
1/2 cup olive oil
1/2 cup dry sherry
3 tablespoons sherry vinegar
3 garlic cloves, minced
2 teaspoons Worcestershire sauce, preferably white wine style
1 teaspoon sugar
1 teaspoon dried oregano, preferably Mexican
1 chile de árbol or cayenne, crushed
1/2 teaspoon salt, or more to taste

8 bone-in, skin-on chicken thighs

Mesquite chips or beans

The night before you plan to cook the chicken, combine the marinade ingredients in a small bowl. Loosen the skin on the thighs with your fingers, then place the chicken in a plastic bag. Pour the marinade over the chicken, rub some of the liquid under the skin, and refrigerate overnight. Drain the chicken, reserving the marinade.

At least 30 minutes before you plan to begin cooking, put a large handful of mesquite chips or beans in water to soak. Prepare your smoker for barbecuing, following the manufacturer's instructions. When the smoker is ready, spread the mesquite on the fire and pour the remaining marinade into the water pan, adding water to fill it.

Transfer the chicken to the smoker and cook it about 1 $^{1}/_{4}$ to 1 $^{1}/_{2}$ hours. To test for doneness, insert a skewer in one of the thighs to see if the juices run clear. Serve the chicken immediately.

TOPOPO CHICKEN SALAD

Many of today's mostly forgettable taco salads had their genesis in a Monica Flin creation for El Charro Cafe in Tucson. According to Carlotta Dunn Flores, Monica's niece, the cook came back from a visit to Mexico inspired by a volcano to create a salad in this style. The lively concoction gives real meaning to the expression "a mountain of food."

Serves 6

DRESSING
2/3 cup vegetable oil
1/3 cup vinegar, preferably white wine
2 tablespoons Salsa del Norte (page 38) or other salsa
1/4 teaspoon salt

Vegetable oil for pan-frying
6 corn tortillas
1 cup Refried Beans (page 378) or other well-seasoned cooked,
     mashed pinto beans
Crisp interior leaves of 3 small heads of romaine, shredded
2 carrots, grated
6 chicken breasts, poached or baked, skins removed, and sliced thin
6 ounces pepper jack or Monterey jack cheese, sliced thin
2 medium avocados, sliced thin
4 ounces mild cheddar cheese, grated
1/2 cup pickled jalapeño slices

The legendary founder of Tucson's El Charro Cafe, Monica Flin died in 1975 after a long and colorful life that revolved around food. In addition to creating the topopo salad, she probably conceived the chimichanga and the cheese crisp, or at least was among the first to promote them.

She opened her restaurant in 1922 with little more than ambition. When the first customers arrived, Monica ducked out the back door to a nearby Chinese grocer and sweet-talked him into giving her the food she needed to prepare a meal. When she started making profits later, she thought the taxes on her hard work unfair and wrote out her I.R.S.

checks to Los Ladrones—the thieves.

Monica presided over the restaurant's La Mesa Redonda, The Round Table, an institution as spirited as the one of the same name and era at New York's Algonquin Hotel. Lacking a liquor license, she served her group martinis disguised as tea, with olives floating on top of the alcohol in dainty cups. Today, Carlotta Dunn Flores and her husband, Ray, run the restaurant in a similar spunky way out of the old family home, still filled with Monica's mementos, curios, and photos.

1/4 cup sliced green olives
1/4 cup sliced black olives, preferably brine-packed
6 cherry tomatoes

In a lidded jar, combine the dressing ingredients and refrigerate. The dressing can be prepared a day ahead.

Warm $1/2$ inch of oil in a skillet over high heat. When the oil ripples, fry each of the tortillas until crisp but not brown. Drain.

Spread the tortillas with refried beans and place each on an individual plate.

In a bowl, toss together the lettuce and carrots with enough dressing to coat. Arrange equal portions of lettuce on each plate in a mountain-like mound. (At El Charro, the lettuce is actually packed into a giant funnel and unmolded to get the distinctive shape.) Arrange the chicken, jack cheese, and avocado slices decoratively around the lettuce mounds. Scatter the cheddar cheese, jalapeños, and olives over the salads and top each with a cherry tomato. Serve the salads immediately, accompanied with the remaining dressing.

Regional Variations: Chicken salads go back on the border to at least the turn of the century, when an El Paso cookbook included a recipe with cubed potatoes, onions, and sliced green olives. Mark Preston, in his tribute to *California Mission Cookery* (Border Books, 1994), presents a version that may have even older roots, studded with black olives and mild green chiles, and flavored with oregano and a mustard-and-wine-vinegar dressing. On the other end of the time scale and the region, Texas chef Stephan Pyles features an exquisite contemporary chicken salad in *The New Texas Cuisine* (Doubleday, 1993), combining tastes of cilantro pesto, mayonnaise, lime juice, tri-colored bell peppers, and Granny Smith apple chunks.

CHICKEN SALPICÓN

A *salpicón* makes a tasty medley out of a hodgepodge of ingredients, as in this San Antonio salad.

Serves 8

6 bone-in, skin-on chicken breasts

3 cups chicken stock

1 cup canned crushed tomatoes

2 dried mild red chiles, preferably ancho or New Mexican, stemmed
    and seeded

1/2 medium onion, chopped

2 garlic cloves, sliced

1 bay leaf

3 tablespoons extra-virgin olive oil

1 tablespoon vinegar, preferably cider

15 1/2-ounce can garbanzo beans, rinsed and drained

6 ounces Monterey jack cheese, diced

1/2 cup chopped roasted mild green chile, preferably New Mexican or
    Anaheim, fresh or frozen

1/2 yellow, orange, or red bell pepper, diced

2 small tomatoes, preferably Roma or Italian plum, diced

2 Haas avocados, cubed

1/4 cup minced fresh cilantro

Lettuce leaves, for garnish

In a Dutch oven or large saucepan, combine the chicken, stock, tomatoes, chiles, onion, garlic, and bay leaf. Bring the mixture to a boil, reduce the heat to a low simmer, and cover. Poach the chicken in the liquid for about 20 to 25 minutes, until cooked through. Remove the chicken with a slotted spoon and set it aside until cool enough to handle. Discard the bay leaf.

Transfer the cooking liquid to a blender in two batches and purée. Return the liquid to the pan and simmer over medium heat for 35 to 45 minutes, until reduced to about 1 $^{1}/_{2}$ cups. Add the oil and vinegar to the reduced sauce to make a dressing.

Shred or cube the chicken and place it in a nonreactive bowl or dish. Pour about two-thirds of the dressing over the chicken and refrigerate it for at least 2 hours or up to overnight. Drain the chicken of any remaining dressing, if you wish. Mix the chicken with the garbanzos.

Assemble the salad on a decorative platter, layering the chicken mixture first. Scatter the remaining ingredients over the salad attractively and if you wish, drizzle some of the remaining dressing on the top. Tuck lettuce leaves around the platter and serve. If you would prefer to use the *salpicón* as a party appetizer, serve it with tostada chips.

CHICKEN ENCHILADAS VERDE

Probably the most popular poultry dish on both sides of the border, green chicken enchiladas show how simple regional preparations can also be stout, spirited, and satisfying. The chicken is a basic *deshebrada*, just stewed and shredded. This version of the enchiladas comes from Mexico, but instead of the customary whole chicken we use only the breast.

Serves 4

CHICKEN *DESHEBRADA*
4 bone-in, skin-on chicken breasts
3 cups chicken stock
1/2 onion, chopped
3 garlic cloves, minced
1 teaspoon dried marjoram or oregano, preferably Mexican
1/2 teaspoon salt
2 bay leaves

2 to 2 1/2 cups Tubac Chile Verde (tomatillo version, page 55)
1 cup Crema (page 63) or crème fraîche
Vegetable oil for pan-frying
12 corn tortillas
1/2 cup minced onion
8 ounces Monterey jack, asadero, or cheddar cheese, grated

In a large saucepan, bring the chicken and other *deshebrada* ingredients to a boil. Reduce the heat to a low simmer and cook the chicken until cooked through and very tender, 25 to 30 minutes. Let the chicken cool for a few minutes in the liquid. Remove the breasts to a plate and let them sit for a few more minutes, until cool enough to handle. Shred the chicken into bite-size pieces. Save the cooking liquid for soups or sauces. (The chicken can be prepared ahead to this point and refrigerated for 1 or 2 days, or frozen for several months.)

Preheat the oven to 350° F. Grease a large baking dish.

In a shallow bowl or dish, combine the sauce with the crema.

Spread about $1/2$ cup of the sauce mixture thinly in the baking dish.

Heat $1/2$ to 1 inch of oil in a small skillet until the oil ripples. With tongs, dunk a tortilla in the oil long enough for it to go limp, a matter of seconds. Don't let the tortilla turn crisp. Repeat with the remaining tortillas and drain them.

Dip a tortilla into the sauce. Top it with about $1/3$ cup of chicken, a couple of teaspoons of onion, and about a tablespoon of cheese. Roll up the tortilla snug but not tight. Transfer the enchilada to the baking dish. Repeat with the rest of the tortillas and filling. Top the enchiladas with any remaining onion and pour the sauce evenly over them. Scatter the rest of the cheese over the sauce.

Bake the enchiladas for 15 to 18 minutes, until they are heated through and the sauce is bubbly. With a spatula, serve the enchiladas immediately.

Regional Variations: In Mexico, these are enchiladas *suisas*, or Swiss, because they call for crema. Central Texans might substitute sour cream instead. Farther west in El Paso and north into New Mexico, both would be nixed in favor of Monterey jack or cheddar cheese, the enchiladas might be flat rather than rolled, and the area's green chiles would flavor the sauce, rather than share the billing with tomatillos. Out in California, their former home, *Bon Appétit* columnists Jinx and Jefferson Morgan made a version with jalapeños, sour cream, and spinach, a rendition so beloved that they proposed it as a substitute for turkey at Thanksgiving.

One of the best restaurants anywhere for home-style northern Mexico cooking is in Albuquerque, New Mexico. Originally from Chihuahua, the Nuñez family run El Norteño with cheer and talent, offering an extensive menu that ranges from a dozen varieties of soft tacos to full cabrito dinners.

These deep-fried "flutes" of tender chicken use the same *deshebrada* as the previous enchiladas to a very different end.

Serves 6

3 tablespoons cream or half-and-half
1 garlic clove, minced
Chicken *Deshebrada*, warmed (see page 283)
2 tablespoons minced fresh cilantro

Vegetable oil for deep-frying
18 thin corn tortillas

Guacamole (page 123)
Crema (page 63), crème fraîche, or sour cream
Serrano Salsa Verde (page 43) or other salsa

Warm the cream with the garlic in a saucepan over medium heat. Add the chicken *deshebrada* and simmer until the cream is absorbed. Stir in the cilantro.

Pour 1 1/2 inches of oil into a deep skillet or heavy saucepan. Heat the oil until it ripples. With tongs, dunk a tortilla into the hot oil long enough for it to go limp, a matter of seconds. Don't let the tortilla turn crisp. Repeat with the remaining tortillas and drain them.

Spoon 1 1/2 to 2 tablespoons of filling on a tortilla and roll up tight. Secure the flauta with a toothpick. Repeat with the remaining filling and tortillas.

Reheat the oil to 375° F. Add several flautas to the oil and fry for about 2 minutes, turning as needed to cook evenly golden brown and crisp. Repeat with the remaining flautas. Remove the toothpicks and serve immediately. Accompany with guacamole and crema. Serve salsa over the flautas, or on the side.

Regional Variations: Similar fried foods are sometimes called taquitos, particularly south of the border. Persnickety people may distinguish between the two by size and toppings, with taquitos being tightly rolled, unadorned finger food and flautas being plumper plate fare served with a salsa or, sometimes in Texas, with chile con queso. Alex Diaz in Santa Barbara blows all the logic, making fat "taquitos" loaded with chunks of chicken and shreds of Monterey jack cheese, topped with a sturdy salad of iceberg lettuce, green onions, tomatoes, mild salsa, and more Monterey jack.

TACOS WITH CITRUS CHICKEN ASADA

The Yucatán method of marinating chicken in a citrus-and-achiote-flavored liquid has gained favor fast along the border in recent years. The technique pairs well with grilling, as in these tacos.

Serves 6

8 boneless, skinless chicken breasts, each pounded to 1/2-inch thickness and halved

MARINADE
1/2 cup orange juice
1/2 cup vinegar, preferably white
1/4 cup extra-virgin olive oil
1/2 small onion, chopped
4 garlic cloves, minced
1 1/2 tablespoons achiote paste (see "Technique Tip")
2 teaspoons dried oregano, preferably Mexican
1 teaspoon salt
1/2 teaspoon ground allspice
1/2 teaspoon crushed dried rosemary
1/2 teaspoon fresh-ground black pepper
1 bay leaf

Mesquite chips or beans
Vegetable oil for frying
18 corn tortillas
Pickled Onions (page 64), chilled

Shredded lettuce, minced fresh cilantro, julienned jícama, and
   crumbled queso añejo or Cotija cheese, or grated Monterey jack
   or asadero cheese, for garnish
Crema (page 63) or crème fraîche (optional)

At least several hours before you plan to grill the chicken, place it in a shallow, nonreactive dish. In a bowl, combine the marinade ingredients and pour the mixture over the chicken. Refrigerate, covered, for several hours or up to overnight.

About 30 minutes before grilling, take the chicken from the refrigerator and let it sit in the marinade at room temperature.

On an outdoor grill, fire up enough charcoal to form a single layer of coals beneath the chicken. At the same time, put a few handfuls of mesquite chips or beans in water to soak.

When the charcoal is covered in gray ash, scatter the wood chips or beans over it. Drain the chicken and place it directly over the fire. Grill the chicken, partially covered with the grill's lid (damper open), to trap some of the mesquite smoke. Cook the chicken 5 to 6 minutes per side, or until the meat is firm and the juices run clear.

Let the chicken sit at room temperature until just cool enough to handle. Shred the chicken into bite-size pieces, tent it with foil, and keep it warm. (The chicken can be made ahead and refrigerated for a day. Rewarm the chicken before proceeding.)

Heat 1 inch of oil in a skillet until the oil ripples. With tongs, dunk a tortilla quickly in the oil long enough for it to go limp, a matter of seconds. Don't let the tortilla turn crisp. Repeat with the remaining tortillas and drain them.

Fill each softened tortilla with about 3 tablespoons of chicken and fold in half. Transfer to a heat-proof tray or baking sheet. When all the tacos are filled, crisp them under the broiler for just 1 or 2 minutes, so that the texture becomes nicely chewy. Top with chilled pickled onions.

Serve immediately with lettuce, cilantro, jícama, and cheese, accompanied with crema if you wish.

Technique Tip: Achiote paste is a blend of annatto seeds (used to color butter and cheese) with garlic and spices. It's essential to Yucatecan cooking, an inspiration we borrow here. Inexpensive, the rusty red paste can be found in a growing number of gourmet food stores and in Hispanic and Latino markets. The brands that currently have greatest U.S. distribution are El Yucateco and La Perla from Mexico.

Regional Variations: The most common filling for a chicken taco is stewed *deshebrada* or just leftovers from another meal. In Tesuque, New Mexico, Gayther and Susie Gonzales, who do a lot of smoking, like to put extra chicken or turkey into their pit to create deliberate leftovers just for tortilla dishes. The smoked poultry works great, mixed in a taco perhaps with a little sliced green onion, minced jalapeños, and a scattering of cilantro for color and complementary spice.

TAMALES CON PAVO O POLLO

These savory turkey or chicken tamales, which evolved from a combination of California recipes, are studded with raisins and olives and encased in a buttery masa dough.

Makes 24 large tamales, about 12 main-dish servings

FILLING
3 1/2 cups shredded smoked or baked turkey or chicken
6 garlic cloves, roasted and minced
1 cup turkey or chicken stock
3/4 cup canned crushed tomatoes
1/4 to 1/2 cup chopped roasted mild green chile, preferably New
    Mexican or Anaheim, fresh or frozen
1/3 cup raisins
2 tablespoons vinegar, preferably sherry
1 tablespoon dried oregano, preferably Mexican
1/2 teaspoon cumin seeds, toasted and ground
Salt to taste (optional)
1/3 cup sliced green or black olives

6-ounce package dried corn husks

DOUGH

1 cup butter, at room temperature

6 ounces Monterey jack cheese, grated

6 tablespoons lard or vegetable shortening

1 teaspoon salt

3 cups masa harina

2 1/4 cups warm turkey or chicken stock, or more as needed

Californio Colorado (page 53) or other mild red chile sauce (optional)

In a large, heavy skillet, combine the filling ingredients, except the olives, and bring just to a boil over medium-high heat. Reduce the heat to a low simmer and continue cooking for 20 minutes, or until the mixture is very thick but not dry. Stir frequently toward the end of the cooking time. Mix in the olives and reserve the filling. (The filling can be made ahead and refrigerated for 1 or 2 days. It can be used without rewarming.)

In a deep bowl or baking pan, soak the corn husks in hot water to cover. After 30 minutes the husks should be softened and pliable. Separate the husks and, if needed, rinse them under running water to wash away any grit or brown silks. Keep them covered with water until you are ready to use each one.

To prepare the dough, beat the butter, cheese, and lard in a large bowl with an electric mixer until the mixture is light and fluffy. Mix in the salt, half of the masa harina, and half of the stock. If your mixer is powerful, continue using it to blend the dough. If not, switch to a sturdy spoon or your hands to avoid burning out the mixer's motor. Add the remaining masa and stock and keep mixing until smooth. When well blended, the masa should have the consistency of thick cake batter. Add more stock if needed for the preferred consistency. Keep the dough loosely covered while working.

To assemble the tamales, use approximately equal amounts of masa and filling. To make 2 dozen 4-ounce tamales, use 2 tablespoons of masa and 2 tablespoons of filling for each tamale.

Hold a corn husk flat on one hand, smooth side up. (You may, depending on the size of the corn husks, need to overlap two husks to form one tamale. Spread the dough over the husks together, just as if they were one.) With a rubber spatula, spread a thin layer of masa across the husk, but not to the edges. Top with filling spread more thickly through the dough's center, stopping short of the dough's edges. Make sure that the dough's edges meet to enclose all of the filling. Secure the tamale by folding the wrapper over or tying it. Repeat the procedure until all the filling and masa are used.

Place the tamales in a steamer, packing loosely in crisscross directions, or stand them on end. Allow enough space between them for the steam to rise effectively. Cover the pot and cook over simmering water for about 1 to 1 1/4 hours, until the masa is firm and no longer sticks to the corn husk. Unwrap one tamale to check its consistency. If it is still doughy, rewrap it, return it to the pot, and continue steaming for a few more minutes.

Tamales should be eaten warm. When tamales are served unadorned, the husks are usually left on, to be removed by each guest before eating. If serving the tamales with sauce, remove the husks first and serve the tamales with the sauce spooned over them.

ROAST TURKEY AND CORN BREADS DRESSING

Serves 8

6 tablespoons butter, at room temperature
1 tablespoon ground dried mild red chile, preferably ancho or New
    Mexican
3 garlic cloves, minced
1/2 teaspoon salt
1/2 teaspoon dried sage
12-pound to 13-pound turkey, fresh or frozen
1 1/2 cups turkey or chicken stock

DRESSING

1/4 cup butter

1/2 medium onion, chopped

2 stalks celery, chopped

1/2 red bell pepper, diced

1/2 cup chopped roasted mild green chile, preferably New Mexican or
    Anaheim, fresh or frozen

3 garlic cloves, minced

1 teaspoon dried sage

1 teaspoon dried thyme

1/2 teaspoon salt, or more to taste

4 cups dried cornbread crumbs

8 corn tortillas, sliced very thin and toasted until crisp

2 eggs, beaten

1 3/4 cups turkey or chicken stock, or more as needed

The night before you plan to cook the turkey, start preparations. In a small bowl, combine the butter with the chile, garlic, salt, and sage until smooth. Loosen the turkey's skin with your fingers, being careful not to tear it. Rub the turkey inside and out with the butter, especially under the breast skin. Place the bird in a large plastic bag and refrigerate overnight. Remove the turkey from the refrigerator about 1 hour before you plan to begin cooking it.

Preheat the oven to 400° F. Grease the rack of a roasting pan.

Transfer the turkey, breast side down, to the roasting pan. Roast in this position for 1 hour to naturally baste the bird, reducing the oven temperature to 325° F after the first 20 minutes. Using sturdy, long-handled spoons, turn the turkey breast side up. Again, try to avoid tearing the skin or piercing the flesh. Baste the bird with some of the stock and accumulated pan juices. Allow a total baking time of about 17 to 18 minutes per pound, until the internal temperature reaches 175° F to 180° F. Continue basting every 20 to 30 minutes or so during the remaining baking time. The breast can be covered with foil toward the end of the cooking time if it appears to be browning too quickly, but keep basting.

While the turkey bakes, prepare the dressing. Butter a shallow baking dish. In a skillet, melt the butter over medium heat. Add the onion, celery, bell pepper, green chile, garlic, sage, thyme, and salt. Sauté for about 5 minutes until the vegetables are softened. Transfer the mixture to a large bowl. Stir in the breadcrumbs and tortilla strips, followed by the eggs. Add enough stock to make the mixture moist but not soupy. Cover the dressing and place it in the oven about 30 minutes before you expect the turkey to be done.

Take the turkey from the oven when done. Uncover the dressing and bake it an additional 10 to 15 minutes. Transfer the turkey to a platter, tent it with foil, and let it sit for about 20 minutes before carving.

Add all remaining stock to the turkey drippings. Scrape up any browned bits from the bottom of the roasting pan, degrease the liquid, and pour it into a small saucepan. Bring the liquid to a boil and reduce as needed to make a thin sauce that can be spooned over the bird like gravy. Add salt and pepper to taste.

Slice the turkey thin and serve it on a platter with the sauce, accompanied with the dressing.

Regional Variations: Border cooks stuff their turkeys with enthusiasm and a wide range of interesting mixtures. Tamales appear in dressings frequently, both savory and sweet varieties. In Texas, cornbread may be mixed with fruit and spices, while in California, the bread might be sourdough, enriched with ground beef, garlic, and red wine. We've found ground pork with apples in New Mexico, and giblets with black olives, red chile, and raisins in Arizona. A particularly elaborate version features crystallized fruit, walnuts, green chiles, stuffed green olives, breadcrumbs, and a pantry's worth of spices.

In April 1598, when the fabled Pilgrim fathers and mothers were boys and girls in England, a party under Don Juan de Oñate made its way through barren north Chihuahua to the banks of the Rio Grande at El Paso del Norte. Grateful for surviving the trek and finding the pass, the soldiers and priests staged a fiesta and invited the local Native people. According to many Texans, including former governor Ann Richards, that was the original American Thanksgiving. The present residents of El Paso commemorate the event annually at the city's Chamizal National Monument, celebrating an April Thanksgiving.

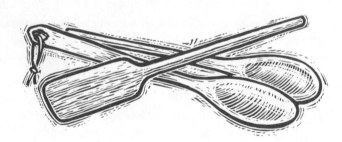

Serves 4

1/2 cup pepitas (shelled pumpkin seeds)
1 whole fresh serrano or jalapeño
3 garlic cloves, unpeeled
1/4 cup mayonnaise
1/4 cup sour cream
2 tablespoons fresh lime juice, or more to taste
Salt to taste
4 cups shredded smoked or baked turkey
1 cup jícama, cut into matchsticks
3 to 4 tablespoons minced fresh cilantro

Lettuce leaves or shredded lettuce, preferably red, for garnish

In a skillet over medium heat, toast the pepitas until they begin to snap and crackle. Spoon the pepitas into a large bowl.

Place the chile and garlic in the hot skillet and raise the heat to high to blacken and blister both. Halve and seed the chile and peel the garlic.

Transfer the chile and garlic to a blender or food processor and add the mayonnaise, sour cream, lime juice, and salt.

Add the turkey and jícama to the pepitas and spoon the dressing over. Mix well. Refrigerate the salad for at least 30 minutes. Stir in the cilantro shortly before serving. Arrange the salad on lettuce and serve chilled.

In an oft-told tale, a Dominican nun in Puebla created *mole poblano* in the 1680s as a special dinner for the viceroy of New Spain. When her bishop asked Sister Andrea de la Asunción to concoct the best dish possible for the occasion, she combined one hundred Native and Spanish ingredients into a startling dark mixture that became Mexico's most distinctive and renowned culinary contribution. As Paco Ignacio Taibo has pointed out, the Mother Superior must have been shocked, seeing before her in the kitchen a final, total break from Old World tastes. Today, there are numerous *moles* in southern Mexico, but it's mainly the original one that migrated north. On the way to the border, it lost some of the complexity and became primarily an enchilada dish. Most versions use leftover chicken, but we prefer turkey. Substitute equal amounts of chicken if you wish.

Serves 6 (plus enough sauce for another batch of enchiladas)

MOLE SAUCE

12 ounces whole dried red chiles, preferably a
    mix of anchos and pasillas

1 to 2 chiles de árbol or dried chipotles

Water

6 tablespoons sesame seeds

1 teaspoon anise seeds

1/2 teaspoon cumin seeds

4 tablespoons peanut oil or lard

3/4 cup chopped pecans or walnuts

6 garlic cloves, unpeeled

6 whole small tomatoes, preferably Roma or Italian plum, unpeeled

4 cups chicken stock

1 medium onion, chopped

1 day-old corn tortilla, torn into quarters

2 ounces unsweetened chocolate

1 1/2 ounces Mexican chocolate, such as Ibarra or Mayordomo (or
    substitute an equal amount of bittersweet chocolate with a pinch
    of cinnamon)

1 teaspoon ground canela or other cinnamon
1/2 teaspoon salt
6 whole cloves

3 cups shredded smoked or baked turkey

Vegetable oil for pan-frying
18 corn tortillas
3/4 cup minced onion
3 ounces crumbled queso fresco or grated asadero or Monterey jack
  cheese

Crema (page 63) or crème fraîche
Minced fresh cilantro and toasted sesame seeds, for garnish

Break the stems off the chiles and remove the seeds. Rinse the chiles. Toast the chiles until fragrant in a large, heavy skillet, turning them frequently. Transfer the chiles to a large saucepan and cover with water. Simmer over medium heat for about 30 minutes until softened.

While the chiles simmer, toast and roast the other ingredients. Toast the sesame seeds over medium heat in the skillet. Watch them carefully as they begin to release their fragrance, browning lightly and dancing in the pan. Don't let them burn. Spoon the seeds into a blender. Toast the anise and cumin seeds in the skillet until fragrant and add them to the blender. Pour 1 tablespoon of the oil into the warm skillet and stir in the nuts. Sauté until lightly colored and fragrant. Transfer the nuts to the blender.

Wipe out the skillet and increase the heat to medium-high. Scatter the garlic cloves in the skillet, turning the cloves occasionally so that they soften and darken on all sides, which takes a few minutes. Remove the garlic from the skillet and set it aside until cool enough to handle. Add the tomatoes to the skillet, turning occasionally as they soften and darken. The skins will split a bit during the process. Remove the tomatoes and set them aside until cool enough to handle. Remove the skins from the garlic and tomatoes and add both to the blender.

Pour about 1 cup of the stock into the blender. Purée the mixture for

2 minutes. The sauce will become smooth but a little grainy. Pour the sauce into a large bowl.

Drain the chiles lightly from their cooking liquid, reserving 1 cup of the liquid. Place the chiles and about $^{1}/2$ cup of the reserved liquid in the blender and purée. Pour the chiles into the bowl with the tomato sauce.

Add 1 more cup of stock to the blender with the remaining sauce ingredients and purée for 2 minutes. This mixture too will become smooth but a little grainy. Pour it into the bowl and stir together.

Wipe out any tomato residue from the skillet and add the remaining oil. Warm the oil over medium heat. Spoon in the sauce and fry it for about 10 minutes, stirring up from the bottom constantly. Mix in the remaining stock and reserved chile cooking liquid, reduce the heat to low, and simmer for 30 minutes. (The sauce can be made ahead and refrigerated for 1 or 2 days, or frozen for several months. Rewarm the sauce before proceeding.) Reserve half of the sauce for another batch of enchiladas or other use.

Add the turkey to the remaining sauce and simmer together for 15 minutes.

Heat 1 inch of oil in a small skillet until the oil ripples. With tongs, dunk a tortilla in the oil long enough for it to go limp, a matter of seconds. Don't let the tortilla turn crisp. Repeat with the remaining tortillas and drain them.

Heat the oven to 350° F. Grease a 9-by-13-inch baking dish.

Dip a tortilla into the sauce. Top it with about $^{1}/3$ cup of turkey drained from the sauce with a slotted spoon, and a couple of teaspoons each of onion and cheese. Roll up the tortilla snug but not tight. Transfer the enchilada to the baking dish. Repeat with the rest of the tortillas and filling. Top the enchiladas with any remaining onion and pour the remaining sauce evenly over them. Scatter the rest of the cheese over the sauce.

Bake for 15 to 18 minutes, until the enchiladas are heated through and the sauce is bubbly. Serve immediately, with spoonfuls of crema drizzled over and a scattering of cilantro and sesame seeds.

Most border *moles* may be less complex than those to the south, but that's not always the case. In a version at La Serenata de Garibaldi restaurant in Los Angeles, the kitchen takes three hours to toast, roast, and otherwise prepare thirty-one ingredients, and another four hours to cook the *mole*. If you find the process daunting, Don Alfonso Foods in Austin sells a good commercial paste (see "Mail-Order Sources"), ground with a *molino*, or mill, from Monterrey.

Baja's San Telmo Valley, southeast of Ensenada, claims the world's greatest concentration of quail. Coveys of three to five hundred birds are common, and some range up to a thousand. During the season, from mid-October to January, Americans stream across the border to nearby hunting camps, which make all the necessary arrangements for permits, guides, and outfitting.

The premier game bird of the borderlands, quail now show up frequently in supermarkets. The recipe works for broiling as well as grilling.

Serves 4

8 whole quail, about 6 to 7 ounces each

MARINADE
Juice of 2 oranges
1/4 cup vinegar, preferably red wine
1/4 cup extra-virgin olive oil
1 tablespoon molasses or dark brown sugar
2 garlic cloves, minced
1/2 teaspoon ground coriander
Dash of hot sauce

8 bacon slices
1 large onion, sliced thick

Corn tortillas, warmed
Pico de Gallo (page 40) and Serrano Salsa Verde (page 43) or sliced
  avocados

Place the quail in a shallow, nonreactive dish or large, zipper-lock bag. Combine the marinade ingredients in a small bowl and pour the mixture over the quail. Marinate the quail, refrigerated, for at least 4 hours and up to 12 hours, turning them occasionally.

About 30 minutes before cooking, take the quail from the refrigerator and drain. Reserve the marinade, pour it into a small saucepan, and boil it vigorously for several minutes over high heat. Keep the liquid warm.

Wrap each quail with a strip of bacon, making sure it covers the breast, and secure the bacon with a toothpick.

On an outdoor grill, fire up enough charcoal to form a single layer beneath the quail. When the coals are covered with gray ash, spread them in a single layer.

Place the quail directly over the fire and the onion slices a little to the side, and grill for about 12 to 14 minutes total, turning the quail frequently and basting them and the onions with the reserved marinade. Be careful of flare-ups as you baste the birds, either dousing any flames or moving the quail to another area of the grill. As you check the meat for doneness, remember that quail will look a little pinker than chicken, so don't overcook them.

Transfer the quail and onions to a platter and serve hot, with or without the bacon, as you wish. Encourage diners to use their fingers in eating the tiny birds, picking off the meat and wrapping it in the tortillas, garnished with the salsas or avocado slices, or both.

All along the Rio Grande from Chihuahua to Tamaulipas, game dinners featuring quail are a fixture on border-town restaurant menus. The small birds often come prepared in this fashion, fried and bathed in brick-colored chile gravy.

Serves 4

8 quail, whole or split, about 6 to 7 ounces each
3 cups milk
2 garlic cloves, minced
1 cup all-purpose flour
2 teaspoons ground dried mild red chile, preferably ancho or New Mexican
1/2 teaspoon cumin seeds, toasted and ground
1/2 teaspoon salt
1/4 teaspoon fresh-ground black pepper
1/8 teaspoon ground canela or other cinnamon
Vegetable oil for pan-frying
1 cup sliced mushrooms, preferably wild varieties
3 cups chicken stock

Arrange the quail in a single layer in a shallow dish. Pour the milk over, add the garlic, and soak the birds for at least 1 hour, but preferably two or three times as long. Blot the quail lightly with paper towels to eliminate some of the surface moisture. Discard the milk.

Combine the flour with the chile, cumin, salt, pepper, and canela in a shallow dish. Reserve 4 tablespoons of the flour mixture. Dredge the quail in the seasoned flour.

Add enough oil to a cast-iron skillet to measure 1 inch and heat the oil to 350° F. Cook the quail for 3 minutes on each side until golden and crispy outside and juicy when you crack open the crust. Transfer the quail to a serving platter, tent with foil, and keep warm.

Pour off all but $^1/_4$ cup of the oil through a strainer and discard it. Return any cracklings from the strainer to the skillet. Warm the drippings over medium heat and add the mushrooms. Sauté until the mushrooms become soft. Add the reserved seasoned flour, stirring well to avoid lumps. Pour in the stock and simmer, stirring often, until the liquid has thickened into a rich brown gravy, about 3 minutes. Taste and adjust the seasoning.

Pour the gravy over or around the quail. Serve hot.

Technique Tip: Quail are often cooked whole because deboning the tiny birds is a time-consuming nuisance. Commercially marketed quail may be partially deboned, or even cut into drumsticks and boneless breasts, but that won't affect the preparation method.

Doves are seldom available commercially, but they are a favorite game bird in many border areas. This preparation combines elements from Texas and California recipes.

Serves 4

12 whole doves, dressed
Salt to taste
Fresh-ground black pepper
2 tablespoons bacon drippings or extra-virgin olive oil
1 medium onion, chopped
2 garlic cloves, minced
1 teaspoon dried oregano, preferably Mexican
1/2 teaspoon dried thyme
1 crushed chile de árbol or cayenne or 2 crushed chiltepíns
1 cup red wine
1 cup chicken stock
1/4 cup sherry

Fresh thyme sprigs, for garnish (optional)

Rub the doves with salt and pepper. Warm the bacon drippings in a large skillet over medium heat. Brown the doves well, turning once. Transfer the doves to a plate.

To the hot fat, add the onion, garlic, oregano, thyme, and chile and sauté until the onion is softened. Return the doves to the skillet and add the wine, stock, and sherry. Bring the liquid to a boil, reduce the heat to a low simmer, cover, and cook for 30 minutes.

Transfer the doves to a platter. Reduce the sauce for a few minutes if it seems thin, and pour a little of the sauce over the birds. Garnish, if you wish, with the thyme and serve.

Technique Tip: If you don't have a hunter friend to supply you with doves, Cornish game hens can substitute. Use one hen per serving rather than a trio of dove and add about 10 minutes to the baking time.

FISH AND SEAFOOD

Most people don't think of fish and seafood in connection with the border. When you trace the long boundary line between Mexico and the United States on a map, you scan a lot of desert and scrubland, even along the Rio Grande. The Native Americans in the heart of the area seldom ate fish, and even early Spaniards who had braved the Atlantic Ocean didn't show much interest in seafood.

The appeal grew gradually but inevitably, because as that map indicates, the region is actually surrounded by water. From the Gulf of Mexico on the eastern edge to the Sea of Cortés and the Pacific Ocean out west, the borderlands abound with opportunities to enjoy fresh fish and seafood. One authority estimates that the coasts of Baja California alone offer eight hundred different possibilities. With that kind of natural abundance, it's only natural that cooks developed many tasty ways to prepare the catch of the day.

PUERTO NUEVO LOBSTER

On the Pacific coast of Baja California, no seafood rivals the spiny lobsters of Puerto Nuevo in fame. Different from the large-clawed Maine crustacean, and less expensive, the Baja variety often comes packaged as frozen rock lobster tails. Many cooks in the tiny fishing village prepare the local specialty plain, sometimes just fried, but we side with those who think that it needs a little extra help from the kitchen, and grilling or broiling, to reach its full potential.

Serves 4

Two 1-pound spiny rock lobster tails, fresh or frozen
Vegetable oil
5 tablespoons butter
Juice of 2 limes
Juice of 1 orange
2 garlic cloves, minced
1 teaspoon dried oregano, preferably Mexican
Pinch of salt

Lime and orange wedges and avocado slices, for garnish
Pico de Gallo (page 40) or other salsa

Split the lobster tails in half vertically with a cleaver or other heavy knife. Be careful of your fingers because the shells tend to be slick. Oil the shell and meat of each tail section well.

In a small saucepan, melt the butter and add the fruit juices, garlic, oregano, and salt. Keep warm.

On an outdoor grill, fire up enough charcoal to make a single layer beneath the shellfish. When the coals are covered in gray ash, place the lobsters directly over the fire, cut side down. Grill the lobsters for 3 minutes, then turn them shell side down. Baste the meat of each lobster thickly with the butter mixture and grill 8 to 9 more minutes, or until cooked through.

Transfer the lobsters to a serving platter, shell side down, and spoon additional butter over them. Garnish festively with limes, oranges, and avocado slices and serve immediately with pico de gallo. In Puerto Nuevo,

The fishing village of Puerto Nuevo, a few square blocks big, looks like one giant restaurant. Every building seems to house a café and all of them specialize in the local lobster, which gives some indication of how tasty it can be. On our first visit, a friend had told us to seek out the Ortega family restaurant for a fine meal. We spotted an Ortega's sign right off, but before we could park we came across four others, all labeled by number. The extended clan is pulling in the lobsters and the diners both. If you find yourself in a similar predicament, try number two, or for a truly baroque lobster experience, go to the nearby Rosarito Beach Hotel, the aging grande dame of Baja resorts.

lobster is always accompanied with beans, either Refried Beans or Frijoles de Olla, and flour tortillas.

Technique Tip: Typically in Baja, whole fresh lobster is split on the half shell. We suggest the use of tails instead because they are easier to locate. Split open or not, any fresh lobster should be cooked the day of purchase.

DIABLO SHRIMP

Much of Baja California's ocean bounty comes from the Sea of Cortés (also called the Gulf of California), the giant finger of water that forms the eastern boundary of Baja and the western shore of Sonora. Known to anglers as the world's largest fish trap, the sea produces the most succulent shrimp in the Americas. Cooks in coastal towns often prepare the delicacy in this fiery "devil's" style, popular throughout Mexico but never as lusty and luscious anywhere else as in the north.

Serves 6

Diablo Sauce (page 58)
2 pounds medium or large shrimp, peeled but tails left on, deveined if you wish

In a heavy skillet, bring the sauce to a simmer over medium heat. Add the shrimp to the sauce and simmer only until they turn pink and firm, a matter of just a couple of minutes. Do not overcook or the shrimp will toughen. Serve hot, accompanied with rice or potatoes to help soak up the tasty sauce.

Regional Variations: The small, homey San Carlos Bay Seafood Restaurant in Phoenix serves its *diablo* shrimp over plump French fries. The cross-cultural anomaly tastes great, with the potatoes soaking up the incendiary sauce and providing a crispy accent to the texture. In Mexico, white fish fillets, especially sea bass, are often prepared *en diablo*. They can be simmered in the sauce as our shrimp are, or broiled or grilled separately and combined later with the sauce.

DESERT DROWNED SHRIMP

This simple but unusual preparation comes from the desert country of Arizona, where farmers actually raise shrimp commercially today.

Serves 4 to 6

2 pounds medium or large shrimp, unshelled
1/2 cup fresh lime juice
1/2 cup fresh lemon juice
1/2 cup water
1 teaspoon salt
1 tablespoon extra-virgin olive oil
1 tablespoon coarse-ground black pepper

Lime and lemon wedges, for garnish

Place the shrimp in a saucepan. Add the lime and lemon juices, water, and salt and bring just to a boil. Pour the mixture into a shallow dish, refrigerate it, and marinate the shrimp in the liquid for 45 to 60 minutes.

Drain the shrimp and add the oil and pepper to them. The shrimp can be served immediately or refrigerated for several more hours before serving. Arrange the shrimp on a decorative platter, garnished with lime and lemon. Since the shrimp are intended to be peeled at the table, supply plenty of napkins.

An old folk saying, or *dicho*, teaches the importance of staying alert and prepared. It goes, "Camarón que se duerme se lo lleva la corriente," or "The shrimp that sleeps is carried away by the stream."

Serves 4 to 6

1 1/2 pounds large shrimp, peeled and butterflied
Juice of 1 lime
2 tablespoons vegetable oil
1/2 teaspoon salt
12 ounces link chorizo, sliced in 1-inch sections
18 fresh serranos, halved lengthwise
2 medium onions, chunked

In a bowl, toss the shrimp together with the lime juice, oil, and salt.

In a skillet, fry the chorizo sections until browned and just cooked through. Drain them.

Heat the broiler.

Skewer the shrimp, wrapping each around one of the serrano sections, alternating with small chunks of onion and chorizo sections. Arrange the skewers on a baking sheet and broil for 3 minutes. Turn the skewers and broil an additional 3 minutes, or until cooked through. Serve immediately.

Regional Variations: Shish kebabs, or *alhambres*, are popular on both sides of the border, though beef is usually the main ingredient rather than seafood. In ranch country in northern Mexico, the meat might be basted with a simple vinaigrette laced with dried red chile, and alternated on the kebab with chunks of poblano chile.

CORPUS CHRISTI SHRIMP SALAD

What the Sea of Cortés provides to Baja and Sonora, the Gulf of Mexico supplies to Texas and Tamaulipas. Contemporary cooks in the Lone Star State love to put the shrimp catch into salads.

Serves 6

6 cups water
2 tablespoons salt
1 large onion, chopped
6 garlic cloves, halved
1/4 cup pickling liquid from a jar of pickled jalapeños
1 chile de árbol or cayenne, crushed
2 pounds medium or large shrimp, unshelled
6 ounces jícama, sliced into small matchsticks

DRESSING
1/2 cup mayonnaise
3 tablespoons minced red onion
2 pickled jalapeños, minced
4 garlic cloves, roasted and mashed
Zest and juice of 1 lime
2 teaspoons tequila

1 Haas avocado, cubed
1/4 cup minced fresh cilantro

Lettuce leaves
Avocado slices and pickled jalapeño slices, for garnish (optional)

In a large saucepan, combine the water, salt, onion, garlic, pickling liquid, and chile and bring to a boil over high heat. Reduce the heat to a simmer and cook for 10 minutes. Add the shrimp, simmer just until they begin to turn pink, and immediately remove the pan from the heat. Place the pan in the freezer if you have space, or in the refrigerator, to cool. Chill for 30 to 60 minutes, then drain and peel the shrimp. Halve the shrimp lengthwise.

Combine the shrimp and jícama in a large bowl. In a small bowl, mix together the mayonnaise, red onion, jalapeños, garlic, lime zest and juice, and tequila. Pour the dressing over the shrimp and jícama and mix well. Refrigerate for at least 1 hour or until ready to serve.

Mix the avocado chunks and cilantro into the salad and arrange the salad on a platter of lettuce leaves. Garnish, if you wish, with avocado and jalapeño slices, and serve.

Regional Variations: Pickled shrimp salads are another popular style in Texas. Cooks first marinate the peeled crustaceans overnight in vinegar flavored with serranos or hot sauce, and spices such as cilantro, ground coriander, and marjoram. Before serving, they toss the shrimp with olive oil, additional cilantro, and a healthy grinding of black pepper. On the Pacific coast, California salads are likely to add more vegetables. One version mixes boiled shrimp and halved cherry tomatoes with a puréed salad dressing of olive oil, white wine vinegar, avocado, green onion, and a little mild green chile.

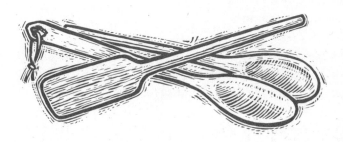

SHRIMP AND NOPALES TOSTADAS

Serves 6

1 pound shrimp, boiled as for Corpus Christi Shrimp Salad (page 308),
    peeled, and chopped
1 cup prepared nopales, diced
1/2 cup onion, chopped
3 small tomatoes, preferably Roma or Italian plum, diced
3 garlic cloves, roasted and mashed
1 canned chipotle chile plus 1/2 to 1 teaspoon adobo sauce
Juice of 1 1/2 limes
2 tablespoons extra-virgin olive oil
Salt to taste

Vegetable oil for pan-frying
12 thin corn tortillas
Shredded lettuce and minced fresh cilantro
Lime wedges, for garnish

In a bowl, mix together the shrimp, nopales, onion, tomatoes, garlic, chipotle and adobo sauce, lime juice, and olive oil. Add salt to taste. Refrigerate the mixture for 30 minutes to 1 hour.

In a skillet, warm 1 inch of oil over high heat. Fry the tortillas flat, until they become crisp, a matter of seconds. Remove the tortillas with tongs and drain. Spoon the shrimp mixture onto the tortillas and top each with sprinklings of lettuce and cilantro. Garnish with lime wedges and serve.

Rivers in Texas and Tamaulipas sometimes teem with crawfish. Cooks in both states incline toward spicy preparations like this one. If you can't find crawfish, substitute 2 pounds of unshelled shrimp.

Serves 4

4 ounces whole dried mild red chiles, preferably ancho or guajillo, stemmed, seeded, and rinsed

3 cups seafood stock or bottled clam juice

6 tablespoons extra-virgin olive oil

2 cups minced onions

1/2 cup vinegar, preferably white wine

3 garlic cloves, minced

1 pickled jalapeño, minced, plus 2 tablespoons pickling liquid

1 teaspoon sugar, or more to taste

1/2 teaspoon dried thyme

1/2 teaspoon dried marjoram, preferably, or Mexican oregano

12 whole pimiento-stuffed green olives

1 bay leaf

1 1/2 pounds blanched crawfish tails

Minced fresh cilantro and parsley, preferably the flat-leaf variety, for garnish

In a heavy skillet over medium heat, toast the dried chiles briefly, just until they become fragrant. Transfer the chiles to a saucepan, add the stock, and simmer over medium heat for 15 minutes, or until the chiles are soft.

While the chiles simmer, use the skillet that toasted the chiles for cooking the onions. Warm 4 tablespoons of the oil in the skillet over medium-low heat, add the onions, and sauté slowly, until the onions are very soft but not brown. Transfer the onions and oil, and the dried chiles and liquid, to a blender. Add the vinegar, garlic, jalapeño and pickling liquid, sugar, thyme, and marjoram and purée.

Warm the remaining oil in a skillet or saucepan over high heat. Pour in the sauce, being careful to avoid splatters as the liquid hits the hot oil.

When the most insistent sputtering dies down, reduce the heat to medium-low and add the olives and bay leaf. Simmer, uncovered, for 30 minutes, stirring occasionally.

Add the crawfish tails and simmer another 5 to 7 minutes, until the crawfish is cooked through. Serve the crawfish immediately, topped with light sprinklings of cilantro and parsley. Pair the dish with mild-flavored rice or *fideos*.

Technique Tip: Freshwater crustaceans related to lobsters, crawfish have a texture similar to shrimp, but a distinctive flavor of their own. From November through early summer, look for fresh blanched tails. Frozen crawfish work fine in this and other dishes as long as they haven't been encased in ice for long. Don't bother with blanched tails that are uncurled, an indication that the crawfish were already dead when cooked.

TAMAULIPAS STUFFED CRABS

Anywhere crabs flourish, cooks will stuff them in their own local style. This approach is typical around Tampico, a major Gulf fishing center.

Serves 4

3 tablespoons butter
1/2 medium onion, chopped
1 garlic clove, minced
2 small tomatoes, preferably Roma or Italian plum, chopped
1 tablespoon minced pickled carrots, rinsed, preferably, or 1
    tablespoon minced carrot, blanched and drained
1 fresh serrano or jalapeño, minced
1 pound crabmeat, fresh or frozen, picked over well to remove any
    pieces of shell
2 tablespoons minced fresh cilantro

TOPPING
2 tablespoons butter
1/4 cup dried breadcrumbs

Preheat the oven to 350° F. Butter 8 scallop shells or a shallow baking dish.

In a heavy skillet, warm the butter over medium heat. Add the onion and garlic and sauté briefly until limp. Stir in the tomatoes, carrots, and chile and cook until well softened. Remove from the heat and mix in the crab and cilantro. Pack the mixture into the prepared shells or dish.

In a small pan, melt the butter over low heat. Remove the pan from the heat and stir in the breadcrumbs until coated. Spoon the crumbs evenly over the crab and bake, uncovered, for 18 to 20 minutes, until crispy on top but still moist inside. Serve immediately.

Technique Tip: If you have access to whole crabs, and are willing to fuss with them to get the meat, bake the crab mixture in their shells for a beautiful presentation. Be sure to use crabs small enough to hold an individual serving.

Regional Variations: Some Tamaulipas cooks add 1 or 2 teaspoons of minced capers to the crab, and they may use the stuffing without the breadcrumb topping to fill a tortilla dish, such as deep-fried taquitos. Farther up the coast in Texas, the crab might be mixed with mayonnaise, cracker crumbs, and bell peppers, and the fresh chiles might be replaced with a combination of Tabasco sauce and horseradish.

CRAB SALPICÓN

Serves 4 to 6

1/2 medium red bell pepper, diced
1/4 cup diced seeded, peeled cucumber
2 tablespoons minced red onion or sweet onion
2 fresh serranos, minced
1 tablespoon minced fresh cilantro
1/2 teaspoon dried epazote
1/2 teaspoon sugar
1 tablespoon vegetable oil
1 tablespoon extra-virgin olive oil
1 tablespoon rice vinegar, or 2 teaspoons white wine vinegar and
    1 teaspoon water
1 tablespoon fresh lime juice
1 pound crabmeat, fresh or frozen, picked over well to remove any
    pieces of shell
Salt to taste
1 Haas avocado, diced

Lime wedges, for garnish

In a bowl, combine the bell pepper, cucumber, onion, serranos, cilantro, epazote, sugar, oils, vinegar, and lime juice. Gently stir in the crab and the salt. The salad can be refrigerated for up to 2 hours at this point. Just before serving, mix in the avocado and garnish with the limes.

Regional Variations: To stretch the *salpicón*, some people would serve it as an appetizer with chips or, for a more formal presentation, eliminate the avocado from the recipe and present each portion over an avocado half. Other coastal cooks make a seafood *salpicón* with cooked snapper, tuna, or mackerel in place of the crab, or combined with it. A simple Baja *salpicón marinero* might use equal portions of crab, fish, and peeled shrimp, along with just enough olive oil and lime juice to bind the mixture. Smoked fish, popular on Mexico's Pacific coast, works well in the blend.

Mexican cookbook author and chef Zarela Martínez considers enchiladas of this style to be a good example of contemporary *mestizo* cooking styles that have evolved in the borderlands. This creamy version comes from landlocked New Mexico.

Serves 4 to 6

FILLING
2 tablespoons butter
1/2 medium onion, chopped
1 garlic clove, minced
1 fresh jalapeño, minced
1/2 teaspoon dried epazote
8 ounces cream cheese, at room temperature
1 pound crabmeat, fresh or frozen, picked over well to remove any
    pieces of shell
2 tablespoons minced fresh cilantro

Tubac Chile Verde (tomatillo version, page 55)
Vegetable oil for pan-frying
12 corn tortillas

Crema (page 63) or crème fraîche
Minced fresh cilantro, for garnish

Preheat the oven to 350° F. Butter a shallow baking dish.

In a heavy skillet, warm the butter over medium heat. Add the onion, garlic, jalapeño, and epazote and sauté briefly until limp. Stir in the cheese and cook until well softened. Remove the skillet from the heat and mix in the crab and cilantro.

In a saucepan, warm the sauce.

Heat $^{1}/_{2}$ to 1 inch of oil in a small skillet until it ripples. With tongs, dunk a tortilla quickly in the oil long enough for it to go limp, a matter of seconds. Don't let the tortilla turn crisp. Repeat with the remaining tortillas and drain them.

Dip a tortilla in the sauce to coat it lightly. Lay the tortilla on a plate, sprinkle 2 $^1/_2$ to 3 tablespoons of filling over it, and roll it up snug. Transfer the enchilada to the baking dish. Repeat with the remaining tortillas and filling. Top with the remaining sauce, seeing that each enchilada is submerged in the sauce, and bake for 20 to 25 minutes, until heated through and bubbly.

Spoon crema over the enchiladas and sprinkle with cilantro. With a spatula, serve the enchiladas immediately.

Julio's Casa Corona has served tourists and locals alike in Ciudad Juárez for more than a half century. Julio and Lupe Ramirez founded the family business in 1941, specializing in authentic home cooking. The gracious service and value prices attract an eclectic clientele from both sides of the border for a wide range of dishes, including *salpicón, carne asada a la tampiqueña,* and *mole poblano.*

The railroad made oysters into inveterate travelers a century ago, long before most other seafood found its way inland. Packed in ice and sawdust, and fed cornmeal, the little bivalves made a splash as far from home as Arizona mining towns. This recipe is modeled on a cool-weather dish developed by the Ramirez family in Ciudad Juárez, owners of Julio's Casa Corona restaurant, who also add asadero cheese to the topping.

Serves 4

16 oysters with liquor, shells reserved
Juice of 1/2 lime
1/4 pound bulk chorizo
2 bacon slices, chopped
Ground dried red chile, preferably New Mexican or ancho
1 green onion, minced

Lime wedges, for garnish

Heat the broiler.

Arrange the oysters on the half shell on a baking sheet or in a heat-proof dish. Pour the oyster liquor and lime juice over the oysters.

In a small skillet, fry the chorizo over medium heat until browned and crisp. With a slotted spoon, remove the chorizo and drain it. Add the bacon to the skillet and fry over medium heat until browned and crisp. Drain the bacon. Scatter the chorizo and bacon evenly over the oysters. Sprinkle lightly with chile.

Broil the oysters for 1 to 2 minutes, just long enough to heat them through. Be careful to avoid overcooking or they will toughen. Scatter the green onion over the oysters. Serve immediately, garnished with limes.

OYSTERS GUAYMAS

The Sonoran coastal city of Guaymas is best known for its shrimp, but the local San Carlos Bay fishing fleet also hauls in plenty of oysters. A version of this dish always opens our Christmas dinner. If your oysters come without shells, serve the shellfish on toasted flour tortilla wedges.

Makes 24 oysters on the half shell

24 oysters with liquor, shells reserved
8-ounce bottle clam juice
1/4 cup extra-virgin olive oil
3 green onions, minced
1 bay leaf
4 garlic cloves, roasted and mashed
1 to 2 chiles pequins or 1 cayenne, crushed
3/4 teaspoon salt
1 teaspoon fresh-ground black pepper
1/2 teaspoon dried marjoram, preferably, or Mexican oregano
2 tablespoons vinegar, preferably white
Juice of 2 medium limes

Lime wedges, for garnish

Measure the oyster liquor. The amount will vary depending on the particular batch of oysters and the skill of the shucker. Add as much of the clam juice as is needed to equal 1 cup of liquid. Reserve the liquid.

In a large, shallow saucepan, warm the oil over medium heat. Add the onions and bay leaf and sauté until the onions are very soft. Stir in the garlic, chile, salt, pepper, and marjoram and sauté for 1 additional minute. Pour in the oyster-liquor mixture and vinegar and bring the mixture to a boil. Add the oysters and reduce the heat to a simmer. Poach the oysters for about 3 to 4 minutes, stirring as needed to make sure they cook quickly and evenly, until their edges curl and they begin to plump. Remove the oysters from the heat and add the lime juice.

Refrigerate the oysters in the poaching liquid, covered, for at least 1 hour.

Place the oysters on the half shell with equal amounts of the poaching liquid. Garnish the oysters with lime wedges and serve.

Regional Variations: Mexican culinary authority Patricia Quintana shares a delectable Guaymas version of poached oysters in her *Cuisine of the Water Gods* (Simon and Schuster, 1994). She uses jalapeño for heat and enough fruit vinegar to fully pickle the oysters after cooking. Sharon Cadwallader, in her enjoyable travel guide-cum-cookbook, *Savoring Mexico* (Chronicle Books, 1987), reminisces fondly about a warm version of Guaymas oysters, broiled on the half shell with a similar sauce rather than poached. Other coastal cooks might flash-sauté the oysters first in olive oil, for a chewier seared surface, and then chill them in the spicy marinade.

SANTA CATALINA ABALONE

Once abundant along the Pacific coast of the Californias, subtly flavored abalone, or *abulón*, is a little more difficult to find these days, especially in other parts of the country. Conch or squid make reasonable substitutes in the recipe.

Serves 4 to 6

2 pounds prepared abalone (see "Technique Tip")
1 1/2 cups white wine
Juice of 2 limes or lemons
1 1/2 teaspoons salt
3 eggs
2 cups all-purpose flour
1/2 teaspoon fresh-ground black pepper
1 teaspoon ground dried mild red chile, preferably New Mexican or ancho (optional)
Olive oil and butter for pan-frying

Lime or lemon wedges and black olives, for garnish

Place the abalone in a shallow, nonreactive dish. Pour the wine and lime or lemon juice over it and add $1/2$ teaspoon of the salt. Let the abalone marinate for 30 minutes at cool room temperature. Drain it and blot lightly to remove excess moisture from the surface.

Break the eggs into a shallow dish and beat lightly.

In another shallow dish, combine the flour with the pepper, the remaining salt, and the chile, if you wish.

In a heavy skillet, warm enough of an equal mixture of oil and butter so that the abalone will be half-immersed in it during the frying. Heat the fat until foamy. Dredge the first abalone steak in the seasoned flour, dip it in the egg, and then coat it with more seasoned flour. Fry the steak until just golden and crispy, about 1 or 2 minutes on each side. If overcooked, the abalone will be tough. Drain the steak and keep it warm. Repeat the process with the remaining steaks, preparing and cooking them one or two at a time, adding more oil and butter if needed for the frying.

Technique Tip: The abalone meat is a tough muscle that requires special treatment to bring out its best. The abalone should be trimmed until only white meat shows, sliced with a sharp knife to less than $1/2$-inch thickness, and pounded with a mallet to half that thickness.

Pollution has substantially reduced abalone supplies over the years. Look for it fresh, particularly in the fall. If your regular seafood supplier doesn't have it, check an Asian market, which also might carry it frozen at other times during the year. Don't bother with the canned varieties usually found in the same stores.

Like abalone, clams can be found along the coast of both Californias. White-shelled pismos and brown-shelled *chocolatas* are among the most-prized varieties, but any fresh hardshell clams can be prepared in this fashion. Ask your fishmonger to open the clams, leaving them on the half shell.

Serves 4 to 6

3 dozen small or medium clams on the half shell
4 tablespoons extra-virgin olive oil
1 1/2 tablespoons fresh lemon juice
1 tablespoon dried breadcrumbs
1 teaspoon ground dried mild red chile, preferably ancho
1 garlic clove, minced

Lemon wedges, for garnish
Jalapeño Hot Sauce (page 49), Tabasco sauce, or other hot pepper
     sauce

Heat the broiler.

Arrange the clams in a single layer in a shallow baking dish. Combine the oil, lemon juice, breadcrumbs, chile, and garlic and drizzle the mixture over the clams.

Broil the clams until sizzling, about 1 to 2 minutes, depending on their size. Avoid overcooking the clams or they will toughen. Garnish with lemons and serve immediately with hot pepper sauce.

Technique Tip: Purchase clams on the half shell the day you intend to use them, and then keep them packed on ice until you are ready to cook. Some people still eat clams raw, but it isn't considered safe today.

CEVICHE QUE CANTA

Probably brought to Mexico in the sixteenth century from the South Seas, via early Spanish trade routes across the Pacific, ceviche developed into a national passion south of the border. The idea of cooking fish and seafood chemically with citrus juice took longer to catch on in the States, but it's gaining ground, particularly in the Southwest. This version "sings" with freshness and flavor.

Serves 4 as an appetizer

3/4 pound firm-fleshed white fish fillets, such as sea bass or snapper, as fresh as you can buy, sliced into bite-size pieces
1/4 pound quartered sea scallops, whole bay scallops, or halved peeled shrimp
1/3 cup fresh lime juice
Juice of 1/2 medium orange
1 small tomato, preferably Roma or Italian plum, halved, squeezed to eliminate the juice and seeds, and minced
1/4 cup thin-sliced green olives
2 tablespoons minced red onion
1 to 2 fresh serranos, sliced in very thin rings
1 tablespoon minced fresh cilantro
1/4 teaspoon salt
3 tablespoons extra-virgin olive oil, one with a full fruity flavor
1 Haas avocado, cubed

Lime slices, for garnish

In a nonreactive bowl, marinate the fish and scallops in the lime juice for 30 to 45 minutes. Drain the liquid from the bowl and gently mix in the remaining ingredients except the avocado. Refrigerate the ceviche for 30 to 45 minutes.

Stir in the avocado and spoon the ceviche into parfait glasses, margarita glasses, or glass bowls to show off its colors. Garnish with lime slices and serve chilled.

Regional Variations: In Mexico, cooks make ceviche (also called *cebiche* and *seviche*) with a wide range of fish and seafood, depending on what's fresh at the market, a critical factor in success. At a museum reception in California, the caterer took the diversity of possibilities to its logical West Coast conclusion, creating a ceviche buffet. The staff laid out separate bowls of lime-marinated scallops, shrimp, and three kinds of fish, and served the other traditional recipe ingredients as a sauce on the side along with extra chopped tomatoes, onions, serranos, cilantro, lime wedges, and warm tortillas. It was a festive presentation, easily prepared, reasonably priced, and expandable to any size group.

PESCADO MOJO DE AJO

No fish preparation is more pervasive in Mexico than *mojo de ajo*, "soaked in garlic." While the style works with almost any fish or shrimp, it has a special affinity for the flavors of the freshwater fish found most commonly in the border region, lake bass and catfish.

Serves 4

**Four 6-ounce to 8-ounce lake bass or catfish fillets, other white fish
      fillets, or 1 1/2 pounds peeled shrimp**
Juice of 2 limes
2/3 cup all-purpose flour
1/4 teaspoon dried epazote (optional)
1/4 teaspoon salt, or more to taste
1/4 cup butter
2 tablespoons vegetable oil
10 to 12 garlic cloves, sliced thin
Generous grinding of black pepper

Minced fresh parsley and lime wedges, for garnish

Place the fish in a single layer in a shallow, nonreactive dish. Pour the lime juice over the fish, turning the fish once to coat evenly. Set the fish aside.

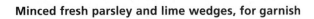

On a plate, mix together the flour, epazote, and salt.

In a large, heavy skillet, warm the butter and oil over medium-low heat. Add the garlic and cook slowly, until it just begins to color. Do not let the garlic color beyond the nutty, light-golden stage or it will become bitter in taste. Remove the garlic with a slotted spoon and reserve it. Keep the butter-oil mixture warm.

Drain the fillets and pat them dry. Raise the heat under the skillet to medium. Dip the fish lightly in the seasoned flour. Fry the fish, 1 or 2 fillets at a time, until lightly browned on both sides and cooked through, about 4 minutes cooking time total per $^1/_2$ inch of thickness.

Sprinkle the garlic back into the skillet and serve the fish immediately with equal portions of the garlic and sauce. Sprinkle parsley over the fillets and accompany with lime wedges.

FLOUNDER FILLETS REGALO

These subtly scented, roasted fillets come to the table wrapped like a present, or *regalo*, in a banana leaf, a common treatment in subtropical areas of the borderlands.

Serves 4

Four 6-ounce to 7-ounce flounder or sole fillets
Olive oil
Salt to taste
4 prepared banana leaves (see "Technique Tip")

1/4 cup minced fresh cilantro
2 garlic cloves, sliced thin
2 fresh serranos, preferably 1 red and 1 green, sliced in very thin rings
4 small green onions, tops trimmed to 1 inch
8 thin lemon slices

Salsa Shoyu (page 48), Roasted Garlic–Piñon Sauce (page 60),
    or other salsa

Texas and Coahuila consume more catfish than any other states in their respective countries, and northern Mexico and south Texas boast some of the best lake black-bass fishing in the world. Guerrero Lake, fed by five rivers and regulated by one of the world's largest dams, is a particularly popular spot to angle for bass. Near Ciudad Victoria, the capital of Tamaulipas, it regularly attracts organized groups from the United States. Chihuahua cooks in Ciudad Juárez and Ciudad Chihuahua prize the black bass from Boquilla Lake. Plenty of restaurants in those cities feature the fish, but the best place for bass may be Crosby's in Ciudad Acuña, Coahuila, a gracious old Tex-Mex establishment.

Preheat the oven to 400° F. Oil a 9-by-12-inch baking dish.

Rub the fillets lightly with oil and sprinkle them with salt.

Place a banana leaf on a platter and place a fillet lengthwise in the middle of it. Scatter one-fourth each of the cilantro, garlic, serranos, and green onions over the fish. Arrange 2 lemon slices over all. Fold first the narrow sides of the leaf and then the longer sides over and around the fish. Repeat with the remaining leaves, fish, and toppings.

Lay the packages seam sides down, overlapping a bit, in the baking dish. Bake the fish for 7 to 8 minutes, opening one of the fillet packages to make sure it is cooked through. Rewrap the fillet and bake an additional 1 or 2 minutes if needed.

Serve the fillets in their leaves, seam sides up, for each guest to unwrap at the table. Provide a separate plate for the discarded leaves. Accompany the fish with salsa or sauce.

Technique Tip: Look for banana leaves in refrigerated or frozen sections of Hispanic, Latino, or Asian markets. If you can't find them locally, you can order from the Seaside Banana Farm, 6823 Santa Barbara Avenue, La Conchita, California, 805-643-4061. A special spot in a remarkable microclimate, the garden and fruit stand is just off the coastal highway between Ventura and Santa Barbara.

Truly fresh leaves, like the ones the banana farm sells, keep refrigerated for up to two weeks, and the frozen ones last for months. Purchase young, supple leaves if you have any choice. When you are ready to use them, slice out any portion of the central vein that is tough. Wilt the leaves over a stove burner on high heat by holding the leaf flat and running it back and forth quickly, 1 or 2 inches above the burner for 3 to 4 seconds on each side, until pliable. Be careful to avoid burning the leaf or your fingers in the process. Let the leaves cool before proceeding.

Regional Variations: Mexican cooks frequently wrap fish, tamales, and other dishes in leaves or husks to preserve taste and texture, particularly when the food might dry out easily. One of the most distinctive flavors comes from the leaves of the herb *hoja santa*, sometimes used with mild fish in southern Tamaulipas. They lend an assertive tang reminiscent of fennel or sassafras.

PESCADO RANCHERO

Serves 4

Four 6-ounce firm-fleshed white fish fillets, such as snapper, dorado, redfish, or grouper
Juice of 2 limes
Salt and fresh-ground black pepper to taste
Ranchero Sauce (page 57)

Chopped tomato, preferably yellow, and lime wedges, for garnish

Place the fish in a single layer in a shallow, nonreactive dish. Squeeze the lime juice over the fish and allow it to sit for 10 minutes. Drain the fillets and sprinkle them lightly with salt and pepper.

In a skillet or other heavy, shallow pan, bring the sauce to a boil. Arrange the fish on top of the sauce, pushing each fillet into the sauce just a bit. Reduce the heat to medium-low, cover, and poach the fillets in the sauce until they are just cooked through and flaky, about 5 to 7 minutes.

Serve the fish immediately, with the fillets surrounded by a small sea of sauce, and garnished with tomato and limes.

TILAPIA AND PIPIÁN

Tamaulipas cooks make a style of *pipián* sauce simpler and creamier than most. Here it's paired with grilled freshwater tilapia fillets, common in the state's Río Tancoco and available at supermarkets throughout the United States. Catfish is the best substitute for tilapia here, but the sauce goes well with any firm-fleshed white fish.

Serves 6

SAUCE
1/4 cup butter
1 1/2 cups pepitas (shelled pumpkin seeds)
2 cups chicken stock
1/2 cup whipping cream
1 to 2 fresh serranos or jalapeños, halved and seeded
Salt to taste

Six 6-ounce tilapia, catfish, snapper, dorado, redfish, or other firm-fleshed white fish fillets
Vegetable oil
Salt and fresh-ground pepper to taste
Ground dried mild red chile, such as New Mexican or ancho (optional)

Toasted pepitas (shelled pumpkin seeds) and minced fresh parsley, for garnish

Warm 3 tablespoons of the butter in a heavy skillet over medium heat. Stir in the pumpkin seeds and sauté for 2 to 3 minutes until fragrant. Do not brown the seeds or they may become bitter.

Transfer the seeds to a blender and add the stock, cream, serranos, and salt. Purée until the seeds are ground fine.

In a heavy saucepan, warm the remaining butter over medium-high heat. Pour the sauce into the pan, being careful to avoid splatters, and stir. Reduce the heat to medium-low and simmer for about 5 minutes until slightly thickened. (The sauce can be made ahead and refrigerated for a day. Reheat the sauce before proceeding.)

Prepare an outdoor grill, firing up enough charcoal to make a single layer under the fish.

Rub the fillets with a thin coat of oil. Salt and pepper them to taste and add a light sprinkling of red chile, if you wish.

When the coals are covered with gray ash, place the fish directly over them. Grill until cooked through, about 4 minutes per $1/2$ inch of thickness. Serve the fillets hot, topped with spoonfuls of the warm sauce, and garnished with pepitas and parsley.

PAN-FRIED TRUCHAS MONTAÑAS

Native to the Americas, freshwater trout, or *truchas*, thrive in the mountain streams of New Mexico, source of this fish, chile, and pecan combo.

Serves 4

2 eggs
1/2 cup milk
1 garlic clove, minced
1/2 cup all-purpose flour
1/2 cup stone-ground cornmeal
2 to 3 teaspoons ground dried mild red chile, preferably New
    Mexican or ancho
3/4 teaspoon salt, or more to taste
2 tablespoons vegetable oil
2 tablespoons butter
6 trout fillets, about 6 ounces each
1/2 cup fish, seafood, or chicken stock
Juice of 1 lemon
2 teaspoons Worcestershire sauce
1/2 cup chopped pecans, toasted

High in northern New Mexico's Sangre de Cristo mountains, the town of Truchas sits near streams loaded with its namesake fish. It remains an Old World outpost, true to its Spanish frontier heritage, which is why Robert Redford chose it as the location for his film version of John Nichols's novel *The Milagro Beanfield War*. At the terrific Truchas Mountain Cafe, the Romero family hands out maps to the site of the movie's fabled beanfield.

In a shallow dish, combine the eggs, milk, and garlic and beat lightly. In another shallow dish, stir together the flour, cornmeal, chile, and salt.

In a heavy skillet, warm the oil and butter together over medium-high heat. Dredge the trout in the seasoned flour, dunk it in the egg mixture, and then coat it with more seasoned flour. Fry the fillets, one or two at a time, until lightly browned and crispy, about 2 minutes per side. Drain the fish and arrange them on a warm serving platter. Add the remaining ingredients to the pan drippings and heat through. Taste and adjust the seasoning if needed. Serve the drippings as a sauce with the trout.

Few things are simpler or more impressive to guests than the presentation of a whole fish. This Pacific coast version features *cabrilla*, or black sea bass, and it's grilled, or *a la parrilla*. Other types of bass, snapper, redfish, or any mild-flavored fish substitute well, depending on what you find fresh.

Serves 6 to 8

1 cup vegetable oil
2 dried mild red chiles, preferably guajillo, ancho, or New Mexican, cut into thin strips
1 teaspoon cumin seeds, toasted and ground
5-pound sea bass or other whole, mild-flavored fish, gutted and cleaned
Juice of 3 limes
Salt to taste

In a small saucepan over low heat, combine the oil, chiles, and cumin. Cook until the chiles just begin to sizzle, and then remove them immediately from the heat. Set the oil aside to steep for 30 minutes. (The oil can be prepared ahead and refrigerated for a day. Bring the oil back to room temperature before proceeding.)

Place the fish on a platter or on foil and pour the lime juice over it. Let the fish sit at room temperature for 30 minutes.

Prepare an outdoor grill, firing up enough charcoal to form a single layer under the fish.

Rub the fish inside and out with 2 tablespoons of the seasoned oil, reserving the remaining oil. Sprinkle the fish with salt.

When the charcoal is covered with gray ash, transfer the fish to a greased grill basket or directly to the grill, and place it right over the coals. Cover the fish loosely with a foil tent, to help retain moisture, and cook for a total of 8 minutes per inch, turning it once. Be careful to avoid overcooking, which will dry out the fish.

Transfer the fish to a serving platter and accompany it with a bowl of the remaining seasoned oil. We like it served with a tangle of fried or grilled onion rings. Add the complementary flavor of Guajillo Mild Sauce if you want to serve salsa with the fish.

Regional Variations: The preparation of any grilled fish, whole or filleted, is pretty straightforward, but the range of accompanying sauces offers infinite possibilities for creative contemporary cooks. For this kind of mild-flavored white fish, some Southwest chefs offer a hot version of traditional American corn relish. In his *Janos: Recipes and Tales from a Southwest Restaurant* (Ten Speed Press, 1989), Tucson's Janos Wilder takes a more sophisticated approach with a warm salad-like salsa of corn, black beans, bell peppers, and bay scallops. Tropical fruit–based salsas now seem as common with fish as tartar sauce. Mary Sue Milliken and Susan Feniger, chefs at the Border Grill in Los Angeles, headed the other direction and developed a savory compote to accompany their fish. As they describe in *Mesa Mexicana* (William Morrow, 1994), they combine generous amounts of olive oil–sautéed onion and garlic with capers, chopped green olives, tomatoes, jalapeño, and fresh oregano, all enlivened with a little red wine vinegar and honey.

Serves 4

Four 10-ounce swordfish steaks cut no thicker than 1 inch
Chipotle-Tomatillo Salsa (page 39)
1/4 cup extra-virgin olive oil

Place the fish in a shallow, nonreactive dish. In a blender or mini–food processor, purée $^1/_4$ cup of the salsa with the oil and pour the mixture over the fish. Marinate at room temperature for 30 minutes.

Place the rest of the salsa in a serving bowl.

On an outdoor grill, fire up enough charcoal to form a single layer of coals beneath the fish. When the coals are covered in gray ash, drain the steaks from the marinade, discard the marinade, and place the steaks directly over the coals. Grill for about 4 minutes per side, if the steaks are 1 inch thick. Reduce the cooking time slightly for thinner steaks.

Serve the steaks hot, accompanied with the salsa.

TUNA MACHACA

Called a *machaca* because it uses small pieces of fish, this dish is based on one from Ana Lidia Corrales Morales. Her original version won a Baja California cooking contest for recipes from grandmothers.

Serves 4

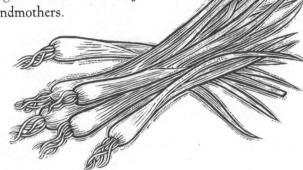

MARINADE
1/2 cup olive oil
Juice of 1 lemon
3 garlic cloves, minced
2 teaspoons Maggi seasoning or soy sauce
1 teaspoon dried thyme
1 fresh serrano, minced

1 1/2 pounds fresh tuna steak, cut in 1/2-inch to 3/4-inch dice
1 small tomato, preferably Roma or Italian plum, chopped
1 small onion, minced
1 to 2 fresh serranos, minced
Tops of 2 green onions, minced
1 tablespoon butter

In a shallow dish, combine the marinade ingredients. Stir in the tuna and let the mixture sit at room temperature for 15 minutes.

Warm a large, heavy skillet, preferably cast iron, over high heat. Drain the tuna from the marinade. When the skillet is very hot, place the tuna and the marinade that still clings to the pieces in the skillet. Immediately add the tomato, onion, serranos, and green onion tops. Fry just 1 or 2 minutes, stirring constantly. Avoid overcooking or the tuna will become dry. It should be seared on the outside with just a hint of pink remaining at the center. Stir in the butter just before removing the *machaca* from the heat, and serve immediately. Arroz Verde makes a good accompaniment.

Regional Variations: Some Baja fish *machacas* resemble the better-known beef versions more closely than this one. Often made with shredded manta ray or cabrilla, they may call for fish to be steamed and well drained or dried in the sun or oven. The fish is then sautéed with a tomato, onion, and chile mixture similar to ours.

ENSENADA TACOS DE PESCADO

Brandy and beer, two of northern Mexico's most popular beverages, blend together better than you might expect in these fried fish tacos.

Serves 4 to 6

1 1/2 to 1 3/4 pounds mild, firm-fleshed white fish fillets, such as
    snapper, dorado, or grouper, cut in fat finger-size strips
3/4 cup inexpensive brandy
1 teaspoon prepared yellow mustard
1 garlic clove, minced
1/4 teaspoon ground chile de árbol, cascabel, or cayenne

BATTER
1 cup all-purpose flour
2 teaspoons salt
1 teaspoon dried oregano, preferably Mexican
1/4 to 1/2 teaspoon ground chile de árbol, cascabel, or cayenne
12 ounces beer
2 teaspoons prepared yellow mustard
2 garlic cloves, minced

Vegetable oil for deep-frying
12 to 16 corn tortillas, warmed
Ensalada de Col (page 135) or shredded red cabbage
Jalapeño Hot Sauce (page 49), Búfalo Salsa Picante (see "Technique
    Tip"), or other hot sauce
Lime wedges, for garnish

Place the fish in a shallow dish and cover it with the brandy, mustard, garlic, and chile. Set aside at room temperature.

For the batter, stir together the flour, salt, oregano, and chile in a large bowl. Mix in the beer, mustard, and garlic.

Fill a large, heavy pan with at least 4 inches of oil. Heat the oil to 350° F.

Dip the fish in the batter a few pieces at a time, and transfer to the oil, taking care to avoid crowding the pieces. Fry the fish until it is golden brown, for 2 to 3 minutes, and drain it. Repeat the process until all the fish is fried, transferring it to a platter.

Serve the platter of fish along with the tortillas, *ensalada* or cabbage topping, hot sauce, and limes. Let the guests make their own tacos, wrapping two or three pieces of fish in a tortilla and adding salad and sauce as they wish.

Technique Tip: For some fifty years, savvy travelers to Mexico have returned home with tall, thin bottles of Búfalo Salsa Picante, a deep-red guajillo-and-vinegar sauce. Festin Foods Corporation of Carlsbad, California, is now importing the sauce and distributing it nationally. Look for the buffalo on the label in supermarkets and specialty food stores. Mixed with lime juice, Búfalo makes a good quick baste for grilled fish or seafood.

The old Baja fishing port of Ensenada, a little more than one hour by car from San Diego, got a facelift in recent years. Consider a visit at *carnaval,* the same time and occasion as New Orleans's Mardi Gras, or in late September during the Feria Internacional del Pescado y del Marisco. Food lovers will delight in the seafood tacos and enchiladas, abalone, oysters, shrimp, and smoked deep-water fish.

Mexicans have long filled tacos, enchiladas, and other *antojitos* with fish, but the idea didn't take off in the United States until recent decades. California cooks led the way north of the border with treats such as these soft tacos. While best hot off the grill, the fish can be broiled instead with good results.

Serves 4

2 cups chopped romaine or other sturdy lettuce
2 small tomatoes, preferably Roma or Italian plum, chopped
3 tablespoons minced red onion
2 tablespoons minced fresh cilantro
Juice of 3 limes
2 to 2 1/2 pounds white fish fillets or steaks, such as snapper,
**   swordfish, or sea bass**
1 tablespoon extra-virgin olive oil
2 garlic cloves, minced
Salt and fresh-ground black pepper to taste

Salsa del Norte (page 38) or other tomato-based salsa
Vegetable oil for pan-frying
16 thin corn tortillas
Haas avocado slices

In a small bowl, mix the lettuce, tomatoes, onion, and cilantro together with the juice of $1/2$ lime. Refrigerate until serving time.

Squeeze the remaining lime juice over the fish, rub the fillets with the oil and garlic, and sprinkle them lightly with salt and pepper.

Prepare an outdoor grill, firing up enough charcoal to make a single layer under the fish. When the coals are coated with gray ash, place the fish directly over the coals. Grill until cooked through, about 4 minutes per side per inch of thickness. Pull or chop the fish into bite-size pieces and transfer them to a bowl. Mix the fish gently with enough salsa to make the mixture moist. Keep the fish mixture warm while you prepare the tortillas.

Heat $1/2$ to $3/4$ inch of oil in a small skillet until the oil ripples. With tongs, dip a tortilla in the oil long enough for it to go limp, a matter of seconds. Don't let the tortilla turn crisp. Repeat with the remaining tortillas and drain them.

To assemble the first taco, place 1 tortilla on top of a second tortilla. (This makes a stronger base for what will be a large taco.) Spoon on several heaping tablespoons of the fish mixture, then top with a generous mound of the salad garnish. Repeat with the remaining ingredients, providing two tacos per serving.

The tacos are served flat and can be eaten that way with a fork or scooped up with the fingers and folded over. Eat immediately, with more salsa, avocado slices, and lots of napkins.

Regional Variations: Texas cooks are developing their own local takes on fish tacos. We had a catfish variation in Houston in a hard taco shell, topped with lettuce and a spicy rémoulade dressing. The cultural combo sounded odd, but the taste buds didn't complain at all.

Restaurants and food stands all over Baja and *alta* California offer fish tacos, but you won't find a better version than Alex Diaz makes at Chileto's in Santa Barbara. You order at a window and sit at umbrella-covered tables outside, munching fish so fresh you'll swear it swam to the kitchen. A flavorful but mild salsa comes with the tacos, but you can juice them up with a half dozen other options made daily. The hottest are kept behind the counter, out of easy reach for good reason.

No restaurant in the United States has refined Mexican seafood to an art more than La Serenata de Garibaldi, in the Boyle Heights neighborhood of east Los Angeles. Chef-owner José Rodríguez, from Torreón, Coahuila, masterfully combines fish with a dazzling array of salsas and sauces. His enchiladas inspired our version.

Serves 4 to 6

SAUCE
2 tablespoons vegetable oil
2 cups chopped husked tomatillos, preferably fresh
1/2 cup chopped roasted mild green chile, preferably poblano
1/4 cup chopped onion
1 fresh serrano, chopped
3 garlic cloves, roasted
3/4 teaspoon salt, or more to taste
1/2 teaspoon dried thyme
1/4 teaspoon ground coriander
1 cup fish stock
1/4 cup white wine
1/4 cup whipping cream
3 tablespoons minced fresh cilantro
Pinch of sugar (optional)

FILLING
1 1/2 pounds poached or grilled firm-fleshed white fish fillets, such as
    sea bass, mahimahi, or grouper, shredded or chopped
1 small tomato, preferably Roma or Italian plum, minced
3 tablespoons minced fresh cilantro
1 fresh serrano, minced
Salt to taste (optional)

Vegetable oil for pan-frying
12 corn tortillas

Chopped tomato and minced fresh cilantro, for garnish

To prepare the sauce, warm the oil in a saucepan over medium heat. Add the tomatillos, chile, onion, serrano, garlic, salt, thyme, and coriander. Sauté until the mixture is soft, for about 10 minutes. Add the stock, wine, and cream and reduce the heat to medium-low. Simmer for an additional 20 minutes. Transfer the sauce to a blender, add the cilantro, and purée. Taste the sauce and if the flavor seems overly tart, add the sugar. Keep the sauce warm.

Preheat the oven to 400° F. Grease a shallow baking dish. Spoon about $1/4$ cup of sauce into the baking dish.

In a bowl, combine the filling ingredients, adding salt if needed to heighten the flavor.

Heat $1/2$ to 1 inch of oil in a small skillet until the oil ripples. With tongs, dunk a tortilla in the oil long enough for it to go limp, a matter of seconds. Don't let the tortilla turn crisp. Repeat with the remaining tortillas and drain them.

Dip a tortilla into the sauce. Top it with about $1/3$ cup of the fish mixture. Roll up the tortilla snug but not tight. Transfer the enchilada to the baking dish. Repeat with the rest of the tortillas and filling. Pour the remaining sauce over the enchiladas.

Bake for 8 to 10 minutes, until the enchiladas are heated through and the sauce is bubbly. With a spatula, serve the enchiladas immediately, garnished with tomato and cilantro.

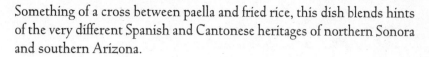

We first enjoyed fisherman's rice in Phoenix at the San Carlos Bay Seafood Restaurant, where the cooking is always creatively down-home. One of the city's leading chefs tipped us off to the inauspicious café, a favorite hangout of his when he wants a break from fancy food.

Something of a cross between paella and fried rice, this dish blends hints of the very different Spanish and Cantonese heritages of northern Sonora and southern Arizona.

Serves 3 to 4

4 ounces bulk chorizo
1 teaspoon vegetable oil
1/2 medium onion, chopped
2 garlic cloves, minced
1 cup uncooked rice
2 cups seafood or chicken stock or bottled clam juice
1 teaspoon Maggi seasoning or soy sauce
1/2 teaspoon vinegar, preferably white
1 bay leaf
12 ounces mixed cooked seafood, such as crab, scallops, oysters, or peeled and halved shrimp
1/2 Haas avocado, diced
2 medium tomatillos, husked, roasted, and puréed

Crema (page 63) or crème fraîche, for garnish (optional)

In a heavy skillet, fry the chorizo in the oil over medium heat. When just browned, add the onion, garlic, and rice and sauté briefly until the rice is translucent. Pour in the stock, Maggi, and vinegar, add the bay leaf, and bring to a boil over high heat. Reduce the heat to low, cover, and simmer for 15 to 18 minutes, until most of the liquid is absorbed.

Stir in the remaining ingredients, cover again, and continue cooking for 2 more minutes. Remove the pan from the heat and let the rice steam, covered, for at least 10 minutes (it will hold 30 minutes). Give the rice a good stir and serve hot.

VERSATILE VEGETABLES

Vegetables seldom stand alone as a separate dish or course in traditional border cooking. Mexican markets and the proliferating farmers' markets of the Southwest abound with produce of all kinds, often overflowing huge bins and piles, but most of the vegetables go into sauces, salsas, soups, stews, and other dishes where they are team players rather than spotlighted stars.

The trend toward healthier eating is beginning to change the role, however. Vegetables take center stage increasingly in tamales, tacos, and other *tipico* preparations, particularly in the Southwest, and they appear more frequently now as major accompaniments throughout the region. In the past, you seldom saw anything fresh on the side except garnishes, squash, green-chile *rajas* (strips), and grilled green onions, but both the range of choices and their prominence on the plate have grown substantially in recent years. Vegetables are ready for prime time in border cooking.

GREEN CORN TAMALES

A summer specialty of Arizona, California, and Sonora, green corn tamales epitomize the flavor potentials of vegetables in border cooking and also the growing popularity of the idea. Still little known outside a limited area, these tamales have become so hot in Los Angeles that some of the most skilled kitchens have to limit the number sold at a time. Like many Southwestern versions of the unconventional tamale, this one relies on the freshest, sweetest corn available at the market.

Makes 10 to 12 large tamales, enough for 5 to 6 main-dish servings

DOUGH
**4 cups fresh sweet corn kernels, from 4 to 5 large ears with husks
    removed and reserved (see "Technique Tip")**
1/2 cup butter
1 cup masa harina
1/2 cup stone-ground cornmeal
1 teaspoon sugar, if the corn isn't very sweet (optional)
1 teaspoon baking powder
1 teaspoon salt
Pinch of cayenne
1 to 3 tablespoons milk (optional)

FILLING
6 to 8 ounces mild cheddar cheese, grated
**1 1/2 cups mild green chile, preferably New Mexican or Anaheim, fresh
    or frozen, roasted and cut into thin strips**

Cover the reserved corn husks with a damp cloth.

In a food processor, purée 2 cups of the corn with the butter, reserving the remaining whole kernels. Add the rest of the dough ingredients, except the milk, to the puréed corn mixture. The dough should be thick but soft and spreadable. Add some or all of the milk if needed for the desired consistency. Stir in the reserved corn kernels.

Pick out 12 large corn husks, or find smaller husks that can be put together to wrap the tamales. Tear several other thinner husks into strips to tie the tamales. Hold a corn husk or pair of husks flat on one hand, smooth side up. Measure a generous $1/3$ cup of the dough. With a spoon or spatula, spread half of that dough on the husk in a rectangle about $1/4$ inch thick. Top the dough with about $1 \, 1/2$ tablespoons of cheese and an equal amount of chile strips. Spread the other half of the dough over the filling, covering as much of the cheese and chile as you can manage. Make sure all the dough is enclosed in the corn husk, and tie the packet loosely with a strip of husk. Repeat with the remaining tamales.

Place the tamales in a steamer, packing loosely in crisscross directions. Allow enough space between them for the steam to rise effectively. Steam the tamales for about 45 to 50 minutes, until the masa is firm and no longer sticks to the corn husk. Remove one tamale and check the consistency. If it is still doughy, rewrap it, return it to the pot, and continue steaming for a few more minutes.

The tamales should be eaten warm. Serve them in their husks, to be removed by each guest before eating. While many tamales are good with sauce or salsa, these are best unadorned. Eat leftovers within a couple of days, because the dough sours quickly. The tamales freeze well for a month or two, or can be used in Tamale Hash.

Technique Tip: When using fresh corn husks as tamale wrappers, first remove any dried or loose outer husks. Then, with a small, sharp knife, slice through the husks at the base of the ear, as close to the stem as possible, and carefully pull the husks away from the corn. Rinse them before using.

Regional Variations: Sonoran cooks usually make these tamales with young (hence "green") field corn so full of starch that you need no masa harina or cornmeal in the preparation. Recipe ingredients may be as simple as corn, lard, salt, and a load of sugar. Even using sweet corn, some Southwestern cooks add up to a cup of sugar to the dough, though we think it masks the corn taste. Purists may skip the cheese in the dish, and others may mix it into the dough rather than the filling, a tasty alternative.

ZUCCHINI, CHILE, AND CHEESE TAMALES

Another twist on vegetable tamales, these are a year-round treat and more traditional in style than the summertime green corn variety.

Makes 24 medium tamales, enough for 8 to 12 main-dish servings

Half a 6-ounce package dried corn husks

FILLING
3 pounds fresh zucchini, grated
1 tablespoon salt
1 cup chopped roasted mild green chile, preferably Anaheim or
    New Mexican, fresh or frozen
2 tablespoons minced onion
1 tablespoon minced garlic

6 ounces mild cheddar cheese, grated

4 cups masa harina
2 teaspoons salt
1 1/4 cups vegetable oil
4 cups water, or more as needed

Hatch Green Chile Sauce (page 54) (optional)

Soak the corn husks for at least 30 minutes in hot water to cover. The husks will become soft and pliable. Separate the softened corn husks and rinse them under warm running water to wash away any grit or brown silks. Soak them in more water until you are ready to use them.

To prepare the filling, first place the zucchini in a colander. Toss the zucchini together with the salt and drain it for at least 20 minutes. Squeeze the zucchini with your fingers to drain more of its accumulated liquid.

In a small saucepan over medium-low heat, simmer together the green chile with any of its juices, the onion, and garlic. Cook just until the mixture is dry but not browned. Stir the chile mixture and the cheese into the zucchini and reserve it.

Vegetable tamales have been gaining increasing acceptance in recent years, but they aren't a new notion. Diana Kennedy has found examples in Mexican cookbooks as far back as 1877, and in the Southwest, one appears in 1936 in a San Antonio publication, *Gebhardt's Mexican Cookery for American Homes.*

To prepare the masa, or dough, stir the masa harina and salt together in a large bowl. Pour in the oil, working it into the masa harina with your fingertips. Add the water and mix with your fingers, a sturdy spoon, or powerful electric mixer. When well blended, the masa should have the consistency of a moist cookie dough. Add more water if needed for the preferred consistency. Keep the dough loosely covered while working.

To assemble the tamales, use approximately equal amounts of masa and filling. To make 2 dozen 4-ounce tamales, use 2 tablespoons each of masa and filling for each tamale.

Hold a corn husk flat on one hand, smooth side up. (You may, depending on the size of the corn husks, need to overlap two husks to form one tamale. Spread the dough over the husks together, just as if they were one.) With a rubber spatula, spread a thin layer of masa across the husk, but not to the edges. Top with filling spread more thickly through the dough's center, stopping short of the dough's edges. Make sure that the dough's edges meet to enclose all of the filling. Secure the tamale by folding the wrapper over or tying it. Repeat the procedure until all the filling and masa are used.

Place the tamales in a steamer, packing loosely in crisscross directions, or stand them on end. Allow enough space between them for the steam to rise effectively. Cover the pot and cook over simmering water for about 1 to 1 $^{1}/_{4}$ hours until the masa is firm and no longer sticks to the corn husk. Unwrap one tamale to check its consistency. If it is still doughy, rewrap it, return it to the pot, and continue steaming a few more minutes.

The tamales should be eaten warm. Serve the tamales in their husks, to be removed by each guest before eating. The tamales are also good topped with green chile sauce, but the husks should be removed before adding the sauce.

RED PEPPER-PIÑON ENCHILADAS

Several years ago, Lia Rupp in Ramah, New Mexico, introduced us to her imaginative bell pepper, leek, and almond enchiladas. We experimented with similar concepts and arrived at this combination of flavors.

Serves 4 to 6

FILLING
2 tablespoons extra-virgin olive oil
2 medium onions, chopped
2 red bell peppers
1 yellow bell pepper, or an additional red bell pepper
1 fresh poblano chile, preferably, or New Mexican chile
1/4 teaspoon salt
1/4 cup plus 1 tablespoon piñon (pine) nuts, toasted

Vegetable oil for pan-frying
12 corn tortillas
Cilantro Cream Sauce (page 60)
Chopped fresh cilantro, for garnish (optional)

Preheat the oven to 350° F. Grease a 9-by-13-inch baking dish.

In a heavy skillet, warm the oil over medium-low heat. Add the onions and sauté them for 25 minutes, stirring occasionally, and reducing the heat if they begin to brown.

Roast the bell peppers and the chile over the stove or under a broiler until the skins char. Transfer the peppers and the chile to a small plastic or paper bag to steam until cool enough to handle. Peel, stem, seed, and chop the bell peppers and the chile and add them to the onions. Stir in the salt and all but 1 tablespoon of the piñons. Keep the filling warm.

Heat $^{1}/_{2}$ to 1 inch of oil in a small skillet until it ripples. With tongs, dunk a tortilla quickly in the oil long enough for it to go limp, a matter of seconds. Don't let the tortilla turn crisp. Repeat with the remaining tortillas and drain them.

Dip a tortilla in the sauce to lightly coat. Lay the tortilla on a plate, sprinkle 2 $^{1}/_{2}$ to 3 tablespoons of filling over it, and roll it up snug.

Lia Rupp runs the kitchen and everything else at the Blue Corn Restaurant in Ramah, easily the best place to eat in the sparsely populated Navajo and Zuni country near the New Mexico and Arizona line. Like many other creative Southwestern cooks today, Lia started with a solid grounding in regional food traditions and then began elaborating on the heritage. She proves once again that the deeper you sink your roots, the taller you can grow.

Transfer the enchilada to the baking dish. Repeat with the remaining tortillas and filling.

Top the enchiladas with the remaining cilantro sauce, seeing that each enchilada is submerged in the sauce, and bake for 20 to 25 minutes, until heated through and bubbly. Sprinkle immediately with the reserved piñons and a scattering of cilantro, if you wish. Using a spatula, serve immediately.

Regional Variations: Some of the most common Southwestern vegetable enchiladas combine either corn or cooked potato chunks with sour cream, cheddar cheese, and green onion, topped with a traditional red or green sauce. More elaborate versions might use anything from sautéed spinach and pickled jalapeños to wild mushrooms and leeks. California cooks seem especially fond of meaty strips of sautéed eggplant, which mix well with red bell peppers and the creamy cilantro sauce in our recipe.

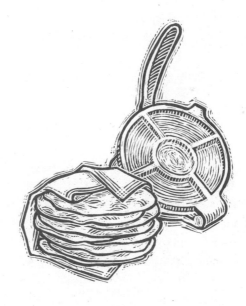

THE HONORABLE HENRY B.'S SOFT TACOS

Long-term San Antonio congressman Henry B. Gonzalez gave us this recipe for his favorite tacos, an uncommon and delectable variation on the vegetable theme. They look like enchiladas, but they aren't because you don't dip the tortillas *en chile*. In this case, boiling the chiles rather than roasting them works well, yielding a lighter, less intense tang that enhances the dish.

Serves 4 to 6

FILLING
4 mild green New Mexican or Anaheim chiles or poblanos
4 small green bell peppers
Water
2 tablespoons vegetable oil
1 medium onion, minced
1 garlic clove, minced
2 cups canned crushed tomatoes
4 ounces mild cheddar cheese, grated
2 ounces Monterey or pepper jack cheese, grated

Vegetable oil for pan-frying
12 corn tortillas

Stem and seed the chiles and bell peppers. Place them in a large saucepan, cover with water, and bring to a boil. Reduce the heat and simmer the chiles and bell peppers for about 20 minutes, until quite soft. Drain the vegetables and allow them to cool. With a table knife, scrape the pulp of the chiles and bell peppers away from their skins. Discard the skins, and mash and reserve the pulp.

In a skillet, warm the oil over medium heat. Sauté the onion briefly until softened. Stir in the garlic, tomatoes, and chile pulp and simmer for about 5 minutes. Mix about three-fourths of each cheese into the filling and reduce the heat to very low. Keep the filling warm while preparing the tortillas.

Heat $^{1}/_{2}$ to 1 inch of oil in a small skillet until it ripples. With tongs, dunk a tortilla quickly in the oil long enough for it to go limp, a matter

In 1857, *The New York Times* sent Frederick Law Olmsted to Texas to report on his impressions of the frontier state. The journalist liked to travel on his stomach, and he provided detailed accounts of his food experiences. Olmsted expressed disgust with the fare of poor southerners in east Texas, but he relished the Mexican cooking in the southern part of the state. He described women patting out tortillas, which he called corn slap jacks, and was delighted by the way that they wrapped the bread around bits of food when eating and dispensed with silverware. He also enjoyed a cabrito hash and beans served with a chile butter sauce.

of seconds. Don't let the tortilla turn crisp. Repeat with the remaining tortillas and drain them. Keep the tortillas warm.

Lay a tortilla on a plate, sprinkle 2 $^1/_2$ to 3 tablespoons of filling over it, and roll it up snug. Transfer the taco to a warm serving plate. Repeat with the remaining tortillas and filling. Scatter the remaining cheese over the top and serve immediately.

TACOS DE RAJAS

Isidoro Gonzales's La Super-Rica in Santa Barbara, a homey open-air café, serves great tacos *de rajas* and other creative *tipico* dishes featuring vegetables. Hardly a vegetarian restaurant, though, it wins acclaim for all its cooking, even from such a California cuisine authority as chef Alice Waters.

Strips of green chile, or *rajas*, frequently garnish meat plates in northern Mexico. In southern California, they sometimes fill soft tacos like these.

Serves 4

1 medium-size white onion, preferably sweet, sliced in thin strips
1 teaspoon vegetable oil
1/2 red bell pepper, sliced in thin strips (optional)
1/4 teaspoon cumin seeds, toasted and ground
2 to 2 1/2 cups mild green chile, preferably poblano or Anaheim, fresh
or frozen, roasted and sliced in thin strips
3 ounces asadero or Monterey jack cheese, grated

8 thin flour tortillas, preferably 5 to 6 inches in diameter, warmed

Toss the onion slices with the oil. On a griddle or in a heavy skillet, cook the onions over medium heat until limp. Add the bell pepper, if you wish, and the cumin. Continue cooking until the onions and bell pepper are very soft, but not browned. Add the chile strips and heat them through. Stir in the cheese and remove the mixture from the heat. There should be enough cheese to bind the vegetables together without the cheese becoming a predominant flavor.

Spoon the mixture equally onto the flour tortillas, folding each in half for serving.

BAKED VEGGIE CHIMIS

Serves 4

FILLING
4 tablespoons butter
8 ounces mushrooms, sliced thin
3 celery stalks, chopped
1 medium onion, chopped
1 garlic clove, minced
2 tablespoons all-purpose flour
1 teaspoon salt
1/8 teaspoon white pepper
1/4 cup evaporated milk
2 to 3 tablespoons minced pickled jalapeño, plus 1 tablespoon
   jalapeño pickling liquid
10 ounces fresh spinach
4 ounces mild cheddar cheese, grated

4 thin flour tortillas, preferably 7 to 8 inches in diameter
Melted butter
Grated mild cheddar cheese and pickled jalapeño slices, for garnish

Preheat the oven to 350° F. Grease a baking sheet.

Melt the butter in a heavy saucepan over medium heat. Add the mushrooms, celery, onion, and garlic and sauté the vegetables briefly, until they are softened. Mix in the flour, salt, and pepper. Add the milk, jalapeño and pickling liquid, and spinach and stir to combine. Cover and simmer for several minutes, just until the spinach is wilted. If the mixture is soupy, remove the lid and cook 1 or 2 additional minutes. Stir in the cheese and remove the pan from the heat. Taste and add a little more salt or pickling liquid to give the mixture more tang. Set the filling aside to cool for 10 minutes. (The filling can be made ahead and refrigerated for a day. Rewarm the filling before proceeding.)

Warm the tortillas for a few seconds on a griddle or in a heavy skillet until pliable. Transfer them to a plastic bag to stay soft.

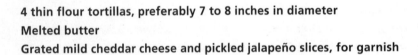

Spoon equal portions of the vegetable mixture onto the center of each tortilla. Fold the sides in and then roll up into a tight package, securing the chimichangas with toothpicks. Repeat with the remaining tortillas. Brush each chimi with melted butter.

Bake the chimis for 10 minutes or until lightly crisp and golden brown. Remove the toothpicks, scatter cheese and jalapeños over the top, and serve the chimis immediately.

CHILES RELLENOS CON PAPAS

A lot of foods taste great stuffed inside a chile—even mashed potatoes.

Serves 6

2 pounds baking potatoes
1 tablespoon salt
Water
3/4 cup whole milk
6 tablespoons Crema (page 63) or crème fraîche
4 tablespoons butter
Pinch of ground canela or other cinnamon
Salt and fresh-ground black pepper to taste

6 fresh large mild green chiles, preferably Anaheim or poblano, roasted and peeled

Grated mild cheddar cheese, for garnish (optional)
Ground dried mild red chile

Place the potatoes and the tablespoon of salt in a large, heavy pan and cover with water by at least 1 inch. Cook over moderate heat until tender, about 25 to 35 minutes, depending on their size. Drain the potatoes.

Preheat the oven to 350° F. Grease a baking sheet or medium baking dish.

While the potatoes cool slightly, pour the milk and crema into a medium pan and scald them. Watch that the mixture doesn't foam over as it heats. Reserve the mixture and keep it warm.

Peel the potatoes when they are cool enough to handle. Rice or mash the potatoes in their original pan. Put the pan over low heat and stir the potatoes continually for 2 or 3 minutes to dry them out thoroughly.

Stir the butter into the potatoes, a tablespoon at a time. Pour in the milk mixture about $^1/_4$ cup at a time, while continuing to stir. Add as much liquid as the potatoes can absorb without becoming soupy. Taste the potatoes for seasoning and add the canela and, if needed, the salt and pepper. Use the potatoes right away, or keep them warm for up to 1 hour in the top of a double boiler.

Slit the chiles on one side from top to bottom. Gently pull back the two side "flaps." Spoon the potato mixture equally into the chiles and place them on the baking sheet or in the baking dish. Top each chile with a sprinkling of cheese, if you wish, and a light dusting of chile. Bake the chiles for 10 minutes.

Serve hot.

Regional Variations: We serve potato rellenos as a side dish for a dressy "company" dinner, but chef Norman Fierros of La Pila in Phoenix goes a step further. He makes a similar preparation into the centerpiece of a meal by topping it with shredded grilled chicken and a light green chile sauce. If you want to try it that way, you can approximate Fierros's sauce by combining half a batch of the Tubac Chile Verde (tomato version) with about $^1/_3$ cup extra chicken stock.

In his monumental cookbook, *Authentic Mexican* (William Morrow, 1987), Chicago chef Rick Bayless talks about living in a Mexico City apartment directly above a neighborhood café. The popular gathering spot provided him, he says, a sense of community in a foreign land, and also contributed to his love for calabacitas. The kitchen served the squash medley as a main dish, and he continues the practice, adding a salad and tortillas.

Probably the border's most popular vegetable side dish over the years, other than simple garnishes at least, calabacitas is a superb way to enjoy squash. This is a straightforward, traditional version from Sonora.

Serves 6 to 8

2 tablespoons butter
2 tablespoons vegetable oil
5 cups sliced zucchini or a mix of zucchini and summer squash (about 2 pounds)
1 medium onion, chopped
2 cups corn kernels, fresh or frozen
1/2 cup chopped roasted mild green chile, preferably New Mexican or Anaheim, fresh or frozen
1/2 teaspoon salt
1/4 teaspoon ground canela or other cinnamon
4 green onions, sliced
2 tablespoons minced fresh cilantro or fresh mint (optional)

In a large skillet, warm the butter and oil over medium heat. Add the squash and onion and sauté for about 10 minutes, until well wilted. Stir in the corn, chile, salt, and canela and cook, covered, for another 10 minutes. Add the green onions and, if you wish, the cilantro or mint and heat through. Serve immediately.

Regional Variations: In northern Mexico, the squash normally used in this dish is more bulbous and lighter green than the zucchini found in most American versions. It's usually known simply as *calabacita*, or "little squash." Traditional New Mexico renditions of the dish, still a favorite in the state, often contain a little milk and a sprinkling of Monterey jack or cheddar cheese but skip the canela, cilantro, and mint. Some Arizona cooks load up the cheese, but others in the Southwest forgo it in favor of additional vegetables. A turn-of-the-century El Paso preparation, which one cookbook called merely "Mexican Dish," used squash, green peppers, green corn, tomatoes, and onion.

Topped with a cheese sauce, this calabacitas cousin from Texas acquires richness and refinement.

Serves 6 to 8

SAUCE
1 tablespoon butter
1 tablespoon extra-virgin olive oil
1 garlic clove, minced
Two 5-ounce cans evaporated milk
1/4 cup Crema (page 63) or crème fraîche
4 ounces pepper jack cheese, grated

2 tablespoons butter
2 tablespoons extra-virgin olive oil
5 cups zucchini, cut in fat matchsticks (about 2 pounds)
1/2 medium onion, sliced in thin strips
1 garlic clove, minced
1 large red bell pepper, sliced in thin strips
2 small tomatoes, preferably Roma or Italian plum, sliced in thin strips
1/2 teaspoon dried oregano, preferably Mexican
1/2 teaspoon salt

Queso añejo or Cotija or feta cheese, crumbled (optional)

In a large skillet, warm the butter and oil over medium heat. Add the garlic, evaporated milk, and crema and heat through. Stir in the cheese, cover the pan, and remove it from the heat. Stir again in several minutes if needed to melt the cheese evenly. Keep the sauce warm.

In a large skillet, warm the butter and oil over medium heat. Add the squash, onion, and garlic and sauté for about 5 minutes, until wilted. Stir in the bell pepper, tomatoes, oregano, and salt and cook for another 10 to 15 minutes, until the zucchini is very tender.

Serve hot with spoonfuls of the cheese sauce and, if you wish, the queso añejo for a sharp flavor.

Tula Borunda Gutierrez probably became the first Tex-Mex restauranteur when she opened the Old Borunda Cafe in Marfa in 1887. The business lasted almost one hundred years, until failing health forced Carolina Borunda Humphries, the last owner, to shut down her stove in 1985. Another Texan, Mike Martínez, created the oldest chain of Mexican restaurants in the country. His original El Fenix in Dallas dates back to 1918, when a fancy hotel fired him for cooking better than the chef.

Less common today, unfortunately, than in the past, colache is a Western variation on succotash. This is an early California rendition.

Serves 6

3 tablespoons extra-virgin olive oil
1 medium onion, chopped
1 garlic clove, minced
2 1/2 cups yellow summer squash, sliced in 2-inch matchsticks (about 1
    pound), or a similar amount of peeled acorn squash, cubed
1/2 pound thin green beans, sliced in 2-inch lengths (about 1 1/2 cups)
1 mild green chile, preferably Anaheim or New Mexican, fresh or
    frozen, roasted and chopped
1 cup corn kernels, fresh or frozen
2 small tomatoes, preferably Roma or Italian plum, diced
1/2 cup chicken stock
1/2 tablespoon vinegar, preferably wine
1/2 teaspoon salt

In a large skillet, warm the oil over medium heat. Add the onion and garlic and sauté for several minutes until the onion begins to soften. Stir in the squash, green beans, and green chile and sauté for another 5 minutes. Add the remaining ingredients and cover the skillet. Reduce the heat to medium-low and simmer the mixture for about 30 minutes until the squash and beans are very tender.

Serve warm.

FABIOLA'S BAKED PUMPKIN

Pumpkins pop up all over New Mexico in the fall, and Fabiola Cabeza de Baca Gilbert knew exactly what to do with them, as she explained in her 1949 book *The Good Life* (Museum of New Mexico Press reprint, 1982). If you can find tiny, individual serving-size pumpkins such as "Little Jack Horners," use them for a delightful presentation.

Serves 6

One 3-pound pumpkin, seeded and sliced in 6 wedges, or 6 miniature
    single-serving pumpkins, tops cut off "jack-o-lantern" style and
    seeded
Vegetable oil
Salt to taste
6 tablespoons butter
4 tablespoons brown sugar
1/2 teaspoon ground canela or other cinnamon
1/4 teaspoon ground dried red chile, preferably New Mexican or
    ancho
1/4 teaspoon ground coriander seeds

Preheat the oven to 350° F.

Place the pumpkin wedges or baby pumpkins (with "lids" on) in a shallow baking dish. Coat thinly with oil, sprinkle with salt, and bake for 50 to 55 minutes, until soft.

In a small pan, melt the butter and mix it with the remaining ingredients. Keep the mixture warm.

Spoon the butter mixture over the pumpkin wedges or drizzle inside the baby pumpkins, replacing their "lids" afterward. Bake for an additional 10 to 15 minutes until the pumpkin is very soft.

Serve hot.

A living museum of the Spanish colonial heritage in New Mexico, El Rancho de las Golondrinas (505-471-2261) hosts spring and fall harvest festivals each year, usually on the first weekends of June and October. The well-restored La Cienega ranch, which dates to the seventeenth century, vividly re-creates the way of life on the northern frontier of New Spain. Food and the agricultural cycle are always featured, but particularly at the harvest celebrations.

Serves 6 to 8

3 cups corn kernels, preferably fresh
1 cup stone-ground cornmeal
4 ounces mild cheddar cheese, grated
4 ounces fresh goat cheese or cream cheese, at room temperature
1/2 cup butter, melted
1/2 cup chopped roasted mild green chile, preferably New Mexican or poblano, fresh or frozen
4 green onions, sliced
1 teaspoon sugar
3/4 teaspoon salt
1/2 teaspoon baking soda
1/8 teaspoon ground canela or other cinnamon
3 eggs
1 1/2 cups buttermilk

Preheat the oven to 350° F. Grease a medium baking dish.

In a food processor or blender, purée 2 cups of the corn. Transfer the puréed corn and the remaining kernels to a large mixing bowl. Mix in the remaining ingredients. Pour the batter into the prepared dish.

Bake the pudding for 50 to 55 minutes, until lightly browned and just firm. Serve warm. We sometimes accompany the pudding with spoonfuls of mild Arizona Chile Colorado for a change of pace.

GRILLED CORN

As long ago as the 1790s, a Sonoran missionary recommended cooking fresh ears of corn in hot embers. Ignaz Pfefferkorn said the grill-like method "indisputably improves their flavor," which he compared to roasted chestnuts. We take the Jesuit's advice and add a twist of our own at the end.

Serves 6

6 ears of fresh sweet corn, unhusked
2 quarts salted water

6 tablespoons unrefined corn oil (see "Technique Tip") or extra-virgin olive oil
2 to 3 tablespoons pickling liquid from a jar of pickled jalapeños
1/2 teaspoon cumin seeds, toasted and ground
1/4 teaspoon salt
Pinch of sugar (optional)

Ignaz Pfefferkorn remained Germanic in his perspective even after eleven years of missionary work in northern Mexico. About corn, he wrote, "Sonorans eat maize with the greatest pleasure and with especial appetite when it is fresh from the field, ripe but still very tender. . . . For this reason *elotes* [ears of corn] are sold in the city markets just as are vegetables in Europe."

Remove any loose husks from the corn. Pull the husks back carefully almost to their base and remove the silks from the corn. Slice off the tip of the ear of corn if it is undeveloped or otherwise unattractive. Pull the husks back up. Soak the corn in the water for 10 to 20 minutes.

In a lidded jar, combine the oil and 2 tablespoons of the pickling liquid with the cumin, salt, and, if you wish, sugar. Taste the mixture and add more of the pickling liquid if desired. The mixture should taste a little hot and sharp because it will mellow when slathered over the corn. Pour the mixture into a serving dish.

On an outdoor grill, fire up enough charcoal to make a single layer under the ears. When the coals are covered in gray ash, place the corn, fully encased in the husks, directly above the coals. Grill the corn, turning once or twice, until the husks are somewhat browned and the corn is soft, about 20 minutes.

Pull the husks back down to expose the ears of corn. Don't remove the husks; they provide a "handle" at one end of the cob and add a nice rustic look. Serve the corn hot with the oil-and-pickling liquid mixture.

Technique Tip: The less refined an oil, the more it resembles the original food in character. Unrefined oils are not good for frying because of low smoke points, but they can be great for drizzling. The corn oil suggested here should smell and taste of summer corn, and should be kept in the refrigerator to preserve that flavor. Spectrum Naturals from California and Arrowhead Mills from Texas are two good brands with reasonable national distribution.

Regional Variations: Mexicans love fresh ears of corn as much as any Iowa native does. Vendors sell them in the streets during the summer, usually grilled and still wrapped in their husks. Norteños like to add cheese or cream, or even both. Southwesterners go for chile flavor, usually mixed with butter rather than the oil in our recipe. Arizona culinary authority Barbara Pool Fenzl takes a different approach, putting jalapeño pickling liquid in the boiling water she uses for cooking the corn.

ORLANDO'S CHICOS

You may have to plan ahead and shop by phone to make chicos, but the dish is definitely worth the effort. A dried roasted sweet corn, chicos originated as a method of preserving the late summer bounty. In many areas they are a lost classic, but they remain popular in New Mexico because of their superlative, lightly smoky taste. Our recipe is named for Orlando Casados, who processes some of the state's finest chicos and sells them through the New Mexico suppliers listed in "Mail-Order Sources."

Serves 8

2 tablespoons vegetable oil

2 medium onions, minced

6 garlic cloves, minced

2 cups chicos

1 teaspoon salt, or more to taste

2 bay leaves

6 cups chicken stock

1/2 cup chopped roasted mild green or red chile, preferably New Mexican or Anaheim, fresh or frozen (optional)

In a large saucepan or Dutch oven, warm the oil over medium heat. Stir in the onions and garlic and sauté for about 5 minutes, until very soft. Add the chicos, salt, bay leaves, and stock and bring the mixture to a boil. Reduce the heat to a simmer and cook, uncovered, for 1 1/2 hours, or until the chicos are well softened but still a little chewy. Add water if the chicos begin to dry out. Add the chile if you like a little heat, and a little more salt if needed, and cook for another 15 to 20 minutes. The chicos should have some liquid but not be soupy.

Serve warm. The chicos keep for several days, and in addition to being eaten as a side dish, they can be added to Frijoles de Olla, New Mexico's Best Green Chile Stew, or soups.

Regional Variations: Chicos are somewhat more common south of the border today than in any area of the Southwest except New Mexico. In Sonora, they may end up in a stew, cooked with beef short ribs or oxtails and a couple of chopped tomatoes. The meat is removed from the pot when it's tender, pulled into small shreds, and returned later when chile is added.

The owner of Ranch O Casados, near Española, Orlando Casados, Jr., prepares his chicos in *hornos,* beehive-shaped outdoor adobe ovens. He heats the *hornos* with an aspen fire, removing the embers with a hoe when the oven reaches the right temperature. Workers place moistened ears of sweet corn inside in their husks and seal the door and vent hole, leaving them to roast overnight. They then husk the ears, allow them to dry in the sun, and separate the kernels from the cob with a shelling machine. In their finished form the chicos resemble wrinkly, shrunk nuggets of popcorn.

Savory variations of flan—the border's best-loved dessert—have caught on with contemporary cooks as side dishes. Our first experience with this rich, garlic lover's version came from the kitchen of Donna Nordin, the creative force behind Cafe Terra Cotta in Tucson and Phoenix.

Serves 6

CUSTARD
2 whole heads of garlic
Vegetable oil
2 cups half-and-half
5 large egg yolks
1/4 teaspoon salt
Pinch of ground cayenne or other hot ground dried red chile

VINAIGRETTE
2 tablespoons vegetable oil
2 tablespoons walnut or other nut oil
2 tablespoons Salsa del Norte (page 38) or other mild
    tomato-based salsa
1 to 2 tablespoons vinegar, preferably rice

3 tablespoons piñon (pine) nuts, toasted (optional)

Preheat the oven to 350° F. Lightly grease 6 custard cups or small ramekins.

Pull any especially loose, papery skin from the garlic heads. Slice the tops off of the heads to expose just the tops of the cloves. Grease the heads with a thick coat of oil and place them in a small heat-proof dish. Bake about 45 minutes, until the cloves are quite soft.

Remove the garlic from the oven but leave the oven on. When cool enough to handle, squeeze the softened garlic out of each clove's skin into a blender. Add the remaining custard ingredients and purée. Strain the mixture and pour equal portions into the prepared cups or ramekins.

Place the flans in a baking pan large enough to accommodate all of the cups with a little room for air circulation. Add warm water to the pan, enough to cover the bottom third of the cups. Cover the pan with foil and bake for 35 minutes. If the flans are not well set in the center, bake for an additional 3 to 5 minutes. Be careful to avoid overbaking. Let the flans sit at room temperature for 15 minutes.

To prepare the vinaigrette, combine the oils and salsa in a small bowl. Stir in the smaller amount of vinegar, adding more if needed to get a tangy but not puckery dressing.

Unmold the first dish by running a knife between the custard and the cup. Invert onto a serving plate. Repeat with the remaining flans. Spoon about 1 tablespoon of vinaigrette over each flan, top with a sprinkling of piñons, if you wish, and serve warm.

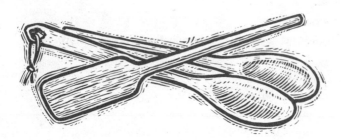

In *Gathering the Desert* (University of Arizona Press, 1985), Gary Paul Nabhan talks about the popularity of wild amaranth greens in Arizona, Baja California, and Sonora from pre-Hispanic times to the present. They usually germinate with the first big summer rainstorm—which folklore says should come on June 26, following the Feast of San Juan—and because of that, amaranth is often called *quelites de las aquas*. The wild greens contain eighteen times more vitamin A and thirteen times more vitamin C than lettuce. One Sonoran old-timer said they were "the meat of the poor people."

When early Spanish settlers in the borderlands had fresh, tender greens, or *quelites*, they sometimes prepared a traditional dish similar to this. The greens then were often wild foods—such as the amaranth of the Sonoran Desert—but cultivated varieties work just as well in our updated version.

Serves 4 to 6

2 tablespoons extra-virgin olive oil
2 garlic cloves, minced
1 1/2 pounds tender greens such as purslane, mustard greens, or spinach, still damp from cleaning
Salt and fresh-ground black pepper to taste
1/3 cup piñon (pine) nuts or fresh breadcrumbs, sautéed in extra-virgin olive oil until browned (optional)

Lemon wedges or vinegar, for accompaniment

Warm the oil over medium heat in a high-sided skillet or Dutch oven. Stir in the garlic and sauté until it just begins to color. Quickly add the *quelites*. Cover the greens, reduce the heat to medium-low, and cook for about for 5 minutes, until the greens are well wilted but still deep green. Add salt and a generous grinding of pepper. If necessary, cook the mixture for another 1 or 2 minutes, uncovered, to reduce any accumulated liquid.

Transfer the *quelites* to a serving dish and sprinkle with the piñons or breadcrumbs if you wish. Serve hot, accompanied with lemon wedges or vinegar.

Regional Variations: During Lent, many cooks add pinto beans to *quelites* to make a stalwart nonmeat meal. To prepare the dish in this way, put 1 cup of Frijoles de Olla or other prepared beans into the sautéing garlic, along with about $1/3$ cup of the bean cooking liquid. Stir the *quelites* into the beans and proceed with the recipe. Some people beef up the mixture even further with a cheese topping, or by using the mixture as a filling for enchiladas or tacos. Southwestern cooking authority Jane Butel gets extra heft and flavor in a lighter manner, adding cherry tomatoes to *quelites*.

A chunkier, earthier dish than *quelites*, these greens get some of their flavor from ingredients used in beans *a la charra*.

Serves 6

3 bacon slices, chopped in 3/4-inch pieces
1 small onion, chunked
2 garlic cloves, minced
2 small tomatoes, preferably Roma or Italian plum, minced, or 1/2 cup
   canned crushed tomatoes
1 crushed chile de árbol or minced fresh jalapeño
1 pound fresh chard, tender stems minced and leaves roughly chopped
1/2 cup chicken stock
Salt to taste

In a large skillet, fry the bacon over medium heat until browned and crisp. With a slotted spoon, remove the bacon from the drippings and drain it.

Sauté the onion and garlic in the bacon drippings until the onion is soft. Add the tomatoes and chile and simmer for another 5 minutes. Mix in the chard, stock, salt, and reserved bacon. Cover the chard, reduce the heat to medium-low, and simmer for about 5 minutes, until well wilted but still deep green. The sauce should be thin but not soupy. If necessary, cook the mixture uncovered for 1 or 2 minutes more, to reduce the sauce.

Serve hot.

Some of the earliest efforts to assimilate Mexican cooking outside the Southwest look a little peculiar today. A 1902 Philadelphia cookbook gave a recipe for dishes such as "chile con-cana" and explained that "enchilades" came from Spain, where cooks made the tortillas with "the ordinary thin, French pancake batter" instead of Mexican masa. That certainly would have surprised Spanish cooks, who wouldn't have known an enchilada from a Liberty Bell.

This fast and easy dish combines the complementary sweet flavors of fresh carrots and velvety *mole*. The recipe includes a simple *mole* sauce, but it's even better with a more elaborate leftover version.

Serves 4 to 6

QUICK *MOLE* SAUCE
1 tablespoon vegetable oil
3 tablespoons minced onion
1 garlic clove, minced
6 tablespoons ground dried mild red chile, preferably half New Mexican and half ancho
1 cup chicken or vegetable stock
1 ounce Mexican chocolate, such as Ibarra or Mayordomo, preferably, or 1 ounce bittersweet chocolate with an extra pinch of ground canela or cinnamon
2 teaspoons creamy peanut butter
1/4 teaspoon salt
Pinch of ground canela or other cinnamon

10 medium carrots, sliced in rounds and steamed until soft

2 teaspoons sesame seeds, toasted
Minced fresh cilantro, for garnish (optional)

In a saucepan, warm the oil over medium heat. Stir in the onion and garlic and sauté for a minute. Add the rest of the sauce ingredients and simmer for 20 to 25 minutes. Stir in the carrots and simmer for a couple of minutes, until the carrots are heated through and well coated with the sauce.

Serve the carrots warm, sprinkled with sesame seeds. Top with cilantro if you wish.

JÍCAMA HASH BROWNS

Most frequently eaten raw in salads or as an appetizer, jícama makes a crunchier, slightly sweeter substitute for fried potatoes. Try it in place of French fries or as a breakfast side dish.

Serves 4

3 cups grated jícama
Juice of 1 lime or 2 tablespoons pickling liquid from a jar of pickled
    jalapeños
1 teaspoon salt
1 egg, lightly beaten
2 tablespoons all-purpose flour
2 teaspoons ground dried mild red chile, preferably New Mexican or
    ancho
1 tablespoon minced onion
2 garlic cloves, minced

Vegetable oil for pan-frying
Salsa de Chiltepín (page 45) (optional)

Place the jícama in a large colander and toss it with the lime juice and salt. Let the jícama drain for 20 minutes, squeezing once or twice with your fingers to help eliminate the moisture. Squeeze the mass of jícama again and then roll it up in a clean dishtowel. Squeeze the towel over the sink to eliminate any additional moisture you can wring out.

Transfer the jícama to a bowl and mix in the egg, flour, chile, onion, and garlic. Form the jícama mixture into 8 to 10 patties, about 3 inches in diameter.

Warm $1/4$ inch of oil in a heavy skillet over medium heat. Fry the patties, in batches, cooking until they are richly brown and crisp on the outside. The interior should be soft and a little creamy. Serve immediately, accompanied with salsa if you wish.

The statuesque saguaro cactus provides less food than its prickly-pear cousin, but the fruit at the top of the tall arms is edible. Some Tohono O'Odham families spend three weeks each year gathering it in southern Arizona. The harvest marks the beginning of the traditional O'Odham calendar, when religious ceremonies encourage the desert's summer rains. The collectors use poles made from skeletons of dead saguaros to reach the fruit, which they cook into syrup or jam.

Serves 4

2 bacon slices, chopped
1/2 medium onion, minced
3 tablespoons diced red bell pepper, or a combination of red and yellow bell peppers
2 garlic cloves, minced
1/2 teaspoon cumin seeds, toasted and ground
2 cups prepared nopales, sliced in thin ribbons
3 tablespoons vinegar, preferably cider
1 1/2 teaspoons sugar, or more to taste

Slivers of red radish, for garnish (optional)

In a heavy skillet, cook the bacon over medium heat until crisp. With a slotted spoon, remove the bacon and drain it. Sauté the onion, bell pepper, garlic, and cumin in the bacon drippings until softened, about 5 minutes. Mix in the nopales and heat through.

Add the vinegar and sugar to the skillet and cook until the sugar has dissolved.

Serve hot or warm, garnished with the radish slivers for extra color if you wish.

Technique Tip: You can make this medley with canned nopales or nopalitos, or fresh pads of prickly-pear cactus prepared as described on page 22.

GRILLED GREEN ONIONS AND RAJAS

In northern Mexico, *cebollitas asadas* and green-chile *rajas* often accompany grilled meat, and they make a perfect match. Look for green onions with the biggest bulb you can find—the ones used south of the border commonly have heads up to an inch in diameter.

Serves 6

3 fresh poblano chiles or large New Mexican chiles
12 large green onions
1 tablespoon vegetable oil
Dash of Maggi seasoning, or pinch of salt
Juice of 1/2 lime

On an outdoor grill, fire up enough charcoal to make a single layer under the vegetables. When the coals are covered with gray ash, place the chiles directly over the fire. Grill the chiles, turning them frequently, until their skins are blackened. Transfer the chiles to a plastic bag to steam until cool enough to handle. Peel the chiles, using rubber gloves if your skin is sensitive, and cut the chiles into $^{1}/_{4}$-inch strips. Keep the *rajas* warm.

Trim any wilted portion of green from the tips of the onions. Rub the onions with the oil and the Maggi seasoning, if you are using it.

Tear a piece of aluminum foil about 6 inches wide. Place it on one side of the grill. Arrange the onions so that their green portions are on the foil and the bulbs are directly over the fire. Grill, turning frequently, until the bulbs are soft and lightly browned, about 5 to 10 minutes, depending on size. Squeeze lime juice over the onions and sprinkle salt over them, if you are using it.

Serve with the *rajas* and *carne asada* or another grilled meat.

This is our version of a recipe that originated in Parral, Chihuahua, where farmers raise peas in fertile river valleys. If you can't find tender pea pods, use snow peas as a substitute.

Serves 4 to 6

5 whole small tomatoes, preferably Roma or Italian plum, roasted
1 small onion, chunked
1 fresh jalapeño, halved and seeded
1 garlic clove
1/2 teaspoon salt
3 tablespoons vegetable oil
3/4 cup chicken or vegetable stock
1 pound pea pods, preferably fresh

In a blender or food processor, purée the tomatoes, onion, jalapeño, garlic, and salt.

Warm the oil over medium-high heat in a heavy skillet. Add the blended mixture, being careful to avoid spatters as the liquid hits the hot oil. When the most insistent sputtering dies out, stir in the stock, reduce the heat to low, and cook the mixture for 10 minutes. Stir in the pea pods. Cover the skillet and cook for 5 minutes, or until the peas are tender but still have a touch of crunch.

Serve hot.

The inspiration for this robust dish comes from early California, where they thought the potato rounds resembled doubloons, or *tostónes*.

Serves 6

4 baking potatoes, boiled or baked until tender
3 tablespoons extra-virgin olive oil
1 medium onion, chopped
3 garlic cloves, minced
1 cup Californio Colorado (page 53) or other red chile sauce
4 ounces asadero or Monterey jack cheese, grated
Sour cream, minced green onion, or chopped fresh cilantro, for garnish
   (optional)

Heat the broiler.

Peel the potatoes, if you wish. Slice the potatoes into thick rounds.

In a large, heavy, ovenproof skillet, warm the oil over medium-high heat. Add the onion and garlic and sauté until the onion is translucent. Stir in the potatoes, reduce the heat to medium, and fry until the potatoes are crisp and a little browned.

Pour the chile sauce over the potatoes and scatter the cheese over the top. Place the potatoes under the broiler just long enough for the cheese to melt.

Serve immediately, topped if you wish with sour cream, green onion, or cilantro.

The main national holiday in Mexico is Independence Day, September 16, but Southwestern Hispanics are more likely to celebrate Cinco de Mayo, May 5. Observed on a smaller scale in Mexico than in the United States, Cinco de Mayo commemorates the Mexican victory against French invaders at the Battle of Puebla in 1862. The winning general, Ignacio Zaragoza, was born in Texas, but that doesn't explain the fervor of holiday fiestas in cities such as San Antonio and Los Angeles. Some speculate that Cinco de Mayo is important to Mexican-Americans because it represents what they wish had happened two decades earlier, when the U.S. Army invaded the Southwest.

Spicy yet soothing, these potatoes are hearty border comfort food, a mainstay on our table both on the side and in the center, with just a green salad.

Serves 6

4 baking potatoes
1 tablespoon salt
Water
1 cup chopped roasted mild green chile, preferably New Mexican or
**   poblano, fresh or frozen**
3 small tomatoes, preferably Roma or Italian plum, chopped
2 garlic cloves, minced
3 cups chicken stock
Additional salt to taste

Place the potatoes and the tablespoon of salt in a saucepan and cover with water by at least 1 inch. Cook the potatoes over moderate heat until they are just barely tender, about 25 minutes, and drain them.

When the potatoes are cool enough to handle, peel them and cut them into bite-size chunks. Put the potatoes back in the pan and add the remaining ingredients. Cook the potatoes over medium heat for about 15 to 20 minutes, stirring up from the bottom frequently, or until the potatoes become very soft and a thick sauce has formed. Taste and add more salt as needed.

Serve warm.

BEANS, RICE, AND BREADS

No meal in the Americas, perhaps in the world, has sustained more people than tortillas and beans. During the frontier era in the borderlands, as in many other places and periods on the continent, the two formed the backbone of the diet and often constituted the entire daily fare.

People continue to eat beans and tortillas together in a variety of dishes, and whether combined or alone, they are still essential components of regional cooking. Though rice holds a less revered position—the European import was barely known until recently in some areas, such as New Mexico—it has gained acceptance as another major staple. Few borderlands residents today live on just one or even all three, but breads, beans, and rice definitely remain the staff of life.

When you're dealing with beans, it's best to start with the basics. These simple, unpretentious "pot" beans simmer on the backs of thousands of border stoves daily, and they form the bedrock of all elaborations. Don't skimp on the garlic, which mellows during the cooking, and add other seasonings to your taste, such as the ones suggested in "Regional Variations."

Serves 6 to 8

2 cups dried pinto beans
8 cups water, or more as needed
1 whole head of garlic, minced
2 dried chipotles
2 teaspoons dried epazote
1 1/2 teaspoons salt, or more to taste

Pick through the beans and rinse them carefully, looking for any gravel or grit. Rinse the beans a second time.

Place the beans in a stockpot or large, heavy saucepan. Cover them with water and add the garlic, chipotles, and epazote. Bring the beans just to a boil over high heat, then reduce the heat to low and simmer the beans, uncovered. Plan on a total cooking time of 2 to 2 1/2 hours.

After 1 hour, stir the beans up from the bottom and check the water level. If there is not at least 1 inch more water than beans, add enough hot water to bring it up to that level. Check the beans after another 30 minutes, repeating the process. Add the salt after the beans are well softened, and continue simmering. Check every 15 minutes, keeping the level of the water just above the beans. There should be extra liquid at the completion of the cooking time, but the beans should not be watery. If you wish, remove 1/2 to 1 cup of the beans, mash them, and return them to the pot for a thicker liquid.

Serve warm. The beans keep for several days and are even better reheated.

Technique Tip: When cooking beans, keep in mind the old Mexican expression "No hay como la lumbre mansa"—"There is nothing like a slow fire." You want the beans to become soft and creamy while holding their shape, and any attempt to speed the cooking tends to disintegrate them instead. The time required depends on the altitude—the higher, the longer—plus the age and obstinacy of the beans (though not the cook). We used to soak and drain beans before cooking, as is usually recommended in the United States, but we've realized that the steps steal some of the flavor and don't significantly reduce the time on the stove.

Regional Variations: Many cooks add meat to *frijoles de olla*, perhaps a ham hock in northern New Mexico, or chorizo in Chihuahua and Sonora. The *frijoles fronterizos* of Nuevo León contain not only chorizo, but also a similar amount of smoky bacon, a tomato or two, a chopped fresh poblano, some onion, and a little vinegar. J. Frank Dobie, the quintessential Texan, cooked the beans plain with a few cubes of salt pork and then served them with chiltepín chiles and raw onion for zest. New York chef Zarela Martínez, who grew up on a ranch in northern Mexico, puts sprigs of fresh epazote in the pot, and at the table finishes the beans with a splash of vinegar and oil, chopped onion, and pico de gallo.

DRUNKEN BEANS

Beer adds an earthy dimension to beans. These *frijoles borrachos* are particularly popular around Monterrey, Mexico's third-largest city and its brewery capital. Don't use a dark beer in the beans, because it can make them too bitter.

Serves 6 to 8

2 cups dried pinto beans

5 cups water, or more as needed

3 cups beer

4 ounces salt pork, chopped, or 1 tablespoon peanut oil

1 1/2 medium onions, chopped

6 garlic cloves, sliced

1 tablespoon vinegar, preferably cider

2 teaspoons dried oregano, preferably Mexican

1 teaspoon salt, plus more to taste

The dappled pinto bean, a relative of the kidney bean, takes the honors as the leading legume of the borderlands. In Texas alone, farmers grow some twenty thousand acres of pintos, but the state still has to import more than a hundred million pounds of the beans each year.

Pick through the beans and rinse them carefully, looking for any gravel or grit. Rinse the beans a second time.

Place the beans in a stockpot or large, heavy saucepan. Cover them with the water and beer and add the remaining ingredients, except the salt. Bring the beans just to a boil over high heat, then reduce the heat to low and simmer the beans, uncovered. Plan on a total cooking time of 2 to 2 $^{1}/_{2}$ hours.

After 1 hour, stir the beans up from the bottom and check the water level. If there is not at least 1 inch more water than beans, add enough hot water to bring it up to that level. Check the beans after another 30 minutes, repeating the process. Add the salt after the beans are well softened, and continue simmering. Check them every 15 minutes, keeping the level of the water just above the beans. There should be extra liquid at the completion of the cooking time, but the beans should not be watery. If you wish, remove $^{1}/_{2}$ to 1 cup of the beans, mash them, and return them to the pot for a thicker liquid.

Serve warm. The beans keep for several days and are even better reheated.

In *Early California Hospitality* (Academy Library Guild, 1952), Ana Bégué de Packman says that rancho cooks "served beans for dinner, more beans for supper, and warmed-over beans, fried dry and crisp, for breakfast. There was never a meal without beans in early California."

Named after the lady of the ranch, these are the most famous beans of northern Mexico, known across the country. The humble pinto doesn't get any dressier or finer than this.

Serves 6 to 8

2 cups dried pinto beans
5 cups water, or more as needed
3 cups beef stock
2 bay leaves
4 bacon slices, chopped
1 medium onion, chopped
4 garlic cloves, sliced very thin
3 to 4 fresh jalapeños or serranos, sliced vertically into thin strips
1 cup canned crushed tomatoes
1 teaspoon salt, plus more to taste
2 to 3 tablespoons minced fresh cilantro

Pick through the beans and rinse them carefully, looking for any gravel or grit. Rinse the beans a second time.

Place the beans in a stockpot or large, heavy saucepan. Cover them with water and stock and add the bay leaves. Simmer the beans, uncovered, over low heat. Plan on a total cooking time of 2 to 2 1/2 hours.

After 1 hour, stir the beans up from the bottom and check the water level. If there is not at least 1 inch more water than beans, add enough hot water to bring it up to that level. Check the beans after another 30 minutes, repeating the process.

In a skillet, cook the bacon over medium heat until browned but not quite crisp. Remove the bacon with a slotted spoon and drain it. Add the onion, garlic, and chiles to the bacon drippings and cook until softened. Stir in the tomatoes and salt and simmer for 5 minutes.

Spoon the vegetable mixture into the beans and continue cooking the beans. Check them every 15 minutes, keeping the level of the water just above the beans. There should be extra liquid at the completion of the cooking time, but the beans should not be watery. If you wish, remove $^1/_2$ to 1 cup of the beans, mash them, and return them to the pot for a thicker liquid. Stir in the cilantro and the reserved bacon just before the beans are done.

Serve warm. The beans keep for several days and are even better reheated.

REFRIED BEANS

One bite of a cook's *frijoles refritos* can tell you how serious he or she is about beans. The ultimate border comfort food, and an essential ingredient in many other dishes, *refritos* don't taste quite right if they are winning any health awards.

Serves 6

1/4 cup lard or bacon drippings, or a mixture of both
1 medium onion, chopped
3 garlic cloves, minced
3 cups Frijoles de Olla (page 374), Drunken Beans (page 376), Frijoles a
    la Charra (page 377), or other cooked whole pinto beans, plus 1
    cup of the cooking liquid
1/2 cup cream or evaporated milk
Salt to taste
1 teaspoon ground dried mild red chile, preferably ancho or New
    Mexican (optional)
Crema (page 63) or crème fraîche, crumbled queso fresco or queso
    añejo such as Cotija, or grated mild cheddar or Monterey jack
    cheese, for garnish

Warm the fat in a heavy skillet over medium heat. Stir in the onion and garlic and fry until softened, about 3 minutes. Add the drained beans to the skillet and smash them with a potato masher or Mexican-style bean masher, adding the cooking liquid and cream a bit at a time, until they reach a fairly smooth and moist consistency. Sprinkle in the salt and, if you wish, the chile. Continue to cook, stirring up from the bottom with a spatula or large spoon, until the beans become a thick paste.

Serve hot, topped with crema or cheese.

Technique Tip: While good beans and a generous hand with seasonings help make superior *refritos*, the lard or bacon drippings in the frying pan account for the magic of their transformation. If you are determined to cut down on the saturated fat, the best alternative is roasted peanut oil, which substitutes a deep, nutty taste for the meat flavor. Look for Loriva brand, in particular, at your supermarket or in specialty food stores.

Regional Variations: The healthiest *refritos* aren't fried at all, just mashed from whole beans. For many contemporary cooks, the tradeoff in taste is worth the fitness value. The richest *refritos* come from Arizona and Sonora, where some cooks double the amount of cream we suggest. Carlotta Dunn Flores, from Tucson's famed El Charro, swears by evaporated milk in the beans she serves at home and at her restaurant. Chihuahua versions, often soupier than others, may be covered with the state's wonderful mild cheese. Ninfa Rodríguez Laurenzo, owner of Houston's chain of Ninfa's restaurants, adds cumin in accordance with her family recipe from the Rio Grande Valley, while other Texans forgo the dried red chile for a sprinkling of minced fresh serrano or jalapeño on top.

TIED-UP BEANS

A major variation on refried beans from northern Mexico, *frijoles meneados* deserves to be more widely known. The name comes from the addition of stringy melted cheese, which laces through the beans. Some recipes today suggest a simple blending of *refritos* and cheese, but the extra steps detailed here result in a much more flavorful mixture. With its richness, we reserve *frijoles meneados* for special occasions, when we relish every last bite.

Serves 4

1 ancho chile (optional)
Water (optional)
2 cups Frijoles de Olla (page 374) or other cooked whole pinto beans,
    plus 1/2 cup of the cooking liquid
1/3 cup milk
1/2 cup lard, butter, or peanut oil
1/2 onion, minced
1 garlic clove, minced
1/2 teaspoon cumin seeds, toasted and ground
4 to 6 ounces asadero or mozzarella cheese, grated

Minced green onion tops or fresh cilantro, for garnish

Flour tortillas, warmed

Preheat the oven to 350° F.

Soak the chile in enough hot water to cover it, if you wish to have a slightly spicy version of the dish. When the chile is pliable, cut it into thin slices.

In a food processor, purée the beans and their liquid with the milk.

In a baking dish, warm the fat over medium heat. Stir in the onion, garlic, cumin, and ancho slices and warm through. Remove the dish from the stove and stir in the beans. Transfer the beans to the oven and bake them for 1 hour, or until they appear very thick and begin to dry out. Stir in the cheese and return the beans to the oven, baking just until the cheese has melted through, about 5 minutes.

Scatter the green onions or cilantro over the top. Serve the beans immediately with flour tortillas. For more heat, pair the beans with Salsa de Árbol or Sweet and Sour Anchos.

Technique Tip: In southern Sonora, a regional cheese called *mocorito* makes an extra-special *frijoles maneados*. Rich but mild in flavor, the cheese is long, slim, and thin. We haven't found it in the States yet, but it's worth knowing about, since Mexican cheeses are becoming increasingly available in American markets.

PINQUITOS SANTA MARIA

Elizabeth Berry pioneered the growth of Southwestern heirloom beans at her Gallina Canyon Ranch in Abiquiu, New Mexico. She has supplied many of the region's best restaurants for years, and now has sufficient production to sell the beans in specialty stores and by mail. For ordering information on some two dozen varieties, call 505-982-4149 or write 144 Camino Escondido, Santa Fe, New Mexico 87501. In California, Valerie Phipps also grows and sells specialty beans. Contact her at the Phipps Ranch, Box 349, 2700 Pescadero Road, Pescadero, California 94060, 415-879-0787.

On the early California ranchos, the bean of choice was often the small, pink *pinquito*. This preparation of the rosy legume takes its name and culinary inspiration from the town of Santa Maria, where farmers grow the beans commercially today on land lodged between the sea and the mountains. If you can't find *pinquitos* locally, you can order them by mail from Righetti Specialties in Santa Maria, 805-937-2402, or substitute small red beans.

Serves 6 to 8

1 pound dried pink beans
8 cups water, or more as needed
1 teaspoon salt, plus more to taste
3 bacon slices, chopped
2 garlic cloves, minced
1/2 cup bottled chili sauce
7-ounce can tomato sauce
2 teaspoons dry mustard
1 teaspoon sugar

Pick through the beans and rinse them carefully, looking for any gravel or grit. Rinse the beans a second time.

In a small stockpot or other heavy pan, combine the beans with the water. Bring the beans just to a boil over high heat, then reduce the heat to low and simmer the beans, uncovered. Cook slowly, stirring up from the bottom occasionally, for about 2 hours, or until the beans are soft but hold their shape. Stir in the salt after the beans have begun to soften. Add more hot water, if needed, to keep the beans just a little soupy while they simmer. Drain the beans, reserving the cooking liquid.

In a large skillet, fry the bacon over medium heat until translucent, just short of crispy. Stir in the garlic and sauté briefly until softened. Add the chili and tomato sauces, mustard, and sugar and simmer 5 minutes.

Simmer the cooking liquid in the original pan, reducing it to 3/4 to 1 cup.

Stir the beans and the sauce into the cooking liquid. Simmer the beans over low heat for 15 to 20 minutes to combine the flavors. The beans should be moist but not soupy.

Serve warm.

SAGE TEPARY BEANS

Cultivated long ago by the Tohono O'Odham and other indigenous peoples in the Sonoran Desert region, the tepary bean has been making a strong comeback in recent years with the help of groups like Native Seeds/SEARCH in Tucson. Higher in protein and fiber than the pinto, it matures quickly and tolerates the top temperatures of southern Arizona. You may have to conduct your own search to find teparies (see the sidebar), but the meaty-tasting beans are worth the effort.

Serves 6 to 8

**2 cups tepary beans, preferably half white and half brown varieties,
    soaked at least 8 hours**
6 cups chicken stock
4 cups water, plus more as needed
1 medium onion, minced
3 garlic cloves, chopped
2 teaspoons crumbled dried sage leaves
**1 1/2 teaspoons crushed or coarse-ground dried jalapeño or 1 minced
    fresh jalapeño**

Native Americans in the Southwest and northern Mexico cultivated New World beans as early as 800 B.C. By the time the Spanish arrived, the indigenous peoples knew and grew many more varieties than exist today, enjoying a wealth of tastes and textures that is just beginning to be rediscovered. Most of the beans were lost or hybridized in the last few centuries, but Native Seeds/SEARCH and other organizations are sponsoring research to revive varieties such as the extraordinary tepary. The Tucson nonprofit group sells dried beans and seeds for many other indigenous crops through a catalog that helps support its preservation efforts. For information and to order, contact Native Seeds/SEARCH, 2509 North Campbell, Suite 325, Tucson, Arizona 85719, 602-327-9123.

1 teaspoon vinegar, preferably sherry
1/2 teaspoon dried thyme
1/2 teaspoon salt, or more to taste

Pick through the beans and rinse them carefully, looking for any gravel or grit. Rinse the beans again. Because of the dryness and density of these desert beans, we recommend soaking them overnight.

Place the beans in a stockpot or large, heavy saucepan. Cover them with the stock and water and add the onion, garlic, sage, jalapeño, vinegar, and thyme. Simmer the beans, uncovered, over low heat. Plan on a total cooking time of approximately 3 to 3 $^{1}/_{2}$ hours.

After 1 hour, stir the beans up from the bottom and check the liquid level. If there is not at least 1 inch more liquid than beans, add enough hot water to bring it up to that level. Check the beans after another 30 minutes, repeating the process. Add the salt after the beans are well softened, and continue simmering. There should be extra liquid at the completion of the cooking time, but the beans should not be watery. If you wish, remove $^{1}/_{2}$ to 1 cup of the beans, mash them, and return them to the pot for a thicker liquid.

Serve warm. The beans keep for several days and are even better reheated.

HABAS AND OLIVE OIL

Technically a broad term for several kinds of bean, *haba* usually refers to the fava or horse bean in the Southwest. Farmers who raise them today in New Mexico and California use the beans fresh, just stripped from their tough pods. Our recipe calls for the dried version, which is more common in stores. Limas make a satisfactory substitute.

Serves 4 to 6

1 pound dried haba, fava, or horse beans
8 cups water, or more as needed
1 medium onion, minced
3 garlic cloves, minced
2 bay leaves
1/2 teaspoon salt

Extra-virgin olive oil
Minced fresh cilantro, fresh mint, or both, for garnish

In a large, heavy saucepan, combine the beans with the water, onion, garlic, and bay leaves. Bring to a boil over high heat, then reduce to a simmer. Cook slowly, stirring up from the bottom occasionally, for about 2 hours, adding more water if the beans begin to seem dry. Stir in the salt in the last 20 to 30 minutes of cooking. The beans should hold their shape and be soft, not mealy.

Drizzle the beans with olive oil and sprinkle them generously with the herbs. Serve warm.

Technique Tip: Often sold in their pods in Middle Eastern and Asian markets, fresh favas taste even better in the recipe. Avoid pods in which the beans bulge visibly, an indication they are old. After shelling, cook the beans in a smaller amount of water, just a couple of cups, and reduce the cooking time to about 30 minutes. Fresh or frozen lima beans can be treated in a similar fashion.

Californians grew garbanzos in the mission period and sometimes cooked them with tender spring greens such as lamb's quarters. We use spinach instead to make the tasty combination a year-round dish.

Serves 4 as a side dish or 2 as a main dish

2 teaspoons extra-virgin olive oil
4 ounces bulk chorizo, crumbled
1/2 medium onion, chopped
1 garlic clove, minced
Pinch of oregano, preferably Mexican
1 small tomato, preferably Roma or Italian plum, chopped
1/4 pound fresh spinach, chopped
2 cups canned or pre-cooked garbanzos, drained
6 green olives, sliced
Salt to taste

In a skillet, warm the oil over medium heat. Add the chorizo and cook until lightly browned. Stir in the onion, garlic, and oregano and cook until the onion is softened. Add the remaining ingredients and cook for 10 minutes.

Serve warm.

BEAN BURRITOS ENCHILADA STYLE

Most bean burritos are filled with *refritos*, but we prefer the lighter result you get with whole beans. This California-inspired version gains special flavor from salad toppings and a mild red chile sauce. The sauce makes it an "enchilada-style" burrito, or a "smothered" one in the terminology of some places.

Serves 6

SALAD GARNISH
4 small tomatoes, preferably Roma or Italian plum, chopped
3 crisp inner leaves of romaine, chopped
1/2 cup black olives, preferably brine-packed, sliced
4 green onions, sliced
2 tablespoons minced fresh cilantro
1 tablespoon minced onion
Juice of 1/2 lime
Salt to taste

6 thin flour tortillas, preferably 7 to 8 inches in diameter
6 to 8 cups drained Frijoles de Olla (page 374) or Refried Beans
    (page 378), or other well-seasoned pinto beans, warmed
1/2 cup minced onion
4 cups Californio Colorado (page 53) or other mild red chile sauce
Grated Monterey jack or asadero cheese

Heat the broiler.

In a small bowl, combine the garnish ingredients.

To assemble the burritos, take one tortilla and place it on a heat-proof plate. Spoon a generous cupful of the beans down the center of the tortilla and top with a sprinkling of onion. Roll up the tortilla snug around the filling, arranging it seam side down on the plate. Repeat with the remaining tortillas, beans, and onion.

Top the burritos with equal portions of the chile sauce and cheese. Melt the cheese under the broiler.

Spoon portions of the salad over each burrito and serve immediately.

Sleepy Mesilla, New Mexico, now known mostly for chile farms and pecan orchards, used to bounce back and forth in nationality between the United States and Mexico. The founders established the town on the Mexican side of the Rio Grande, to escape the authority of the U.S. Army during the 1846–48 war, but the river kept changing its course. Until the Gadsden Purchase settled the situation permanently, residents didn't know for sure on a given day what country they might wake up in.

Katy Camuñez Meeks learned to cook in her mother's kitchen, where the motto was "Panza Llena, Corazón Contento"—"Full Stomach, Contented Heart." When she opened the famed La Posta restaurant in Mesilla, New Mexico, in 1939, Katy used family recipes for most of the dishes, but she invented her own for "dressed-up" tostadas. Her best-selling version inspired this one.

Serves 4 to 6

12 corn tortillas
Vegetable oil for deep-frying
2 cups Refried Beans (page 378), warmed
1 1/2 cups Dora's Carne con Chile (page 198), warmed
Shredded lettuce, chopped tomatoes, and grated mild cheddar cheese, for garnish
Guacamole (page 123), for garnish

Pour enough oil into a deep, heavy skillet to measure at least 3 inches in depth. Heat the oil to 375° F.

While the oil is warming, cut 4 evenly spaced 1 1/2-inch-deep slits in the tortillas' edges. Fry the tortillas as described in the accompanying "Technique Tip" until crisp and lightly colored, about 20 to 30 seconds. Drain the tortilla shells.

Spoon 2 heaping tablespoons of beans onto a tortilla shell, followed by about 1 1/2 tablespoons of carne con chile. Top with lettuce, tomatoes, cheese, and guacamole. Serve immediately.

Technique Tip: To fry the tortillas in the proper upturned shape, you need some kind of round but flat-ended tool, perhaps a wooden flour tortilla roller or a cylindrical bean or potato masher. Place the tortilla into the hot oil and immediately press down on it with your chosen device. The hot oil will force the tortilla back up toward your tool, forming it into a cup. Use a slotted spoon in your other hand to help mold the cup shape uniformly. Have a few extra tortillas on hand when you first try these little nests, but they become easy with practice. Commercially available tools to mold the tortilla cups take more effort to use.

Regional Variations: In some areas, Katy Meeks's style of cupped tostadas would be called *chalupas*, and the term *tostadas* might be reserved for a similar flat tortilla dish, at least if the latter weren't already known as *tapatias*. By whatever name, the most basic versions call for little more than beans, cheese, and salad, but a lot of cooks add special local touches, like Katy does with the New Mexican carne con chile or Texans do with crab from the Gulf of Mexico.

BEAN GORDITAS

Makes eight 5-inch to 6-inch gorditas, enough for 4 main-dish servings

2 cups masa harina
1/2 teaspoon salt
1 1/3 cups warm water, or more as needed
1 cup mashed or Refried Beans (page 378), with 1 or 2 tablespoons of
    water added to make the beans spread easily
Ground dried red chile, preferably ancho or New Mexican
Minced fresh serrano

Salsa del Norte (page 38), Cactus Relish (page 47), or other salsa

In a small bowl, stir together the masa harina and salt. Add the water and mix into a soft dough. It is important for the masa to be quite moist, but sturdy enough that it can be rolled into balls.

Form the dough into 12 balls approximately 1 $^1/_2$ inches in diameter. Cover the balls with plastic wrap to keep them from drying out. If any of the balls do seem dry before cooking, knead more water into them. Unlike the dough for flour tortillas, this dough can be reworked.

Place one ball of dough in a tortilla press between the two sheets of plastic sometimes sold with the press, or use two plastic sandwich bags. (If you do not have a press, see "Border Basics" for instructions about rolling out dough.) Press the ball until it is flattened to the desired thickness, generally about $^1/_4$ to $^1/_3$ inch. Lay the dough on a medium-hot griddle or heavy skillet. Cover the tortilla with a heaping tablespoon of

beans and sprinklings of red chile and serrano. Form a second tortilla of the same size and place it over the first tortilla and filling. While cooking, press down on the top tortilla, especially around the edges, squashing some of the filling into the masa. Avoid pressing so much that beans ooze out the side. (You can form the remaining tortillas from the balls of dough while the first *gordita* is cooking.) Cook for about 2 minutes on each side, until speckled with brown flecks and a little leathery on the surface.

Transfer the *gordita* to a serving platter and keep warm while you repeat the process with the remaining tortillas and filling.

Serve warm with lots of salsa.

Regional Variations: In the *Blonde Chicana Bride's Mexican Cookbook* (Filter Press, 1981), Helen Duran gives a recipe for a dish similar to these *gorditas*, but made with a traditional American buttermilk corncake batter. She explains that her recipe is an attempt to capture the flavor of a market treat she ate in Mexico. As some people would have said in the 1970s, the food just keeps on trucking.

MEXICAN RED RICE

Mexican rice is usually sautéed before cooking, which gives a nuttier flavor to the grain. We prefer to use fragrant Texas-grown Texmati rice in this dish, though any medium- or long-grain rice will work. Choose between beef or chicken stock on the basis of what else you plan to serve.

Serves 4 to 6

2 tablespoons peanut oil or lard
1 medium onion, minced
2 garlic cloves, minced
1 cup uncooked rice
2 small tomatoes, preferably Roma or Italian plum, chopped,
    or 1/3 cup drained, chopped canned tomatoes
2 cups beef or chicken stock
1 tablespoon ground dried mild red chile, preferably ancho or New
    Mexican
3/4 teaspoon salt

In a medium saucepan, warm the peanut oil or lard over medium heat. Sauté the onion and garlic until softened. Add the rice and tomatoes and sauté for another couple of minutes, stirring to coat all the grains of rice with oil. Pour in the stock, sprinkle in the chile and salt, and bring to a boil. Reduce the heat to a simmer, cover the pan, and cook the rice for 15 to 18 minutes, until all the liquid is absorbed. Remove the pan from the heat and let the rice steam, covered, for 5 to 10 minutes.

Fluff up the rice with a fork and serve warm.

Technique Tip: Many Mexican cookbooks suggest washing and rinsing rice to remove the talc and dust. These steps can be skipped when working with U.S. products. The same books may also call for more liquid than you add to rice in the States. Mexican rice absorbs more because it is less refined. Our recipes are written with U.S. rice in mind.

Regional Variations: Rice shows up less in northern New Mexico than elsewhere in the border region, but when it does, it's often flavored heavily with tomatoes. A cook might reduce the chile to 1 teaspoon and add an 8-ounce can of tomato sauce and a stalk or two of chopped celery. Descendants of California rancho cooks often use olive oil as the fat, which contributes another dimension of taste, and they sometimes get the rosy color from Spanish saffron rather than tomato. Tex-Mex cooks might also skip the tomato, and would likely substitute commercial chili powder, heavily flavored with cumin and garlic, for the dried red chile. A handful of fresh corn kernels or minced carrot are favorite vegetable additions. We like to add a cup of cooked garbanzos during the simmering for a heartier dish that can serve as an entrée.

ARROZ VERDE

Traditionally in Mexico, the day might dictate the color of the rice. Using the three colors of the Mexican flag, cooks served white rice for christenings, red at regular meals, and green for holidays. The custom is disappearing, but this green version from Austin still stands up to a celebration and can turn any dinner festive.

Serves 4 to 6

1 green bell pepper, chopped
3/4 cup well-packed chopped fresh cilantro
10 green onions, chopped
**2 to 4 fresh serranos, chopped (depending on your heat tolerance and
    what the rice will accompany)**
1 1/2 teaspoons salt
2 3/4 cups water
3 tablespoons butter
1 1/2 cups uncooked rice
1/2 cup peas, fresh or frozen (optional)

In a blender or food processor, purée the bell pepper, cilantro, onions, and serranos with the salt and the water.

In a heavy saucepan, warm the butter over medium heat. Sauté the rice until translucent. Pour in the sauce and bring the rice to a boil. Reduce the heat and simmer, covered, for 15 to 18 minutes, until all the liquid is absorbed. If you wish to use the peas, stir them into the rice. Remove the pan from the heat and let the rice steam, covered, for 5 to 10 minutes.

Fluff up the rice with a fork and serve warm.

Regional Variations: In the late 1980s, Mexico's Banco Nacional de Crédito Rural published a solid series of cookbooks about the *Comida Familiar* (popular foods) of the various states in the country. The Baja California edition describes a green rice with almonds that derives its hue from green onions, chopped celery, and parsley. In other states, cooks use lettuce leaves, chives, and sprigs of basil or other green herbs to provide color and flavor.

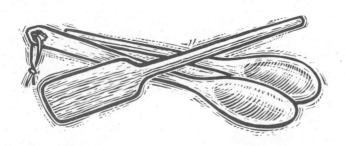

The inspiration for this recipe comes from a slim but terrific 1914 cookbook, Bertha Haffner-Ginger's *California Mexican-Spanish Cook Book*. Probably the first effort to address the state's Hispanic culinary heritage in a broad way, it remains one of the best. Few copies seem to have survived, but one is in the rare book collection at the Los Angeles Public Library.

Yerba buena, or mint, goes well in rice, as California cooks knew from an early period.

Serves 4

2 cups chicken stock
1/3 cup loosely packed fresh mint leaves
1 tablespoon bacon drippings
2 tablespoons minced onion
2 garlic cloves, minced
1 cup uncooked rice
1 teaspoon salt
1/2 teaspoon ground dried mild red chile, preferably ancho or
    New Mexican
1 tablespoon minced fresh mint

In a saucepan, bring the stock and the mint to a boil. Remove the stock from the heat and let it steep.

Warm the bacon drippings in a heavy saucepan over medium heat. Add the onion and garlic and sauté until soft. Mix in the rice and continue cooking until it is translucent.

Strain the stock (discarding the mint) and pour it over the rice. Sprinkle in the salt and chile. Reduce the heat, cover the pan, and simmer the rice for 15 to 18 minutes, until all the liquid is absorbed. Remove the pan from the heat and let the rice steam, covered, for 5 to 10 minutes. Sprinkle in the minced mint, re-cover the pan, and let the mixture sit for 10 more minutes.

Fluff up the rice with a fork and serve warm.

CREAMY RICE CASSEROLE

Serves 6

2 tablespoons butter
1/2 medium onion, chopped
1 1/2 cups corn kernels, fresh or frozen
1/2 cup chopped roasted mild green chile, preferably poblano or New Mexican, fresh or frozen
3 cups cooked rice, preferably cooked in chicken stock
4 ounces asadero or Monterey jack cheese, grated
1/2 cup Crema (page 63), crème fraîche, or sour cream
Salt to taste
3 tablespoons minced fresh cilantro

Preheat the oven to 350° F. Grease a baking dish.

Warm the butter in a skillet over medium heat. Add the onion and sauté until soft. Stir in the corn and chile and cook for about 5 minutes.

Transfer the corn and chile mixture to a large bowl. Stir in the rice and the remaining ingredients. Spoon the mixture into the baking dish and bake, covered, for 25 minutes. Uncover the dish and bake for 5 minutes more.

Serve warm.

The grande dame of Texas cooking, Neiman Marcus chef Helen Corbitt collaborated with Mexican food authority Maria de Carbia on a 1961 cookbook, *Mexico Through My Kitchen Window*. Some of the dishes, such as this soft-textured spoonbread, put an unusual twist on Tex-Mex traditions.

Serves 4

1 cup Mexican Red Rice (page 390) or other well-seasoned cooked rice
1/4 cup stone-ground cornmeal
1 teaspoon salt
1/2 teaspoon baking soda
2 tablespoons melted butter or bacon drippings
2 tablespoons minced green onion tops
2 eggs, lightly beaten
2 cups buttermilk

Preheat the oven to 325° F. Grease a baking dish.

In a bowl, mix together all the ingredients and pour into the baking dish. Bake for 55 to 60 minutes until lightly browned and puffed.

Serve warm.

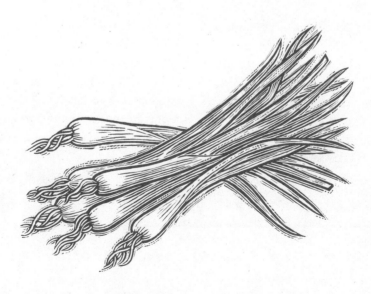

Fideos is the Mexican name for vermicelli, a thin pasta used in Spanish cooking but popularized in Mexico partially by Italian immigrants. In this Americanized version of a Sonoran preparation, the noodles are combined with rice, which early Spanish settlers imported from Asia via the Philippines. So what's so new about fusion cooking?

Serves 4 to 6

1 tablespoon butter
1 tablespoon bacon drippings or vegetable oil
1 cup uncooked rice
1/3 cup *fideos* or vermicelli
1 small onion, chopped
2 garlic cloves, minced
2 tablespoons chopped roasted mild green chile, preferably New
     Mexican or poblano, or 1/2 green bell pepper, chopped
2 1/3 cups stock, chicken or beef
3/4 teaspoon salt
Fresh-ground black pepper to taste
1 tablespoon minced fresh parsley

Heat the butter and bacon drippings in a heavy skillet until medium-hot. Add the rice and *fideos* to the fat. Sauté briefly until medium brown. Add the onion, garlic, and chile or bell pepper and continue heating for another couple of minutes, until the vegetables begin to soften. Pour in the stock and sprinkle in the salt and pepper. Cover the pan, reduce the heat to a low simmer, and cook until the liquid is absorbed and the vermicelli tender, about 15 minutes. Sprinkle in the parsley, re-cover the pan, and let the mixture sit for 10 minutes.

Fluff up the rice and *fideos* with a fork and serve warm.

Technique Tip: *Fideos* are usually sold in little nests. Separate the strands and break them into smaller pieces before measuring.

Local produce markets in Mexico usually sell a wide variety of pastas. They come in wheels, curlicues, and more whimsical shapes, and in colorful hues that replicate the Mexican flag.

As founder of La Sociedad Folklórica de Santa Fe, Cleofas M. Jaramillo was an authority on all aspects of New Mexico folk life and foods, subjects that she covered together in her 1942 cookbook, *The Genuine New Mexico Tasty Recipes*. Señora Jaramillo made her own noodles for *fideos*, flavoring them with mint and the local *azafrán*. We've borrowed her tasty idea and adapted it to ready-made pasta.

Serves 8

2 3/4 cups chicken or beef stock
1/3 cup tightly packed fresh mint leaves
1/4 cup extra-virgin olive oil
10 ounces *fideos* or vermicelli
1 large onion, minced
2 garlic cloves, minced
1 tablespoon plus 1 teaspoon New Mexican *azafrán,* or a pinch of
     saffron threads, crumbled (see "Technique Tip")
1 1/2 teaspoons salt
1/2 teaspoon ground dried mild red chile, preferably New
     Mexican or ancho

1/4 cup piñon (pine) nuts, toasted
2 tablespoons minced fresh mint, for garnish

In a saucepan, bring the stock and the mint to a boil. Remove the stock from the heat and let it steep.

Heat the oil in a heavy skillet until medium-hot. To the oil, add the *fideos* or vermicelli, crumbled lightly from the "nests" that they usually come in. Sauté briefly until golden brown. Add the onion and garlic and continue heating for another couple of minutes until the vegetables begin to soften.

Strain the stock (discarding the mint) and pour it over the pasta. Sprinkle in the remaining seasonings. Cover the pan, reduce the heat to a low simmer, and cook until the liquid is absorbed and the *fideos* tender, about 15 minutes.

Stir in the piñon nuts, sprinkle the mint over the *fideos*, and serve warm.

Technique Tip: *Azafrán* is the Spanish word for saffron, but in New Mexico it means something a little different. True saffron comes from the stamen of a particular variety of crocus. When the early settlers arrived in New Mexico, they found a substitute in the safflower. It doesn't have the full redolence of the original, but it also lacks the hefty price tag. Look for it in Hispanic markets or order from the Santa Fe School of Cooking (listed in "Mail-Order Sources"). If you want to substitute true saffron, a pinch of crumbled threads will be sufficient.

Regional Variations: In most border areas, cooks brown *fideos* in a neutral vegetable oil, lard, or bacon drippings, and rely more heavily than Señora Jaramillo on a tomato sauce for flavor. They probably would leave out the *azafrán* and mint, add a cup of chopped fresh or canned tomatoes, and reduce the stock to about 2 ¹/₂ cups. Texans might throw in a pinch of cumin. People with a pot of *frijoles de olla* on hand sometimes use bean liquid in place of all or part of the stock. After cooking the *fideos,* many people top the noodles with cheddar cheese today, though we prefer Pauline Wiley-Kleeman's approach from her 1929 California cookbook, *Ramona's Spanish-Mexican Cookery,* where she suggests a covering of goat cheese.

Some Sonoran tortillas are larger than a pizza and thinner than the fine lines in a loan agreement. You don't need to go quite that far to duplicate the taste.

Makes ten 8-inch, eight 10-inch, or six 12-inch tortillas

2 cups high-gluten bread or all-purpose flour
3/4 teaspoon salt
3 tablespoons vegetable shortening
3/4 cup warm water

Stir together the flour and salt in a large bowl. With your fingertips, mix in the shortening. Add the water, working the liquid into the dough until a sticky ball forms.

Dust a counter or pastry board with flour and knead the dough vigorously for 1 to 2 minutes. The mixture should be soft but no longer sticky. Let the dough rest, covered with a damp cloth, for about 15 minutes. Divide the dough into 6 or 8 balls, cover them again with the damp cloth, and let them rest for at least 45 minutes longer. (If not for use immediately, the dough can be greased lightly and refrigerated for up to 12 hours. Bring the dough back to room temperature before proceeding.)

Cover the counter or pastry board with waxed paper, place a ball of dough in the center of it, and top with another piece of waxed paper. A tortilla roller (much like a short section of broomstick) is easier to use than a conventional rolling pin. Roll the dough from the center outward, then turn the tortilla a few inches and roll again, attempting to keep the growing circle even. Roll out the dough into a circle as thin as possible, preferably $1/16$ to $1/8$ inch thick. Remove the waxed paper and pull on the dough with your fingertips too, being careful to avoid tearing it. If you didn't succeed in creating a nicely rounded tortilla, trim off any ragged edges and discard them.

Heat a dry griddle or large, heavy skillet over high heat. Cook the first tortilla 10 seconds on each side, then flip back and forth for another 10 seconds per side, cooking just until the dough looks slightly dry and wrinkled and a few brown speckles form on both surfaces. Repeat with the remaining tortillas.

Fold each tortilla in quarters and serve warm in a napkin-lined basket, with butter or salsa, or reserve for another use.

Technique Tip: We suggest rolling the dough between waxed paper because it's the easiest method for people who don't make tortillas on a daily basis. The traditional technique, if you want a challenge, is to roll out a disk of dough about 6 or 7 inches in diameter, place it over a closed fist, and pull it out gently with your other hand, lightly greased, similar to the way pizza masters prepare their crust. As the circle of dough enlarges, its position shifts up the arm, draping you from wrist to elbow, or with the largest tortillas, from fingertips to armpit. Griddles in Sonora, sometimes made out of the lids of oil drums, are often oversized to handle massive tortillas, but you can cook one in stages if you lack the extra capacity. Drape half of it across the cooking surface, while supporting the other half with your hands during the brief cooking. Flip the tortilla over, continuing to hold the second half. When the first half is cooked on both sides, turn it 180° and cook the other half in similar fashion. The technique isn't as awkward as it might sound, and if you've gotten this far, you're obviously not easily daunted anyway.

Flour tortillas are indispensable to border families, as fundamental as a crusty baguette to the French. In *California Rancho Cooking* (The Olive Press, 1988), Jacqueline Higuera McMahan recalls her Aunt Emma's wonderfully light tortillas, which all the women in the family tried to emulate. They were so prized at parties that Emma doled out the tortillas personally from a seat of honor instead of setting them on the table with the others.

The passion for seeking out the best continues today, even from commercial sources. A Tucson friend, displaced to Hawaii, manages by any means possible to get regular shipments of her favorite hometown St. Mary's Sonoran-style

tortillas. In New Mexico, people make pilgrimages to the famous Santuario de Chimayó, and also to an open-air food stand in a corner of the church's parking lot, where Léona Tiede sells fabled fresh-grilled tortillas. The talented but unassuming cook developed the small business into a Southwestern institution, supplying her Léona's de Chimayó brand of tortillas to area grocery stores and to fans nationwide (call 505-351-4660 to order). In addition to thick and chewy traditional tortillas, made in the local style from white or whole-wheat flour, she now also sells versions flavored with butterscotch, basil, apples, jalapeños, and more.

TEXAS FLOUR TORTILLAS

The best-known style of flour tortilla is thicker and chewier than its Sonoran cousin. Unlike the previous recipe, you use leavening and a softer wheat or lower-gluten flour for flakier, more tender results.

Makes about 8 tortillas, approximately 7 to 8 inches in diameter

2 cups low-gluten pastry or all-purpose flour
1 teaspoon salt
1 1/2 teaspoons baking powder
1 1/2 teaspoons vegetable oil
3/4 cup lukewarm milk or water

Sift together the flour, salt, and baking powder into a large bowl. Pour in the oil and mix with your fingertips to combine. Add the milk or water, working the liquid into the dough until a sticky ball forms.

Dust a counter or pastry board with flour and knead the dough vigorously for 1 minute. The mixture should be "earlobe" soft and no longer sticky. Let the dough rest, covered with a damp cloth, for about 15 minutes. Divide the dough into 8 balls, cover them again with the damp cloth, and let them rest for another 15 to 30 minutes. (If not for use immediately, the dough can be refrigerated for up to 4 hours. Bring the dough back to room temperature before proceeding.)

Dust a counter or pastry board with flour again and roll out each ball of dough into a circle or oval approximately $1/4$ inch thick. A tortilla roller (much like a short section of broomstick) is easier to use than a conventional rolling pin. If you want nicely rounded tortillas, trim off any ragged edges and discard them. To avoid toughening the dough, try not to reroll it.

Heat a dry griddle or heavy skillet over high heat. Cook the tortillas 30 seconds on each side, or until the dough looks dry and slightly wrinkled and a few brown speckles form on both surfaces.

Serve warm in a napkin-lined basket, with butter or salsa, or reserve for another use.

Technique Tip: Many people today use microwave ovens to reheat flour tortillas, wrapping them in plastic so they steam. It's an acceptable technique if you're planning to bury the tortilla in sauce or filling. If you plan to eat it alone as bread, it deserves better treatment. Heat a griddle or heavy skillet—we especially like cast iron—and warm the tortilla briefly on both sides. It becomes soft and pliable, but also develops an appealing crustiness on the surface.

For holding warm tortillas before serving, the best container is a *chiquihuite* basket, woven of reeds with squared-off sides. It works better than the popular ceramic models because moisture escapes more freely, preventing the bread from getting soggy.

Regional Variations: In Coahuila, some tortillas are small and fat, good for stand-up buffets. You can make them using this same recipe, starting with 12 balls of dough and rolling out each about 4 inches in diameter. In northern New Mexico and a growing number of other areas, many people prefer whole-wheat tortillas, for which you substitute that kind of flour for half of the low-gluten or all-purpose flour. Lucy M. Garza from the Rio Grande Valley in Texas recommends tortillas *de azucar*, a tasty sweet variety made with anise tea. Add 1 or 2 tablespoons of sugar to the dry ingredients and, in place of the liquid, tea made from anise seeds steeped in water for at least 10 minutes.

José Cordova and his wife, Kathy, operate the Valencia Flour company in tiny Jarales, New Mexico, in a family mill that dates back to 1913. They are properly proud of their Valencia Tortilla and Pastry Flour, a low-gluten product that rolls out into a soft dough and makes light, flaky tortillas as well as great pie crusts. The Cordovas sell their flour—along with good mixes for fry bread and sopaipillas—in many stores in the Southwest and also by mail (P.O. Box 210, Jarales, New Mexico 87023, 505-864-0305).

If flour tortillas are at the heart of border cooking, corn tortillas still form the soul of many dishes. They were the original tortilla, created by Native Americans long before the Spanish arrived, and they remain the dominant form in most of Mexico. The conquerors called them tortillas because of their shape, similar to the omelets that went by the same name in the mother country. Even on the northern frontier, before the Spanish began cultivating wheat extensively, corn tortillas constituted the core of the diet. In late eighteenth-century Sonora, Jesuit missionary Ignaz Pfefferkorn reported with some incredulity that the Natives and Mexican-born Spaniards "eat these cakes with the same relish as Europeans do the very best bread. They even consider them superior to the most excellent wheat bread baked in Mexico City and elsewhere."

Makes twelve 5-inch to 6-inch tortillas

2 cups masa harina
1/2 teaspoon salt
1 1/4 cups warm water, or more as needed

Heat a dry griddle or heavy skillet over medium-high heat.

In a large bowl, mix the ingredients with a sturdy spoon or your hands until the dough is smooth and forms a ball. A food processor can speed up this step. The dough should be quite moist but hold its shape. Add a little more water or masa harina, if needed, to achieve the proper consistency.

Form the dough into 12 balls approximately 1 1/2 inches in diameter. Cover the balls with plastic wrap to keep them from drying out. If any of the balls do dry out before cooking, knead more water into them. Unlike the dough for flour tortillas, this dough can be reworked.

Place one ball of dough in a tortilla press between the two sheets of plastic sometimes sold with the press, or use two plastic sandwich bags. (See the "Border Basics" chapter for instructions about rolling out dough if you do not have a press.) Press the ball until it is flattened to the desired thickness, generally about 1/8 inch. Carefully pull the plastic from the round of dough and lay the dough on the hot griddle or skillet.

Cook the tortilla for 30 seconds. Flip it and cook it for 1 minute on its second side. Then flip it back over to cook about 30 seconds longer on the first side. The tortilla will be speckled with brown flecks.

Cover the cooked tortilla to keep it warm while the remaining balls of dough are shaped and cooked.

Serve warm in a napkin-lined basket with butter or salsa, or reserve for another use. The tortillas taste best the day they are made.

Technique Tip: Many cooks go out of their way to find a special masa harina for corn tortillas. They seldom bother to grind the corn themselves anymore, but they often seek out a personal source for what they consider the most desirable texture and flavor. Some combine two or more masa harinas to create their own blend. Whether or not you go to that effort, try at least to get a "tortilla grind," a fine, almost powdery corn flour, as opposed to a coarser "tamale grind." If you live in an area where you can find fresh masa, the ready-made dough, you can use it to make puffier, lighter tortillas, but the tradeoff is a mixture that sours easily and loses its elasticity within a day.

To reheat corn tortillas, wrap a stack of them in a clean towel and put the package in a steamer. When steam begins to escape from the lid, turn off the heat, and let the tortillas sit, covered, for 10 to 15 minutes. They'll keep warm this way for about 1 hour.

Regional Variations: Blue corn tortillas appear in New Mexico almost as often as their lighter-colored counterparts. Developed by the Pueblo peoples in pre-Hispanic times, and still revered in their culture, blue corn has an earthier taste and more protein than white or yellow corn, but it makes a fragile dough. For easier handling, substitute blue corn masa harina for just half the standard masa harina.

Another half-and-half combination appears in California, at least in the past, mixing flour and masa harina along with a tablespoon or more of lard per dozen tortillas. South Texas recipes of a generation ago sometimes added the same amount of margarine. Earlier, tortillas *de manteca* from the same area included both lard and pork cracklings.

The *Los Angeles Times* published the first of its many cookbooks in 1902. A tiny booklet with a big name, *The Times Prize Cook-book: 453 Good Recipes by California House-Keepers* retailed for 15 cents at the time. It included seventy-six "Spanish Dishes," five less than the number of puddings. The recipes involving flour and corn tortillas ranged from the authentic to the offbeat. One cook made masa from scratch, while another claimed that corncakes could be substituted for tortillas. An Anglo woman derided the "Spanish" for using lard in masa, but hardly an early cholesterol fighter, she replaced it with beef suet. One of the first bilingual cookbooks, the *Times* work printed different recipes in English and Spanish but none in both languages.

Two decades later in southern California, the Presbyterian Ladies Aid Society from a Santa Maria church compiled a cookbook with more interesting but equally eccentric "Spanish" recipes. Among the simplifying substitutions, the ladies suggested switching pancakes for flour tortillas, explaining that the latter were as difficult and frustrating as biscuits. They didn't bother with corn tortillas.

Moors from the arid lands of North Africa taught the Spanish how to make outdoor adobe ovens, and the Spanish in turn introduced the technology to the Native peoples in arid Arizona and New Mexico. Pueblo cooks still make bread in the beehive-shaped *hornos*—a hearty loaf that you can replicate indoors with this recipe. A bread-baking or pizza stone ensures a crisper crust.

Makes one 1-pound loaf

1 teaspoon dry yeast
2 tablespoons warm water
1 1/2 cups water
1 tablespoon lard or vegetable shortening
2 teaspoons molasses
2 teaspoons salt
1 teaspoon cumin seeds, toasted and ground
1 teaspoon dried sage
2 3/4 cups sifted high-gluten bread flour

In a small bowl, dissolve the yeast in the warm water.

In a small saucepan, warm the water, fat, and molasses over medium heat until the fat is melted. Pour the mixture into a food processor and let it cool to warm. Pour in the yeast mixture. Add the salt, cumin, and sage and process just to combine. Add 2 cups of the flour and process until the dough forms a cohesive, somewhat-sticky ball. Scatter 1 tablespoon of the flour on a counter or pastry board. Turn the dough out onto the counter. Knead it several minutes, adding as much of the remaining flour as necessary to make a smooth, elastic dough with a satiny sheen.

Grease a large bowl and place the dough in it, turning it once so that the top of the dough is lightly coated in fat. Cover the bowl with a towel and let the dough rise until it is doubled in size, about 1 1/2 to 2 hours.

Punch the dough back down and fold the dough over itself in thirds to redistribute the yeast. Knead the dough back into a ball, grease and cover it again, and let it rise again until almost doubled in size, about 1 1/4 to 1 3/4 hours. Punch the dough down again and shape it into a 7-inch or 8-inch round.

Place an empty heavy skillet on the lowest rack of the oven and, for the best results, a baking stone like those used for bread or pizza on the middle shelf. If you don't have a baking stone, use a heavy baking sheet. Preheat the oven to 400° F.

Transfer the bread to the heated baking stone or sheet, using a large spatula. Before closing the oven, pour $1/2$ cup water into the skillet to create steam in the oven. Close the oven and immediately turn the heat down to 350° F. Bake the loaf for 55 to 60 minutes, until lightly browned and crusty, with an internal temperature of 200° F.

Serve hot from the oven or at room temperature. Eat within several hours for the best flavor.

BUÑUELOS WITH ORANGE SYRUP

South of the border, buñuelos are traditionally a special-occasion home delicacy, particularly popular around Christmas. When the fried sweet bread spread to the Southwest, it became as much a snack or dessert as a holiday treat. Some versions have a dry sugar-and-spice topping, but most people prefer a flavored syrup when they get a choice.

Makes 12 to 14 buñuelos, approximately 7 inches wide

SYRUP
1 cup brown sugar or 8 ounces *piloncillo*
1 teaspoon ground canela or other cinnamon
1 cup orange juice
1 cup water

BREAD
4 cups all-purpose flour
1 tablespoon sugar
2 teaspoons salt

Adobe is an excellent insulating material, making an efficient outdoor oven, usually built large enough in the Southwest to handle at least twenty-five loaves of bread. Before baking, cooks start a wood fire inside and allow it to die down to coals, which they then sweep out. Experienced bakers can tell the temperature without testing, but those who are less certain may check it by throwing in a handful of oatmeal or a piece of newspaper. If it incinerates right away, the oven must cool further. When the heat is right, loaves are sealed in and baked for up to an hour. After the bread is finished, cakes or cookies might go in, and after that, perhaps turkeys or other large cuts of meat.

2 teaspoons baking powder
1/4 teaspoon ground canela or other cinnamon
2 tablespoons vegetable shortening
3/4 cup orange juice
3/4 cup water

Vegetable oil for deep-frying

Combine the brown sugar and canela in a small, heavy saucepan. Add the orange juice and water and simmer over medium heat until the mixture thickens and forms a light syrup. Remove from the heat and set aside. Rewarm if necessary before serving time.

For the bread, sift together the flour, sugar, salt, baking powder, and canela into a large bowl. Add the shortening and mix with your fingertips to combine. Stir in the orange juice and water, working the liquids into the dough until a sticky ball forms.

Dust a counter or pastry board with flour and knead the dough vigorously for 1 minute. The mixture should be "earlobe" soft and no longer sticky. Let the dough rest, covered with a damp cloth, for 15 minutes. Divide the dough into 12 to 14 balls, each about the size of a golf ball. Cover the balls with the damp cloth and let them rest for another 15 to 30 minutes. (If not for use immediately, the dough can be refrigerated for up to 4 hours.)

Dust the counter or pastry board with flour again and roll out each ball of dough into a circle about $^{1}/_{4}$ inch thick. Trim off any ragged edges and discard them. To avoid toughening the dough, roll it out only once. Cover the buñuelos with the damp cloth. Don't stack the dough circles, because they might stick together.

Pour enough oil into a high-sided, heavy skillet to measure at least 3 inches in depth. Heat the oil to 375° F.

Gently drop the first buñuelo into the hot oil. After sinking in the oil briefly, it should begin to puff and rise back to the surface. Avoid spooning oil over the top of the frying bread, as it will balloon too much. When the buñuelo's top side has bubbled and risen more or less uniformly, turn it over with tongs. Cook the buñuelo until it is just light golden, remove it with tongs, and drain it on paper towels. Repeat the frying process with the remaining dough.

Drizzle the syrup over the buñuelos and serve immediately.

Regional Variations: In Chihuahua, some cooks enrich the buñuelo dough with the state's legendary cheese. If you like the idea, reduce the recipe's shortening to 1 tablespoon and add 3 tablespoons of grated mild white cheese. For anise buñuelos and syrup in an early Californian style, add 1 to 1 $^1/_2$ teaspoons ground anise seeds to the dough, and replace the syrup's orange juice with additional water and 2 teaspoons of crushed anise seeds. In *Christmas in Arizona* (Golden West Publishers, 1992), cookbook author Lynn Nusom puts brandy in the dough and suggests dipping the buñuelos in chocolate. Other people enhance the flavor by topping the pastry with a sprinkling of ground almonds, or by putting $^1/_2$ teaspoon ground cloves in the syrup. One turn-of-the-century El Paso cookbook author implored readers to avoid rolling the buñuelos and, instead, to pull and prod the dough to make a more tender crust, a technique some still espouse today.

Native American fry breads in the Southwest resemble buñuelos in many ways. Often called Navajo, though also made by the Pueblos, the bread owes a big debt to the Spanish, who introduced both wheat and frying techniques to the region. The large, flat disks form the base for a popular fiesta dish, the Navajo or Indian taco, topped with beans, meat stewed with chile, and garnishes of lettuce, cheese, and tomato.

Most of the border region loves buñuelos, but other forms of fried bread predominate in certain pockets. The sopaipillas of New Mexico are the best-known example, though at one time in the past a similar beignet-style bread known as *palillis* or *palillas* enjoyed the same laurels in California. Sopaipillas originated as a bread and are still served that way in New Mexico and occasionally in Sonora and Chihuahua too. Traditionally, they come with honey because the combination of starch and sweet cuts the heat of chiles, but people in other areas thought the accompaniment made the bread into a dessert, which is how it's often presented today away from the Rio Grande.

Makes 12 sopaipillas

HONEY BUTTER
1/2 cup butter, at room temperature
1/4 cup honey

SOPAIPILLAS
2 cups all-purpose flour
1 teaspoon salt
1 teaspoon baking powder
1 1/2 teaspoons sugar (optional)
1 1/2 teaspoons vegetable oil
1/2 cup lukewarm water
1/4 cup milk, at room temperature

Vegetable oil for deep-frying

In a food processor or with a mixer, combine the butter and honey until well blended. Refrigerate the honey butter if you don't plan to use it within a couple of hours. Return the mixture to room temperature before using.

In a large mixing bowl, stir together the flour, salt, baking powder, and, if you wish, the sugar. Pour in the oil and mix with your fingertips to combine. Add the water and the milk, working the liquids into the flour until a sticky dough forms.

Lightly dust a counter or pastry board with flour and knead the dough vigorously for 1 minute. The mixture should be "earlobe" soft and no longer sticky. Let the dough rest, covered with a damp cloth, for 15 minutes. Divide the dough into 3 balls, cover the balls with the damp cloth, and let them rest for another 15 to 30 minutes. (The dough can be refrigerated at this point for up to 4 hours.)

Lightly dust a counter or pastry board with flour again and roll out each ball of dough into a circle or oval approximately $^1/8$ to $^1/4$ inch thick. If you have a tortilla roller, use it rather than a heavier rolling pin, which compacts the dough more. Trim off any ragged edges and discard them. To avoid toughening the dough, try not to reroll it. Cut each circle of dough into 4 wedges.

In a heavy, high-sided saucepan or skillet, heat the oil to 400° F. Carefully transfer 2 to 3 wedges of dough to the oil. After sinking briefly, the sopaipillas should begin to balloon and rise back to the surface. Spoon some oil over the tops of the sopaipillas. When the top surfaces are fully puffed, a matter of seconds, turn the sopaipillas. Cook just until the sopaipillas are light golden, and drain.

Arrange the sopaipillas in a napkin-lined basket and serve immediately with honey butter. Puncture the sopaipillas as you eat them, filling the center with a drizzle of the butter.

Technique Tip: Make sure you use fresh oil when cooking sopaipillas. The smoke point of oil drops with every use, and you need to have very hot oil for the sopaipillas to balloon properly. Spooning the oil over the sopaipillas as they fry is also essential to success.

Regional Variations: New Mexicans sometimes eat unsweetened stuffed sopaipillas as a main dish. They can be filled with almost any combination of meat and beans, but they are particularly delicious bulging with New Mexico Carne Adovada and topped with chopped tomato and lettuce.

Although at least one Southwestern food authority claims green chile cornbread to be an "ancient Pueblo tradition," most hot and spicy cornbreads are a recent creation, based on the standard commercial cornmeal that Mexicans call *maiz americano.* Even in Texas, the adopted home of the jalapeño, few cookbooks suggested the peppery addition until after LBJ left the White House. We gave the recipe for our favorite jalapeño cornbread in *Texas Home Cooking* (Harvard Common Press, 1993).

This spicy, south-of-the-border hushpuppy may remind you of jalapeño cornbread.

Serves 6

2/3 cup stone-ground cornmeal
6 tablespoons all-purpose flour
1 teaspoon baking powder
1/2 teaspoon salt
1/4 teaspoon crushed chile de árbol or cayenne
1 egg, lightly beaten
1/2 cup milk
1/4 cup minced onion
3 to 4 pickled jalapeños, minced
2 garlic cloves, minced

Vegetable oil for deep-frying

In a large bowl, stir together the cornmeal, flour, baking powder, salt, and chile. Mix in the egg and milk, followed by the remaining ingredients.

In a heavy saucepan or skillet, heat at least 3 inches of oil to 350° F. Drop tablespoons of the batter into the oil and fry until puffed, golden brown, and crisp, about 1 1/2 minutes. Turn them or spoon oil over them while frying to ensure even cooking. Drain the fritters. Repeat with the remaining batter. Serve immediately.

Try the fritters with soups, especially Coahuila Catfish Soup, or serve them as an appetizer, with the more traditional accompaniments of guacamole and salsa.

SWEET ANISE MOLLETES

This New Mexico version of an anise-flavored bun, sometimes called a *bollete* instead of a *mollete*, would have been known as a *semita* in early California cooking. To compound the confusion, a *mollete* in south Texas lacks the anise, making it more akin to a California *biscochuelo*.

Makes about 12 rolls

ROLLS
1/4-ounce package dry yeast
1/4 cup warm water
1/2 cup milk
3 tablespoons butter
3 tablespoons vegetable shortening
1/2 cup sugar
2 tablespoons anise seeds, toasted and ground
1/2 teaspoon salt
1/2 teaspoon vanilla
1 egg, lightly beaten
2 1/4 to 2 1/2 cups sifted all-purpose flour

TOPPING
1/3 cup sugar
1 teaspoon ground canela or other cinnamon
1 teaspoon anise seeds, toasted and ground
1/2 cup melted butter

Sprinkle the yeast over the water in a small bowl and let it dissolve.

Heat the milk with the butter and shortening in a small saucepan until the fats are melted. Pour the milk mixture into a large mixing bowl and stir in the sugar, anise, salt, and vanilla. Cool to lukewarm and add the yeast mixture. Mix in the egg. Add the flour gradually, mixing in only as much as is needed to make a smooth dough.

Turn out the dough onto a floured surface and knead until its surface has a satiny sheen. Rinse and dry the bowl and coat it lightly with butter. Place the dough back in the bowl, turning it over so that all sides have a film of butter. Cover the bowl loosely and set it aside in a warm

Though cooks north of the border frequently use *mollete* to refer to a sweetened egg yeast bun, the term can apply to any baked roll. Throughout Mexico, including the north, the most popular flour roll is the *bolillo,* which gained favor during the French occupation in the 1860s. A country cousin of the baguette, it's tapered at both ends and split on top. When Mexicans serve toasted *bolillos* for breakfast, spread with beans and cheese, they call them *molletes.*

place until the dough rises to double its original size, about 1 1/2 hours.

Punch down the dough, knead it several times, and cover it once more. Let it rise again until doubled in size, about 1 1/2 hours. Divide the dough into balls about twice the size of a golf ball. Flatten each ball with a rolling pin to about 1/2 inch in thickness. Transfer the dough to a baking sheet, spacing the flattened balls about 1 inch apart.

To prepare the topping, combine the sugar with the canela and anise in a small bowl. Brush the rolls with the melted butter and sprinkle them with the sugar mixture. Cover the rolls and let them rise until nearly doubled, about 1 hour. Slash the tops of the rolls in crisscross directions.

Preheat the oven to 375° F.

Bake for 20 to 25 minutes, or until golden. Serve the *molletes* warm.

Often offered at traditional afternoon teas, the rolls are just as good with a glass of cold milk. *Molletes* can be made as a breakfast treat too, prepared the evening before and rewarmed in foil.

LEMON-CORIANDER CHURROS

Churros get their name from a special type of sheep, because the piped batter looks like the long, wavy churro wool so prized for weaving. The fluted, deep-fried fritters are a popular street food in northern Mexico and, in the Southwest, a favorite at fiestas and fairs. This is a refined version, more delicate in taste and texture than most of the mass-produced treats. You might want to top them with the goat's-milk caramel called *cajeta* (see page 435), a beloved combination in Monterrey and other Mexican cities.

Makes 12 to 15 churros, serving 5 to 6

6 tablespoons sugar
2 teaspoons ground coriander
Peel of 2 lemons, 1 in zest, 1 in large pieces
Juice of 1 lemon plus water to make 1 cup
1/2 cup butter
1 teaspoon ground canela or other cinnamon
1/2 teaspoon salt
1 cup all-purpose flour
4 eggs

Vegetable oil for deep-frying

On a plate, stir together 4 tablespoons of the sugar and 1 teaspoon of the coriander. Set the mixture aside.

In a saucepan, combine the lemon zest, lemon juice–water mixture, butter, canela, salt, and remaining sugar and coriander. Bring the liquid to a rolling boil. Stir in the flour, all at once, and remove immediately from the heat. Stir the mixture until it becomes a thick paste with a satiny sheen. It will pull away from the sides of the pan.

Transfer the dough to a mixer bowl. Add the eggs one at a time, beating well after each addition, and for 2 to 3 minutes after all the eggs have been incorporated.

Transfer the batter to a pastry bag with a large star tip.

In a large, heavy pan, heat about 3 inches of oil to 365° F. Add the large pieces of lemon peel to the oil, being careful to avoid any spattering

As the commercial tortilla industry has boomed in the last decade—up to estimated sales of $5 billion in 1995—brands have begun to fight for shelf space. When big California manufacturers moved into the New Mexico market, local companies banded together behind an effective advertising campaign, running pictures of a laid-back tortilla wearing sunglasses and asking, "Do You Know Where Your Tortilla Was Last Night?"

oil. With a slotted spoon, strain and discard the peel when the edges just begin to brown.

Pipe the batter into the hot oil in ribbons about 6 to 8 inches long. Fry briefly until golden brown and crisp. Drain the churros and roll them in the reserved sugar mixture. Serve immediately.

Try the churros as a snack with a cup of tea or hot chocolate, or on cool evenings with a snifter of brandy.

CROSS-CULTURAL DESSERTS

Desserts demonstrate the expanding role of the borderlands in integrating the disparate cooking traditions of Mexico and the United States. Some foods—from beef to beans—are so entrenched and widely loved throughout the border region that new notions about them from the outside scarcely penetrate at all. Desserts occupy the opposite camp, with such a thin hold on heritage that they adapt readily to contemporary influences from elsewhere in the two countries.

For hundreds of years, until the coming of the railroad, sugar was scarce in both the Southwest and northern Mexico. Spanish settlers had honey and grew a little sugar cane even in areas as unlikely as the foothills of the New Mexico mountains, but they ate desserts only for special occasions and limited their sights to just a few treats. After ample sugar finally became available, cooks began importing recipes for sweets from both American and Mexican sources, bending and blending ideas to suit local ingredients and tastes. Desserts quickly settled into the hottest spot in the melting pot of border cooking.

RANCHO DE CHIMAYÓ FLAN

Among the few desserts enjoyed in the frontier period, flan was the border favorite from the first, and it still retains that position, not only in the region but in all of Mexico. Spanish settlers brought the baked caramel custard directly from the mother country, seldom introducing notable changes in the classic European preparation. This version from Chimayó, New Mexico, is different from most, as dense and thick as it is moist and silky. The family of Arturo Jaramillo developed the technique of long, low baking that produces the delectable texture, and they gave us the recipe originally for our *Rancho de Chimayó Cookbook: The Traditional Cooking of New Mexico* (Harvard Common Press, 1992).

Serves 8

CUSTARD
2 1/4 cups canned evaporated milk (1 1/2 12-ounce cans)
1 1/2 cups sugar
3/4 cup water
6 eggs
1 1/2 teaspoons vanilla

CARAMEL
1/4 cup sugar

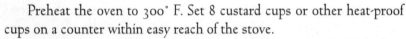

Preheat the oven to 300° F. Set 8 custard cups or other heat-proof cups on a counter within easy reach of the stove.

To prepare the custard, combine the ingredients in a double boiler's top pan. Beat with a whisk, or with a hand mixer at medium speed, for about 1 minute, or until the mixture is well blended and begins to froth at its rim.

Insert the pan over its water bath and heat the mixture over medium-low heat until it is warm throughout. Do not let the custard boil. Keep it warm over very low heat while preparing the caramel.

To prepare the caramel, place the sugar in a small, heavy saucepan or skillet. Cook over low heat, watching as the sugar melts into a golden-brown syrup. There is no need to stir unless the sugar is melting

Florence Jaramillo and her staff continue to make flan in this fashion at the Restaurante Rancho de Chimayó. Famous for its New Mexican cooking and gracious Spanish-American character, the restaurant occupies the nineteenth-century hacienda where Arturo Jaramillo grew up. He and Florence founded the business in 1965 as a way to restore the house and help preserve the historic traditions of Chimayó, a village that dates back three hundred years.

unevenly. When the syrup turns a rich medium brown, immediately remove the pan from the heat. Carefully pour about 1 teaspoon of caramel into the bottom of each custard cup. The syrup in the cups will harden almost immediately. The quantity of syrup allows a little extra in case some of it hardens before you get all 8 cups filled.

To assemble the flan, pour the warmed custard mixture equally into the cups, and place them in a baking pan large enough to accommodate all the cups with a little room for air circulation. Add warm water to the pan, enough to cover the bottom third of the cups, and bake for 1 3/4 hours. Check to see if the custard is firm and its top has just begun to color a light brown; if not, bake for up to 10 minutes more.

Remove the cups from the oven and let them cool for 15 to 20 minutes at room temperature. Cover the cups and refrigerate them for at least 3 hours or overnight.

Just prior to serving, take the cups from the refrigerator and uncover them. Unmold the first dessert by running a knife between the custard and the cup. Invert onto a serving plate. Repeat with the remaining flans and serve.

Regional Variations: Other traditional flans throughout the border region are made with similar ingredients but come out lighter in texture due to higher-heat baking and a shorter cooking time. Contemporary versions today tinker with extra flavors rather than techniques, adding almond, coffee, coconut, chocolate, pumpkin, strawberry, and more. We think some of the supplements confuse rather than complement the taste, so we seldom change anything more than the evaporated milk, substituting a goat's milk version of the same.

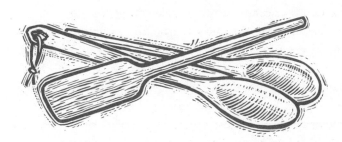

Flan is one of many egg-rich sweets that dominate Mexican dessert cooking. Spanish nuns brought the tradition intact from convents in the Andalusia sherry region. Sherry producers clarified their wines with egg whites and gave the yolks to sisters in the area, who devised ways to use them in desserts. An offspring of this heritage, the floating-island custard called *natillas* became a favorite in the borderlands, particularly in New Mexico.

Serves 8

1/4 cup all-purpose flour
4 eggs, separated
1 quart half-and-half
3/4 cup sugar
2 tablespoons anise seeds, toasted
Pinch of salt
1 teaspoon vanilla

Sprinkle the flour into the top half of a double boiler. Add the egg yolks, two at a time, stirring well after each addition. Pour $1/3$ cup of the half-and-half slowly into the egg mixture and stir it into a thick paste. Add the rest of the half-and-half and stir in the sugar, anise, and salt.

Insert the pan over its water bath. Heat the mixture over medium-low heat, stirring constantly, until the mixture thickly coats the back of a spoon, about 20 minutes. Do not let the custard boil. Stir in the vanilla and remove from the heat. Strain the custard through a fine sieve, to remove the anise seeds and any coagulated egg bits.

Let the custard cool at room temperature, stirring occasionally until no more steam rises. Then refrigerate the custard, covered, for at least 1 hour.

Before serving, beat the egg whites, preferably in a copper bowl, until stiff peaks form. Drop spoonfuls of the meringue over the custard, and then spoon a little of the custard lightly over a few of the meringue puffs. The result should be custard *empedrada*, "flecked with clouds." Serve cold. To gild the lily, offer the *natillas* spooned into piping-hot sopaipillas or onto buñuelos.

The vanilla that flavors *natillas* and so many Mexican desserts comes from the only edible bean produced by some twenty thousand varieties of orchid, a type that's native to Central America. The Aztecs knew how to cure the bean for eating, and they treasured it as an aphrodisiac, reserving the entire harvest for the royal court. Vanilla is now a commercial crop in Madagascar and a few other places, but the plants grown in the original Mexican soil still produce some of the world's best beans.

Technique Tip: Since *natillas* features uncooked meringue, you may want to avoid it if you have safety concerns about your egg source. Egg whites, however, are generally considered to be less of a risk uncooked than yolks. The custard can be prepared without egg whites, but it will be very rich and dense.

Regional Variations: In northwest Mexico, *natillas* may come topped with raisins, cherries, or walnuts. Farther east in Coahuila, close to sugar cane country, we've found a version laced with the local rum. Other cooks spike the custard with a couple of spoonfuls of brandy. In any of these variations, eliminate the anise first.

CALIFORNIA JIRICALLA

In Mexico, *jericalla* is a popular baked custard, but in California rancho cooking the similar word *jiricalla* embraced a broader range of egg-based puddings. We modeled this recipe on one from Ana Bégué de Packman's *Early California Hospitality* (Academy Library Guild, 1952). The masa harina used to thicken the boiled custard gives it a subtle sweet-corn flavor.

Serves 4 to 6

2 cups whole milk
3 eggs, separated
1/2 cup sugar
1/2 teaspoon vanilla
1/4 teaspoon salt
1/4 teaspoon ground canela or other cinnamon
1/8 teaspoon ground nutmeg
1/4 cup masa harina mixed with 1/4 cup water and strained
    through a sieve

Ground canela or other cinnamon

Preheat the oven to 350° F. Grease an 8-inch baking dish.

In a heavy pan, stir together all the ingredients except the egg whites and 1 tablespoon of the sugar. Beat with a whisk, or with a hand mixer at medium speed, for about 1 minute or until the mixture is well blended and begins to froth at its rim.

Heat the mixture over medium-low heat until it coats a spoon but runs off quickly. Do not let the custard boil.

Pour the custard into the baking dish. Let the custard cool at room temperature, stirring occasionally, until no more steam rises, about 10 minutes.

Beat the egg whites, preferably in a copper bowl, until soft peaks form. Add the remaining tablespoon of sugar and continue beating until stiff peaks form. Spread the meringue over the custard.

Bake for 6 to 8 minutes, until the meringue is just set and is lightly browned. Cool at room temperature for 20 to 30 minutes, then refrigerate for at least 1 hour.

Serve chilled, topped with a sprinkling of canela.

CHIHUAHUA CARAMEL-TOPPED MERINGUE

At its source in Chihuahua, this egg-white treat is called a flan, because of its shape and caramel top, though it's really a meringue.

Serves 8

CARAMEL
1 1/3 cups sugar

MERINGUE
10 egg whites
1/4 teaspoon cream of tartar
1/4 teaspoon salt
2/3 cup sugar
2 teaspoons vanilla
3/4 teaspoon almond extract

TOPPING
1 cup whipping cream
1 tablespoon sugar
1 teaspoon vanilla
1/4 teaspoon almond extract

1/2 cup slivered almonds, toasted, for garnish

Preheat the oven to 350° F. Butter a bundt pan or ring mold of at least 2 quarts in size.

To make the caramel, melt the sugar in a small, heavy saucepan or skillet over low heat. Watch carefully as the sugar melts into a golden-brown syrup. There is no need to stir unless the sugar is melting unevenly. When the syrup turns a rich medium brown, immediately remove the pan from the heat. Pour the caramel carefully into the prepared pan. Tip the pan if necessary to spread the syrup quickly throughout the pan. The syrup will harden almost immediately.

Beat the egg whites in a large bowl, preferably copper. When they become frothy, add the cream of tartar and salt. Gradually beat in the sugar and continue beating until stiff peaks form. Beat in the vanilla and almond extract. Spoon the mixture into the caramel-lined pan and smooth its surface.

Place the pan in a heat-proof dish large enough to provide a little air circulation. Add warm water to the dish, enough to cover the bottom third of the pan, and bake for 50 to 55 minutes. The meringue balloons in the pan while baking, so be sure to have several inches of clearance between the top of the pan and other oven racks or the oven's top. Turn the oven off and let the pan sit in the oven for 10 minutes. Remove the pan, and the water bath, from the oven and let it sit for another 15 minutes. The meringue will deflate and shrink some while it cools.

Pour boiling water into the dish that held the pan while baking, and set the pan back in the dish for a couple of minutes to loosen the meringue. Unmold the dessert onto a decorative serving platter. Refrigeration changes the meringue's texture, so plan to serve it warm or at room temperature within 1 or 2 hours.

For the topping, whip the cream in a bowl with the sugar, vanilla, and almond extract. Serve slices of the dessert with spoonfuls of the topping and the almond garnish.

The most popular egg-white dessert in the borderlands, *almendrado* looks more interesting than it tastes. A Technicolor but flavorless froth of egg whites and gelatin, dyed the colors of the Mexican flag, it's usually buried in a thin custard sauce, whipped cream, and a shower of almonds. A mortified Arizona friend recalls eating mounds of *almendrado* as a child in the 1940s, telling the story with the same kind of embarrassment that Madison Avenue has gotten us to associate with eating Kellogg's Frosted Flakes.

Padre Eusebio Kino planted orange orchards at the missions he established in southern Arizona and northern Mexico, establishing the fruit in the region long before it became a commercial crop in California and Texas. When border cooks make capirotada, a style of bread pudding enjoyed in many areas of Mexico, they sometimes add orange juice, along with the ubiquitous cheeses of the area. The dessert is often associated with Lent, or served for Easter dinner, because of the religious symbolism of bread.

Serves 8

1/2 cup raisins
1/2 cup brandy
10 to 12 white bread slices
1/2 cup chopped pecans, toasted
1 cup grated cheddar, asadero, or Monterey jack cheese (4 ounces)
2 cups sugar
2 1/2 cups hot water
1 cup orange juice, preferably fresh
1/4 cup butter
2 teaspoons vanilla
1 teaspoon ground canela or cinnamon
Pinch of cloves

Whipped cream, for garnish (optional)

Place the raisins in a small bowl and pour the brandy over them. Set aside to soften.

Preheat the oven to 350° F. Butter a baking dish.

Tear the bread into bite-size pieces. Transfer the bread to the baking dish. Add the pecans and the cheese to the bread, mixing both in lightly. Scatter the raisins over the top, including any brandy not absorbed by the fruit.

Pour the sugar into a large, heavy saucepan. Warm over medium-high heat until the sugar melts and turns a deep golden brown, about 8 to 10 minutes. Stir occasionally to ensure even melting. Pour the water into the molten sugar, standing back from the pan to avoid the steam that will rise as the water hits the sugar. The mixture will partially solidify. Continue cooking until liquid again, stirring occasionally. Add the orange juice, butter, vanilla, and spices to the syrup.

Ladle the syrup carefully over the bread. When the preparation is complete, the syrup should be about level with the top of the bread. If any bread pieces aren't coated, push them into the syrup.

Bake for 20 to 25 minutes, until the syrup has absorbed and the cheese has melted into the pudding.

Serve the pudding hot, topped with whipped cream if you like.

Regional Variations: At Tamayo restaurant in Los Angeles, the kitchen blends passion fruit juice with the orange, and uses whole eggs and extra yolks to enrich the mixture. Other cooks eliminate juice in favor of chopped fruit, including bananas, prunes, or peaches. We've never seen it served this way, but Ernest Camou Healy in his *Cocina Sonorense* (Instituto Sonorense de Cultura, 1990) recommends adding tomato, onion, and cilantro. Almost every kind of bread makes it into someone's capirotada, from bolillos to buñuelos.

MANGO CHIMICHANGAS

Serves 4

6 ripe mangoes, peeled and diced, or a 26-ounce jar sliced mangoes in syrup, diced
2 tablespoons sugar, or more to taste, if using fresh mangoes
2 tablespoons Triple Sec or other orange-flavored liqueur
Juice of 2 limes
2 teaspoons butter
1/3 cup fine-ground toasted almonds

Several other starch-based puddings thrive in border cooking. The most common derives from rice, and is prepared usually in a simple, standard style, though it might be sprinkled with pistachios or laced with sherry or brandy. On the rare end of the spectrum, *panocha* seldom ventures outside New Mexico and doesn't often appear there except during Lent. Similar to "Indian pudding," it's made from special sprouted-wheat flour that has a subtle natural sweetness. In the past, people washed whole wheat, set it behind a warm stove for several days to germinate, ground it, and made the pudding with little else. Today, cooks buy prepared *panocha* flour (see the New Mexico suppliers listed in "Mail-Order Sources") and generally add molasses and other flavorings.

4 thin flour tortillas, preferably 7 to 8 inches in diameter
Vegetable oil for deep-frying
Powdered sugar
Whipped cream, for garnish (optional)

In a heavy saucepan, combine the fresh mangoes and sugar or jarred mangoes with syrup. Add the Triple Sec and half of the lime juice and bring to a boil over medium-low heat. Simmer until the mixture is very thick, like preserves, stirring constantly toward the end. Stir in the butter, almonds, and as much of the remaining lime juice as needed to make the flavor sparkle. Set the mixture aside to cool. (The filling can be made 1 day ahead and refrigerated. Bring the filling back to room temperature before proceeding.)

Warm the tortillas for a few seconds on a griddle or in a heavy skillet until pliable. Transfer them to a plastic bag to stay soft.

Spoon one-fourth of the fruit mixture onto the center of a tortilla. Fold the sides in and then roll up into a tight package, securing the chimichanga with toothpicks. Repeat with the remaining tortillas and fruit.

Pour at least 3 inches of oil in a heavy, deep skillet. Heat the oil to 365° F. Fry the chimichangas, one or two at a time, until light golden, 4 to 5 minutes. Drain and sprinkle with powdered sugar shaken through a sieve.

Serve immediately, topped with spoonfuls of whipped cream if you wish.

Regional Variations: In Arizona, the birthplace of the chimichanga, cooks have turned the dish into a wonderful dessert in recent years, filling it with all manner of sweets. Along with the mango version, our other personal favorite comes from chef Norman Fierros of La Pila restaurant in Phoenix. He puts chunks of a chocolate-and-almonds candy bar inside bite-size, envelope-shaped pieces of thin flour tortilla, fries the diminutive chimis, and serves them dusted with powdered sugar. They are better even than a childhood "somemore."

BAJA DATE CAKE

An oasis in the Baja California desert, Mulegé brims with lush date palms. Maria Teresa Noriega Uribe used fruit from the trees to create this simple snacking cake, which she made moist with the American trick of adding mayonnaise to the batter.

Makes an 8-inch to 9-inch cake

1 1/2 cups chopped dates
1 cup hot water
2 cups all-purpose flour
3/4 cup sugar
1 teaspoon ground canela or other cinnamon
1/2 teaspoon baking soda
1/2 teaspoon salt
1/4 teaspoon powdered ginger
1 cup mayonnaise
1/2 cup chopped walnuts or pecans, toasted
1 tablespoon vanilla

Powdered sugar

Preheat the oven to 350° F. Butter a 9-inch cake pan.

Cover the dates with the water and let them sit for 30 minutes.

In a large bowl, stir together the dry ingredients. Mix in the dates and their soaking liquid along with the remaining ingredients. Spoon the batter into the prepared pan, smoothing the surface. Bake for 50 to 55 minutes, or until a toothpick inserted into the center comes out clean.

Eat the cake warm or at room temperature, sprinkled with powdered sugar. Top the cake with Natillas for a fancier dessert or serve alongside a scoop of Vanilla Ice Crema. It's also great for breakfast, unadorned.

Date palms thrive in the deserts of Arizona and California as well as Baja. Imported from the Middle East around a century ago, the trees often grow in "harems," with a single male surrounded by as many as fifty females.

It's become common in the States to have coffee ground to order, but Mexico is a step ahead with chocolate, probably because it originated there. Mexican chocolate mills allow you to customize your own blend, choosing between different grades of the product and mixtures of spices and nuts, particularly canela and almonds. Even packaged brands such as Ibarra and Mayordomo feature heady aromas and tastes. This moist, dense cake pairs the fragrant Mexican chocolate with an old-fashioned Texas-style buttermilk batter.

Makes an 8-inch layer cake, serving 8

CAKE

1 1/2 cups all-purpose flour, sifted
1 3/4 cups sugar
1 heaping teaspoon baking powder
1 teaspoon salt
3/4 cup plus 1 tablespoon butter
2/3 cup water
6 ounces Mexican chocolate, such as Ibarra or Mayordomo
1 tablespoon cocoa
2 eggs, beaten lightly
3/4 cup buttermilk
2 teaspoons vanilla
1/2 cup fine-ground toasted almonds

ICING

6 tablespoons butter
3 ounces Mexican chocolate, such as Ibarra or Mayordomo
1 tablespoon cocoa
2 to 3 tablespoons half-and-half
2 cups powdered sugar
1/2 teaspoon vanilla

Chopped almonds, toasted, for garnish

Preheat the oven to 350° F. Grease and flour two 8-inch round cake pans.

Sift together the flour, sugar, baking powder, and salt in a bowl and reserve.

Melt together the butter, water, chocolate, and cocoa in a heavy saucepan over medium heat, stirring well. Cook for 3 to 5 minutes and remove from the heat. Stir the sifted dry ingredients into the chocolate mixture. In a bowl, combine the eggs, buttermilk, and vanilla and mix well with the chocolate mixture. Stir in the almonds.

Spoon the cake batter into the prepared pans and bake for 30 minutes or until a toothpick inserted in the center comes out clean.

Allow the layers to stand in their pans for about 5 minutes. Run a knife around their edges, invert them onto cake racks, and remove the pans. Let them cool.

While the layers cool, prepare the icing. Melt the butter together with the chocolate and cocoa in a heavy saucepan over medium heat. Add 2 tablespoons of the half-and-half and heat through. Mix in the remaining ingredients and blend well. Stir in the remaining half-and-half if needed for easy spreading consistency.

To assemble the cake, place one layer on a decorative serving plate. Ice the top and sides of the cake layer. Repeat with the remaining layer and frosting.

Technique Tip: The United States imports more Ibarra chocolate from Mexico than Mayordomo, but the latter is richer and higher in quality. If you can't locate either or another Mexican brand, substitute equal quantities of bittersweet chocolate in both the cake and the icing, adding a healthy sprinkling of ground canela or other cinnamon and enough almond extract to be discernible. It's not quite the same, but you'll get a similar range of flavors.

Along with honey, molasses made from sugar cane was the primary sweetener in the borderlands before the railroad broadened the options. Pioneer families crushed cane stalks, often by feeding them through rollers driven by horses, cooked down the juice to the desired consistency, and put it into jars or barrels. Sometimes people ate it just with fresh goat cheese as a dessert.

Sweet tamales, unlike regular varieties, contain no filling because the flavoring ingredients go into the masa itself. They are enjoyed throughout
the borderlands, but styles of sweetening vary in different locales. Our
approach derives from El Paso and southern Arizona.

Makes approximately 24 small tamales, enough for 12 dessert servings

6-ounce package dried corn husks
2 cups butter, at room temperature
1/2 cup dark brown sugar
3 1/2 cups masa harina
1/2 teaspoon ground canela or other cinnamon
1/2 teaspoon salt
8-ounce can crushed pineapple in its own juice
Water
1/3 cup sherry
1 teaspoon vanilla
3/4 cup chopped pecans, toasted

In a deep bowl or baking pan, soak the corn husks in hot water to
cover. After 30 minutes the husks should be soft and pliable. Separate the
husks and rinse them under warm running water to wash away any grit
or brown silks. Soak them in more warm water until you are ready to use
them.

With a mixer, beat together the butter and brown sugar until light
and creamy.

In a large bowl, stir together the masa harina, canela, and salt. Drain
the pineapple juice into a large measuring cup. Add water to the juice to
equal 2 $^{1}/2$ cups. Add the juice mixture, pineapple, sherry, and vanilla to
the masa. With a powerful mixer, a sturdy spoon, or your fingers, mix to
combine. Whip in the creamed butter and sugar, and the pecans.
Continue mixing until all the ingredients are well combined and the consistency is like soft cookie dough, about 3 to 5 minutes. If the dough
seems dry, add a little more water.

To make approximately 2 dozen tamales, use about 3 tablespoons of masa for each tamale.

Hold the first corn husk flat on one hand. With a rubber spatula, spread a thick layer of masa across the husk. Roll the tamale into a fat cylinder or another desired shape. Repeat the procedure with the remaining dough.

Cook the tamales over simmering water for 1 hour, or until the masa is firm and no longer sticks to the corn husk. Unwrap one tamale to check its consistency. If necessary, rewrap it and return it to the pot for a few more minutes.

The tamales should be eaten warm. The corn husks are usually left on when tamales are served, for each guest to remove before eating. Accompany the tamales with Rompope-Canela Helado or vanilla ice cream, or with sautéed apples. The tamales are also good for breakfast, accompanied with slices of fresh pineapple.

Regional Variations: Though sweet tamales are usually dessert or breakfast dishes on the U.S. side of the border, in Mexico they appear traditionally for *merienda*, as late-afternoon tea snacks. Because of that, some Mexican cooks use chicken stock for the liquid, which makes the tamales more savory. Others accomplish the same goal by replacing the butter with lard. In the past, the flavoring elements depended on locally available ingredients. An 1889 Phoenix cookbook, *Housekeeping in the Salt River Valley*, recommended using raisins, almonds, and anise, which would have been popular choices in many places at the time.

European styles influence desserts more than any other part of a Mexican meal. The Spanish imported egg-based sweets from the mother country at an early period, as well as such key ingredients as sugar, cream, and almonds. The prevalence of pastries today is one of the few lasting consequences of the French occupation during the 1860s. Even the idea of finishing with a dessert course comes from Europe. Aztecs and other Native Americans usually mixed sweet and savory flavors throughout a meal, instead of ending with one or the other.

The border version of a cheese blintz, this is dressed to impress. Our initial inspiration came from Maria de Cardenas, whose family founded Cacique, the Mexican-cheese company based in Los Angeles.

Serves 6

CRÊPES
1 cup all-purpose flour
Pinch of salt
1 egg
1 cup milk
1/4 cup water, or more as needed
2 tablespoons melted butter

1/2 cup prickly-pear jam or marmalade, or apricot jam
1 tablespoon butter
Vegetable oil for pan-frying
10 to 12 ounces crumbled queso fresco or ranchero, farmer, or ricotta cheese
1/2 cup Crema (page 63) or crème fraîche

Toasted piñon (pine) nuts, for garnish (optional)

For the crêpes, combine the flour, salt, and egg in a large bowl, and then mix in the milk, $^1/_4$ cup water, and butter until the batter is very smooth and thin. Refrigerate the batter for 1 to 2 hours.

Take the batter from the refrigerator. To form the best crêpes, the batter needs to be very pourable, with a consistency between whipping cream and buttermilk. Add more water if needed for the proper consistency.

Warm a 7-inch or 8-inch skillet, preferably nonstick, over medium-high heat, and brush lightly with oil. Using a $^1/_4$ cup measuring cup, pour 3 to 4 tablespoons of batter (just enough to thinly coat the skillet) into the skillet quickly. Swirl the batter around to cover the pan evenly. Fry the crêpe until the surface is no longer shiny and the edges begin to dry, about 45 seconds. Loosen the crêpe with a table knife or narrow spatula and flip it over. Cook another 45 seconds and slide the crêpe from the pan. (The crêpes may be made ahead, separated by waxed paper and wrapped tight, and refrigerated for a day. Warm the crêpes to room temperature before continuing.)

Preheat the oven to 325° F.

In a small saucepan, warm the jam or marmalade with the butter over low heat until syrup-like. Keep the mixture warm.

Spoon about 2 generous tablespoons of cheese and $1/2$ tablespoon of crema onto a crêpe and fold into quarters. Transfer the crêpe to a heat-proof decorative platter. Repeat the process until you have a dozen filled crêpes. Cover the crêpes with foil. (The crêpes can be prepared and filled 1 hour before you plan to eat.)

Bake the crêpes, covered, for 10 minutes to warm them through. Spoon the jam syrup over the crêpes. Top with spoonfuls of crema and, if you wish, piñon nuts and serve.

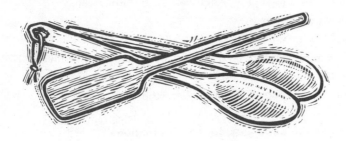

Both Arteaga, Coahuila, and Velarde, New Mexico, celebrate their local crops in annual festivals. The spring event in Arteaga, the Día de San Isidro Labrador, honors St. Isidro the farmer, and the fall fiesta in Velarde salutes the apple harvest.

Apple orchards flourish in scattered areas of the borderlands, from Arteaga in southeast Coahuila to Velarde in northern New Mexico. This is a luscious way to eat the fruit, stuffed with pecans from the same region, baked, and lapped with tangy *cajeta*, a goat's-milk caramel sauce. While some people dislike the assertiveness of goat's milk, virtually everyone loves this combination. If you are unconvinced, or just can't find goat's milk, substitute cow's milk in the *cajeta*.

Serves 6

CAJETA
1 quart fresh goat's milk, or 2 cups canned evaporated goat's milk plus 2 cups water
1 cup sugar
1 tablespoon light corn syrup
1/4 teaspoon baking soda

APPLES
6 ounces *piloncillo* (see page 26), softened, or 1/2 cup dark brown sugar
1/2 cup coarse-chopped pecans, toasted
3 tablespoons butter
1 tablespoon all-purpose flour
6 baking apples such as Romes, Winesaps, or Granny Smiths, sliced in half vertically and cored
1 1/2 cups apple cider
Ground canela or other cinnamon

In a large, heavy saucepan, prepare the *cajeta*. Combine the milk, sugar, and syrup and cook over medium heat. When the mixture comes to a boil, add the baking soda, which will cause the mixture to bubble up merrily. Lower the heat so that the mixture simmers steadily. Cook the milk for about 1 hour, stirring occasionally at first and more frequently as the mixture thickens and turns golden brown. When done, the *cajeta* should have the consistency of a spoonable syrup.

Cajeta can be used immediately or stored in the refrigerator, covered, to be used as needed. When rewarming it, add a little water or milk if the caramel seems too thick.

Preheat the oven to 375° F.

Wrap the *piloncillo* in foil and heat in the oven for 10 to 20 minutes or until soft enough to chop roughly with a knife or food processor.

Combine the chopped *piloncillo*, pecans, butter, and flour and mound the mixture into the apples' hollowed-out centers.

Arrange the apples in a baking dish. Pour the cider around the apples. Sprinkle the canela over the top.

Cover the apples and bake them for 45 to 50 minutes. Uncover the apples and return them to the oven for another 15 minutes, or until the apples are soft and the cider has reduced and thickened into a light syrup.

Serve the apples warm, in individual bowls, with generous spoonfuls of *cajeta* poured over them.

Refrigerated leftover *cajeta* keeps indefinitely. Serve it with waffles, baked bananas, sliced mangoes, or vanilla ice cream.

Regional Variations: Originally from the central Mexican state of Guanajuato, *cajeta* caught on in the north partially because many farmers in the region raise goats. Some cooks like to add a teaspoon of vanilla to the caramel sauce, and others spike it with a few tablespoons of sherry or brandy. Early this century, the El Paso branch of the Robert E. Lee Chapter of the United Daughters of the Confederacy suggested making the *cajeta* into a kind of "turtle" candy. In a self-published cookbook, the authors called for simmering the syrup down to candy consistency and mixing in chocolate or nuts.

Simple fruit desserts are welcome treats in the heat of a border summer or after a spicy meal anytime. Top berries or watermelon chunks with crema. Scoop out cantaloupe or honeydew balls and mix with fresh mint. Baste bananas with guava juice and bake until soft, adding a bit of rum if you like. Drizzle rounds of mild fresh goat cheese with honey and accompany with dried or fresh apricots and raisins. Hollow out a whole pineapple and mix the fruit with berries, melon, and a hefty dose of brandy, or try fresh pineapple chunks and orange sections with splashes of tequila and Triple Sec. Perhaps best of all, marinate whole, unstemmed cherries in tequila, add a splash of vanilla and brown sugar to taste, warm through, and serve as a finger-food dessert.

Serves 4 to 6

SANGRIA SYRUP
2 cups fruity red wine
6-ounce can orange juice concentrate
2 to 3 tablespoons Triple Sec or other orange-flavored liqueur
2 tablespoons brandy (peach- or apricot-flavored varieties are especially good)
1 to 2 tablespoons sugar
2 teaspoons fresh lemon juice
1 teaspoon lemon zest

2 pounds firm but ripe peaches, peeled and sliced

In a heavy saucepan, combine all the syrup ingredients, using the smaller amounts of Triple Sec and sugar. Bring the syrup to a boil over medium heat. Reduce the heat and let the mixture simmer for 5 minutes. Taste the syrup. Add the remaining Triple Sec or sugar, or both, if needed for a pleasantly sweet but not cloying mixture. Continue simmering for another 5 minutes. Remove the syrup from the heat and let it cool for at least 10 minutes.

Place the peaches in a nonreactive bowl. Pour the syrup over the peaches, cover, and refrigerate for at least 4 hours.

Serve the peaches chilled, with some of the syrup spooned over.

From San Antonio to Los Angeles, soft, spiced piglet cookies are among the best-loved sweets in Mexican bakeries. Our recipe is more complexly seasoned than most and enhanced with sour cream.

Makes about 2 1/2 dozen cookies, each about 1 by 3 inches

3 cups all-purpose flour, sifted
1 tablespoon powdered ginger
1 1/2 teaspoons ground canela or other cinnamon
3/4 teaspoon baking soda
1/2 teaspoon salt
1/2 teaspoon ground cloves
1/4 teaspoon white pepper
1/2 cup butter, at room temperature
1/2 cup brown sugar
1/2 cup sour cream
1 egg
1/4 cup honey
1/4 cup molasses
1 teaspoon vanilla

GLAZE
1 egg white
1 tablespoon water

Preheat the oven to 350° F. Grease two large baking sheets.

Sift together the flour, ginger, canela, baking soda, salt, cloves, and pepper into a bowl. In a large bowl, cream together the butter and sugar. Add the sour cream, egg, honey, molasses, and vanilla. Stir in the dry ingredients and mix again until well combined. The dough should be fairly moist.

Refrigerate the dough, covered, for at least 1 hour and preferably 2. Dust a counter or pastry board lightly with flour. Roll the dough out to about 1/3-inch thickness and cut cookies with a pig-shaped cutter. If you can't locate an appropriate cutter, you can make the cookies in any shape

Like many merchants in the past, bakers and other cooks used to sell their goods on the streets. In a 1963 issue of *Arizona Highways*, Arnulfo D. Trejo recalled the food vendors of his youth in early twentieth-century Tucson. Doña Ramona lured customers by gossiping and chanting "Tamaleees! Tamaleees calientes!" while El Canario (the canary) brought in business with a melodious voice that sang about *pan de huevo, semitas, polvorones,* empanadas, and more. The shrewdest of the roving bakers was called El Venadito (the deer). When he got to the neighborhood, he gave a *cochinito* to the first child he saw, which led to crowds of youngsters yelling his name down the street and announcing his arrival.

you wish, though technically they will no longer be *cochinitos*. Transfer the cookies to the baking sheets, spacing them 1 $^1/_2$ inches apart.

To prepare the glaze, combine the egg white and water in a small bowl. Brush the cookies lightly with the glaze.

Bake the cookies for 10 to 12 minutes. Do not overbake because the *cochinitos* should be soft and chewy. Cool the cookies for about 5 minutes and then transfer them to absorbent paper to finish cooling. Covered, they keep several days.

PUCHITAS

The californios made these delicate anise-flavored shortbread cookies as an afternoon-tea snack for *merienda*. Because they could grow anise locally, cooks used the spice extensively in baking, the way people use vanilla today. We've reduced the amount of lard in the old recipe—but kept some to maintain the fine texture—and added butter for extra flavor.

Makes 2 $^1/_2$ to 3 dozen cookies

1/2 cup water
1 1/2 heaping teaspoons anise seeds, toasted and ground
Juice and zest of 1/2 medium lemon
2 1/4 cups low-gluten pastry or all-purpose flour
1 cup sugar
1 teaspoon baking powder
1/2 teaspoon salt
1/4 cup chilled lard
1/4 cup chilled butter
1 egg, beaten

Pour the water into a small saucepan and add the anise plus the lemon juice and zest. Bring the water to a boil, then remove from the heat and place the mixture in the freezer to steep and cool.

Sift together the flour, sugar, baking powder, and salt into a medium bowl. Cut in the lard and butter. Mix in the egg. Strain the chilled liquid and add as much of it as is needed to make a loose dough. As with a pie crust, add no more of the liquid than is necessary for the dough just to hold together. Refrigerate the dough for 30 minutes.

Preheat the oven to 400° F. Grease two baking sheets.

Form the dough into walnut-size balls. Space the balls at least 1 inch apart on the baking sheets.

Dip a fork into flour and press down on the first ball in crisscross fashion, to flatten the ball and make the kind of markings many cooks associate with peanut butter cookies. Repeat with the remaining cookies, dipping the fork back in flour as needed to eliminate sticking.

Bake the cookies for 10 to 12 minutes, until lightly colored. Remove from the baking sheets and cool on racks. Eat warm or at room temperature.

Regional Variations: In New Mexico, a similar dainty, flaky cookie, the *biscochito* or *bizcochito*, has won recognition by the legislature as the official state cookie. Like the *puchita*, it's flavored with anise, but may also have a splash of brandy or sweet wine in the dough. Traditionally, bakers shape it like a fleur-de-lis or roll it into curlicues like a tightly corkscrewed pig tail. Next door in Arizona and south to Sonora, the same style of sweet changes names to *biscochuelo* and assumes different forms, especially wreaths. In each case the cookies are closely associated with Christmas and other major occasions like weddings.

Border bakeries brim with cookies, many covered in a multitude of exuberantly colored sugar sprinkles. Two of the best choices lack the bangles—the *oregas* (ear-shaped cookies made of puff pastry rolled with cinnamon and sugar) and the *pasteles de bodas* (Mexican wedding cakes). *Betty Crocker's Cookbook* popularized the latter across the United States years ago, though the editors of more recent editions changed their name to Russian Tea Cakes.

APRICOT-PINEAPPLE OR PUMPKIN-ANISE EMPANADITAS

Little fruit-filled turnovers, empanaditas can be delicious tidbits if you avoid the common mistakes of a leaden crust and a cloying center. This version features a flaky cream-cheese pastry wrapped around your choice of two fillings bursting with fruit flavor. The popular apricot-pineapple mixture springs up all along the border, while the less familiar pumpkin-anise combination deserves to be better known.

Makes 3 1/2 dozen 3-inch empanaditas

PASTRY

8 ounces butter, at room temperature

8 ounces cream cheese, at room temperature

2 cups low-gluten pastry or all-purpose flour

1 tablespoon sugar

1/2 teaspoon salt

1/2 teaspoon anise seeds, toasted and ground, if you are preparing the pumpkin-anise filling

1 to 2 tablespoons cold water (optional)

APRICOT-PINEAPPLE FILLING

1 cup water

Two 6-ounce bags dried apricots

8-ounce can crushed pineapple with juice

1/2 cup apricot jam or preserves

1/3 to 1/2 cup sugar

1/8 teaspoon salt

4 to 6 tablespoons dried breadcrumbs

PUMPKIN-ANISE FILLING

1 pound canned pumpkin

1/2 cup brown sugar

1/4 cup almonds, toasted and ground

2 teaspoons anise seeds, toasted and ground

1 teaspoon vanilla

GLAZE
1 egg
1 tablespoon water
2 tablespoons sugar

Using a food processor, a bowl with a pastry blender, or your fingers, cut the butter and cream cheese into the flour, sugar, salt, and, if you wish, anise seeds. Whatever method you choose, be careful not to over-work the dough, which would reduce the flakiness. If the dough isn't holding together, add the water, a little at a time, until a soft dough forms. Divide the dough into two balls. Wrap each in plastic and refrigerate for at least 2 hours. The dough can be prepared a day ahead.

Preheat the oven to 375° F.

For the apricot-pineapple filling, pour the water over the apricots in a heavy saucepan and add the other filling ingredients, except the bread-crumbs. Simmer over medium heat until the apricots are quite soft and the liquid is thick. Purée the mixture in a food processor. Add the smaller quantity of breadcrumbs and combine them with the mixture. If it is not yet stiff, mix in additional breadcrumbs. The filling should be firm but still moist.

For the pumpkin-anise filling, blend all the filling ingredients together in a medium bowl.

Remove the first ball of dough from the refrigerator. On a floured surface, roll out the dough to about $1/8$ inch in thickness. Cut the dough into rounds with a 3-inch biscuit or cookie cutter. Top each with about 1 tablespoon of filling. Fold the first round in half, pinch the edges to seal, and crimp with a fork. Transfer the empanadita to an ungreased baking sheet. Repeat with the remaining assembled rounds. Dust the surface with flour again, and roll out the second round of dough. Repeat the assembly with the remaining dough and filling.

To prepare the glaze, whisk together the egg and water in a small bowl. With a pastry brush, paint a light coat of glaze over each empana-dita and sprinkle them with sugar.

Bake the empanaditas for 20 minutes or until light golden brown and flaky. Serve warm or at room temperature. While empanaditas are best the day they are made, leftovers can be sealed in an airtight container to eat the following day.

The first candy in the borderlands probably featured pumpkin. In *Cooking and Curing with Mexican Herbs: Recipes Gathered in Múzquiz, Coahuila* (The Encino Press, 1977), Delores L. Latorre describes how generations of Mexican families glazed pumpkin during the sugar cane harvest, dropping pieces into the huge cauldrons used to make molasses out of the cane juice. In *Early California Hospitality* (Academy Library Guild, 1952), Ana Bégué de Packman says *dulce de calabaza* "was to California what pumpkin pie was to New England."

Serves 4 to 6

1/4 cup sugar
2 teaspoons ground canela or other cinnamon
4 thin flour tortillas, preferably at least 7 to 8 inches in diameter, cut
    in 8 wedges each
Melted butter

1 to 1 1/2 cups *cajeta* (see page 435), warmed
1/2 cup pecan or walnut pieces, toasted

Preheat the oven to 400° F.

Stir together the sugar and canela on a plate.

Brush both sides of the tortilla wedges generously with melted butter. Rub both sides of each wedge with a sprinkling of the sugar mixture. Transfer the tortillas to a baking sheet or sheets. Bake for approximately 10 minutes, or until crisp.

Arrange the warm tortilla wedges in a single layer on a large decorative platter. Drizzle with *cajeta* and sprinkle with nuts. Serve immediately. The nachos are best eaten as finger food.

Regional Variations: Espartaco Borga takes dessert nachos another step at his ZuZu cafés, making them the base for luscious, *cajeta*-topped sundaes. Unlike most of its fast-food Tex-Mex competition, the Dallas-based chain offers handmade dishes to order that are inspired by real south-of-the-border fare.

PILONCILLO PRALINES

A raw Mexican sugar, *piloncillo* is much deeper in flavor than American brown sugars, which are actually the white variety darkened with a little molasses. Becoming more common in the United States, sometimes under the name of *panela* or *panocha*, *piloncillo* makes these pralines especially rich.

Makes 1 1/2 dozen medium pralines

1 1/2 cups sugar
8 to 9 ounces *piloncillo*, softened and chopped, or 3/4 cup dark
     brown sugar
1/2 cup plus 2 tablespoons whole milk
6 tablespoons butter
1 1/2 cups pecan pieces, toasted
1/2 teaspoon ground canela or other cinnamon
2 teaspoons vanilla

Grease a 2-foot sheet of waxed paper. Set it on several thicknesses of newspaper to avoid ending up with wax on your table or counter.

Combine all the ingredients except the vanilla in a heavy saucepan. Bring to a boil slowly so that the *piloncillo* melts and continue cooking, stirring constantly, until the mixture reaches the soft ball stage, 238° F to 240° F.

Add the vanilla, remove the pan from the heat, and continue stirring as the candy cools. When the mixture becomes creamy and cloudy, and the pecans remain suspended while stirring, spoon the mixture onto the waxed paper. You can make pralines of any size, but using about 1/4 cup of the mixture per praline produces about 1 1/2 dozen. Work quickly, before the candy hardens in the pan. The pralines set as they cool.

While best the day they're made, the pralines can be kept, tightly covered, for several days. Crumble leftover pralines over ice cream— vanilla, peach, and butter pecan are especially good matches.

Regional Variations: The milk used in the recipe, or even cream, is common in the beefy states of Chihuahua, Sonora, and Texas. Elsewhere, water may be substituted. The combination of sugars varies widely, and so can the presentation. Some cooks spoon the mixture into a pan, cool it, and cut it like fudge. In Nuevo León, the same candy ingredients may become a nut brittle, loaded with the pecans grown in the area.

ROMPOPE-CANELA HELADO

A favorite of many Mexican ice-cream shops, this cooling treat combines the flavors of Mexican eggnog and cinnamon.

Makes about 1 quart

3/4 cup sugar
1/2 tablespoon cornstarch
2 teaspoons ground canela or other cinnamon
Pinch of salt
2 eggs plus 4 egg yolks
2 1/2 cups whole milk
1/2 cup whipping cream
2 teaspoons brandy
1/2 teaspoon vanilla

In a heavy saucepan, stir together the sugar, cornstarch, canela, and salt. Add the eggs and beat or whisk to combine well. Pour in the milk and the cream and place the pan over medium-low heat. Stir the mixture continuously as it thickens, about 20 minutes, until it coats a spoon thinly. Stir in the brandy and vanilla and remove the mixture from the heat. Pour the custard through a strainer into a bowl. Chill it thoroughly.

Transfer the custard to an ice-cream maker and process it according to the manufacturer's directions. After churning, place the ice cream in the freezer until serving time. It's best eaten within 1 or 2 days.

VANILLA ICE CREMA

Mexican crema makes a wonderfully rich yet refreshing frozen dessert, offering a tang that balances sweetness.

Makes about 1 quart

2 cups Crema (page 63) or crème fraîche
2 cups buttermilk
1 cup sugar, or more to taste
1 tablespoon fresh lemon juice
1 teaspoon vanilla

In a blender, combine all the ingredients until the sugar has dissolved. Chill the mixture thoroughly.

Transfer the mixture to an ice-cream maker and process it according to the manufacturer's directions. After churning, place the ice cream in the freezer until serving time. It's best eaten within 1 or 2 days. Try it with Mexican Chocolate Cake or your favorite apple pie.

Among the exotic foods featured at Tucson's La Fiesta de los Chiles, chiltepín ice cream probably takes the cake. If you can't get to the fall festival, held on the grounds of the local botanical gardens, you can make your own version of the treat by adding a just-tolerable amount of the crushed little pods to softened vanilla ice cream. We won't promise anything about the taste, but it will allow you to chill out and chile out at the same time.

For a light frozen dessert with a border tang, nothing is more bracing or beautiful than this simple ice, or *nieve*, based on the popular beverage made from hibiscus flowers.

Makes about 1 quart

4 cups Jamaica Tea (page 465)
1/2 cup sugar
Lemon or lime juice to taste

Strawberries, orange sections, or mint sprigs, for garnish (optional)

In a medium bowl, stir together the tea and sugar and add 1 or 2 tablespoons of fruit juice as needed to balance the tangy and sweet flavors.

Transfer the mixture to an ice-cream maker and process it according to the manufacturer's directions. After churning, chill the ice in the freezer until serving time. It tastes best when eaten within 1 or 2 days. Top individual portions with strawberries, oranges, or mint, if you wish.

BEVERAGES AND BOTANAS

If the border region has an ambassador in the United States, her name is margarita. The popular drink wins more friends for the area than any other single food or beverage, and does it with a sassy vitality that represents the spirit of the people and place. Her only fault, perhaps, is flamboyance, a tendency to upstage and overshadow other worthy beverages, both alcoholic and not.

Hardly anyone in the borderlands has a cocktail or beer without *botanas*, zesty tidbits that don't have an exact counterpart in standard American cooking. Not quite snacks, or hors d'oeuvres, or appetizers, they can serve in any of those roles, depending on the occasion, and they certainly add spice to a celebration. The duo of drinks and *botanas* always inspires cheer.

PANCHO'S ORIGINAL MARGARITA

Ciudad Juárez bartender Francisco "Pancho" Morales invented the margarita on the Fourth of July, 1942, according to the most plausible of many stories about the drink's creation. Pancho says a woman wandered into his bar and ordered a "magnolia," a gin cocktail. He didn't know the drink, so he made up a Mexican substitute based on tequila and called it a "margarita," the Spanish word for daisy. Ridiculing most versions of the cocktail as impostors, Pancho insists it should be made with clear silver tequila, Cointreau, and the juice squeezed from half of a *limón* (key-style Mexican lime). This is our rendition of his margarita, modified slightly for home preparation.

Serves 1

Cracked ice
1/2 lime, preferably the small, key-type *limón*
Salt
2 ounces premium silver tequila
1 ounce Cointreau

Fill a cocktail shaker or lidded jar with cracked ice. Squeeze the juice from the lime into the container and then rub the lime half around the rim of an 8-ounce glass.

Place a thin layer of salt on a saucer and dip the lime-rubbed glass into the salt. Shake off excess salt to leave only a light sprinkling on the rim of the glass.

Pour the tequila and Cointreau into the container with the ice and lime juice and shake to blend. Strain the margarita into the prepared glass and serve.

Technique Tip: By Mexican government regulations, all tequila must contain at least 51 percent distilled liquor from the blue agave plant. The best brands, for our tastes at least, use 100 percent agave. They come in three types, depending on the degree of barrel aging: *plata*, or silver (no aging), *oro*, or gold (aged in wood up to a year), and *añejo*, or old (aged in oak, usually for several years). Make margaritas with silver or gold tequila and reserve the *añejo* for serious sipping, like a cognac.

Regional Variations: The typical margarita proportions are 3 parts tequila to 1 part lime juice and 1 to 2 parts orange-flavored liqueur, usually Cointreau or Triple Sec. From that starting point, the troops depart in all directions. Some people alter the ratios in favor of the tequila or lime juice, some like it frozen or "on the rocks" instead of "up," some have a strong preference for either the "pure" taste of silver tequila or the "rich" body of the gold variety. Cookbook author Jane Butel, founder of the Albuquerque cooking school that bears her name, adds part of an egg white for a little froth. The most unusual variations change the liqueur, substituting Curaçao perhaps to make a blue margarita, or they combine another fruit flavor, from cranberry to prickly pear, with the Cointreau or Triple Sec.

MAJESTIC MARGARITA

Los Angeles's El Cholo restaurant serves more than a thousand margaritas a day and claims the distinction of being the world's largest single purchaser of Cuervo 1800 premium tequila. Though the kitchen has been in the vanguard of border cooking in California since 1927, margaritas are a relatively recent addition to the menu, dating back only to 1967. Before then, say the Salisbury family owners, diners usually ordered beer, sherry, or California "claret" with their meals.

Born on the border but bred for worldly esteem, the margarita single-handedly brought international acclaim to tequila. This is the most elegant of the many margarita styles, dressed up in finery befitting the stature.

Serves 1

Salt
Lime wedge
2 ounces premium, 100 percent agave tequila such as Herradura, Porfidio, or El Tesoro
1 ounce Grand Marnier
3/4 ounce fresh lime juice
Cracked ice

Place a thin layer of salt on a saucer. Rub the rim of an 8-ounce glass with the lime wedge and dip the rim into the salt. (Omit this step if you prefer your margarita *sin sal*, without salt.)

Pour the tequila, Grand Marnier, and lime juice into a cocktail shaker or lidded jar, add several pieces of cracked ice, and shake to blend. Strain into the prepared glass and serve.

TEQUILA SOUR

Americans often assume that the margarita is the national drink of Mexico, but this variation on the whiskey sour is actually more popular south of the border.

Serves 1

2 ounces gold tequila
2 ounces simple syrup (see "Technique Tip")
1 1/2 ounces fresh lemon juice
Several ice cubes
Lemon slice, for garnish

In a cocktail shaker or lidded jar, combine all of the ingredients. Strain into a sour glass. Garnish the rim of the glass with the lemon slice and serve.

Technique Tip: To make simple syrup, heat together 1 part sugar to 2 parts water until the sugar dissolves. The syrup keeps well if refrigerated.

CHIMAYÓ COCKTAIL

When the Restaurante Rancho de Chimayó opened in the New Mexico village of Chimayó in the 1960s, the Jaramillo family owners wanted to create a cocktail flavored with the cherished local apples. This was the result of the experimentation, still the restaurant's signature drink.

Serves 1

Ice cubes
1 1/2 ounces gold tequila
1 1/2 ounces apple cider, preferably unfiltered
1/4 ounce fresh lemon juice
1/4 ounce crème de cassis

Unpeeled apple slice, for garnish

Long before the Spanish arrived, Native Americans fermented the juice of the agave plant, producing pulque. Even in a remote corner like Baja California, Padre Junípero Serra found the indigenous peoples carefully cultivating agave, which produces its *aquamiel* only when it blooms, after eight to ten years of growth. The Spanish introduced the Old World technique of distillation, which turned the pulque into mescal. Tequila is a refined version of mescal, much as cognac is a superior type of brandy. To earn the name, it has to be made from the special blue agave plant raised in a small agricultural region near the town of Tequila, about forty miles from Guadalajara.

Despite a disastrous 1971 freeze that destroyed much of the commercial crop, apple pressing remains a spirited fall ritual in Chimayó to this day. At Rancho Manzana, the appropriately named proprietors, Jody and Chuck Apple, invite their friends and family to join them in gathering bushel baskets of fruit from their orchard. They take turns grinding up the whole apples in a hand-cranked machine, and then press the pulp to expel the unfiltered juice. With or without tequila, nothing tastes better on a crisp autumn afternoon.

Half-fill an 8-ounce glass with ice cubes. Pour all of the ingredients over the ice and stir to blend. Garnish the rim of the glass with the apple slice and serve.

ARIZONA SUNSET

What the margarita didn't accomplish for the tequila industry, the Rolling Stones did. On a 1972 tour, the rock band announced to their American fans that the tequila sunrise was their favorite drink. Suddenly, the Technicolor combination of tequila, orange juice, and grenadine soared in fame. This Arizona version substitutes the local prickly-pear-cactus syrup for the grenadine, a pomegranate-flavored syrup.

Serves 1

1 1/2 ounces gold tequila
6 ounces orange juice, preferably fresh
1 ounce prickly-pear syrup (see "Technique Tip")
Several ice cubes

Orange slice, for garnish

In a cocktail shaker or lidded jar, combine all of the ingredients. Pour into a 12-ounce glass. Garnish the rim of the glass with the orange slice and serve.

Technique Tip: Found in shops specializing in Southwest food products and in some well-stocked supermarkets, prickly-pear syrup boasts a delicious berry-like sweetness. If you don't have a local source, you can order it from many of the places listed in "Mail-Order Sources" or get it directly from a Tucson manufacturer, Cheri's Desert Harvest (800-743-1141 or 602-623-4141). Cheri Romanoski and her family make the syrup and other prickly-pear products in small batches to keep the quality high.

VAMPIRO

A shot of tequila with a sangrita chaser is a longtime cantina classic in Mexico. It never caught on in the United States, though, possibly because the tomato, citrus, and chile mixture in the sangrita seemed strange. Now a new combination of the two drinks, put together Bloody Mary style, is raging through south Texas like a prairie fire.

Makes 2

SANGRITA
1 cup tomato juice
1/2 cup fresh orange juice
2 tablespoons fresh lime juice
1 tablespoon chopped onion
2 teaspoons Worcestershire sauce
1 fresh serrano or jalapeño, seeded and chopped

Salt
Lime wedges
Ice cubes
3 ounces tequila

Place all the sangrita ingredients in a blender and purée them. Chill the mixture for at least 1 hour. (It can be made up to a week ahead.)

Place a thin layer of salt on a saucer. Rub the rim of an 8-ounce glass with a lime wedge and dip the rim into the salt. Repeat with a second glass. (Omit this step if you prefer your vampiro *sin sal*, without salt.)

Half-fill the two 8-ounce glasses with ice cubes. Pour the tequila equally into the glasses. Top with portions of sangrita and serve.

The original vampire of agave drinks, and still the champ in some areas of northern Mexico, is homemade mescal. In stories about his life in Arizona's Santa Cruz Valley in the late nineteenth century, James Cabell Brown said the local mescal was so potent that three drinks "would drive a fellow into voluntarily kissing his mother-in-law." Just a little farther south in Sonora, bootleggers still make the wild and raw mescal *bacanora*, the equivalent of Kentucky moonshine, and deeper into the countryside, *paisanos* produce a liquor with such a kick that it's called mescal *bronco*.

Everyone associates wine with California, but the Spanish padres who planted the first grapes in that state did the same throughout the borderlands. In need of sacramental wines, and too isolated to import them, the priests started vineyards anywhere they could. Both west Texas and southern New Mexico produced wine long before California, and in levels that exceeded that of the Pacific state until the last century or so.

The padres planted vineyards in Baja about the same time as in *alta* California, propelling the area on the path to becoming the hub of the modern Mexican wine industry. Centered in Ensenada and the nearby Guadalupe Valley, the industry is booming, particularly at large wineries such as Santo Tomás and Casa Pedro Domecq, both open for visits and tastings. Probably the best producer in the country, the local Monte Xanic makes wines that rival award winners from Napa.

An import from Spain, sangria is an unsurpassed party punch. This version contains a hefty dose of tequila, which you can weaken by using the larger amount of sparkling water suggested in the recipe.

Makes about 2 quarts

2/3 cup sugar
1/3 cup water
4 cups fruity red wine
1 1/2 cups orange juice, preferably fresh
1 cup fresh lime juice
3/4 cup tequila
1/4 cup Triple Sec or other orange-flavored liqueur
1 to 2 cups sparkling water

Orange, lime, and lemon slices, for garnish
Ice cubes

Boil the sugar and water together in a small saucepan until the sugar dissolves and the liquid is clear. Set the syrup aside to cool.

In a large pitcher or punch bowl, mix together the sugar syrup, wine, juices, and liquors. Just before serving time, stir in the sparkling water. Add the fruit slices and a lot of ice either to the sangria or to the individual glasses or cups. Serve chilled.

Technique Tip: If you frequently make drinks with fresh limes, invest in a bartender-style squeezer, sold in kitchen and restaurant supply stores. The handheld mini-vise makes easy work of the process, and typically takes less time than setting up an electric juicer, using it, and cleaning it.

Regional Variations: Though the name *sangria* comes from the Spanish word for blood, some people make the punch from white instead of red wine. In that case, the fruit garnish may switch to strawberries, grapes, or even kiwi, and champagne or sparkling wine may replace the tequila and some of the fizzy water. In red versions, brandy is more common than tequila as a bracer, and truer to the European roots.

BAJA MANGO DAIQUIRIS

Serves 8

2 large, ripe mangoes, peeled and chunked
16-ounce jar or can of mango slices, undrained
2 to 3 cups ice cubes
10 ounces light rum
2 ounces dark rum
Juice of 2 limes

In a blender, purée all the ingredients in two batches, and pour into a pitcher. Store in the freezer briefly or serve immediately.

Technique Tip: If you can't find fresh mangoes, use a 26- to 28-ounce jar or can of the fruit with syrup in the recipe. You may want to add a little more lime juice to counterbalance the sugar in the processed version.

New Orleans puts up a good argument for the invention of this gin-based beverage, but Nuevo Laredo's venerable Cadillac Bar also lays a convincing claim. Now called El Dorado, after a dispute forced a name change, the brassy bar is the most famous watering hole on the border.

Serves 1

2 ounces whole milk
1 ounce gin
3/4 ounce fresh lemon juice
1 egg white
1 tablespoon powdered sugar
Splash of orange-flower water
Several ice cubes

Place all the ingredients in a cocktail shaker or lidded jar and shake to blend. Strain and pour into a tall glass. Serve immediately.

A few of these Bloody Mary clones and you'll be farther out to sea than a Guaymas shrimp boat.

Serves 1

4 ounces tomato juice
1 1/2 ounces pepper-flavored vodka
1/4 ounce fresh lime juice
1/4 teaspoon Maggi seasoning or Worcestershire sauce
Several ice cubes
Celery salt
Fresh-ground black pepper
Boiled shrimp and celery stick, for garnish

Place the tomato juice, vodka, lime juice, and Maggi or Worcestershire sauce in a cocktail shaker or lidded jar, add several ice cubes, and shake to blend. Pour into an old-fashioned glass and top with a sprinkling of celery salt and pepper. Garnish the rim of the glass with the shrimp, add a celery stick, and serve.

On the border, you don't need a Red Tide or similar concoction to get a chile fix from your drink. An Albuquerque company makes a green-chile wine, and several microbreweries in the region have created chile beers with varying degrees of heat and success. We especially like the fire and flavor of Cave Creek Chili Beer from Black Mountain Brewing Company (800-228-9742) in Cave Creek, Arizona, just north of Phoenix. Sold throughout the United States in select locations, "Crazy Ed" Chilleen's serrano-laced brew comes complete with a chile in the bottle. It's guaranteed to warm your belly.

The Mexican version of eggnog, *rompope* is made from a rich cooked custard base rather than from the cold cream-and-eggs mixture that is standard in the United States.

Serves 10 to 12

4 cups whole milk
1 cup sugar
2 sticks canela or other cinnamon
Pinch of salt
8 egg yolks
2 teaspoons vanilla
1 cup brandy, or to taste

Ground canela or other cinnamon, for garnish

In a heavy saucepan over medium-low heat, warm the milk, sugar, canela, and salt until the sugar is dissolved. Set the mixture aside to steep.

In a large bowl, beat the egg yolks for several minutes, until the mixture forms thick ribbons. Remove the canela from the milk and pour the milk slowly into the yolks, continuing to beat. Return the mixture to the saucepan and place it over medium-low heat. Stir the mixture continuously as it thickens. Do not let it boil or you will find yourself with scrambled eggs. The *rompope* base is ready when it coats a spoon thinly. (It will thicken further when chilled.) Stir in the vanilla and the brandy. Strain the mixture into a pitcher or bowl and refrigerate for at least 2 hours or preferably overnight.

Pour into small glasses or cups, topped with generous sprinklings of canela, and serve immediately.

Regional Variations: Sonoran cooking authority Alfonso C. Pain, author of *Western Mexican Cookbook* (Post Litho Printing, 1981), adds $^1/_4$ cup of ground almonds to the custard base, an idea we like. Some cooks today make a simplified *rompope*, using a can of sweetened condensed milk and an equal amount of whole milk, enriched with 4 to 6 egg yolks and brandy to taste. It's good and fast if you feel confident in the safety of your raw eggs.

RAIN OF GOLD PUNCH

Tucson's St. Ann's Society promoted this punch in its 1909 *The Mission Cook Book*. The ladies in the organization seemed to have liked their liquor. We had to reverse the proportion of cider to brandy to get the golden taste suggested in the name. Our version makes a refreshing, light alternative to more potent party drinks.

Makes about 2 quarts

1 quart apple cider, preferably unfiltered
1 1/2 cups good brandy
Minced zest and juice of 2 lemons
Minced zest and juice of 4 oranges
1 to 2 tablespoons sugar
12 ounces ginger ale, or sparkling apple juice or water

Ice cubes
Lemon and orange slices, for garnish

Combine all the ingredients in a punch bowl and stir to dissolve the sugar. Add a lot of ice, garnish with the fruit slices, and serve.

You probably never thought of watermelons as speedy, but they once were, according to the experts at Native Seeds/SEARCH in Tucson. After the Spanish introduced the watermelon, originally from Africa, Native Americans traded its seeds northward so rapidly that the fruit actually reached the Colorado River plateau before the Spanish.

Aguas frescas are blends of water and ripe fruit, wonderful with fiery food or as a morning eye-opener. *Fruterías* in Mexico often show off giant glass jars of multicolored *aguas*, glimmering like jewels in the sun. We make this version with watermelon, a border favorite.

Serves 6

8 cups loosely packed seeded watermelon chunks
1/4 cup packed fresh mint leaves
12 ounces sparkling water
Sugar

Ice cubes
Mint sprigs, for garnish

In a blender, purée the watermelon in batches, adding the mint leaves to one of the batches. Pour the watermelon juice into a large pitcher. Stir in the sparkling water and taste. Perfectly ripe, peak-of-the-season fruit doesn't require sugar, but add 1 tablespoon or more if needed to get a well-balanced sweet and fruity taste. Chill for at least 1 hour.

Pour over ice in tall glasses and garnish each with a mint sprig if you wish.

Regional Variations: Like watermelon, mangoes and blood oranges pair well with mint in *aguas frescas*, and also create lovely hues. Banana mixes smartly with honey, particularly when served with a canela stick. Add milk instead of water for a *licuado*, a south-of-the-border fruit milk shake especially good with strawberries, alone or with cantaloupe. Another popular fresh-fruit drink, *limonadas* are a lime-juice equivalent of an American lemonade, sometimes enhanced by sparkling water.

HORCHATA

Sort of a rice pudding in liquid form, milky-looking *horchata* soothes the tongue after hot border foods.

Makes 1 quart

1 cup uncooked rice
1/4 cup slivered almonds
2 sticks canela or other cinnamon
1 quart water
1/4 cup sugar
1/2 teaspoon vanilla

Ice cubes

In a blender, grind up the rice for 2 minutes, until it resembles coarse meal. Transfer the rice to a bowl and add the almonds, canela sticks, and water. Stir the mixture well. Cover the mixture loosely and let it sit overnight.

Transfer the mixture to the blender in two batches and purée until the grittiness disappears, about 2 to 3 minutes per batch. Strain into a pitcher through several layers of dampened cheesecloth. Don't skimp on either of these steps or the drink will come out tasting like chalk. Mix in the sugar and vanilla and stir until the sugar dissolves.

To serve, pour the *horchata* into tall, ice-filled glasses. Leftovers keep, refrigerated, for several days.

At some point in the past, an ingenious Mexican cook discovered how to make a delicious drink out of ingredients most people throw away.

Makes about 2 cups

**Seeds and pulp scooped from 2 large cantaloupes or 2 small
     honeydew melons, measuring about 1 1/2 cups**
1 1/2 cups water
1 1/2 tablespoons sugar, or more to taste
1 1/2 tablespoons fresh lime juice, or more to taste

Ice cubes
Melon balls or cubes, for garnish (optional)

Combine all the ingredients in a blender and blend until seeds are ground fine.

Refrigerate the mixture in the blender container for at least 2 hours, or up to 8 hours. Blend the mixture again, at least 2 minutes, to recombine and further grind the seeds. Strain the liquid through a very fine sieve, or several layers of damp cheesecloth, discarding the solids. Don't skimp on either of these steps or the drink will come out chalky. Add a little more sugar or lime juice if needed to make the drink lightly sweet and zesty.

Serve the *horchata* in tall, ice-filled glasses, topped with a few melon balls or chunks if you wish. The drink is best the day it's made.

HOT VANILLA

A delightful change from hot chocolate, this Mexican treat deserves to be better known north of the border.

Serves 2

14 ounces whole milk
2 ounces whipping cream
1/2 vanilla bean
1 1/2 teaspoons sugar, or more to taste

Ground canela or other cinnamon, for garnish

In a heavy saucepan, combine the ingredients and warm over low heat. When small bubbles appear around the sides of the pan, remove it from the heat and let the mixture sit at room temperature for 15 to 20 minutes. Place the pan back on the stove and rewarm the mixture, whisking it briefly to redistribute the skin that forms on the milk's surface. Remove the vanilla bean half, scrape out its seeds with a sharp knife, and return the seeds to the milk. Pour the vanilla milk into two 8-ounce mugs and top with sprinklings of canela. Drink hot.

Regional Variations: Both vanilla and chocolate, New World products, are popular in Mexico as hot beverages. The chocolate version we prefer, sometimes called French-style, uses a little cream, which allows it to be frothed in a blender before serving. Heat 1 1/4 cups milk and 3 tablespoons whipping cream just to a boil, add them to a blender with 1 1/2 ounces Mexican chocolate, such as Ibarra or Mayordomo, and whip until frothy. Another old Mexican drink, *champurrado* combines sweetened chocolate and ground corn, blended with steaming water or milk. It has many fans along the border, but you want to acquire the taste from an early age.

Hot vanilla and chocolate make great breakfast beverages, but most Mexicans want coffee to start the day, either the dark, strong brew once typical or, increasingly, the weakened form known as *americano*. The country raises a lot of coffee beans today in the southern highlands, but in the past the supply often ran short, particularly on the frontier. Borderlands substitutes included beverages made with burnt wheat, mesquite beans, and in Arizona at least, jojoba seeds, now used mainly for making shampoos and body care products.

Dried hibiscus blossoms gained repute in the United States in recent decades as the core ingredient in red zinger tea, but they have enjoyed even greater esteem south of the border for much longer.

Makes 2 quarts

5 ounces (about 2 cups) dried hibiscus blossoms, rinsed
8 cups water
1/3 cup sugar or simple syrup (see "Technique Tip," page 452), or more to taste (optional)

Ice cubes
Lime wedges, for garnish

In a saucepan, bring the blossoms and the water to a boil over high heat. Reduce the heat to medium-low and simmer for 5 minutes. Remove the pan from the heat and let the tea steep for at least 10 minutes. Strain the tea into a pitcher and add the sugar or syrup, if you wish. Without any sugar, the tea is exceedingly tart. The amount we call for cuts some of the acidity while keeping the tea refreshingly tangy.

Serve over a lot of ice, garnished with limes.

Technique Tip: Look for dried hibiscus blossoms in health or whole foods stores, or as an alternative, shop in the same places for *jamaica* concentrate, usually labeled something like "instant concentrate for hibiscus flower tea." The brand we see most commonly is Del Tropico, distributed by California's Los Altos Foods.

CACAHUATES CON CHILE

From baseball stadiums to bars, chile-coated peanuts are likely to show up anywhere people eat *botanas*.

Makes 3 cups

2 tablespoons peanut oil, preferably a roasted variety
1 head of garlic, minced
2 tablespoons ground dried mild red chile, preferably New Mexican or ancho
1/4 to 1/2 teaspoon ground chile de árbol or cayenne
1 teaspoon salt, or more to taste
1 pound shelled raw peanuts (about 3 cups)

Preheat the oven to 325° F.

In a heavy skillet, warm the oil over low heat. Add the garlic and sauté slowly until well softened. Do not let the garlic brown or it will become bitter. Stir in the chiles and salt and mix well. Sprinkle in the peanuts and stir to coat.

Transfer the peanuts to a baking sheet. Bake for 20 minutes, stirring once. Allow the peanuts to cool on absorbent paper. Stored in a closed jar, they will keep for several weeks.

Technique Tip: Some cooks prefer to use powdered garlic, onion, or both to season the nuts, because the spices adhere more easily. If you go this route, make sure you have fresh, high-quality powders or the nuts will taste tired.

Despite its reputation for fine wine, California consumes more beer than any other American state. Even Texas lags behind, though it takes second place. In both states and the rest of the Southwest, the beer of choice is frequently Mexican. Monterrey breweries, far closer to the Rio Grande than to Mexico City, make most of the top national brands, including Bohemia, Carta Blanca, Corona, Superior, and the seasonal La Navideña for Christmas. The biggest producer of all, Cervecería Cuauhtémoc offers visitors not only a beer garden for tastings, but also a contemporary art museum and the Mexican Baseball Hall of Fame.

Closely related to cashews, as well as mangoes and poison ivy, pistachio nuts are another border favorite. California, Arizona, and New Mexico rank first, second, and third, respectively, in pistachio production in the United States, raising the trees in areas where the climate resembles that in the Middle Eastern lands of origin. At the Eagle Ranch Pistachio Groves in Alamogordo, New Mexico, Marianne and George Schweers add green chile to some of their nuts, which are sold under the brand name "Heart of the Desert" by several of the suppliers listed in "Mail-Order Sources."

Pine nuts and pumpkin seeds are common border snacks on their own, but they are even better mixed together.

Makes 1 1/2 cups

1 tablespoon butter
1 tablespoon sugar
3/4 cup piñon (pine) nuts
3/4 cup pepitas (shelled pumpkin seeds)
1 to 1 1/2 tablespoons ground dried mild green chile, preferably New Mexican or Anaheim

In a heavy skillet, warm the butter and sugar over medium heat. Stir in the piñon nuts and pepitas and coat them with the butter-sugar mixture. Add the chile and continue stirring to coat well, and warm through, just until the pepitas begin crackling. Pour the nuts onto a baking sheet to cool briefly.

Serve warm, or cool thoroughly and store in a tightly covered jar for up to several days.

BLACK BEAN TORTILLA PINWHEELS

Usually filled with cream cheese and chile, flour-tortilla pinwheels or roll-ups have swept the Southwest as a party finger food. This California version is almost as fast and easy as any other, but it offers more flavor. Though the approach works with tortillas of any thickness, we prefer thin ones.

Makes about 4 dozen pinwheels

8 ounces cream cheese, at room temperature
1 teaspoon cumin seeds, toasted and ground
1 garlic clove, minced
4 thin flour tortillas, preferably 9 to 10 inches in diameter, warmed
3/4 cup cooked black beans, canned or freshly prepared, drained
3/4 cup chopped roasted mild green chile, preferably New Mexican or
    Anaheim, fresh or frozen, well drained
6 tablespoons grated mild cheddar cheese
1/4 cup chopped pimiento-stuffed olives
2 tablespoons minced fresh cilantro (optional)

Salsa del Norte (page 38) or other salsa

Combine the cream cheese, cumin, and garlic in a food processor.
Spread the mixture evenly over the tortillas. Sprinkle the beans, chile, cheddar cheese, olives, and, if you wish, cilantro equally over the cheese mixture and roll the tortillas up snug. Wrap in plastic and chill for at least 2 hours.
Cut into 3/4-inch slices with a sharp knife. Let the slices sit, covered with plastic wrap, at room temperature for a few minutes before serving them, accompanied with salsa.

Another crunchy border snack, *chicharrones,* or fried pork rinds, originated as a way to make full use of a pig for food. Originally rendered in large copper or iron kettles in the fall at hog-killing time, they flavored beans and occasionally substituted for cured bacon. People from outside the region often frown at the idea of *chicharrones,* but some southern Arizona groceries sell them in the deli section, boxed to-go with ketchup, and in Los Angeles the upscale Tamayo restaurant serves them as a complimentary appetizer along with chips and salsa.

Anyone can buy corn tortilla chips. For real raves, make your own to pair with a special salsa or dip.

Makes 48 or 72 chips, enough for 4 to 6 people

Vegetable oil for deep-frying
12 thin corn tortillas
Salt or garlic salt to taste

Pour enough oil into a heavy skillet to measure at least 1 inch in depth, and heat to 375° F.

While the oil warms, cut each tortilla into 4 or 6 wedges. Fry 6 to 8 tortilla wedges at a time, for just a few seconds. The chips should turn crisp but not brown. Drain the chips and repeat with the remaining tortillas. Salt, if you wish, and serve warm with salsa, guacamole, or other dishes.

Tostadas can be kept for a couple of days in an airtight container. Rewarm the chips, uncovered, in a 250° F oven for the best flavor.

Technique Tip: For the crispest chips, start with the thinnest tortillas you can make or buy, and let them dry out for at least an hour, covered with a towel, before frying. It's more difficult to prepare great chips with Mexican tortillas, which tend to be relatively thick and high in moisture content, making them better for eating fresh than frying.

Regional Variations: Chip-addicted, health-conscious cooks are switching to baked flour tortilla snacks. They taste best fresh, eaten within a couple of hours, but it's easy to prepare a batch. Simply slice flour tortillas into wedges, place them on a baking sheet, and toast each side under a broiler for a minute or two. Thin tortillas, such as the Sonoran style, make the crunchiest chips.

DEVILED CORN DIP

We picked up the idea for this salsa-based dip at Albuquerque's Fiery Foods Show.

Makes about 2 cups

1 cup cooked corn kernels, preferably roasted in the husk as in Grilled Corn (page 358)
1/2 cup Salsa del Norte made with chipotles (page 38), or other chipotle salsa
2 ounces sharp cheddar cheese, grated fine
1 1/2 tablespoons sour cream
1 tablespoon minced fresh cilantro (optional)

Mix all the ingredients together and refrigerate for at least 30 minutes. Serve with tostadas or other corn chips.

Perhaps the best place in the world to fire up your taste buds on spicy dips, salsas, sauces, and more, the National Fiery Foods Show takes over the Albuquerque Convention Center one weekend each year in early March. Condiment manufacturers from the United States, Mexico, and other countries offer their wares for tasting to the retail trade and to individual chile lovers, presenting peppery versions of everything from chocolate to wine. Call 505-873-2187 for details.

AZ-TEX CALENDAR

A product of recent generations, party bean dips probably owe their origin to the Mexican practice of serving refried beans with a few chips for scooping. Southwestern creations continue to get more elaborate, as reflected in this recipe that combines influences from Arizona and Texas. In Phoenix, some people call their version of this dip an Aztec Calendar, because of its ornate design.

Serves 10

3 cups Refried Beans (page 378) or other well-seasoned mashed beans, warmed
1 1/2 cups Guacamole (page 123), mashed to eliminate any avocado chunks
3/4 cup sour cream

3/4 cup chopped roasted mild green chile, preferably Anaheim or New Mexican, fresh or frozen
1/2 cup Salsa del Norte (page 38) or other tomato-based salsa
3 ounces mild cheddar cheese, grated fine
3 ounces Monterey jack cheese, grated fine
3/4 cup diced tomato
4 green onions, sliced in very thin rings
Shredded romaine lettuce

On a decorative round platter of at least 10 inches, spread the beans evenly almost to the edge. Spoon a thin layer of guacamole over the beans, leaving a border of 1 inch of beans showing around the edge. Stir the sour cream well to make it more spreadable, and spoon a thin layer over the guacamole, leaving a 1-inch border of guacamole showing. Scatter the chile over the sour cream, and top with the salsa.

Sprinkle the cheeses in alternating color wedges over the sour cream or salsa. Sprinkle the tomato and green onions along the lines where the different cheeses meet. Arrange the romaine around the outside edge of the beans.

Serve while the beans are still warm, with tostada chips.

Regional Variations: Another of our favorite bean dips comes from Californian Ronald Johnson, author of *Southwestern Cooking* (University of New Mexico Press, 1985). He makes a purée of garbanzos, pine nuts, sour cream, and generous amounts of cilantro, sautéed onion, and garlic. The most common bean dips are much simpler, often just mashed or refried pintos flavored with salsa and shredded mild cheese, still a good alternative for everyday munching.

PUERTO PEÑASCO SHRIMP SPREAD

Just an hour's drive from Arizona's Organ Pipe Cactus National Monument, the seaside village of Puerto Peñasco overflows with shrimp, just like this spreadable dip.

Makes about 2 cups

1/2 pound cooked shrimp, peeled
6 ounces cream cheese, at room temperature
4 ounces fresh goat cheese, at room temperature
3 tablespoons minced fresh cilantro
3 tablespoons fresh lime juice
1/4 teaspoon crushed or ground chile de árbol or cayenne
1/8 teaspoon Worcestershire sauce
Salt to taste
1/3 cup finely diced jícama

In a food processor, combine the shrimp, cheeses, cilantro, lime juice, chile, Worcestershire sauce, and, if you wish, salt. Process until well blended but a little texture of the shrimp remains. Transfer the mixture to a bowl and stir in the jícama. Chill for at least 1 hour.

Serve cool with bread, crackers, or cucumber slices.

VERDE VEGETABLE DIP

Makes about 2 1/2 cups

1 1/2 cups sour cream
3/4 cup chopped peeled, seeded cucumber
1/4 cup minced fresh parsley
3 ounces queso añejo or Cotija or feta cheese, crumbled
2 tablespoons minced fresh cilantro
6 garlic cloves, roasted and mashed

2 tablespoons chopped roasted mild green chile, preferably New
    Mexican or Anaheim
1 tablespoon fresh lemon juice
1 fresh serrano, roasted, halved, and seeded
1 1/2 teaspoons dried oregano, preferably Mexican
1/2 cup finely diced jícama (optional)
Salt to taste

In a food processor, purée all the ingredients except the jícama and salt. Stir in the jícama, if you wish, and add salt to taste. Chill for several hours or overnight.

Serve with raw vegetables, chips, or baked potatoes.

JÍCAMA Y PEPINO

Perhaps the most pervasive vegetable *botana* south of the border, crunchy slices of jícama and cucumber make a quick and easy snack.

Serves 6

6 ounces jícama, cut in large bite-size slices
1 small cucumber, peeled and sliced
Juice of 1 lime
Salt to taste
Ground dried mild red chile, preferably New Mexican or ancho
    or, for more heat, chile de árbol or cayenne

Arrange the jícama and cucumber slices on a decorative plate. Squeeze the lime juice over them. Sprinkle with salt and chile and serve.

HONGOS RELLENOS

These stuffed mushrooms ooze flavor from a filling inspired by a California recipe.

Makes 12 mushrooms

12 large button mushrooms
3 tablespoons butter
1/2 medium onion, chopped
2 tablespoons minced red bell pepper
1 garlic clove, minced
1 tablespoon sherry vinegar
2 tablespoons minced fresh parsley
1/4 teaspoon dried rosemary
1/4 teaspoon dried thyme
2 ounces Chihuahua or Muenster cheese, grated
1/4 cup wheat germ, preferably, or 3 tablespoons dried breadcrumbs
Salt to taste

Preheat the oven to 375° F.

Carefully remove the stems from the mushrooms and chop the stems.

Warm the butter in a skillet over medium heat. Sauté the mushroom caps quickly on all sides. Remove the caps and reserve them. Add the chopped stems, onion, bell pepper, and garlic to the skillet and sauté until the onion is well softened. Add the vinegar, parsley, rosemary, and thyme and simmer for 1 or 2 minutes. Transfer the mixture to a bowl. Stir in the cheese and wheat germ and add salt to taste.

Stuff the mushroom caps with the filling mixture. Bake for 10 minutes, or until heated through and bubbly. Serve immediately.

Not all jalapeños are as fiery as they used to be, thanks to the taming efforts of Texas A&M chile expert Dr. Ben Villalón (a.k.a. Dr. Pepper). He advises southwest Texas growers, who account for much of the U.S. production. Each year Laredo honors the area crop at its Jalapeño Festival, where Austinite Braulio Ramirez set a world record in 1992 by eating 141 of the hot pods in just fifteen minutes.

Jalapeño chiles come from the state of Veracruz, but no state has embraced them with more enthusiasm than Texas. Though the cream cheese filling helps cool the bite in this Lone Star tidbit, we wouldn't serve these to any timid eaters.

Makes 2 dozen

6 tablespoons chunky peanut butter
1 1/2 ounces cream cheese, at room temperature

12 whole pickled jalapeños, halved, seeded, and deveined
Minced fresh cilantro, for garnish (optional)

In a small bowl, blend together the peanut butter and cream cheese. Spoon the mixture into the jalapeños, mounding it up in the center. Chill for at least 30 minutes and up to overnight.

Serve at cool room temperature, with cilantro scattered over the top if you wish.

OLIVOS NEGRO Y ROJO

These infused black olives are Spanish in inspiration but identifiable as a border dish today with their generous dose of chile *rojo*.

Makes 1 1/2 cups

10-ounce to 12-ounce jar brine-packed black olives
3 tablespoons sherry vinegar
1 tablespoon crushed or ground dried mild red chile, preferably New Mexican or Anaheim
4 garlic cloves, halved and lightly crushed
2 bay leaves
1 teaspoon cumin seeds, toasted
1 teaspoon dried oregano, preferably Mexican
Extra-virgin olive oil

Prepare the olives at least 3 days before you plan to serve them. Drain the liquid from the olive jar and reserve 3 tablespoons of the liquid and the jar itself. Place the olives and the reserved liquid in a small bowl and combine with the vinegar, chile, garlic, bay leaves, cumin, and oregano. Transfer the olive mixture back to the jar. Fill the jar to the top with olive oil. Let the olives sit at room temperature for 3 days, turning them occasionally.

Serve at room temperature, but refrigerate any leftovers. The olives keep for weeks.

Brought to California by the first padres, olive trees still flourish in areas of the state that enjoy a subtropical climate. The early settlers prized olives primarily for oil, used for lighting as well as cooking. They cured them for preservation in the fall, in barrels or rawhide bags filled with rock salt and water.

Makes a 12-inch pizza

CRUST

1 package dry yeast

3/4 cup warm water

1 teaspoon sugar

1 1/2 cups flour, preferably high-gluten bread flour, or
all-purpose flour

1/2 cup stone-ground blue or yellow cornmeal

1 1/2 tablespoons extra-virgin olive oil

3/4 teaspoon salt

1 garlic clove, minced

1 tablespoon extra-virgin olive oil

3/4 to 1 cup Arizona Chile Colorado (page 52) or other mild red chile
sauce

1 to 2 small tomatoes, preferably Roma or Italian plum, sliced thin

1/3 cup chopped roasted mild green chile, preferably Anaheim or New
Mexican

1/3 cup chopped red onion

1/3 cup sliced green or black olives

1 tablespoon minced fresh cilantro

2 to 3 tablespoons crumbled queso añejo or Cotija or Romano cheese
(optional)

3 to 4 ounces grated asadero, mozzarella, or Monterey jack cheese

Combine the yeast with the water and sugar in a small bowl and let sit until foamy. With a heavy-duty mixer or in a food processor, mix the yeast with the rest of the dough ingredients for several minutes, until the dough becomes smooth and elastic.

Transfer the dough to a well-floured pastry board or counter, knead at least 2 more minutes, until no longer sticky, and form into a ball. Place the dough in a greased bowl and cover with a damp cloth. Set the dough in a warm spot and let it rise until doubled in size, about 1 hour. Punch the dough down on the floured pastry board and let it rest for 10 minutes. Form the dough into a thin disk, about 12 inches in diameter, stretching and prodding it with your fingers. (The dough can be refrigerated or frozen at this point. Bring it back to room temperature before proceeding.)

Preheat the oven to 500° F.

Brush the oil over the crust and bake 5 minutes. Remove the pizza from the oven and top it with the chile sauce. Scatter the remaining toppings over the pizza. Bake for another 8 to 10 minutes. Let the pizza sit at room temperature for 5 minutes, slice into thin wedges, and serve hot.

Regional Variations: La Zona Rosa in Austin has perfected the Mexican pizza, offering an array of toppings that includes two sauces, three cheeses, chopped tamales, chili con carne, pickled carrots and jalapeños, chorizo, and shrimp. To the west in El Paso, W. Park Kerr favors chorizo, chopped grilled shrimp, and green chile as the toppings. As he and Michael McLaughlin suggest in *Burning Desires* (William Morrow, 1994), you can grill the crust and then the assembled pizza over a charcoal or gas grill. Cooks needing to save time often start with a thick flour tortilla as a base, or in Arizona even a thin cheese crisp (like one of our Tucson Cheese Crisps), instead of making the crust from scratch.

Serves 6 to 8

SAUCE
6 tablespoons Guajillo Mild Sauce (page 50), commercial Búfalo Salsa Picante, or other tomato-based salsa
6 tablespoons mayonnaise
2 1/2 tablespoons prepared Dijon mustard
Juice of 1 1/2 limes
2 tablespoons minced fresh parsley

1 pound fresh, meaty fish steak or fillet, such as sea bass, swordfish, or tuna, minced
2 tablespoons brandy
1 small celery stalk, minced
1/4 cup minced fresh parsley
1/4 cup minced onion
1/4 cup dried breadcrumbs
1 tablespoon Guajillo Mild Sauce, commercial Búfalo Salsa Picante, or other tomato-based salsa
2 teaspoons prepared Dijon mustard
1/2 teaspoon salt
1 egg

Vegetable oil for deep-frying

In a small serving bowl, combine the sauce ingredients and refrigerate. (The sauce can be made a day ahead.)

Toss the fish together with the brandy in a large bowl until the liquid is absorbed. Mix the remaining ingredients into the fish. Form into 1-inch balls.

Heat at least 3 inches of oil in a heavy skillet or saucepan to 365° F. Fry the fritters, a few at a time, for about 1 minute, until the fish is lightly crisp. Drain and serve immediately with the sauce.

PORK AND PUMPKIN EMPANADITAS

Tiny turnovers, empanaditas come with a wide variety of savory fillings throughout the border region. Here's a New Mexico version, plump with pork and pumpkin. The traditional filling hails from Nolia Martínez of Española, but we've updated the crust and we bake the turnovers rather than fry them in the old style.

Makes 4 dozen 3-inch empanaditas

PASTRY
2 cups low-gluten pastry or all-purpose flour
1/2 teaspoon salt
8 ounces cream cheese, in chunks
4 ounces vegetable shortening
4 ounces butter, in chunks

FILLING
1 cup raisins
1/2 cup brandy or inexpensive Madeira
1-pound pork loin
1 medium onion, minced
1 teaspoon salt, or more to taste
2 cups water
2 cups canned pumpkin
1/2 cup pecans or piñon (pine) nuts, toasted and chopped
1 tablespoon minced fresh cilantro (optional)
1 teaspoon ground dried mild red chile, preferably New Mexican or
    Anaheim
1 teaspoon ground allspice

GLAZE
1 egg
1 tablespoon water

In a food processor, combine the flour and salt. Scatter the cheese, shortening, and butter over the flour and pulse quickly until a soft dough forms. Divide the dough into two balls, wrap the balls in plastic, and refrigerate them for at least 2 hours. (The dough can be made a day ahead.)

Preheat the oven to 350° F.

In a small bowl, combine the raisins and the liquor and set aside.

Place the pork, onion, and salt in a baking dish, pour the water over, and cover the dish. Bake for about 1 ^{1}/2 hours, or until the meat is cooked through and tender. Remove the pork from the stock, reserving both. When the meat is cool enough to handle, shred it fine.

Transfer the pork to a large bowl and mix in the pumpkin, nuts, cilantro, chile, and allspice. Mix in enough of the pork stock to make the filling moist but not runny. (The filling can be made a day ahead and refrigerated.)

Raise the oven temperature to 375° F.

On a flour-covered pastry board or counter, roll out the dough to ^{1}/8-inch thickness. Cut the dough into rounds with a biscuit or cookie cutter. Top each round with a couple of teaspoons of filling. Fold the dough over, seal the edge, and crimp with a fork. Transfer the empanaditas to a baking sheet.

Combine the glaze ingredients in a small bowl. Brush the empanaditas lightly with the glaze. (The empanaditas can be frozen at this point for later use. Do not thaw them before proceeding, but plan to bake them a couple of extra minutes.) Bake the empanaditas for 20 minutes, or until lightly browned and flaky.

Serve warm or at room temperature.

Technique Tip: Traditional cooks still fry empanaditas in lard, which does add a rich taste to the turnovers. Peanut oil, heated to 350° F, accomplishes much of the same effect with a lot less saturated fat.

Regional Variations: Santa Fean Eloisa Rivera, grandmother of famed Southwestern chef John Rivera Sedlar, mixes pork with applesauce in her empanaditas. Early Californians sometimes worked with minced beef or sweetened pink beans. In Baja California, coastal cooks fill empanaditas with chopped cooked fish and vegetables. To the east in cowboy country, a ground beef picadillo would be the norm in a savory version. Dessert empanaditas, loaded with fruity jam-like mixtures, abound (see page 441).

CHARD EMPANADITAS WITH A GOAT CHEESE CRUST

You often find goat cheese inside an empanadita, but in this case it's also in the crust, making a particularly tender pocket of pastry to wrap around greens and chorizo.

Makes approximately 4 dozen 3-inch empanaditas

PASTRY
2 cups low-gluten pastry or all-purpose flour
1/2 teaspoon salt
6 ounces vegetable shortening
6 ounces creamy fresh goat cheese
4 ounces cream cheese, in chunks
1 to 2 tablespoons milk (optional)

FILLING
6 ounces bulk chorizo
1/2 medium onion, minced
3 garlic cloves, minced
1 teaspoon cumin seeds, toasted and ground
1 to 1 1/4 pounds chard, tough stems discarded and leaves minced
3 tablespoons chicken stock or water
1 teaspoon vinegar, preferably white
2 ounces creamy fresh goat cheese

GLAZE
1 egg
1 tablespoon water

In a food processor, combine the flour and salt. Scatter the shortening and cheeses over the flour and pulse quickly until a soft dough forms. Add a little milk if necessary to get the proper texture. Divide the dough into two balls, wrap the balls in plastic, and refrigerate them for at least 2 hours. (The dough can be made a day ahead.)

Preheat the oven to 375° F.

In a large skillet, sauté the chorizo over medium heat until it is richly browned. If the chorizo has rendered enough fat to pour off, do so. Add the onion, garlic, and cumin to the chorizo and sauté for an additional couple of minutes. Stir in the chard, stock, and vinegar and reduce the heat to low. Cover and cook for 10 minutes, until the chard is soft. If the mixture has any liquid remaining, cook, uncovered, for an additional 1 or 2 minutes. Stir in the cheese until melted and remove the filling from the heat. (The filling can be made a day ahead and refrigerated.)

On a flour-covered pastry board or counter, roll out the dough to $^1/8$-inch thickness. Cut the dough into rounds with a biscuit or cookie cutter. Top each round with a heaping teaspoon of filling. The dough is a little more fragile than some other pastries, so let the empanaditas sit unfolded for 5 minutes, for the dough to warm and soften briefly.

Combine the glaze ingredients in a small bowl. Brush the outside edge of each dough circle with a thin coat of glaze. Gently fold the dough over, seal the edge, and crimp with a fork. Transfer the empanaditas to a baking sheet.

Brush the empanaditas lightly with the glaze. (The empanaditas can be frozen at this point for later use. Do not thaw them before proceeding, but plan to bake them a couple of extra minutes.) Bake the empanaditas for 20 minutes, or until lightly browned and flaky.

Serve warm or at room temperature.

MAIL-ORDER SOURCES

The following Southwestern companies carry broad lines of products useful in border cooking, and they are set up to ship their goods across the country. All will provide a catalog or brochure that details the offerings. Other companies that supply a single specialty product, or a small line of products, are mentioned as sources in appropriate recipes earlier in the book and are also listed in the People, Places, and Products Index.

Coyote Cafe General Store
132 West Water Street
Santa Fe, NM 87501
800-866-HOWL
505-982-2454
Fax: 505-989-9026
American Express, Discover, MasterCard, Visa
Products developed by chef Mark Miller plus a wide range of other contemporary Southwestern foods and wares

Don Alfonso Foods
P.O. Box 201988
Austin, TX 78720
800-456-6100
512-335-2370
Fax: 512-335-0636
MasterCard, Visa
Among the finest sources in the United States for food products and utensils imported from Mexico, plus fresh, dried, and frozen chiles, and the company's own line of sauces and condiments

El Paso Chile Company
909 Texas Avenue
El Paso, TX 79901
800-274-7468
915-544-3434
Fax: 915-544-7552
American Express, Discover, MasterCard, Visa
Broad brand-name line of Southwestern condiments created by the Kerr family, as well as chiles, spices, and more

Mo Hotta–Mo Betta
P.O. Box 4136
San Luis Obispo, CA 93403
800-462-3220
805-544-4051
Fax: 805-545-8389
MasterCard, Visa
Fiery foods specialists, with especially strong selections of salsas and sauces; fresh tamales too

Native Seeds/SEARCH
2509 North Campbell, Suite 325
Tucson, AZ 85719
602-327-9123 for catalog or information;
    orders by mail or fax (602-327-5821) only
No credit cards; personal checks accepted
Seeds, beans, grains, herbs and spices, and books and other educational materials on cooking, indigenous agriculture, and ethnobotany, sold by a nonprofit organization working to preserve traditional crops and wild foodstuffs in the Southwest and northern Mexico

Old Southwest Trading Company
P.O. Box 7545
Albuquerque, NM 87194
800-748-2861
505-836-0168
Fax: 505-836-1682
MasterCard, Visa
Minimum credit card order: $15
Specialists in fiery foods, with fresh chiles in season

Salsa Express
P.O. Box 3985
Albuquerque, NM 87190
800-437-2572
505-888-3816
Fax: 505-884-5266
Southwest condiments with an emphasis on the hot and spicy, along with tableware, flours, and fresh tamales and chiles rellenos

Santa Cruz Chili and Spice Company
P.O. Box 177
Tumacacori, AZ 85640
602-398-2591
No credit cards; personal checks accepted
Producers of a private line of chile staples, with a particular emphasis on products made from the mild red pods favored in Arizona

Santa Fe School of Cooking
116 1/2 West San Francisco Street
Santa Fe, NM 87501
505-983-4511
Fax: 505-983-7540
American Express, MasterCard, Visa
Minimum mail order: $10
Specialists in New Mexican products, including sauces, condiments, fresh chiles in season, cookbooks, cookware, and tableware

Stonewall Chili Pepper Company
P.O. Box 241
Stonewall, TX 78671
800-232-2995
210-644-2667
Fax: 210-644-2377
MasterCard, Visa
Minimum credit card order: $20
Private-label condiments with a special emphasis on jalapeño and habanero chile products, other food items, seeds, and cookbooks

Territorial Gourmet
P.O. Box 228
Cortaro, AZ 85652
800-798-7328
602-297-9646
Fax: same as phone
No credit cards; personal checks accepted
Brand-name line of food products based on frontier and western recipes, and related Arizona-style condiments

ACKNOWLEDGMENTS

As the old *dicho*, or folk saying, maintains, "Libros y amigos, pocos y buenos"—"Books and friends, few and good." Both inspired us in this effort, providing knowledge, encouragement, and most important, a love of border cooking.

We're most indebted to other cooks who have allowed us to peer over their shoulder during the past three decades, friends who've taught us about food, culture, and more. Many of them are credited in particular recipes, but a few special people deserve broader thanks. We're honored to have learned and shared so much with Jessie Perez, Gayther Gonzales, Bell Mondragón, Laura Jaramillo Swendsen, Florence Jaramillo, and Genoveva Martínez.

We mention in the text most of the books that have contributed to our thinking, cooking, and eating pleasure in this project. The cookbook authors and food writers who provided the most assistance and enlightenment include Rick Bayless, Louise DeWald, Fabiola Cabeza de Baca Gilbert, Bertha Haffner-Ginger, Jacqueline Higuera McMahan, Mark Miller, James W. Peyton, and Patricia Quintana. Nach Waxman, Greg Ohlsen, and librarians from Monterrey to Monterey tracked down books for us. Publisher Bruce Shaw, Associate Publisher Dan Rosenberg, and editor Chris Keane got this book in print in an adept and supportive way.

Dino DeConcini, Dotty Griffith, Bob Jamison, W. Park Kerr, Jacqueline Higuera McMahan, Terry Melton, Janet Mitchell, and Jason and Brian Stuart introduced us to border cooks and dishes in their home territories. Jane and Michael Stern's writings always provide great advice on down-home restaurants in the Southwest, and author Dave DeWitt suggested other possibilities. The Mexico Tourism Office offered guidance south of the border.

We got valuable product information from Dr. Paul Bosland, María de Cárdenas, Richard and Shirley Jones, José Marmalejo, and Andy Robinson. At home, Art Pacheco, Paula Garcia Jones, Chris Martínez, and Patrice Harrison-Inglis gave generously of their expertise on meat and cheese. Seva Dubuar took a particularly active and enthusiastic role in aiding us with everything from cabrito to abalone.

Others who've shared professional expertise include Jo Ann Casados, Susan Curtis, Norman Fierros, Roger Hayot, Kathi Long, Adair Margo and staff, and Grace Saez. Susie Gonzales, Betty Alters, Myrna Richard, and Kyle Nelson helped test recipes. Skilled cooks Red Caldwell, author of *Pit, Pot, and Skillet* (copyright 1990 by Don Caldwell), Roque Garcia, and the Honorable Henry B. Gonzalez gave us permission to use their recipes.

PEOPLE, PLACES, AND PRODUCTS INDEX

RECIPE INDEX

Grilled Quail and Onions, 297
Guacamole, 123
Guajillo Mild Sauce, 50

H

Habanero Ketchup, 67
Habas and Olive Oil, 384
Harvest Corn Pudding, 357
Hash
    Rio Bravo Brisket Hash, 83
    Tamale Hash, 82
Hatch Green Chile Sauce, 54
Homemade Tostadas, 469
Hongos Rellenos, 474
Honorable Henry B.'s Soft Tacos,
    The, 348
Horchata, 462
Hot Vanilla, 464
Huevos con tostaditos. *See* Tex-Mex
    Migas
Huevos Rancheros, 86

I

Ice creams and ices
    Jamaica Ice, 447
    Rompope-Canela Helado, 445
    Vanilla Ice Crema, 446

J

Jalapeño Hot Sauce, 49
Jalapeño Pie, 93
Jalapeños, Stuffed Pickled, 475
Jamaica Ice, 447
Jamaica Tea, 465
Jícama
    about, 23
    Jícama Hash Browns, 366
    Jícama y Pepino, 473
Jiricalla, California, 421
Joe's Breakfast Nachos, 80
Juárez Salpicón, 194

K

Ketchup, Habanero, 67

L

Lamb
    Grilled Pomegranate Lamb
      Chops, 258
    Lamb Shanks Adobo, 260
Lard, about, 20
Limónes, limes, and lemons, about,
    23
Lobster, Puerto Nuevo, 304
Lower Valley Carnitas, 229

M

Machaca. *See also* Carne Seca
    about, 75
    Chicken Machaca, 273
    Machaca Breakfast Burros, 74
    Tuna Machaca, 332
Majestic Margarita, 451
Mama's Papas, 371
Mango Chimichangas, 426
Margaritas
    Majestic Margarita, 451
    Pancho's Original Margarita, 450
Masa and masa harina, about, 21–22
Mayo(nnaise), Green Chile, 66
McAllen Mustard, 69
Melon
    Agua Fresca de Sandía, 461
    Melon Horchata, 463
Menudo, Sonoran, Blanco, 204
Mesquite, about, 186
Mexican Chocolate Cake, 429
Mexican Red Rice, 390
Migas
    Joe's Breakfast Nachos, 80
    Tex-Mex Migas, 79
Milanesa, 190
Mole
    Carrots in Quick Mole, 365
    Mole Enchiladas, 294
Molletes, 99
Mule Mountain Scramble, 91
Mushrooms. *See* Hongos

Mustard, McAllen, 69

N

Nachos
    Cajeta-Nut Nachos, 443
    Creamy Crab Nachos, 145
    Joe's Breakfast Nachos, 80
    Nachos El Norte, 144
Natillas, 420
New Mexico Carne Adovada, 226
New Mexico Salsa Picante, 41
New Mexico's Best Green Chile
    Stew, 203
Nogales Entomatadas, 162
Nopales. *See* Cactus
Northern Tortilla Soup, 107
Nuevo Laredo Ramos Gin Fizz, 457
Nuts
    Cacahuates con Chile, 466
    Sugar-and-Spice Piñons and
      Pepitas, 467

O

Oils, cooking, 20
Old-Fashioned Sonoran-Style Red
    Enchiladas, 160
Olives
    about, 23
    Olivos Negro y Rojo, 476
Omelets. *See* Egg dishes
Onions
    Grilled Green Onions and Rajas,
      368
    Pickled Onions, 64
Orlando's Chicos, 360
Oysters
    Oysters Corona, 317
    Oysters Guaymas, 318

P

Painted Desert Roasted Chile Salad,
    128
Pancakes, Piñon, with Apple Cider
    Syrup, 97